Japanese Film
and the Floating Mind

Japanese Film and the Floating Mind

Cinematic Contemplations of Being

JUSTIN VICARI

McFarland & Company, Inc., Publishers
Jefferson, North Carolina

LIBRARY OF CONGRESS CATALOGUING-IN-PUBLICATION DATA

Names: Vicari, Justin, 1968– author.
Title: Japanese film and the floating mind : cinematic contemplations of being / Justin Vicari.
Description: Jefferson, North Carolina : McFarland & Company, Inc., Publishers, 2016 | Includes bibliographical references and index.
Identifiers: LCCN 2016020571 | ISBN 9781476664989 (softcover : acid free paper) ∞
Subjects: LCSH: Motion pictures—Japan—History. | Ontology in motion pictures.
Classification: LCC PN1993.5.J3 V53 2016 | DDC 791.430952—dc23
LC record available at https://lccn.loc.gov/2016020571

BRITISH LIBRARY CATALOGUING DATA ARE AVAILABLE

ISBN (print) 978-1-4766-6498-9
ISBN (ebook) 978-1-4766-2496-9

© 2016 Justin Vicari. All rights reserved

No part of this book may be reproduced or transmitted in any form or by any means, electronic or mechanical, including photocopying or recording, or by any information storage and retrieval system, without permission in writing from the publisher.

On the cover: Takako (Hiroko Oshima) balances on a surfboard to cheer up her brooding boyfriend Shigeru (Claude Maki) in Takeshi Kitano's *A Scene at the Sea* (*Ano natsu, ichiban shizukana umi, 1991*)

Printed in the United States of America

*McFarland & Company, Inc., Publishers
Box 611, Jefferson, North Carolina 28640
www.mcfarlandpub.com*

For Vivian and Bin,
who are from Hong Kong
and make great Asian food

Table of Contents

Preface: Japanese Film X — 1
Introduction: Paradoxes of Perception: In a Ghostly Theater — 6

Part One: Toward the Last Ontology

1. Moon in Water — 23
2. The Broken Heart of Ontology — 37
3. Anxieties of Change, Changing Anxieties — 52
4. Extremisms — 64
5. The Last Ontology — 101

Part Two: The Floating World

6. Refugees of the Floating World — 109
7. The Meanings of the Wound — 127

Part Three: Emperor Worship

8. The Problem of Emperor Worship — 147
9. Naruse: An Early and Enduring Critic of Emperor Worship — 160
10. Ozu, After Surrender — 166
11. "Just a memory": The Figure of the Emperor in Postwar Melodrama — 176
12. Three Films — 186
    Mizoguchi's *Women of the Night* 186
    Imamura's *Outlaw Matsuo Comes Home* 188
    Wakamatsu's *Caterpillar* 192

Conclusion — 197
Chapter Notes — 205
Works Cited — 215
Index — 221

Preface
Japanese Film X

NICK: I think my favorite film is *Tokyo Story*. I just think Mizoguchi is a great director.
SHEENI: It's a great film. But wasn't that by Ozu?
NICK (rethinking): Who can say?
—dialogue from *Youth in Revolt* (2009)

[Japanese] films have offered [the Westerner] only anachronistic beings, peasants or samurai, who belong less to "Japan" than to the object "Japanese film"…
—Roland Barthes[1]

My hatred for Japanese cinema includes absolutely all of it.
—Nagisa Oshima[2]

We probably imagine that we know everything there is to know about Japanese film. Sweating, shouting males. Blushing women. The despair and horror, wrapped up in Buddhist homilies about resigned surrender to the greater good. Prostitution, double suicides, ghosts. The push and pull between a surreal life of tradition and bewildering modernity. The obsession with "Japaneseness," and the faint but persistent warning that no one who is not Japanese can ever truly understand.

Japanese Studies in the West have been stultified by an unwillingness to disabuse ourselves of these all-too-familiar concepts, or in some cases even acknowledge them. At any rate it has been a matter of either too much or too little. According to most self-effacing Western scholars (and when are Western scholars ever self-effacing except when approaching the subject of Japan?[3] It has become an "academic-tourist" hot spot for trying on an unnatural, unconvincing *shrinkage*…[4]), Japan is the mutant product of the Bomb—the terrorized geisha of a male fantasmatic both tenacious and largely unconscious.[5]

Speaking with non–Japanese Asians begins to give one a sense of how insular and discursive our conception of Japan really is (and how self-serving). For Chinese and Koreans, Japan is a malevolent presence: cruel, imperialistic, racist, murderous. It is not a genteel tea ceremony. But when we turn to the *films* of Japan, we find that their greatest filmmakers also understood this. From Ozu to Wakamatsu, from Naruse to Oshima, from Mizoguchi to Imamura, from Masumura to Miike and the current Extremists, the question of Japanese humanity is blatantly, violently up for grabs. Even if the constant theme of Japan's cinema is regeneration in all its forms, nothing has come to be settled; everything remains in flux. Japanese cinema is an island sending out images to the world—images in which it barely exists as it truly is; images which it itself does not believe in. These images barely resolve the reflexive difficulties of a culture that has been inoculated against itself for centuries.

It is, naturally, easy to draw these conclusions about another culture; but then, our understanding of anything is an inevitable mixture of self and a certain digested alterity. Japanese cinema stages a kind of philosophical theater in which this mixture is rendered plain in every frame of film, while nonetheless nearly passed off as nothing but a stylized by-product of "art" and aesthetics (is it ever only this?); in which we see ambivalence in powerful yet matter-of-fact ways, a sense of tragic fate springing from the deeply undemocratic, anti-individualist tendencies of Japan and calling to an ambivalent, undemocratic part of ourselves, one which is tired of pretending that everything we know and do is for the sake of an abstract, received humanism.

There *is* humanism in Japanese cinema, but it is almost like a "Humanist Hall" in some strange national museum. Because Japanese culture is predominated by belief in fate, it lacks the ability to conceive the most essential ingredient of true humanism: agency. But no one ever said that humanism was anything but a Western phenomenon, in some ways a Western delusion. Just as our cinema is usually driven by protagonists whose epic conflicts force them into an often stale defiance of society and circumstance, the deepest bind that has come to characterize humanism is the suspicion that social progress can only be driven by a petulant individualism which never reconciles with otherness. Acceptance of one's ideas remakes rebellion as mere capitulation; the only successful rebellion is one which fails. In some ways, this tic of irresolvable rebellion arises from the belief that every individual voice is always heard within a democracy; to blend with the majority is to reveal this as a lie, even in situations when blending would make sense. In Japanese cinema, however, protagonists do not seek enormous changes; they are already almost overly reconciled to their existence being niched within a social order whose harmony and fulfillment take precedence over any one person's. If anything, rebels in Japanese cinema are sad figures, self-questioning, forlornly aware that they are making waves. Hence, Japanese cinema frees us from our Western bind temporarily, and allows us to see a world that was never constricted by the need to believe in the ineluctable benightedness of masses and majorities, or only learned this belief late in life and rather badly.

So, inside this Humanist Hall, there is the anti-war diorama, nearly identical to the ones which celebrate war; there, the one modeled on Ibsen's *A Doll's House*; there, the one in which children get to speak out (from behind glass, of course). Meanwhile, cartoon holograms serve plastic display food in restaurant windows, even as offerings of real food are left to rot at sacred places where centuries-old ghosts are memorialized and oblated. Of course, most younger Japanese no longer "believe," yet continue to bring offerings, ironically, superstitiously, ritualistically, or for kicks. The trappings and spirit of ancient feudalism linger on, especially in all displays of protest, winking, swinging a samurai sword that is one more surplus value in a culture whose warriors are capitalist CEOs and political bosses, as far removed from bushido codes or Zen philosophy as is possible to be. Successful businesses, after all, are not run by turning everything over to the often merciless hands of fate.

Where a kind of humanism does emerge in Japanese cinema, it is either consciously modeled on Western concepts, as in much of Akira Kurosawa's work, or it is something unique: a smaller, less grandiose humanism, one which observes intentionality more than actions, and hopes more than consequences. Instead of boasting of itself as a towering mountain all must climb, it claims only what lies below the mountain, below the surface, or in the mountain's shadow. This book is mostly concerned with what we might call the shadow of Japanese cinema—what it does not mean, what it cannot encompass. The empty space, the proverbial "X." Like Siegfried Kracauer with Germany, I am intrigued by common threads; the threads in this book stretch from the 1920s to the present day. I treat genres as if they barely exist (they have, anyway, been covered brilliantly by numerous other writers); auteurs, too, for the most part (where the same holds true). Wherever possible, I ignore or flatten obfuscatory barricades; certainly I try to erect no new ones. The subject is rich and complicated enough as is.

It is impossible to avoid the thought that a great deal of Japanese cinema is a put-on, celebrated abroad for its outrageous novelty while perceived at home as little more

In this vintage Spanish lobby card for Akira Kurosawa's *Stray Dog* (*Nora inu*, 1949), we see the stark contrast of classes so intrinsic to the director's social consciousness. In middle-class suits and hats, Detective Murakami (Toshirô Mifune, far left) and Detective Sato (Takashi Shimura, second from left) have come to a slum dwelling to interrogate the landlady and her laborer husband about a murder case. In defiance, the husband does not stop hammering his barrel during the entire scene.

than bastardizations. Thus, at the 1985 Tokyo Film Festival, it was possible for Japan to fete Akira Kurosawa's *Ran* with department store exhibits and publicly installed *Ran*-themed works of art, and at the same time to treat the film itself (and Kurosawa) almost dismissively, as egregiously Westernized, pretending to authentic Buddhist values.[6] Along with most Japanese popular culture,[7] Japanese movies have been an uneasy fit for the pursuit of *nihonjinron*, what J. Hoberman defines as "the theory of Japanese-ness"[8] and Marilyn Ivy as "discourses on the Japanese,"[9] a philosophy which presented Japan to itself in the 1970s and 1980s all too narcissistically, as a hermetic sign-system hopelessly exotic and unknowable even to the Japanese themselves. Ivy writes:

> Immensely popular works in this genre—written in Japanese by Japanese for Japanese—assert, for example, that the Japanese language is the most difficult in the world, that Japanese are not logical, that Japanese selves are sheerly "relational," and that the Japanese are a homogeneous race. Whether these works put a positive or negative spin on their conclusions, they assert with numbing repetition the uniqueness of Japan.[10]

The Nihonjinronians also spent a lot of energy deconstructing vintage Japanese magazine covers. Try to imagine a U.S. academic cottage industry (with motivational, self-help undertones) devoted to the proposition that *The Saturday Evening Post* was produced by a bunch of space aliens who understood "American-ness" better than we ever could. (Actually, there might be something to that.)

In the practice of *nihonjinron*, Yoshikuni Igarashi maintains, "supposedly ahistorical categories, such as biology or ethnicity, are employed as essentialist sources of Japanese uniqueness."[11] But such reductive absolutes are surely cribbed from a certain segment of Japan's studious and perhaps partly self-disliking identification with bodies of thought from *outside* Japan, namely the Western preoccupation with polarized stereotypes of the Japanese as past-worshipping conservatives or kinky futurists. For example, the Western conception of "un–Japaneseness" (we, too, are invested in our own way in the elusive authenticities and hybridities of Japan) is a blanket term to refute derivations from traditional Japanese aesthetics, what David Desser calls a tautological argument, since it permits nothing that breaks with tradition to be considered truly Japanese, and vice versa.[12] (It is like the Western tourists who go looking for Japanese paintings and invariably buy only kitschy watercolors on silk.)

The problem is that Japanese culture is neither unified or discontinuous, but rather that it sometimes appears (again, to an outsider) to be ever at either extreme: rigidly, even obsessively tradition-bound, or taboo seemingly for taboo's sake alone. In fact, these extremes cohabit flagrantly within Japanese sensibilities themselves. Miryam Sas writes:

> In contemporary Japanese popular speech, heard in the streets or in TV commercials, one frequently notes the use of the prefix *cho-* [meaning] emphasis or excess…. This 'ultra-' can be understood to convey the contemporary excitement (constructed at least in part by the mass media) implicit in the idea of progress, of speed, of convenience (chokakuyasa, ultra-cheap; cho-kosoku, superhighway).[13]

According to Sas, such usage "signifies transcendence as well as transgression"[14]—two things we Westerners have trouble placing together but which the Japanese, in their rather deliberate refusal to mistake representations for realities, or perhaps even to mistake realities for realities, have worked out to a virtual science. The Japanese mean their zeal, their compulsory cuteness,[15] just as they also mean what filmmaker Eiichi Kudo called the obligatory Japanese "sour twist" on everything.[16]

Finally, what interested me in writing this book was the attempt to understand the ontological process of cinema, or *cinematic ontology*, from a viewpoint that is both semi-unified (Japanese) and semi-other (non–Western). My inclination is that something so familiar as the way we absorb and respond to films can only be understood through this mixed approach. "At the cinema," Alain Badiou writes, "as in Plato, genuine ideas are mixtures."[17] And so are the ideas that films generate in us, the viewers. Within the presence of a preponderantly mediated identification, we can approach the symbolic more and more as a pure point of reference to be summarily overcome in relation to our own (self-)consciousness. Put otherwise: we can say, "Of course, 'Japanese Film X' has a symbolic presence and meaning; but given that this may only be *my* symbolic, how can I learn to see beyond what would automatically more than content me in the examination of Western art—how to transcend the symbolic? How to literalize signifiers without losing sight of their signifieds—indeed, literalize them in order to see their signifieds that much clearer?" A repeated Buddhist precept: *the form is empty.*[18]

When I told someone I was writing a book about Japanese film, he asked, "What do you know about the subject?" "Nothing at all," I replied, "I'm a blank slate." The book you hold is what Japanese film wrote (and is still writing) upon me. If I tell you that the slate nonetheless remains blank, perhaps it will help explain things; and then again, perhaps it won't.

Introduction
*Paradoxes of Perception:
In a Ghostly Theater*

In *Briefings on Existence*, Alain Badiou writes of the moment "when existence breaks the ice of its own transparency," coming into visibility as an observable entity. This should be a potentially sublime or transcendent moment, yet it has been rendered definitively moot by post-religious thought.[1] Being emerges into appearance drained of spirit. What now fills the hunger for a being that is both visible (plastic) and transcendent, for Badiou, is a ghostly theater: "But it is only in drama, as in *Hamlet*, that specters cast a semblance of efficacy."[2]

In contrast to a theological world where everything lives (in God) and nothing dies, there is posited a world in which everything seems to live in dramatic representation: the fundamental principle of cinema—indeed, the ontology of appearances in cinema, with its radical disconnect from that fullness of concrete rationality by which we would ideally like to grasp what we see as something "true," remaining fixed for our extended contemplation, our increasing certainty. Whereas in cinema it is precisely opposite: we have powerful impressions that are not usually allowed to attach themselves for very long to their objects, or which contradict stark facts (about reality) even as they co-exist with these facts. This occurs both diegetically, within the unfolding world of the film (its narrative, its visual style), and extra-diegetically, as when we find ourselves laughing at the antics of a comedian whose death we momentarily forget, or when we feel longing for a body whose cinematic appearance we know to have been more or less a production of light and shadow. (In general, the spirit that imbues the visible in cinema is usually nothing more than lighting.)

It is not merely that space-time continuums are broken and rearranged by this cinematic ontology of appearances, it is that cinema would not be possible for us without this dual perception in which one half is always struggling to catch up to the other, and to remind it that nothing is there but projections. Cinematic ontology might very well be a blueprint for all post-metaphysical or non-metaphysical ontology (Badiou's sense of post-religious thought) in the sense that in cinema metaphysics is both omnipresent and completely depleted, redundant perhaps. There is another world within and beyond this one ... and it is there in plain view, its lineaments as specific as millimeter width and scoping, its hues as identifiable as Technicolor. Not unlike the religious-metaphysical world, it makes no bones about being a creation.

For these reasons, cinema is closest to the Aristotelian God which Badiou describes as "exemplary" and "the supreme immobile mover."[3] It only *seems* to change (within a single film, or within different viewings of the same film) when in reality it changes us in relation to itself. Whenever we contemplate cinematic ontology (whenever we watch films), we are close to Badiou's prescription for a God who thinks Himself and has no other conceivable purpose.[4] Moreover, I would argue that cinema helps us make a leap similar to Badiou's characterization of fundamentalist religion's "obscure Subject," who begins by being invested "in the ceaseless reproduction of [God's] death," then moves toward a semi-living "encounter" with a being who entails the risk of certifying (or not certifying) what we have already led ourselves to believe about the world.[5] There is an opening-up of trust and vulnerability in this movement, a laying-aside of abstract dogma in favor of something more personal and tangible. This has everything to do with what is called "the evidence of the eyes." Whether or not we believe in its perception of miracles, Born-Again-ism is about seeing the unseen as an almost commonplace, everyday revelation—and isn't this the same hope of all belated viewers who in their turn seek to give themselves some new account of *Citizen Kane*, *The Searchers* or *Battleship Potemkin*, thereby adding personal significance to the litanic or scriptural?

There is no better example of the confounding, empathetic, self-conscious, exhilarating practice of cinematic ontology than Nagisa Oshima's *The Man Who Left His Will on Film* (*Tôkyô sensô sengo hiwa*, 1970), in which a group of young radical filmmakers are changed by their need to understand the last raw footage shot by their friend, who has recently committed suicide by leaping off a building with the group's communal Bolex. We see this raw footage, described as a cinematic "testament," while we hear the friends' comments in voiceover. There is a multileveled process here: the young filmmaker and his film are both subject (his friends attempt to discover why he was filming certain things, and to engage and grasp his own, now dead subjectivity) and object (the film is an external thing, also an eschatological "last thing," whose meaning therefore they cannot alter or take part in); the dead friend is also subject and object, as the creator of the film, the subjective originator of the footage, and also as the objective mystery to be solved by analyzing this footage. Finally, in their spontaneous commentaries on what they are seeing, the friends appear as both subjects and objects to themselves: perceiving and feeling what they perceive and feel, but wondering how much film in general, life, a friend's tragic fate, and the politics of modern Japan have impinged on their ability to understand what they are watching, or indeed, impinged more directly on the images themselves. The testament film, needless to say, interrogates and even watches *them*. All of these subjectivities and objectivities are in play, and in the very nature of the unrolling filmed images, on one hand "flat" and descriptive (street traffic; buildings) and on the other hand almost three-dimensional in nature, potentially seeded with enigmatic clues to the living filmmaker's final moments on earth.

Giving their analysis yet another layer of meaning, these friends are all committed to forging a radical cinema in conservative Japan, filming leftwing protests and making works that reflect the class struggle (in the manner of the then-current Dziga-Vertov Group of Jean-Luc Godard and Jean-Pierre Gorin), while at the same time arguing among themselves that film is bourgeois and secondhand, and can never adequately address oppression. In fact, film, by its technocratic and financial pedigrees, its institutionalized ways of looking and hearing, only reifies oppression, the divisions of us versus them, inside versus outside, what is shown versus what is hidden. There is nothing original or groundbreaking about this schism; and Oshima depicts the communist-sympathizing would-be radicals as defeated, forever at an impasse, even ridiculous. Suicide is as meaningful (and meaningless) a gesture as all their circuitous debates.

In their direct contemplation of the testament footage, the friends increasingly resist the images they are seeing. The film is all urban and suburban landscapes, sometimes empty and sometimes filled with strangers; its banality, its pure descriptiveness, does nothing to illuminate the filmmaker's state of mind, particularly why he killed himself. "But what was he thinking when he shot this?" we hear one of the group say over images of cars driving on a highway. "Maybe he really was crazy." The need to analyze is a dogged one; at the lowest level of this interpretive subject-object game, one is what one sees. Not to find meaning is a possible failure of one's own subjectivity; not to find anything is a possible indication that one, too, is lacking: "There's got to be something here." "Hard as you look, though, there doesn't seem to be anything there. It's getting on my nerves."

Coming into contact with this film, like any film, means that viewer and film will affect and change each other, leading to the generation (in this case, *re*generation, since the filmmaker has died) of a new and living entity made up of the filmmaker's subjectivity and the viewer's subjectivity, and resulting finally in an ontological hybrid: filmmaker-viewer-film-X. The ontology of this is one where the human is already partly mechanistic, balanced out by the fact that the film is anthropomorphized into a living entity. This transpires whether or not one likes the film or even finds anything in it. And we may as well note that it is not coincidental that we speak of films as spaces "in" or "inside" which things occur: films double for the subjective interior, even as they exteriorize it.

To find something in a film, or indeed to not find anything, is to be forced to become a different person, altered by the attempt to think one's way into the lifelike and multivalent "consciousness" of the film. At the same time, the attempt to find any methodology whatsoever, any structure, however unlikely and abstruse, is shown to be a kind of intellectually received second nature. Even apparent chaos can be sculpted into a worldview. "Maybe he was figuring that by linking meaningless shots he could create meaning by paradox," one of the young filmmakers offers, but the group concludes that such a deviously formalist approach to art is "bankrupt, both politically and artistically." This is essentially a defense against the opening-up that would take place, ontologically, by surrendering to the terms of the film. These terms in themselves seem to be: meaninglessness, paradox for its own sake, hermeticism, the seeming opposite of revolutionary engagement. Inevitably, as we see in *The Man Who Left His Will on Film*, films demand an ultimate movement of empathic otherness, an existential self-sacrifice in which political certainties are often the first bulwark of the self that must be challenged and overthrown.

Instead of this happening, however, the testament-footage only seems to reinforce negative, closed dogmas which the group already holds. One of the friends states, over a shot of railroad tracks along a rather sad backstreet, "You get stuck in the muddy mixture of the feudal and the modern that is Japan, and you slip deeper and deeper into the fetishes of youth and childhood." Oshima neither contradicts nor endorses this

Nagisa Oshima (standing, center) instructs his cast how to play the round-table discussion scene in *Diary of a Shinjuku Thief* (*Shinjuku dorobô nikki*, 1969). The most talented Japanese filmmaker of his generation, Oshima tackled political and social issues with keen intelligence and also with a severe streak of dark irony and absurdism.

observation; however, he does indicate that it has little to do with the actual content of the image that has supposedly inspired it—or rather, the association to the image is random and personal, therefore not rigorous. "It's beginning to scare me," a member of the group says when the footage impassively shifts to an empty sky.

There was a school of Japanese Marxist cinema in the late 1960s, including writer-director Masao Adachi, that held to the practice of editing together different images of landscapes, outdoor locations, rural farms, storefronts and dwellings in non-narrative montages, in order to document socioeconomic structures. I have looked at an example of Adachi's cinema, *A.K.A. Serial Killer* (*Ryakushô renzoku shasatsuma*, 1969), and found it oddly pretty, but vapid and interminably boring. Adachi had co-written a few of Oshima's late-'60s films, but Oshima may have been mocking the landscape school here; later in *The Man Who Left His Will on Film*, when cinema itself has been decisively abandoned by the protagonists, Oshima shoots a Tokyo panorama upside-down, as if to literally overturn the idea of the empty landscape as a meaningful signifier.

Determined to keep watching because it was their comrade's last work (although one of them pointedly yawns at this piety), they nonetheless agree that their friend failed to "achieve proletarian consciousness," and finally conclude that the police stole the real film from the Bolex and kept it as evidence.[6] This feint reveals their need not only to preserve their ideological preconceptions but also to hold onto the idea that a film only derives meaning from its relation to a reality that can be pointed to, as *evidence* of something which could be considered transcendental. The quasi-religious, metaphysical aspect of ontology is still so ubiquitous to their thinking that they avoid and dismiss the actual footage in front of them in favor of a transcendentalist "ideal" footage that would explain everything if only they were permitted to see it. The viewer protects himself or herself from too much self-knowledge, suspending the moment when the self must open up and become other, and indulging in the fantasy that this moment will be an effortless satori, or illumination. The film will revelate; any changes that occur in the watchers will be an automatic transmogrifying, beatification, the form and content of an analysis no longer necessary. But such a point can only be reached by undergoing a process of merging one's subjectivity with the film, and becoming an otherness-in-one, and nothing could be harder and less effortless.

Finally, two of the young filmmakers, Motoki (Kazuo Goto) and Yasuko (Sukio Fukuoka), are left alone. "What could he have been trying to say?" Motoki asks. "To make it his testament," she says quickly, as if the matter were completely obvious. He grows angry and says, "He never existed. The idiot who made this idiot film never existed!" This is, of course, an oxymoron that makes no attempt to deny the fact that the film itself proves its maker's—some maker's—existence. Again, metaphysics envies cinema: the phenomenology of the world might like to prove the existence of some maker but cannot do so because the process of how it came to be is untraceable, unrepeatable, the opposite of a technological or even an epistemological mastery.

However, the testament footage has already begun to perform its unconscious work on Motoki. Shortly after watching it, he is walking on the street lost in thought, and gets accosted by a young man dressed exactly like himself, who looks at him and apologizes, "Sorry, I thought you were someone else." Motoki's exact double misrecognizes him, a dramatization of Motoki's alienated, automorphic consciousness. This is the extension of cinematic ontology into a "real world" in which the viewer's sense of self is temporarily or permanently altered by a film. One no longer knows oneself; at the same time, one is no longer *alone* in oneself; the self has been briefly externalized as a character, or set of characters, moving through the dramatic action. Different aspects of oneself, disguised as elements of the film, as characters, actors, ideas, move within oneself and install themselves. Subject-object ungrounding is taking hold of Motoki.[7] It is also taking over Yasuko, who was lovers with the dead man, and who later attempts to merge her consciousness with the testament-film when she tells Motoki about how he gave her "a silent embrace" on their last morning together, then screens the testament footage on her nude body. The unspoken is a signal of subject-object inversion, just as much as the misspoken (Motoki's encounter on the street with his double).

Motoki's inability to forgive the dead friend—his assertion that this friend "never existed"—is, of course, his refusal of a part of himself that fears his own lack of engaged commitment, his own defeatism, his own ersatzness perhaps. His refusal tries to defer, and at the same time inevitably reifies, the personal mental exhaustion of trying to conceive an impossible "radical cinema." Yasuko also expresses at one point that she now hates her former lover. Death has made the friend's subjectivity an enemy, he can now only be encountered as pure object, pure other. But this too leads to a psychological block for his survivors, which they must circumvent by again trying to come to terms with what he has filmed, to "beat him," as they say, at his own subject-object game.

Oshima seems to suggest, as a master filmmaker telling this tale of earnest young amateurs, that one must stare into those disowned, embarrassing corners of the self, for they contain truths excluded by idealism and dogmatism. Motoki's rejection of the testament-film expresses a need on his part to feel a special distinction. "It's a place like a million others," he says, referring to a location depicted in the footage. "It's a miserable landscape! A filthy landscape like any other!" A film is both there and not there, comparable to the world in so many ways but at the same time definitively removed from the world's reality. Again, it verges on the occult, self-knowledge seeking to protect itself from otherness through a kind of magic blindness which comes and goes, and which affects different viewers to varying degrees. This is similar to the way that the ten-year-old Toshio (Tetsuo Abe) in Oshima's *Boy* (*Shônen*, 1969) tries to escape the dreary reality of his life by imagining that he is a space alien: "I look like a human being but I am really from Andromeda." For Oshima such strategies belong to childhood, to poverty and desperation, or to superstition.

When two people see different things in a film, it is no different than if they see different things in reality. "You're the one who can't see it," Yasuko tells Motoki exactly as if she were speaking of some privileged ghost, Badiou's representation of degraded spirituality as an empty figure. Of course, the more they have watched the testament-footage, the more it *has* merged with their consciousness in spite of their resistance, and become more like a finished film, with its own internal logic and continuity, its own reassuring patterns. They have conditioned themselves to find *something* in the footage, and thus something is now there: themselves. It is largely the unconscious aspect of cinematic ontology that enables it to become so potent and meaningful; films become embedded in different substrata of our consciousness, just like raw experience. Some parts are fully conscious, other parts are subjected to screen-memory and distortion, still other parts work on us below our levels of direct perception. Motoki and Yasuko have, in fact, memorized each detail of the footage, and recite these details to each other like a series of sacred vows while they make love (the footage is here projected on both of their naked bodies). This is like knowledge extracted under hypnotic trance, and Oshima portrays now the objective mingling of three minds, three consciousnesses, three subjectivities, made up of two watchers and one filmmaker—actually, four subjectivities in total if one counts the film as a separate subjectivity which alters its watchers and which has been altered by its maker's death and by the relation of its watchers to it, by the associations they bring to it, etc.

The testament film changes upon different viewings, as Maureen Turim has noted[8]; in this screening of the sacred vows, for example, documentary scenes of a student demonstration appear, interrupting the apathetic landscapes, since political action is on Motoki's and Yusako's minds. The testament footage is a way of breaking open their individual subjectivities and mingling them, like the act of coitus or conversation. In return, the film too is broken up, expanding to include more and more of what they come to "see" in it, and even what they only yearn to see in it. Later in the film, as Motoki and Yusako draw closer to a full merger of subjectivities, the testament footage finally comes to incorporate the opening scene of *The Man Who Left His Will on Film* itself into the chain of intersubjectivities. Consciousness makes and remakes itself relentlessly, even beyond the human; or rather, objects are anthropomorphized as they enter (our) human consciousness. Each breeching of consciousness's borders is the recognition of a larger, indeed endless borderlessness. Otherness is everywhere, it is everything, not only inside oneself but in the space where one would stand if one could look at oneself, especially there. "He's there," Yusako says, "he's watching us from behind the screen."[9] But she might as well be saying "it" instead of "he," the unseen presence being otherness itself. (Ghostliness, too.)

There may very well be something moribund and pathetic in an ontology that comes into focus only via the mediation of closed cinematic texts (no matter how richly ambiguous and significant these texts might be). To an extent, it is an ontological refuge for damaged psyches. Also, this containment of experience—like the relative containment of subject and object (one is always fixed and unchanging in relation to the other: either we accept the film's given reality or alter its meaning to fit our own)—enables a unique paranoia, definitely political in nature, to play out in safe seclusion. (*The Man Who Left His Will on Film* is an early harbinger of the same late-stage revolutionary paranoia that marks other 1970s films, including Luchino Visconti's *Conversation Piece* [*Gruppo di famiglia in un interno*, 1974] and Rainer Werner Fassbinder's *The Third Generation* [*Die Dritte Generation*, 1979]). It is a containment in which the obvious wrongs of the world can be pinned down, pointed to, even studied; and in which every element is potentially heroic—filmmaker, film, viewer—simply for having the temerity to exist, to see, to think. It alternately antagonizes and pacifies a radical-political ontology which, in a conservative nation like Japan, feels itself to be chronically on the outside, manipulated, being sold propagandistic lies and whitewashed histories.

The young radicals in *The Man Who Left His Will on Film* certainly recognize their beleaguered and even dangerous position. Their Bolex is a lifeline; by documenting street protests, they intend not only to spread news of radical activity in Japan but to capture any police brutality against the protesters. By using their shared camera to "leave *his* will on film" (a personal, selfish expression rather than one committed to the group and its struggle), their friend has hijacked, and reoriented, the group's conscious understanding of the world and itself. Inevitably, Motoki and Yasuko, in what they call the "War of Landscapes," go out and find the actual locations, retracing the filmmaker's last steps, placing themselves directly into the space of his subjective vision. This is close to the final stage of opening up and becoming othered by a film. The filmmaker has already merged with his film for one and all; now it their turn.

Initially, they end up chasing phantoms; Yusako feels his presence, strong enough to knock her to the ground, but she can liken it to no recognizable phenomenological experience. As if becoming a shifting actor in an anarchic comedy (Malcolm McDowell in Lindsay Anderson's *If...* [1968], let's say), Motoki himself chases people who vanish; charges across a bridge with an automatic rifle; and suddenly turns up in a highway construction worker's helmet for no apparent reason (seeking the elusive "proletarian consciousness," perhaps). It is as if he is passing rapidly through various degrees of otherness, trying on costumes and poses for fit. It is only when Yusako places herself into the view of Motoki's camera while he re-films the same locations that new, unforeseen things begin to happen; indeed, Yusako and Motoki become sacrifices in an unfolding series of raw experiences that materially alter them: Yusako is arrested and beaten by the police for loitering; she is smacked around by a businessman (or yakuza) who finds her irritating; both young people are kidnapped by a car full of men, one of whom rapes Yusako as Motoki watches sadly. In entering the film as it has entered them, they have become different people, and lost some of the delusional integrity of being defended selves-apart, insular egos that can go through life untouched. They have also materially changed the testament-film's reverential eschatological status as a last thing by creating something new, in defiance of closed-off perceptions.

Meanwhile, resorting to solipsism, the rest of the group of friends is saddened to think that "we're the only ones left who can build a cultural front," meaning the only ones left in all of Japan. (In a hilarious moment of self-referentiality, they talk about asking for help from Nagisa Oshima. This is Oshima congratulating himself on no longer being a struggling young turk; he has passed into the role of Japanese "Elder Statesman.") Yet, again, the film denies the eschatology it invokes as a reference. There is never a "last" anything here; frontlines are continuously pushed backward and forward by life, by reality, or by that "imagination" which the group agrees is necessary to political art and action. Art is regeneration, not only because it can bring about regenerations but because it essentially stems from them. As the postwar intellectual Shûgo Honda noted, "Where joy and fascination do not burst forth from within the artist, where passion does not flow outward from the self—the individual self—of the artist, all art will die."[10] The artist is a privileged citizen, laboring but not a laborer, sympathetic perhaps to collective struggle albeit someone whose purpose derives from following his or her own visions and instincts, a would-be revolutionary but one who finds a way to place his or her own responses to the world above dogmatic sloganeering.

Such championing of individualism has always met with resistance from traditional forms of organized religion as well as from the modern secular corollary of religion, political ideologies; and here I am not only speaking of Japan, although postwar Japan provides many exemplary instances of nascent individualisms running afoul of self-abnegating Buddhists no less than collectivist Marxists. The hopeful artistic imagination and its eventual bourgeois failure already appeared as a theme of Kenji Mizoguchi's *Ugetsu* (*Ugetsu monogatari*, 1953), in which some promise is initially held out for Genjûrô (Masayuki Mori)—as an artist, a potter—to resist the evil tides of war-torn, feudal Japan in the 16th century; we see this in his daydream of bringing home lavish kimonos for his dutiful wife Miyagi (Kinuyo Tanaka). But Mizoguchi argues that this imagination would have to be almost superhuman to overcome such a hard life in a bereft world. The daydream withers quickly in the world's harsh light; its deferred satisfactions do not jibe with the artist's natural spontaneity, his need to draw connections, his ingrained, natural sensuality; also, the trust he must place in people who express the desire to become his patrons. The nature of feudalism itself sets up the negative boundaries, the lack of options, by which even the most miserable and put-upon within its domain are driven to cling to it ever more thoroughly. The most tempting "way out" is to yield to selfish solipsism, thereby reifying the predatory and closed aspects of feudalist life. Indeed, Genjûrô ultimately succumbs to the temptation to betray his wife for an easier, wealthier, more pleasurable marriage with the aristocratic, too-good-to-be-true Lady Wasaka (Machiko Kyô).

In Kenji Mizoguchi's *Ugetsu* (*Ugetsu monogatari*, 1953), Genjûrô (Masayuki Mori) is a peasant attempting to maintain his responsibilities to his devoted wife Miyagi (Kinuyo Tanaka) and their young son Genichi (Ichisaburo Sawamura), while also pursuing a career as a potter in war-torn Medieval Japan. In Mizoguchi's powerful vision, women are left to languish, usually being made to suffer unfairly for the prideful ambitions of the men in their world.

The problem of revolutionary consciousness on both individual and mass levels has been an ongoing one, as Masato Ara writes:

> The masses' feudalistic attitudes and lack of *shutaisei* [subjectivity] could be transcended, not simply through a movement for popular enlightenment, but by means of struggle against the actual feudal relations that constrain them.[11]

So, in Oshima's *The Man Who Left His Will on Film*, Motoki and his friends must try to rise above a different, modern kind of civil war, one where power lines are blurrier, but where the most difficult aspect of life is still maintaining one's own thoughts and convictions while remaining open to experience. Here, in the largest sense, we are interested in a subjectivity that is not strictly bound up within individualism, but open, shattered open in some cases, to the meanings posed by otherness in all its forms; put otherwise, the total breakdown and reorganization of that "unitary, self-consistent nature" which Max Weber determined to be the collective-societal subject.[12] Consciousness is not linear, so political consciousness cannot be either, without becoming a lie.

Also, we note that there can be no vacuum inside subjectivity. Every interior space is filled with consciousness of something—of itself if nothing else. This is why anything can be absorbed into someone's consciousness. Another's consciousness survives in Motoki whether he wants it to or not. Nor does it even die with him in the end, as

Motoki jumps from the same building only to have yet another figure, possibly a regeneration of Motoki himself, make off with the new testament-footage. *The Man Who Left His Will on Film*, Turim writes, "flirts with nihilism, but tips its final hand-off to the imagination, to renewal, to creative regeneration."[13] But this is more of an embryonic hope than a fully realized regeneration within the diegesis as such and also within Oshima's sympathy for the young people's political activity. There is simply nothing in filmmaking that corresponds to the charged blank page of the writer, the space of beginning, of waiting, gravid emptiness, where anything or indeed nothing might happen. Because film is in its essence the intersection of the "natural" world with a recording technology, it is never reducible to just one of these two parts (world or technology). The Bolex itself makes the young filmmakers feel wistful and empowered, but it is as much a superstitious fetish as an actual fully-fledged tool, especially when it is not being used to film anything; and the world itself is a conundrum, in many respects pointedly not natural and also not one which the young filmmakers can claim to have made.

It is a moment as poignant as it is confounding when Motoki visits his mother's house, late in the film, and prepares a snack to eat in his old room, after first making sure that this room has not been co-opted by his younger brother, who still lives at home: he opens the curtains on the window above his desk, and there is the same view from the opening shot of the testament-footage, trees waving with other houses in the background. We see that it is not as simple as saying that film "redeems" subjectivity—subjectivity itself is displaced from its beginning, always an accident for one reason or another, never special, never properly owned by any one person. If we can claim to own some perception of reality, it is only because we have allowed that perception, that reality, to own us in turn. We must sacrifice something on its behalf. The filmmaker's homelife is beyond the purview of even his closest friends, who are not primed to search out such intimacies in their politically charged work, anyway. Yet, this undermines and even disproves the psychical communism of film, if you will, the idea that we can share whole parts of reality through a film, and you will see everything exactly as I do, I will see everything exactly as you do, even without the mediation of language; somewhat like Andy Warhol's Pop Art utopia of the 1960s in which everyone, rich or poor, can drink the exact same Coke,[14] but more troublesome in that we are not talking about the simple consumption of a uniform commercial product. Instead, we are talking about life and death themselves.

To be sure, cinematic ontology is larger in scope, more universally existential and basic than any specific (politicized) agenda which can be associated with it. What Oshima depicts, in *The Man Who Left His Will on Film*, is the way we watch all movies, not always with the same personal urgency but with that reflexive and continuous inversion of subject and object. Perhaps Badiou's sense that fundamentalist belief offers us an obscure Subject is only partly true in relation to cinema (as I am applying it); perhaps it is truer, in fact, to say that it is the (cinematic) Object which is obscure, the sounds and images themselves, the presence of the film's creator(s). How often do we remember a film quite differently from how it actually "happened"? It is the Freudian slip of cinema, the insistence that it happened *this way*, only to have it pointed out to us, by a more objective viewer, that it didn't happen that way at all. To re-watch is to risk disabusing ourselves of faulty and self-deluding memory, which nonetheless serves some consoling or at least creative purpose. And there again is the inescapable conclusion that film is the evidentiary Real for something nonexistent, something undefined: infallible where "we" are prone to make mistakes; forgiving where we are prone to locked-in judgments; patiently revealing itself to the avid and disinterested alike, etc. (Just as certain ceremonies of serving and eating sushi in small quantities at a time ensure that the essence of the food remains: its freshness; its sense of quality over quantity.) The immobile mover has once again changed *us*.

* * * * *

If ontology itself, as Badiou describes it, "lies in the difficult passage whereby it has to explore the thinkable dimension of the pure multiple without ever being able to state the specific conditions a multiple affords,"[15] then film, I believe, is an ideal exemplar of this transitory ontology. Cinema is, to borrow the wording of Kelsey Wood on the *Parmenides*, "the encounter with the other (*to heteron*) that changes the soul of the learner and reconfigures the ordering that is cosmos."[16]

This would make cinema potentially something more than the "re-enchantment of the world."[17] Rather, it would mark a full return of something that might pass for how we would imagine ontological wholeness. Cinema would seem to redeem the ontological impasse whereby, as Wood writes, "Any representation of being is necessarily a misrepresentation."[18] Like the indiscriminate footage of ordinary landscapes shot by the dead filmmaker in *The Man Who Left His Will on Film*, there is always *something* in the representation of the world, a more or less reassuring here-and-now that can be pointed to, even freeze-framed, replayed, comprehensively inventoried and defined. Cinema offers truth "separated from its context," truth that no longer changes because its context no longer changes, unlike the phenomenology of world, which, as Wood reminds us, "is in a constant process of change."[19] (Film can, again, be likened to what Badiou describes as the supreme immobile mover.)

Clearly, this is precisely why cinema is one of the most contested zones of ideology, epistemology, and ontology in our time, since film enacts the birth of aware being in the simultaneous symbolic death of an authorial entity, at the same time using more or less direct life (via recording, realist simulation, documentation). It is when a film passes from its makers' hands to its viewers' eyes that it becomes "ours," the audience who lays correct or incorrect claims to it, and this is, of course, overdetermined by the partisan interpretation of nearly everything in our postmillennial chaos. Film replicates the diffuseness of active organic life, and though it has been ordered, structured, by specific human beings, the imposition of the frame is never the entire picture and must achieve a naturalness or at least the appearance of inevitability if it is not to be questioned. Advocates for plainer, unedited, real-time cinema are often searching for a textual reality that will not throw into question the fantasy that film has immaculate origins, that it doubles for an ineffable world that can be revealed but never fully explained. By this logic, filmmakers are reduced to essentially glorified set dressers of the world. The director did not give birth to the actors, did not plant the trees; locations have an existence outside of the diegesis, etc. Although it is an exemplar of that God-like cinema-as-immobile-mover, or even (in sacrilegious terms) *because* it is, each film inevitably does what Badiou defines as the work of conscious art: it puts its own God to death.[20] Thus, this death of filmic authorship is or should be ordinary and rote, and not truly at the service of some lost or unimagined wholeness, as some would seem to wish; nor even truly definitive as a death of authorship. Quite the opposite, the filmic image is not an irreducible, primary entity that can resolve our human doubts about unitary being; and the most accurate way of reading films finally remains one which places an emphasis on their artifice, their relation to their own times, and their creative intentionality.

For the creative intentionality behind a film is actually nothing but the blueprint for our own understanding of the film, as its watchers. The art of film is in tracing, in space and time, the series of moves by which subjectivity incorporates otherness. What makes ensemble films like George Cukor's *The Women* (1939) or Robert Altman's *Nashville* (1975) so dazzling to experience is that these moves are happening in many directions at once, a kind of cat's-cradle looping back and forth through the stretched fingers of a hand. Badiou points to a non-explicit "negative duty"[21] as the way a single apprehending consciousness splits itself off in order to enter, and be entered by, a multiplicity of phenomena, and we can apply this to any data which inputs into consciousness, living or recorded. Ontological consciousness learns to absorb new uncertainties and find new bearings; as watchers we are constantly taking in the cinematic manifold while automatically unifying it as it unfolds within our consciousness, and simultaneously de-unifying our consciousness as we take in otherness.

Film is finally an objective correlative to the self; as Emiko Ohnuki-Tierney writes, "The self cannot be defined in the abstract. It cannot be without reference to the specific other."[22] Hence, film watching is exemplary watching: it delineates the borders of self, of empathy and identification, of interpretative vagaries and the always messy trade-offs between solipsism and engagement. We note otherness-in-one even as we elide and basically forget it. We do this, too, in a busy café or on a street, where we are confronted with epiphenomenological data which alternately reinforce and erode our personal boundaries. Yet in life, it is all improvisatory, the data and our responses; it precisely lacks the illusion of a form, though we may choose to assign it one (astrology, luck, superstition, physics, politics). With films there is the possibility of rehearsing the performance of response vis-à-vis a closed field of (textual) reality; what eludes our tendency to unify is what strikes us as most providential. The total impression which any film makes upon us is nothing more than the residual impression of the otherness that persists in leaving its trace around the otherness-in-one, thereby causing us to think about mental processes of apprehension and interpretation which would otherwise only be random, reflexive, unstudied, fleeting.

Cinema is no longer the innocent proof that we exist; it is closer to the guilty proof that we have been damaged, that we exist only outside of ourselves, in active discord with our palpable realities. Indeed, the history of cinema from its earliest years has been a history of increasingly complex fragmentations: continuity into discontinuity, omniscience into subjectivity, discrete time into polychronic times, proscenium space into locations, pre-montage into post-montage, uniform silence into layered sounds. One thinks of Claude Lévi-Strauss' assertion, in *The Raw and the Cooked*, that a culture comes to know itself through a visual code that distinguishes between whole and broken objects—for instance, a liquid "homogeneous" inside a vessel versus the same liquid "spilled" upon the ground—and that behind these recognitions of difference there always lurks the largest possible contrast of the visual code, "between visible and invisible."[23] Every operation by which we perceive the world is inherently a proposition in which we learn to apprehend general presence or absence, and more specifically, general wholeness or brokenness.

Cinema's creative secret, its plastic interest—unlike other art forms—lies not in the creation of an approximate form which can substitute for reality, but instead the apprehending of a proximate form that is already made in the image of the real. Each shot bears a recognizable subject which is already a multiplicity, given the co-existence, within the frame, of people and objects who are themselves multiplicities; and each shot-subject exists in relation to its observer, who is also already a multiplicity, and who either chooses to adopt one or more aspects of the shot-subject(s) as his or her reality in a bid to become an even vaster, more occupied multiplicity ... or not.

Actually, the choice is often subliminal, and we can be altered by a film without even realizing or seeking this. In fact, we feel that we are still whole entities even as cinematic ontology works to fragment us into separate strands of otherness-in-one. For example, what happens when we gaze at the filmed image of a woman who is herself gazing into the night, at the sight of moonlight reflected in water? We see the broken object, the absence, the invisible which she (from her site of visibility) is attempting to locate; we see it through objects (woman, water, light) whose wholeness is disguised by framing, lighting, viewpoint, editing. At the same time our yearning is always stronger than the evidence presented to it, and therefore unfulfilled. It is the ontological mark of the broken object that the same thing which awakens our sensitivity of response (to the object's nuances) also leaves us dissatisfied: mortality and immortality no less than actual bodies (of people, of water, of light) are never wholly there, but only from certain partial or oblique angels.[24] We cannot say with certainty that what we are looking at is broken or whole, visible or invisible, real or unreal; ours is the first civilization that fails Lévi-Strauss' test of common-sensical judgment about unitary presence or absence. Although we might retain the illusion of being whole rather than broken objects, we only understand a given film by slipping inside it, becoming part of it, becoming connected to it at many different loci like the suckers of an octopus' tentacles, and therefore losing our own wholeness.

And just as nature becomes culture through a process of adulteration, of breaking-down and incorporation, so the aforementioned general tendency of cinema toward greater fragmentation is in itself a movement from nearly raw nature toward something ever more and more removed from the natural, yet fundamentally unable to finally and fully release itself from that nature from which it came. The separated parts still long for their affiliations to a state of being that has not been previously coded. It is an example of Badiou's "subtractive Being," or what he calls "the theory of inconsistent multiplicities."[25] "This means that what lends itself to the thought of ontology," he writes, "is a manifold without a predicate other than its own multiplicity."[26] More specifically, Emiko Ohnuki-Tierney has written about the moon in water as an ultimate emblem of the self extending itself toward otherness, "striving to reach a transcendental self as symbolized in the mirror—that is, the moon."[27] The enigma of the moon-in-water cannot ever be found, but it is significant that the woman looks for it, that we see her looking for it, and that we identify with her search.

What can block the process of otherness-in-one is something like racism, which takes the form of a hostile projection by which we pass judgment on the other for things that we already consider frightening or shameful. In Oshima's *Death by Hanging* (*Kôshikei*, 1968), R. (Do-yun Yu) is a nameless Korean accused of rape and murder by the Japanese court. When he survives his own execution (in a piece of magic realism), the officers of the court must reconstruct his crimes and, even more, what they take to be his core identity before they can execute him again. In the eyes of the Japanese officials, R. is a predatory animal, deluded into thinking of himself as human. They take the resurrected R. back to the slum where he used to live, and because R. is calm rather than violent, they coach him to "get angry." Instead, R. hangs his head in sorrow. In recreating R.'s supposedly disreputable home life, two of the Japanese play the parts of what they imagine to be R.'s drunken father and dissolute brother; in so doing, the Japanese men begin fighting each other in earnest, acting out the projected violence which they ascribe to the Other. Pretending to be "Korean" (according to their racist views) gives them license to be antisocial and even criminal. A Japanese officer ends up strangling a young woman in his attempts to demonstrate how vile R. is as a Korean.

Death by Hanging is a bit of a one-note symphony, yet it provides key insights into racist projection. Although Japanese and Koreans are both Asian ethnicities, the Japanese have historically treated Koreans in ways that are classically racist: Koreans living in Japan were not allowed to vote, were banned from becoming civil servants, policemen or teachers, and could not get hired by major corporations.[28] Furthermore, the Korean colony was kept in a state of chronic impoverishment during its thirty-six years under Japanese rule.[29] Oshima was frequently vocal in his criticism of these attitudes and policies. *Death by Hanging* deconstructs the visceral "othering" of Korean identity by the Japanese. What is lacking in racist relations is the presence of otherness-in-one; in fact otherness-in-one is the very opposite of projection, the introjection of the other into oneself, a blending in which the best of oneself seeks out the best of the other. R. is dehumanized by being watched over, and by having his captors constantly try to read his thoughts, which they misinterpret and hold against him. They are like a clumsy, imperceptive audience, seeing only what it wishes to see. R. is brought a drink by a waitress in a bar; when he so much as sips the drink, he is accused of wanting to rape the waitress ("Oh, so she was the one you wanted!") even though R. could not be more indifferent to her. The evil thoughts stem from the racist mind and flow toward and into the racialized other; it is the broken looking glass which only ontological otherness-in-one can smooth over. Intriguingly, this same claustrophobic psychological encroachment emerges around the issue of homophobia in Oshima's last film, *Taboo* (*Gohatto*, 1999), where even the slightest attention paid to the androgynous young samurai Kano (Ryûhei Matsuda) within the all-male Shinsen militia is read as an indicator of same-sex desire and leads to rumors of gay sex. This kind of policing projection is how we treat animals, small children, and criminals, and even in these cases it can be abusive; applied to anyone else it is the essence of oppression.

This is all equivalent to saying that the operation of seeing ourselves (the human) in any film is simultaneously the operation of seeing ourselves as otherness, as multiplicities. At the same time, we keep patching over our porous boundaries by knitting the film itself into an overall meaning, and by identifying with its strongest points of

The beautiful androgynous samurai Kano (Ryûhei Matsuda, right) forces Tashiro (Tadanobu Asano), his fellow samurai and ardent admirer, away from his bed at night by knifepoint in a tense scene from Oshima's last film, *Taboo* (*Gohatto*, 1999). Male same-sex desire is viewed as a chaotic ruling principle incompatible with the respect and trust required for militarism; but Oshima denotes this as a shortcoming of militarism itself rather than an indictment of homosexuality.

individual identification: like the woman gazing at moon-in-water, for example. If we step outside of our rationalistic selves and subject the process to a greater degree of honesty, we acknowledge that these identifications are bulwarks, forestallings, against seeing ourselves as we always already truly are, as (broken) multiplicities. It also requires a deeper, more felt relation to the film we are watching. Cinema helps with our coming to see ourselves as multiplicities since it requires the watcher to open up and identify with a variety of human characters and perspectives, including but not limited to the filmmaker's. Cinema is otherness-in-one, or what Kelsey Wood calls "mixed wholeness,"[30] in which "even intelligence itself intimately involves its opposite within itself"[31] and "even the sameness of logical identity is shown to be permeated by nonlogical otherness."[32] And we can break this down even further. Watching a film, we know what we know, and we also know that there are things we do not know, all of which are integral aspects of our knowledge, which is a complex multiplicity. And we begin to sustain all these multiplicities within our consciousness, as they already exist, layered and overlapping, within the film itself.

Part One

Toward the Last Ontology

It is perfectly possible to argue that some distinctive objects are made by the mind, and that these objects, while appearing to exist objectively, have only a fictional reality.

—Edward W. Said[1]

The cinema ... aims at transforming the agitated witness into conscious observer.

—Siegfried Kracauer[2]

The heart itself will be explored by experts, and I doubt if you or I do qualify, for we are strangers to the vagaries of science and history, but not to the contact of the eyes, the touch of pulse, the sound of footsteps on the stairs, and the fragrances of love.

—Nicholas Ray[3]

1

Moon in Water

The archetypal Zen image of a woman looking at the moon reflected in water appears in a Japanese film, Kôji Wakamatsu's *Caterpillar* (*Kyatapirâ*, 2010). The otherness-in-one that we began to explore in the previous chapter is symbolized quintessentially, according to Japanese Zen Buddhism, by the figure of moonlight reflected in different bodies of water. "The moon is but one," Daisetz T. Suzuki writes, "but its reflections are seen wherever there is water."[1] There is synergy between moon and water that is spontaneous and independent of either: "Neither the moon nor water has any preconceived idea of producing the incident designated by us as 'the moon in water.'"[2] Moreover, there is a transcending of individual will, a transcending which comes about strictly through passive, random being. "Again, it is all the same to the moonlight whether there are so many bodies of water, or there is just one little puddle."[3] Fate, serendipity, harmony are all evoked by this simple image.

Wakamatsu's use of this image in *Caterpillar*, however, is bruisingly sarcastic. The protagonists in his film blatantly fail, or never even try, to live up to Buddhist ideals; and their resigned drifting with the currents of history is shown to be heinous and inhumane. The woman, Shigeko (Shinobu Terajima), is an abused wife striving to please her maimed, crippled husband Tadashi (Keigo Kasuya), a veteran of the Pacific Asia War, a brutal man who took part in the Rape of Nanking. Her gazing at moon-in-water demonstrates how slavishness to Buddhist concepts of resignation and passivity has harmed Japan, as well as Confucian concepts of female obedience to males, or youthful obedience to elders. Yet, since these concepts have always played out more flexibly in actual social history than in their religious "ideals," it would be more accurate to say that what harmed the Japanese was the conviction that they *ought* to follow these concepts slavishly. At the same time, for our purposes of understanding Japanese cinema, we can see that on another level Wakamatsu respects the meaning of moon-in-water, its symbolic congruency, its establishment of multiplicity or otherness-in-one. Moon and water change in contact with each other to become a third entity, a beautiful, enhanced entity. This is the ideal. The ability to become like moon-in-water is alien to fundamentally Western paradigms of thinking, in which the philosopher makes an enemy out of reality and situates it permanently outside of himself, not as something to be smoothly and harmoniously blended with, but as an opponent to be faced down and fought against.[4]

There is a place for resistance in Japanese Zen thinking, and in Japanese cinema as well, which has been in different eras among the more violent and confrontational of world cinemas (Wakamatsu, for example, had been making controversial films since the 1960s; *Caterpillar* was one of his late masterpieces), but it is a resistance that takes place decidedly after the failure of blending, of making common cause with otherness. In Akira Kurosawa's *Ikiru* (1952), Watanabe (Takashi Shimura) must finally be disabused of the reactive egoism that cares how others around him might perceive or misperceive his actions; in short, he comes to live truly *for* others (the children whose lives he improves by having a public park built in a slum) only after refusing to live *by* the judgments of others (his disapproving son and daughter-in-law, who live with him and only think the worst of him). And in *Ran*, Kurosawa's version of *King Lear*, old Lord Hidetora (Tatsuya Nakadai) brings about his downfall when he attempts to demonstrate his love for his sons and coax expressions of their love in return; he does not cede power to them because he believes they are ready to rule and because he himself is ready to abdicate and die (these reasons would involve some accurate assessment of reality, and thus a living-for-others), so much as *pretend* to cede power in order to dwell within the same power-relationships, meant to be ameliorated by a greater albeit phony outwardness of mutual affection and trust (living-by-others). Kurosawa makes us see that what is at the heart of *King Lear* is the protagonist's inability to show love in ways that are not materially quantifiable (speech, land) and thus imbricated with, and tainted by, unequal power relations. Hidetora's overestimation of his two older sons' love for him is the fatal flaw in his attempted otherness-in-one; Taro (Akira Terao) and Jiro (Jinpachi Nezu) have never abandoned the way of self-interest, a fact to which Hidetora's pride blinds him. Finally, as a person who comes to achieve a greater modernity, Watanabe in *Ikiru* can overcome personal pride to become an opened, othered self, closer to strangers in the end than to his own flesh and blood, and compatible with being of service to others; but Hidetora is stuck in feudalism: he tries to renounce power and simultaneously maintain it, a state which harms his interests as well as the interests of his kingdom.

Whether serviceable harmony with others is always desirable or not, is a separate question. In Western cinema, as in Western existence, we tend to search for individual happiness or fulfillment; if we cannot find it, we regard that as a negative. But this is not as true in Japanese thought and culture where individual happiness is often relegated to a backseat to the common order, the common good. This concept goes by different names: *giri*, meaning social obligation, and *wa*, meaning group or social harmony. The individual's needs and demands hold no special, preeminent place.

As has often been noted, female characters have been resonant in expressing a longing for individualism, as well as the limitations of that individualism, in Japanese cinema. What jeopardizes *giri* and *wa* often comes to the individual first as a shock, a dare, a dislocation. The jolt of a morally good, conscientious woman having to re-examine her own values under duress is depicted in Yasujirô Ozu's *A Hen in the Wind* (*Kaze no naka no mendon*, 1948), for example, in a series of edits between close-ups of the despairing, penniless Tokiko (Kinuyo Tanaka) staring into a mirror and then her mirror image staring back at her; the shots are angled and framed so that we see almost two distinct women, with differences in posture, sightline, relation to composition, etc. By the time Tokiko has put her face in her hands to weep, Ozu has begun to have louche music playing on the soundtrack, preparing us for a cut to the inside of a geisha house; within an empty room, all the signifiers of prostitution are laid out for us: a bottle of sake, a cigarette in an ashtray, a Western-style bed with a small electric fan perched at its head, faint pulsing neon through a single desultory window. These elements of Tokiko's future (very different from her past, and from her self-image) have been read inside the mirror as if through a magic lantern. Another, distinct self has been extracted from the former self, through a series of traumatic events: her husband has not returned from the war; her child has become seriously ill. Tokiko has never ceased to live *for* the others in her life, earning money through prostitution to save her child's life; but in ceasing to live *by* others (by their moral judgments), Ozu shows us that Tokiko is damned either way, doomed to betray either her child or her husband. Tokiko's potential *self*-betrayal is never at issue for Ozu except insofar as it includes the betrayal of one or another of her familial, societal bonds.

Director Yasuzô Masumura has summarized the situation of emotions in Japanese cinema well:

> In Japanese society, which is essentially regimented, freedom and the individual do not exist. The theme of the Japanese film is the emotions of the Japanese people, who have no choice but to live according to the norms of that society. The cinema has had no alternative but to continue to depict the attitudes and inner struggles of the people who are faced with and oppressed by complex social relationships and the defeat of human freedom.[5]

There are problematic aspects of this. I wish to distinguish between multiplicity and what might be called "adaptation." Many Japanese feel a sense of "isolation"[6] and an inability "to incorporate signs of difference."[7] Mistaken Western assumptions only point to our tendency to reify Western stereotypes of Japan as a compendium of either radically traditional or radically futuristic signs: philosopher Kôjin Karatani has stated, "Japan will remain for the West a place of exteriority rather than being what in fact it is: a discursive space filled with complacency and almost totally lacking in exteriority."[8] Marilyn Ivy calls this "the difficulty for modern Japanese of imagining otherness," and blames it on the tendency of the Japanese to want to see themselves as unique in all things.[9] For our purposes, otherness-in-one is primarily a Zen ideal, and one which we are tracing in the cinema of Japan, where we find much that certainly seems to mitigate against Japanese insularity and complacent self-regard. It is not Tokiko's fault, in *A Hen in the Wind*, for example, that she must bear alone a new shameful secret about herself; nor is it Ozu's fault for showing us that this shame is all but irresolvable according to Japanese decorum. In fact, it is only through the film that we understand something of the nature of this "regimented" social order at all.

Therefore, it is perhaps only through its cinema that Japan becomes brave, progressive, expansive; naturally holistic without strain, empathetic without disgust. That is okay, for what concerns us at the moment is *cinematic ontology*, of which Japanese cinema (in all eras) provides us with numerous strong, exciting, fascinating instances. The mind of a film, its consciousness, is not different from our own; but so much of what the West considers endemic to critical thinking and to the rational appreciation of art often makes it difficult for us to reach this point of otherness-in-one with the cinematic image. It is either us or other, but rarely both at the same time; we are either lost in rapturous identification *or* in objective contemplation. Such is Western ontology. In Japanese cinema we find a startling crossing of these wires. Objectivity is everywhere; in general, for example, there is very sparing use of close-ups, which tend to imitate and valorize subjectivity in film language. Visually, Japan's is a cinema of middle and long distances, equalizing everything within its frame, and in this measured, descriptive distancing, identification is always a question, a challenge.

On top of this we are often asked to contemplate people who are themselves out of place, shifting and squirming, unhappy in their environments, painfully unable to transcend themselves. There is seldom a discrepancy in Japanese cinema between what a character is and what he or she purports to be or imagines being. The only discrepancies come, as with Tokiko in *A Hen in the Wind*, from having to suddenly internalize the realization of an ambivalent otherness. What we witness is more typically a spectacle of fully integrated otherness-in-one which nonetheless disconcerts us because it asks us to ingest this spectacle from the standpoint of our own otherness-in-one: identifying and not identifying, venturing within and remaining without, "understanding" (in its most violent, domineering meaning of using up, getting to the end of something, determining, labeling, finally forgetting) and allowing something to simply be. For example, an adult daughter who lives too much for her aged father, the basis of more than one Ozu film: it is moving and even at times disturbing to identify with how much such a daughter has built her inner conflict, her division, into the keystone of her self, brittle and brave and seemingly without needs of her own.

But Zen otherness-in-one is only half the picture. To a certain extent, this can be true of non–Japanese cinema, of any cinema. What Badiou calls "subtraction from the

In Ozu's last masterpiece, *An Autumn Afternoon* (*Sanma no aji*, 1962), Michiko (Shima Iwashita) is an adult daughter who has put off her own wedding and marriage because she has stayed at home taking care of her father. In this scene she is finally dressing for her wedding after the father has agreed to let her be independent of him. Ozu never shows us the groom, as if the wedding and marriage were merely symbolic; what is crucial is the difficult, complex reordering of the bond between parent and child, one which neither has been eager to sunder.

normative power of the One"[10] leads us to be able to see wholeness as always already divided and disputed, and leads us, too, to some of the most cutting-edge revisions of ontology, for example Catherine Malabou's trauma-theory-derived articulation of "destructive plasticity" in persons who have been radically altered, physically and emotionally, by disastrous events, and who have thereby forged new identities, new self-relationships, out of what could be otherwise perceived as deficits or handicaps. We might think of this in particular in relation to Masumura's description of Japanese emotions as being in continuous struggle against social regimentation. "Destructive plasticity," Malabou writes, "enables the appearance or formation of alterity where the other is absolutely lacking. Plasticity is the form of alterity when no transcendence, flight or escape is left. The only other that exists in this circumstance is being other to the self."[11]

Parts of this book will be indebted to Malabou's concept of destructive plasticity, as she relates it to survivors of trauma whose being has been altered either literally or symbolically. Scars, deformities, neurotic anxieties: what the 19th and 20th centuries were content to call "symptoms" to be managed or if possible eradicated, Malabou centers as ineluctable facts of the 21st century consciousness; obstacles which have become embedded in the subject as part of its inevitable journey. "The individual's history is not definitively breached by the meaningless accident," she writes, "an accident that it is impossible to re-appropriate through either speech or recollection…. How do you speak about emotional deficit since words must be carved by the affects whose very absence is precisely what is in question here?"[12] It is survivors of brain damage, neurally reconfigured, whom Malabou specifically posits as a new standard for post-ontological ontology.

We can think of Malabou's sense of the "accident" as similar to Blanchot's "disaster" in *The Writing of the Disaster*; something positive or at least measurable is produced by otherness, destabilized selfhood, and even physical, emotional and mental damage, as something that can be essentially dynamic, stimulating growth and change. Malabou writes: "Yet destruction too is formative. A smashed-up face is still a face, a stump a limb, a traumatized psyche remains a psyche. Destruction has its own sculpting tools."[13] In Kurosawa's *Ikiru*, after the doctor gives Watanabe his fatal diagnosis, we see him walking slowly and morosely down a city street; in a cut to wide angle, we see a noisy, dusty construction site with a cement mixer behind him, and the busy lanes of trucks on the dirt road in front of him. This image of active building is already a premonition of how Watanabe will use his advanced stomach cancer to completely rebuild his own life.

There is a political component to this; Malabou identifies destructive plasticity as a pre-revolutionary condition rather than a resigned one. "The jobless, the homeless, the sufferers of post-traumatic stress syndrome, the deeply depressed, the victims of natural catastrophes, all begin to resemble one another as the new international"[14]—exemplars of destructive plasticity form a new category of the human which is also an oppressed class. (As if to underscore the potential link between destructive plasticity and dystopian paradigms, Malabou associates destructive plasticity with the Kafkaesque.[15]) This new international performs a kind of alienated labor by simply existing.

At the same time, destructive plasticity is about growth, the opening up of unprecedented possibilities and survivals. It is destructive plasticity which enables us to read the cycle of Oshima's *The Man Who Left His Will on Film*, for example, as essentially a traumatized, uncertain expansion of consciousness wherein subject and object continuously

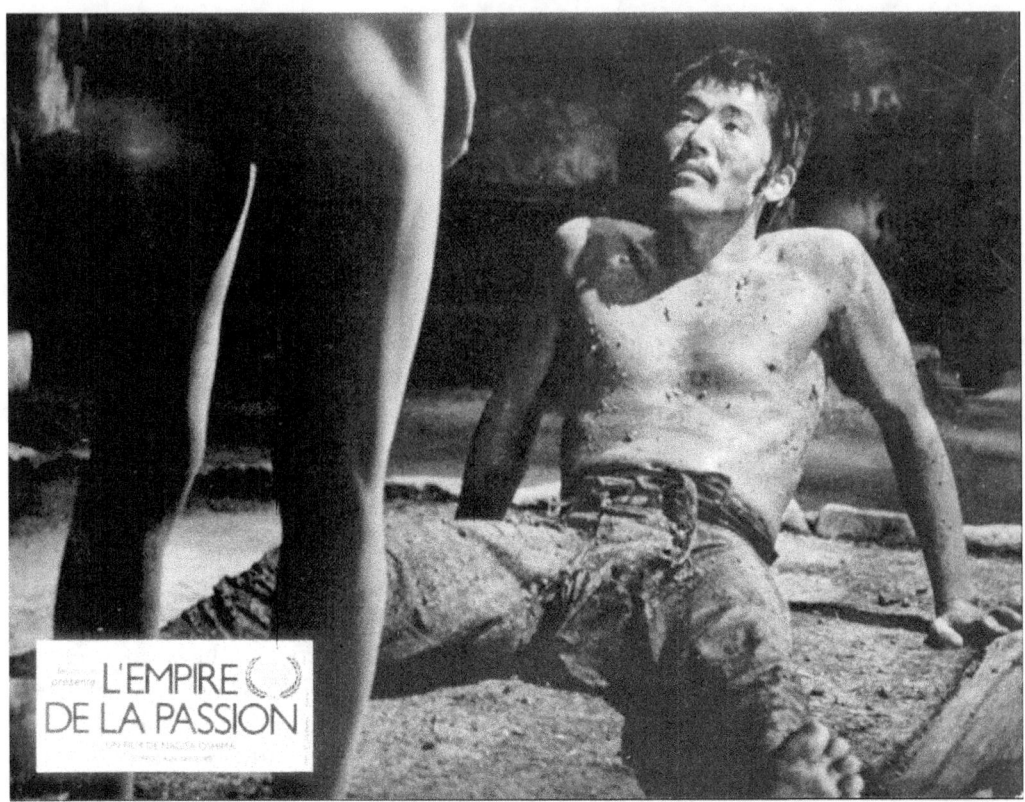

Catherine Malabou writes, "Denial always involved an act of faith, a faith that may be defined as faith in another possible beginning, a source other than the real historical source of what really happened." In this French lobby card for Oshima's *Empire of Passion* (*Ai no bôrei*, 1978), adulterous lovers Seki (Kazuko Yoshiyuki, standing) and Toyoji (Tatsuya Fuji) have been digging in the muddy well where they buried the body of Seki's husband. Their guilty passion renders them increasingly abject; Seki is struck blind by violating the grave.

invert; what appears to be suicide—the organism's willed self-extinction—is in fact merely its change, its expansion as it opens itself to otherness. The subject sees itself as objectively "dead" precisely because it has become other to itself, as part of an ongoing process of living which transforms the subject in constant patterns both randomly apportioned (illness, accidents) and more or less generically preordained (pubescence, aging). Malabou writes, "Denial always involved an act of faith, a faith that may be defined as faith in another possible beginning, a source other than the real historical source of what really happened."[16] This is invoked in repetition compulsion: "In bringing back the scene of the trauma, we simultaneously bring back its denegation, that is, the possibility that nothing happened."[17] Of course, this denial can only be a partial strategy at best, one which recuperates body and psyche until they can function more effectively, also one of the strategies of destructive plasticity. What emerges has withstood its own (symbolic and even material) death.

In Mikio Naruse's *Floating Clouds* (*Ukigumo*, 1955), on one of the occasions when Kengo (Masayuki Mori) turns up after a lengthy absence from the life of the heroine Yukiko (Hideko Takamine), the woman who loves him, he is wearing an eye patch, for a sty, he claims; but in fact we find out later that this patch has only been a ploy to evoke sympathy. Freda Freiberg has noted the radical "compression" which Naruse practices here on the film's source novel.[18] The plot, as if to demonstrate destructive plasticity as a series of traumatic changes that become like effects without direct or perceptible causalities, relentlessly moves the characters forward, so that each time they reunite they are always already deeply embedded in the next phase of their lives. They fill each other in: someone has been murdered, someone else is ill. But Kengo's increasing coldness and Yukiko's increasing frailness are not strictly accounted for by these historical markers, which at any rate are never shown to us directly by Naruse; the events in question belong to the transitory historical realm, whereas Naruse's core drama unfolds within an emotional, ahistorical time where effects and causes are all but incommensurable. In this realm, new relations and identities are tested, while some cling to cruelly shattered hopes; yet every change, for better or worse, is also a moving-forward. As harbingers of survival, the closed, self-centered self and the exploded, fragmented one can be remarkably alike. Likewise, within the context of modern Japan, it is the difficult, engaged, empathetic subjectivity of the young people in *The Man Who Left His Will on Film* that concerns Oshima as a new ideal of Japanese subjectivity, one which will not be militaristic, imperialistic, sexist, racist—and one which will also be able to convert this new acceptance of otherness into original forms of art.

We find the confrontation of a similar psychological block in the surreal, sometimes overheated imagery of Shûji Terayama's autobiographical film, *Pastoral Hide and Seek* (*Den-en ni shisu*, 1974). In a rural village Shin (Hiroyuki Takano), the young son of an imperial officer who died in the war in 1943,[19] experiences enormous conflicts with his absent father and his clinging, neurotic mother; these conflicts are positioned historically as the problem of the postwar generation in general. Terayama shows us photographs of imperial-era officers and geishas, savagely torn and haphazardly stitched back together, so that the pieces barely fit. These pictures seem to have exploded from a too-close proximity of death and life: "In a young woman's loose hair, the word for 'funeral' spelled in roses." Like the young filmmakers in *The Man Who Left His Will on Film*, Terayama's artistic psyche is similarly bursting at the seams, exhausted from having to work within the restrictions of an official image-system. The director's excessive use of zooms implies a frustrated need to run away, to embark impulsively on short flights or leaps that go nowhere; the heart going out, temporarily at least, to something, anything, that captures its imagination. Moreover, many of Terayama's landscapes could be Martian surfaces: Japan, here, is shown as craggy boulders enclosed by drifting, otherworldly mists, a blood-red sun in a black sky (a comment on the "Rising Sun" flag of imperial Japan), and in a particular moment of crisis for Shin (he is sexually assaulted by an aggressive female prostitute), a rippling lake of red-tinged water.

Terayama's imagery is pieced together from the rough edges of theater, camp, and the carnivalesque, somewhat like Werner Schroeter's opera and rock set-pieces in *Eika Katappa* (1969). The need to reconstruct memory, and also to live out a fantasy self—as female, as free, as mad—overrides the ability of the artist to contain his art within linear narrative or realist presentation. (Shin's face is made up with heavy pancake-flour, and in several scenes his mother is played by a transvestite male.) Overwrought women in garish kimonos shriek about not wanting to kill their children, and splash mournfully in rivers like so many ceremonial dolls set adrift inside a philosophical theater. The self is nothing but a series of masks on display, swollen with otherness like the hot-air-balloon wife in a particularly deranged vignette, getting pumped up by her husband, a Mohawked dwarf from a circus sideshow. *Pastoral Hide and Seek* is desperately collaged art, produced by someone seemingly without all the means for, and certainly without much trust in, the processes of making art. The need to reproduce life in art becomes yet another trauma on the copious list, another displaced expectation in which one is forced to confront one's own assumed or voided identities. The film's overripeness, at times rich and kaleidoscopic, at other times merely juvenile, announces both its emotional sincerity and its inability to realize that sincerity in ways that are not also self-undermining and ridiculous—again, as in Masumura's description of "defeated" and "oppressed" emotions within a regimented society, this formlessness and brokenness is not antihuman, it *is* the human, wholly constituted.

So, when David Desser states in *Eros Plus Massacre: An Introduction to the Japanese New Wave Cinema*, "The explicit rejection of the unified subject is a clear indication of the rejection of the humanistic ideal,"[20] we can affirm that this is not true; in fact the de-unified subject, open to a vast range of multiplicities and identifications, holds the objective salvation of the humanistic ideal as an exemplar of otherness-in-one. This is perhaps a condition more familiar to minorities who have experienced traumatic othering. Otherness-in-one is a way of reclaiming that othering as a positive thing, not only because the de-unified subject no longer pretends that it is at war with every other subject, or that the existence of an external world threatens some dubious, pretended claim to wholeness on its part, but also because, as Malabou's destructive plasticity teaches us, the wound itself now is no longer a hot potato to be shunted back and forth between antagonists in an endless blame-game. Instead, the wound is a new existential condition, one which expands the subject in unforeseen ways. There is no identity which is not, to some degree, de-unified. Diminished wholeness or self-sufficiency are points of growth, of identification with otherness. What emerges is a "new, tougher humanism,"[21] one tempered by divestment of ideological falsity.

This seems to be the other half of the picture of Japanese cinema, beyond the typical (if you will) Zen principle of otherness-in-one: an extreme kind of otherness-in-one that speaks relentlessly to damaged selfhood, interrupted and reshaped by traumas. A horrifying image of this occurs in Shion Sono's *Suicide Club* (*Jisatsu sâkuru*, 2001), in the chopped and compressed tangle of bodies that have been mashed together after a large group of high school girls suddenly leaps in front of an express train; in the sprawling mass of meat, stray lumps and stumps stick out. What is suggested here is a new mode of being, displaced of identity and selfhood, beyond trauma and death; the symbolic forging of human multiplicities. Indeed, what Malabou delineates is the underlying weakness inherent in shallow contentment, or the dream of wholeness; the untested existence. "What destructive plasticity invites us to consider," she writes, "is the suffering caused by an absence of suffering, in the emergence of a new form of being, a stranger to the one before."[22] There is something to be said for being able to see oneself from the outside, which is to say, to escape from the confines of the self; or to possess objective "scars" which disallow estrangement from one's past.

* * * * *

Of course, these are not the workings of consciousness as a happy-go-lucky enterprise. There is madness in even the most serene practice of cinematic ontology, since it involves processes that touch on the breakdown and dissolution of the viewer's conscious self. Japanese cinema, more than most national cinemas, has heartily embraced this madness. One of the first great Japanese films, Teinosuke Kinugasa's *A Page of Madness* (*Kurutta ippêji*, 1926), is about a man who works as a groundskeeper in a mental asylum to be near his wife who is confined there. Kinugasa opens with a montage of extreme weather—torrential rain; fires; flooding—then cuts to an allegorical woman in a pixie-like outfit, dancing in front of an endlessly revolving water wheel (painted in expressionist black and white stripes); the camera dollies back to reveal a woman (Eiko Minami) behind bars. The montage pulls us almost bodily into its line of thought. Madness is here understood from the inside, as signifiers immediately comprehensible to the viewer as discrete entities (the extreme weather; dancing), but when taken together, turn out to be indications of mental disorder. To link them as metonyms or even in a cause-and-effect relation is to participate directly in the disorder: an internal state full of storms, flooding, and histrionics.

Kinugasa's montage continues. Other inmates rave and rage; still others grip the bars of their cells warily. Only the first woman continues to dance, wildly, freely, expressing the lightning and rain in her imagination. She is a beautiful woman in a worn black dress, with dramatic dark hair, and in the ongoing cutting, which grows more and more frenzied, her dance is linked to water crashing on a rock, to stylized, animated bolts of lightning, and to close-ups of drums and horns, sometimes with the same crashing water superimposed upon them. No language is used to connect these things; to grasp their connection, again, is already to be drawn into a thought process by which madness is defined as extreme weather of the mind, and also as the expression of intense emotions through physical acts of creativity. This is not necessarily what true clinical madness is, of course. But to understand the film's visual thinking is to participate in an empathetic process by which we are both inside and outside of *the film's* definition of madness, which is a construction of signifiers brought together through montage.

There is a photograph of the dancing woman, which has been ripped in half and pasted to the wall of her cell in disjointed pieces. We have noted similar torn and patched photographs appearing decades later in Terayama's *Pastoral Hide and Seek*, there denoting not merely individual madness but something like family madness, historical madness, imperial madness. (This is perhaps the difference between modernist and postmodernist phenomenologies: the 1926 photograph calls out to a sense of the sundered individual self seeking reunification; the 1974 photographs are despairing indicators of a hopelessly ravaged warehouse of the mind, a status quo of endless disunities and broken histories.) The dancing woman dances until she collapses; but the images in her head, of horns, drums, and flooding, continue, so she gets up again and continues to dance. If the pattern was not evident to us before, it is here made so, through the film's first explicit establishment of a semblance of cause and effect.

This is, of course, yet another dramatic example of what occurs within our subjectivities when we watch any film; the fact that this particular film concerns madness only serves to heighten the idea that this is a process of expanding or otherwise altering the limits of the ontological self in relation to cinematic language. "Madness" is only a particularly suggestive, pungent word for this transmission of the effects of art to human consciousness. In Oshima's *The Man Who Left His Will on Film*, the idea of madness becomes flexible enough to include critical discourse, political analysis, young sexual and romantic love, and something much closer to traditional philosophical ontology (questions such as "Who am I? Why am I here?"). In that film, as we have seen, Motoki and Yasuko go from watching the footage and talking about it, to projecting it on their naked bodies while making love, to scouting out the actual locations, to re-filming the same film—and finally, to re-enacting the filmmaker's suicide. But a compressed version of this movement of "going deeper inside" occurs when we watch any film.

Thus, with *A Page of Madness*, we are going deeper inside not only the disturbed consciousness of the dancing woman, but the asylum itself as both physical and mental space(s). Using a key, the male protagonist (Masuo Inoue) unlocks the ward's barred door at the end of a corridor in wide angle, and moves freely down the hall. He passes the cell of the dancing woman (still whirling about), then moves on to the next cell, where he stops and looks with love and concern at another woman (Yoshie Nakagawa), lying prone on the floor of her cell. This woman has just hallucinated a screaming baby inside a sewer-drain in her cell. Raising her head, she recognizes the man and kneels at the bars, clasping his hand through them. It is through these simple shots (again accomplished without words of any sort) that we understand the bond between the man and this woman, his wife as it turns out, and we feel kinship, not merely to one or both of them, but to their bond itself, since our own subjectivity now includes this bond as an informational entity; more to the point, our subjectivity is responsible for their bond, having created it through our recognition.

How we piece together the action of a film is also how we allow our subjectivity to expand in relation to the film's information. This is generally an instantaneous and mostly unconscious process, rendered conscious only at those moments when we must ask ourselves, "Who is this? What is going on?" Cinema's basic contact points are close-ups and two-shots. The close-ups indicate an "isolated" subjectivity (character/actor) on objective display; the two-shots indicate a relation between two objectively displayed subjectivities. Images that are already emblems of multiplicity, or otherness-in-one (because the multiplicitous subjectivities in the film are already stitched together, through montage and narrative; and because they have meta-contexts, via intertextuality and film history), invoke the movement toward an otherness-in-one that then takes place within our own subjective consciousness. However, in films that we find "uninvolving," it is often difficult to follow the action, even if it is very simple; rather than being free to wander in the film, our identification is more distracted by not finding places for certain aspects of our subjectivity to settle in, to nest, and the whole thing could be taking place (as it is, in fact) entirely without us.

In *A Page of Madness*, in the space where the wife's insanity seems temporarily suspended by her recognition of her husband, we feel like we have been waiting for such a moment, and we flow in to impose a rationally ordered reading of what we are seeing: the seeming connection between her and the man outside her cell. But their love is a tragic, pained one; and Kinugasa's next cut to shrubbery shaken by violent wind and rain outside a barred window not only recalls the former images of extreme weather that symbolize madness, but now also comments on the relation that the film has established (that we have established *with* the film) between these two characters and the other signifiers. Naturally, when we see the husband filmed through the cell bars, gripping them forlornly, he becomes literally like the inmates we have seen; formally, the loss of separate "sides" is a key element of otherness-in-one. He also begins to hallucinate the same screaming baby, thereby both normalizing it as something which an ostensibly sane character might conceivably imagine, and also othering himself, by sharing a trait that has been strongly identified with (the woman's) madness. Thus, the representation of madness is now being extended to a different character who, because he comes and goes from the ward freely, does not seem to be mad and in fact seems closer to how we imagine our own subjectivity, as that of a sympathetic, understanding onlooker. This is why we see his hallucination as normalizing/othering, because our own perspective seeks answers, solutions, to restore the reign of "sense"; and at the same time, we are already invested in the film's evocations of "mad subjectivity." Our own subjectivity pursues both directions at once.

If Japanese films have often stood as exemplary to movie-lovers, scholars and cineastes, it is because these films seem to have been created specially for this kind of interactive expansion of the viewer's subjectivity. The camera is generally placed, as a matter of principle I would say, in such a way that most directly embodies subjective perception becoming objectified through the contents of the composition and the action of the characters. We find this in Kinugasa, Mizoguchi, Ozu, Naruse, Oshima, Imamura,

Loss or blurring of separate sides indicates subject-object inversion, usually with distinct undertones of madness. In Yasuzô Masumura's *Red Angel* (*Akai tenshi*, 1966), army nurse Sakura (Ayako Wakao) finds that she cannot separate herself from her professional duties, or her duties from the battlefield itself, and finally becomes a blood-stained acolyte of imperial madness.

Suzuki, Wakamatsu, Miike—no matter the era, the genre, the subject matter, we find the same confidence in being able to objectivize subjective perceptions. We also find camera placement used to guide and reinforce our sense of being inside the action of the film. Ozu was a master of this: frequently, in shot-reverse-shot dialogue, he has his actors look directly into the camera, as if "we" the audience were the ones being addressed. In *Floating Weeds* (*Ukikusa*, 1959), he frequently films the troubled young couple with their backs to the camera. When the Westerner Jean-Luc Godard uses this technique in the opening scene of *Vivre sa vie* (*My Life to Live*, 1962), it suggests the couple being turned inside-out, cut off from the world and each other, dangerously faceless, anonymous; whereas in *Floating Weeds* Ozu films the couple's backs only to firmly and decorously state, "This is private." In fact, Godard's couple appears in a busy café, so privacy is out of the question; the film begins in a situational realm that is definitively beyond self-protection. Whereas Ozu's couple is always alone when he films them; filming them from the back is his powerful underscoring of the privacy that already exists around them. The contexts are so different that the same technique which alarms us and frustrates our search for meaning (by design) in the Western film, becomes oddly simpatico and consoling in the Japanese one. By extension, what seems almost inhuman in the Western film is, if anything, a heightening of humanity in the Japanese one.

I feel this is due specifically to the impact of Buddhism on Japanese culture. "In the Jodo sect of Buddhism," Karatani writes, "the transcendental other—the object of worship—is regarded merely as absolute emptiness."[23] In striving to grasp and become this emptiness, the subject grows uncannily accustomed to loosening its own rigid bounds, and seeing itself from outside. The form is empty, because it is thing and no-thing. It is what we know it to be, and we know it to be nothing. In that space between fullness and emptiness, there is room for the film-watcher's consciousness to absorb and become absorbed. For neither selfhood nor external objects are transcendental or mysterious; they exist to be seen as they are, to be reduced to the simplest possible representations. Representation, as in the arts, carries no shame in Japanese culture, and no moral responsibility to the forms it represents. The highest grace becomes the achievement of a state that is superficially material, even "full," but again, effectively empty.

Because of this, the issue of "style" recedes to a nearly moot point: Japanese cinema does not appear, it is; it does not explain, it shows. Its film language is almost never florid or gratuitously aestheticized. Whatever extraneous aesthetics are called into play inevitably become further "factual" documentation of the subject-object inversions that are both the necessary and inevitable adjuncts of film-watching—everything becomes a way of seeing, a perception, from the external into the internal and back out again. The hallmark of Japanese film is that it shows us that consciousness (already a hybrid, an otherness-in-one) is always a *depiction* of something; and vice versa: depictions are always aspects of consciousness. This is why we have no record of human consciousness that is not a tangible entity, either a pictogram or the subject for one. This is also why Plato believed that Ideal Forms (accessible only to abstract consciousness) existed as a necessary predicate or inspiration for the thing itself, a resulting and un-abstract depiction.

Cinema has complicated this by giving us numerous technological options for rendering our Ideal Forms into depictions. Yet even the most experimental and tricked-out visualizations function essentially as appeals to tracing subjectivity's expansion into otherness-in-one. For example, in *A Page of Madness*, the next time the husband peers through the bars of his wife's cell, we see him as she sees him, his face distorted by a "fish-eyed" lens. Then we see her, filmed through a normal lens, grimacing, seeming to be laughing and crying simultaneously as she rocks back and forth. Saddened for her, we understand how she "sees," but we also see with other eyes (of sanity), still: the eyes of the man, also sad for her, and the eyes of the film (which know the difference between a distorting lens and a normal one), and of course, our own eyes. Meanwhile, we have rapidly assimilated an ontological lesson: what is normal may appear partly unrecognizable through distortion; what is a case of distortion itself (emotional disorder) might appear with perfect clarity. "Reality" is neither on the side of distortion nor of clarity; it roams between these poles, a free agent, an unmagnetized particle. Reality, too, is an otherness-in-one, which, as we take the film in larger bites so to speak (edits between two shots, montages, entire narrative sequences, the overall story arc), reveals itself more and more as a series of unique, discrete realities, both familiar and requiring active decoding.

Here is an amazing example, a shot that *is* actually rather florid and baroque, and which appears during the "bureaucracy montage" toward the beginning of Kurosawa's *Ikiru*. The fire department chief is telling a patient group of female petitioners that a backed-up sewer-main in their neighborhood is not within his jurisdiction; he stands directly in front of a window whose view is defamiliarized into two columns of narrow horizontal slats, each one seeming to contain a different object. In fact, the view is of a uniformed fireman polishing the rear-view mirror on a fire truck, but the panels bisect in such a way that it takes some looking to make sense of the whole picture. The truck tire in the lower right is cut off from the wheel hub, which appears in the middle right as a flat curved plane, seemingly without function or connectivity to anything. On the left hand side of the window, the truck's fuel system is cut off from the chassis, making it seem to belong almost to a different view altogether, like a flat illustration from an automotive manual. As function is sundered, so some parts come to seem almost threatening: one of the truck's chrome exhaust pipes points directly at the viewer like the barrel of a large gun. The intricate glass windows of the truck's cab are themselves neatly sectioned off from the smooth paneled side of the truck, again disconnecting our sense that these parts belong together.

Above the chief's head, in the panel at the top of the frame, the uniformed fireman—appearing like a smaller version of the chief, a schizo-emanation, and also like a mechanical toy—is engaged in polishing the rear view mirror. It is as if looking backwards were the only thing that mattered, never forwards. The grotesque, imbalanced discrepancies between the parts of the truck as they appear through the various panels are meant to suggest the deformities of the bureaucratic system itself, as it gives an extended runaround to the bedraggled, disoriented posse of well-meaning concerned citizens. Seen through the panels of the window, the constituent parts of the truck become a visual guessing-game, and invoke two folkloric homilies about mismanagement: the first in which a group of blind men must say what animal they are touching, though each man has been given only a small localized part of an immense creature (an elephant); the second in which a giraffe is famously described as having been produced by the compromises and discordant visions of a squabbling committee. Both relate to bureaucracy, and both relate to the oddly disjointed window in Kurosawa's shot, in which the chief, although foregrounded in medium close-up, is really the object, and the disorientingly divided truck in the windows behind him is the subject.

Subject-object inversion completes itself through the dramatic action of *A Page of Madness*. After failing, in an escape attempt, to drag his wife from the asylum (she is terrified of leaving), the husband runs amok and beats a doctor unconscious with a mop handle. Now the husband is insane and gets taken away to a cell of his own; his wife cackles at his downfall. Establishing a relay of subjectivities in its opening quarter, the film goes on, as (narrative) films do, to consolidate that relay into a more diffuse, less dense format: the plotline, involving characters we have grown to know and inhabit. Kinugasa's film echoes and displays the mental processes of consciousness that occur within us as we watch it, in its montage, its visual systems, and also in the strange fate of the male protagonist: being drawn into the subjectivities of a film, becoming the film's object in some ways, lending the film one's own subjectivity and incorporating its subjectivities into oneself, and finally watching what comes or does not come of one's investment of self.

It is true that in more recent cinema, such as the astonishing montage that opens Takashi Miike's *Dead or Alive* (*Dead or Alive: Hanzaisha*, 1999), subjectivity moves and changes too rapidly to establish deep bonds with any of the people (they are not even characters yet) whose exploits we are watching. As Miike's cutting swirls together scenes of excessive sex and violence all occurring during the same night in modern Tokyo, we can parse only the overly familiar cues of the action genre: those men are killing in cold blood, they are yakuza; those men come to the crime scene and pluck clues from a body, they are detectives; that woman is onstage in the nude, dancing on a pole, she is a stripper. After this bravura overture, the rhythm of the film settles into a more or less normal pace, and we slowly do learn more about these figures' various subjectivities; they become characters. But we are denied the ability, at first, to mingle our subjectivities with the film except in very broad reactive ways. This is for two reasons. First, Miike is denouncing Buddhist hybrid consciousness and otherness-in-one as a ludicrous falsity, one which does not hold up in the face of the world's cruelty, disloyalty, and mayhem. And second, the film itself—unlike *A Page of Madness*—is demonstrating psychopathic states rather than merely depicting them. What Kinugasa requires three-quarters of *A Page of Madness* to reveal, that everyone here is insane (even the doctors and staff), Miike insists on having us recognize from the very first seconds of *Dead or Alive*.

2

The Broken Heart of Ontology

If cinema awakens the ontological self to empathic identifications outside of its normal bounds, and redefines it according to these new identifications, then it is ontology's broken heart. Even at its most successful film can only love from a distance, unrequitedly. A problem arises from the fact that it can actually never be broken-hearted enough, since it risks causing us to mistake pseudo-being for being, and pseudo-caring for caring.[1] Some elements are allowed to attain mixed wholeness, but only within certain strictures which exclude some differences albeit not others. "The implication is that being is a coherent unity-in-opposition informed negatively by differences."[2] But this is largely a conservative objection, stemming from a belief that there can ever be a pure holistic identity to which all identities ideally aspire, or let us say an unconditional "moral" set of terms under which all humans should ideally dwell. To worry too much about the otherness part of the otherness-in-one is to suppress the fluid potentialities of being which exist in the margins, against the grain, in hybrid forms. In simpler terms, it is not good manners. Emmanuel Levinas calls it "ontological courtesy, being-for-the-other"[3]; he defines the defense of a unitary personal solipsism as "a threat against all others, a war inherent in this affirmation of oneself."[4] It is also to deny, in some ways, the capacity of damaged organisms to heal themselves through the changes wrought by Malabou's destructive plasticity.

Levinas writes: "The responsibility for the other is the originary place of identification."[5] Much of Japanese cinema stems from this originary place, where the film's responsibility to its "others" (the characters, the actors, the viewers) and the characters' responsibility to each other creates an almost unprecedented quality of respect for human emotions. I believe this is true in kind for recent gore films like Sono's *Suicide Club* or Fukasaku's *Battle Royale* (*Batoru rowaiaru*, 2000) as well as the work of Mizoguchi and Ozu; it is even apparent in a Nikkatsu sex film like *Female Teacher: In Front of the Students* (*Onna kyôshi: Seito no me no maede*, 1982), where the numerous violations against Reiko (Rushia Santô) are not only physical and sexual but threshold-moments where she is asked to take in an entirely new emotional identification, with herself, with her attackers. The attacks, although vicious and sadistic, are almost like spontaneous, intimate bonds of kinship; in the final scene, we see her in her classroom, calmly teaching some of the students who have assaulted her in previous scenes and seeming to share a wistful, gentle understanding with them. This trick ending is versatile: it works if you believe the rape scenes were Belle-de-Jour–esque fantasies, or if you believe that they all really played out as we witnessed them, so intensely polymorphous is the atmosphere of the film, emerging from and mitigating against that loneliness which is omnipresent in this as in most Japanese films.

For the same reason, even some of the most brutal "pink" pornos can also be oddly touching; or the moment in *Suicide Club* where three girls are about to hang themselves and one of them declaims, as if to a theatrical audience, "Kill yourself before you murder someone." Bonds are affirmed even in the midst of the loneliest, most despairing gestures; in fact this is the basic premise of *Ikiru*, an intricate transformational drama only ostensibly about an individual citizen and more accurately about his society. For that matter, the same finesse occurs in Fukasaka's *Battle Royale*, which is quite smoothly and indeed almost effortlessly both a complex ensemble piece about forty-two high school students coming of age and having typical peer and intergenerational conflicts, *and* an ultraviolent, perverse action movie in which the kids are all hunting and killing each other off. They are individuals and not-individuals, and as a result we identify with them as multiplicities, as examples of otherness-in-one. With nearly all the kids in *Battle Royale*, we glimpse the futures they might have had, the loves they might have lived, the friendships they forged or could have forged, and of course we see their pain of a denied and broken life. They have not lived at all, really, and the proof of this is that their deaths take them by surprise. A girl with an arrow shot through her neck stumbles toward a boy, asking helplessly, "What am I going to do? What is this?" Another girl screams, "Why? Stop!" as she is gunned down. This is like the artificial intelligence copied from the dead teenage girl in Takashi Miike's *Andromedia* (*Andoromedia*, 1998), whose first, naive words to the world are, "Is it true that I am dead?" Throughout Fukasaku's film, even the most obnoxious of the kids awaken to a reality that has suddenly become too real, a game too painful to play. *Battle Royale* is, finally, a densely emotional film that swirls like a whirlpool around a free-floating center that is the collective energy of the kids in their combat, living out their last short days under a harsh set of rules that have been imposed upon them.

Fukasaku accomplishes this partly in the manner of all the great Japanese auteurs, for whom economy of action and expression is akin to rigorous wisdom. There is a deep, pleasurably acute sense of context in Japanese cinema: things are always expressed for very specific reasons, otherwise they never would be. (And these expressions are immediately comprehensible. In Naruse's silent films, for example, there are far fewer title cards than in U.S. silent films, and many lines of dialogue that are essentially generic— "Come in, please," as a response to someone knocking on the door, for example—are not conveyed by title cards at all. Why? Because we know, by the way the woman in the kitchen inclines her head expectantly, politely, that she could be saying nothing else; moreover, in the next shot, a gracious messenger walks through the door.) When the emotions are extreme or powerful, they clash with this decorous sense of context in ways that are inherently dramatic—or comedic for that matter; at any rate, always to some degree philosophical in nature. Emotions in Japanese films always constitute a critique, in the sense that every expression of an emotion represents the palpable failure of a system that acts to render such things unnecessary, superfluous, even in some cases taboo; and in so doing, it reestablishes the power of those emotions that escape anodyne conversational code, repressions, and ellipses. The fact that any given emotion shows at all

This Spanish lobby card for Kinji Fukasaku's *Battle Royale* (2000) shows one of the high school students killed with a knife to her forehead as her horrified classmates look on. With nearly all the kids in *Battle Royale*, we glimpse the futures they might have had, the loves they might have lived, the friendships they forged or could have forged, their pain of a denied and broken life. They have not lived at all, and the proof of this is that their deaths take them by surprise.

marks it almost as a societal, even historical event. Thus, though this is a cheeky example, Oshima in *Diary of a Shinjuku Thief* (*Shinjuku dorobô nikki*, 1969) notes that Umeko (Rie Yokoyama) tells her lover Birdey (Tadanori Yokoo), "Let's do it!" at precisely 5 a.m. in the bohemian district of Shinjuku in Tokyo.

In a grander sense, this historicization of emotion is why Kurosawa's *Ikiru* ends up feeling like the Japanese *Citizen Kane*: the spectacle of "individualism" whose spirit drives Kane with monotonous fervor is retroactively conferred upon Watanabe "the Mummy," gray-suited and fedora-wearing bureaucratic cog. Actually it is the opposite of *Citizen Kane*: where Kane in death is revealed to have been far more mediocre and pitiful than anyone knew, Watanabe attains heroic, even legendary proportions only after death. One thing that his survivors recall is that his defiance of the deputy mayor (Nobuo Nakamura) was the only time a bureaucrat ever challenged a City Hall directive (the essence of a historic act, unprecedented and paradigmatic).

Conversely, it is disturbing when emotions are warped into weapons, as we see in Oshima's devastating *Boy*. Toshio's con-artist parents force him to get hit by cars to collect settlement money from the motorists. In some cases, the injuries he sustains are superficial but he must pretend to have suffered damage; he must *act*, in a word. "Father taught me to say 'It hurts' while holding my breath." As the film progresses, however, the repeated "accidents" take their toll: "Since it really hurts now, I no longer have to lie to the doctor." But his body cannot hide the difference. When a doctor finds numerous old bruises during an examination, the parents fall under suspicion and go on the run. The father's solution is to deform his son even more, by making him wear glasses which he does not need and which hurt his eyes, as a disguise to fool the police. Acting, torture, and suppressed emotions are all drawn into a horrible yet matter-of-fact nexus. (Indeed, Oshima often suggests in *Boy* that Toshio has been driven insane by his unloving parents and their machinations.)

This is why it is inadequate to speak of negative and positive emotions in Japanese films; they are all equal emotions, displayed or pointed to, often as if simply for the purpose of instruction. "You, too, can feel like this," many Japanese films seem to say, becoming and also making the audience, once again, exemplars of an otherness-in-one that is innate to the entire ethos of the films. The real which cinematic mimesis aims to copy has never been so distant and wistful, a gaudy notional idea with little underpinning. For example, the hit pop song by the tween girl group in Sono's *Suicide Club* ("I need to hear from you right now or I'll die!") manages to be sinister, ridiculous and poignant all at once. Its perky hysteria accompanies the perky hysteria of the waves of teen suicides, not complicating them, as we would expect a pop song in a Western film to do, but just the opposite: rendering the deadly acts almost self-explanatory.[6] "I'm dying now!" a high school girl grins and waves from the roof of her school with the same exhibitionistic hope to please and entertain as the girl group on TV. Both display an inexplicable *energy* in the face of wanting or threatening to die, and though it is barely an emotion we recognize, it is compelling nonetheless.

The quality of respect for emotions in Japanese cinema is itself calibrated to an awareness of suffering that is both acute and vast. In Naruse's *When a Woman Ascends the Stairs* (*Onna ga kaidan wo agaru toki*, 1960), Keiko (Hideko Takamine) tells her friend Yuri (Keiko Awaji), "I thought you didn't know life, as things have gone well for you." Keiko has only recently discovered that Yuri is unhappy but hides it; her seeming success is only superficial, things are not going as well for her as they appear. But aside from this, it is a strange *ressentiment* on Keiko's part, this accusation of not showing enough pain, an accusation rendered ironic by the fact that, as a nightclub geisha, Keiko herself is discouraged from displaying negative emotions. "Don't be sentimental," her business partner (Tatsuya Nakadai) tells her, "guests pay to have a good time here." This is also an explicit theme of Kenji Mizoguchi's *Sisters of the Gion* (*Gion no shimai*, 1936), in which Omucha (played by Isuzu Yamada) admits bitterly, "I'm a geisha—if I always told the truth I'd be out of business. Sometimes I have to lie." And also, in Mizoguchi's *A Geisha* (*Gion bayashi*, 1953), a geisha in training is given this exhortation: "And you mustn't fall in love. It's bad for business!" Deceit, a spiritual condition involving discordance between one's outer and inner life, is a self-betrayal, shown to be more painful than the scorn which others inflict on us or even loss of livelihood. "And yet, all we did was tell the truth," the disgraced samurai-vassal Tango (Masayuki Yui) says in disbelief in Kurosawa's *Ran*. It is as though the ultimate insult is having to hide one's knowledge, as slaves must. "Isn't life suffering?" goes the secret plaint of the enslaved Tamaki (Kinuyo Tanaka), separated from her children in Mizoguchi's *Sansho the Bailiff* (*Sanshô Dayû*, 1954)—a plaint which, overheard by another slave and passed on, becomes the most popular folk song throughout the entire province. And we hear the same sentiment expressed in the lecture which Shimamura (Sô Yamamura) gives to the acting class on Ibsen at the start of Mizoguchi's *The Love of Sumako the Actress* (*Joyû Sumako no koi*, 1947): "If we let ourselves go to futility, or if we live following a superficial ethic, we're deluding ourselves.... Life is full of conflicts.... In fact, life is suffering." More than foolish, the denial of this conclusion is a species of rudeness, almost a criminal breach of tact.

In their landmark study of Japanese cinema, Joseph L. Anderson and Donald Richie say about Naruse's work: "Happiness is impossible, yet we find a kind of contentment if we are wise enough never to hope."[7] The personal need to be strong no matter what is constantly reinforced in Naruse's films. His trademark racing dollies which zero in on a character's face at decisive moments suggest the world literally rushing in to confront the character, who either remains firm by staring into camera, or loses resolve and looks away. It is like the Japanese children's game "called *kage-fumi* (i.e., stepping on one another's shadows), illustrating in a symbolic way, this infringement of personal space."[8] Shared space is charged with tension and friction for Naruse, who often ends scenes with static shots of two or more people in separate parts of a room, facing away from each other, a tangible, angular hopelessness undermining typically domestic situations where love and happiness are "supposed" to reign. Naruse said: "If they [my characters] move even a little, they quickly hit the wall. From the youngest age, I have thought that the world we live in betrays us; this thought still remains with me."[9]

Like "Isn't life suffering?" this apercus, too, has been rendered into a quotable refrain, the kabuki line, "*If all the world should betray me*," which the stranded traveling actors like to recite among themselves in Ozu's *Floating Weeds*. For Ozu there is irony here, since the actors he depicts are frequently their own and each other's worst enemies: vain, boastful, touchy, boozy, they live on constant thin ice, entrusting their deepest secrets to people whom they have no reason to trust, then worrying and turning despotic when one of their confidants begins to seem petulant or rebellious. It almost never occurs to them that perhaps they should not have

This is the young couple in Yasujirô Ozu's *Floating Weeds* (*Ukikusa*, 1959), Kiyoshi (Hiroshi Kawaguchi, left) and Kayo (Ayako Wakao). Manipulated by the scheming adults in their lives, they find themselves in over their heads, enacting a love as sympathetic and pitiful as it is tragically doomed. Yet, from the tragic potential Ozu crafts a resolution in which the family drama's finally revealed truths end up leading to reconciliation and resiliency.

kept the secret in the first place, since the information is damning only from having been hidden, not necessarily in and of itself. This kind of canny, almost sarcastic awareness of how people set themselves to be "gotten" by others is how Ozu takes a flimsy, essentially melodramatic premise (a son doesn't know his uncle is really his father; the father does not want to tell him the truth and at the same time worries that someone else will tell him) and elevates it to a level of simple tragedy and battered, pained comedy. Few endings are as touching as the reconciliation of the fallen-out friends at the end of *Floating Weeds*, and Ozu also makes us see that this reunion, much like the falling out, might never have happened if not for sheer fate.

Which brings us to a crucial point: to the Japanese, one's life is not a function of characterological essence or even, strictly speaking, behavior, but of fate—an even more unfamiliar concept to the autonomy-obsessed West. In the West, to believe too much in fate is to risk seeming paranoid-delusional, but to the Japanese, any conceivable fear is its own rational justification and, at the same time, nothing that one can or should take steps to try to prevent from coming true, since it either will or won't come true regardless of what one does. Fate is emblemized by the spinning wheels of the rickshaw in Oshima's *Empire of Passion* (*Ai no bôrei*, 1978); we think we are driving the cart but the cart is driving us. As the wise Miyoharu (Michiyo Kogure) says in Mizoguchi's *A Geisha*, "One can never predict one's fate." Similarly, Kenzo Okuzaki, the crusading subject of Kazuo Hara's documentary *The Emperor's Naked Army Marches On* (*Yuki Yukite shingun*, 1987), observes, "We don't have any control over our fate," although Okuzaki implies an idea of fate that encompasses karmic justice; we cannot outrun our due. These are not even matters for speculation or inquiry, as one of the incarcerated juvenile offenders states with equanimity in Susumu Hani's *Bad Boys* (*Furyo shônen*, 1961), "I wonder how we will all end up ... but that's nothing to worry about." For Westerners in the same situation, it might be all we would worry about, as if worrying would make one bit of difference.

Nor does one always understand or even know one's own karma. In Kurosawa's *Ikiru*, Watanabe succumbs to cancer without receiving credit for the city park whose building he has spearheaded. Instead the smarmy, self-aggrandizing deputy mayor has won re-election by claiming the park as his own initiative; but the people know the truth. Grateful citizens come to Watanabe's funeral service and weep for him so much that the deputy mayor is shamed into running away. Watanabe's suffering was not in vain. And suffering itself is not a special, attention-grabbing cult but, according to Buddhism, simply a fact of human life, "caused by men's desires and longings. To get rid of it one must get rid of desire [through] a life of meditation, self-sacrifice, and unselfish service."[10]

We see this in particular in Mizoguchi's *Ugetsu*, several of whose characters are undone by wanting or hoping for more than what they have; they all live to see themselves betrayed by their own dreams and by a hostile world that is, according to a boatman's song, "a temporary abode in which we weep until the dawn comes...." Not even Buddhism itself provides a refuge, as we are forced to recognize when Ohama (Mitsuko Mito) is dragged inside a Buddhist temple by renegade samurais and gang-raped. A tall gold statue of the god himself watches the rape with a serene smile. Other characters in *Ugetsu* call on "Merciful Buddha" at moments that are utterly hopeless; even calligraphic prayers

In Mizoguchi's *Ugetsu*, Ohama (Mitsuko Mito) gets separated from her husband while traveling; she is set upon by renegade samurais who drag her into a Buddhist temple and rape her. A frequent, stern motif of the film is the uselessness of religious trappings—statues of Buddha, prayers, invocations—in a world of cruel, capricious fate. The only enduring peace comes from finding one's true place of belonging, and being content with it.

scrawled on a man's body are shown to be less effective against evil than a sword, and neither one effective at all against abusive, oppressive state-military power. In Ozu's *Floating Weeds*, a theft victim bemoans that the thief "even stole my charm against pickpockets," yet another mockery of Buddhist superstitions, since a charm that can be stolen in the first place could never possess the power to prevent one from being robbed.

If serene acceptance is finally achieved in *Floating Weeds* or *Ugetsu*, it is only with great patience and pain, for peace is not a natural thing of this world. Or rather it is quasi-natural but exotically rare, symbolized by the lotus: "for as the lotus grows in the mud at the bottom of the lake but remains pure and beautiful, so the Buddha walked through the corruption and filth of this world but remained pure and holy."[11] Still, though Buddhism itself was always more of an ideal than a staunch practice in Japan, its philosophy of fatalism and self-abnegation have had long-reaching implications for the Japanese personality. As Joan Mellen writes in *The Waves at Genji's Door*: "to be a good Japanese is never enough. It is always to be tested and ultimately scorned by some sterner judge."[12]

* * * * *

Buddhism carries no inherent feminist message; quite the opposite. Mellen explains, "Buddhism encouraged [women] to acquiesce in their own oppression, to display a calm acceptance of the inevitable. It reminded them that there were no women in Buddha's Western Paradise. In order to enter it, they would first have to be reborn as men."[13] Feminist consciousness was something that the filmmakers Naruse and Mizoguchi added to their own understanding of the religion. In Mizoguchi's *Osaka Elegy* (*Naniwa ereji*, 1936), we see that women are subject to revisionist patriarchal fictionalizing of their own motives, pasts and actions, as in the scene in the police station where Ayoko (Isuzu Yamada) finds herself indicted for a crime that she has been partly led into by the men in her life. These cowardly male accomplices have blamed her and left her to take the fall. Nor is there solidarity among *Osaka Elegy*'s female characters, as when a wealthy wife (Yôko Umemura) hisses at Ayoko, "It's frightening how well you feign innocence!" It isn't that the wife has no cause to feel aggrieved; indeed, Ayoko is having an affair with her husband (Benkei Shiganoya). However, in placing all the blame on Ayoko, the wife is participating in patriarchal logic, in which female guilt is an "always already." At the same time, Mizoguchi is forwardly feminist even in the wife's character, just by making her so outspoken and also childless. According to Anderson and Richie, *Osaka Elegy* can be thought of as fairly unique for its time, since prewar films almost never featured wives except to the extent that they were also mothers. A strong wife, complaining about her husband and talking back to him, and also pointedly a wife who has not produced children, was anomalous in the extreme in imperial-era Japanese cinema.[14]

Mizoguchi's *Sisters of the Gion* concludes that no matter how different women may seem to be in personality or status, they all have oppression in common. The film concerns two sisters, both working as geishas. Omachu, the younger and prettier of the two, is adept at manipulating men. Umekichi (Yôko Umemura), the older, plainer sister, fulfills her geisha role more dutifully, receiving her regular customers even when they fall on hard times financially, in other words when they truly need her emotional support and can give her nothing in return. Her kindliness is chastised by Omachu as foolish disregard for her own self-interests. But for Umekichi there is an ethics that enters into prostitution, perhaps related to the idea of karma. One client, Furasawa (Benkei Shiganoya, the same actor who played the cad husband in *Osaka Elegy*), sponges off Umekichi, staying with her to escape his bankrupt store and nagging wife. As a male, it is Furasawa's prerogative to have two lives, in this sense, both of which he ruins. He holds no special loyalty or attachment to Umekichi apart from what she can give him; when Omachu goes behind her sister's back to bribe Furasawa to leave her sister alone, he takes the money and promptly goes, but does not return to his wife at home. Instead, he takes his buddy out drinking, thus showing, perhaps, the intemperate bad judgment that might have caused his business to fail in the first place.

The function of women is to exalt male vanity, a sexism of which Mizoguchi, of course, strongly disapproves. In *Sisters of the Gion*, Mr. Juwakudo (Fumio Okura)—self-pitying, self-righteous, objectively unworthy of the adoration which he purchases from geishas—asserts that sake must be poured by a beautiful young woman or it "would lose its taste." Ozu noted this, too, in *An Inn in Tokyo* (*Tôkyô no yado*, 1935): when the destitute father of two sons finally lands a job, with the help of the woman he loves, he celebrates by going to a geisha house and having sake served to him. Dressed in a silly-looking kimono that barely fits him, the father talks to the geisha about his new good fortune. "You came here to brag about your woman?" the geisha asks, without blinking. Having seen every kind of behavior there is from a male, she recognizes this too: a man whose sincere love for a good woman is not truly validated until he can boast of it to a geisha.

In *A Geisha*, Mizoguchi composes a shot that expresses this male vanity brilliantly: the male client is preening in the mirror, combing his hair, while the geisha Miyoharu waits for him in the background, on her knees. Under the geisha system, geishas may have appeared as "symbols of Japanese beauty," but this was finally only to be "worthy" of being used by Japanese males, for whom treating women as objects was woven into the savoring of an orderly, well-lived life. Women derive their value from such usage; as a drunken carouser says in Oshima's *Empire of Passion*: "Seki knows the secret of eternal youth is keeping her man happy!"

Of course, the heroic Omachu in *Sisters of the Gion* still has her flaws: she plays dumb with men when it is to her advantage, and she deflects blame when placed on the spot. But she is also on less solid ground. Unlike Furasawa, who can bankrupt his firm and still go on as a businessman, Omachu is at one with her livelihood; being a geisha isn't a job she goes to each day for a certain number of hours, it is who she is, for better or worse. In the end she holds no real advantage—everything she represents is illusory, by male design. "As beautiful as you are," the disconsolate Umekichi upbraids Omachu, "you still have to hustle for a patron." Being young and beautiful is no guarantee for a woman who crosses men. We see this graphically when a vengeful client has Omachu kidnapped and thrown from a speeding car. Patriarchy is so omnipresent in the lives of these geisha sisters that they have already internalized both (losing) sides of their dilemma. Umekichi sobs despairingly, "This is what happens when you treat men like that," while Omachu, bandaged and bed-ridden, vows in anger, "Something like this won't stop me!" Their only responses are either self-fulfilling depression or all-consuming rage, and both are part of their enslavement.

Part of the problem with the geisha system and other forms of prostitution in Japan is that there is no reverse by which women can have their needs met or their loneliness ameliorated the way men (with money) can. Japanese society, at least for a long time, did not seem to recognize that such an outlet might be needed for women, albeit recognizing it as needed on a daily basis for all males, even those who were themselves discriminated against or shunned. In Kazuo Hara's groundbreaking documentary *Goodbye CP* (*Sayonara CP*, 1972), young males suffering from cerebral palsy are asked about their sexual histories, in an obvious and rather self-congratulatory attempt to enlighten the viewer about the disabled being perfectly normal in their sexual needs. "I slept with a woman when I was 18," one of the males says, grinning shyly but clearly proud of this fact. "It was then that I realized I was a man. I went to a red light district.... I kept going for four years." A second CP sufferer did the same at age 16: "I went to a red light district and lost my virginity. I kept going there for quite a while." Japanese prostitution was there to help these disabled men feel like men for the first time in their lives, as they themselves attest; and indeed these CP sufferers struggle inordinately with loneliness and isolation, low self-esteem, and the fear of being impotent. But Hara's film does not even raise the question of what disabled young *women* could do to satisfy similar curiosities, desires and needs, or to make themselves feel attractive. This sexist double standard makes it difficult at times to watch the CP sufferers bragging about their conquests of prostitutes, although in all other respects *Goodbye CP* makes the viewer empathize tremendously with these disabled guys, clearly "second class males" in Japanese society but still with more options than many women.

Japanese geishas, like this unnamed pair from the 1890s, were highly artificial, ornamented productions of extreme femininity. The purpose of their beauty was to exalt the egos of Japanese males, who often paid for their services.

At its best, the geisha system functions as an alternative family for women who are trying to escape dysfunctional families with absent or degenerate parents. So, in *A*

Geisha, Eiko (Ayako Wakao) is sixteen when she asks to join Miyoharu's geisha house: her uncle has told her that she must sleep with him to pay off the cost of her mother's funeral. She eventually develops a mother-daughter relationship with Miyoharu; the scene where Miyoharu introduces the "debutante daughter" of the house to the neighborhood, going door to door and receiving everyone's blessings with thanks, is beautiful and touching. "I feel like a mother marrying off her daughter," Miyoharu enthuses. This is a chosen kinship, in preference to the women's literal backgrounds. Nonetheless, the patriarchal, chattel logic of incest prevails over the general structure of things: Eiko ends up as a geisha in the same house her own father used to frequent, when he was a client of Miyoharu's. As best they try, the generations cannot avoid repeating the same experiences. And of course, the reputation of a Japanese woman could be ruined by even the tiniest slip, something that the rude, drunken, imperious males in *A Geisha* need not worry about.

Mizoguchi was acutely aware of female vulnerability in Japanese society. (He once told someone that no man could understand women until he had been stabbed by one, as he had been by a jilted prostitute.)[15] He had a special horror of seeing refined women exposed to the humiliation of public transportation. It is a motif of *Osaka Elegy* and *Sisters of the Gion*, and it returns in *Women of the Night* (*Yoru no onnatachi*, 1948). It shows the pragmatic side of Mizoguchi's sense of wanting to change Japanese society: he does not overlook the simple daily requirements of material existence. For a woman to take a subway train is for her to become a body among the masses; he always shows his heroines in this situation looking extremely desolate, out of place, reduced in status, especially in the two-shot in *Osaka Elegy*, in which a strange man sleeps in the seat beside Ayoko, who remains sitting upright, staring forlornly off to the side. This slatternly approximation of the "coital" bed in a public (and transitory) space is an affront to Mizoguchi's sense of female honor. In *Women of the Night*, it is at a subway station, surrounded by noises of trains seemingly coming in all directions, that Fusako (Kinuyo Tanaka) finally breaks down sobbing as she acknowledges that her Japan, the world she knew before the war, is gone forever. Mizoguchi renders her sobbing in a close-up, angled from below, which frames Fusako against a blank-white sky as if to shield her from the terrestrial locale (subway station) where she finds herself.

What seems to have appalled Mizoguchi—the thought of women losing their dignity and exalted status on public transportation—is suddenly revealed to us as blasé fact in the Japan scenes of Chris Marker's documentary *Sans Soleil* (1983), where women, now at least one new generation into the postwar, ride subways yawning, sometimes fully asleep themselves, as numb and resigned and hardened to the eyes of strangers as the men are. (No one seems to stare at them anyway.) No longer ashamed or afraid in tawdry commercial spaces, Marker's real Japanese women have no thought of needing to protect themselves or hold themselves apart from the jostling crowds; perhaps this independence is a good thing, and Mizoguchi was wrong to see it only as a coarsening. Nor did this particular bit of modernity seem to bother Ozu, since we see the pretty and outspoken Noriko (Setsuko Hara) happily taking a long subway ride in that director's *Late Spring* (*Banshun*, 1949); nor Yasujirô Shimazu even earlier, in *A Brother and His Younger Sister* (*Ani to sono moto*, 1939), whose independent-minded heroine not only rides the subway without anxieties but sits and gabs with a male acquaintance, raising no eyebrows. By the late 1950s, in Yasuzô Masumura's *Kisses* (*Kuchizuke*, 1957), a young woman runs to stop a crowded bus in pursuit of the young man who has paid her father's jail expenses. And even in Susumu Hani's gritty, early-1960s *Bad Boys*, two delinquents try to set fire to the hair of a "stuck-up" girl on a subway train, but she holds her own, putting them in their place with an imperious glower.

Certainly, to greater or lesser degrees, there are some mixed feelings in all of these sequences about the "Western influence" on Japanese women (if that's what it can be ascribed to); but Ozu, Shimazu and Masumura do not take up a blanket defense of Japanese women on public transportation in the way that Mizoguchi does, as if on the women's own behalf. Here we see in Mizoguchi the presence of an elusive signifier, elusive because it is so smoothly depicted as a cultural generality: the Japanese woman, nervous and humiliated by public transportation both before and after the war. Yet, this is a sign of individuality, of Mizoguchi's own individualistic artistry, rather than of social framing. Mizoguchi's concept of women has only a specific personal meaning for him as an artist, even though he presents it so strongly as a universal truism that we are tempted to read an entire social history into it.

*****

In Naruse's *When a Woman Ascends the Stairs*, the working world of the geisha admits little chance for personal happiness; she must drink with men when she does not want to; she goes to bed with a man or does not go to bed with him largely because of how this will appear to others. All she can imagine for her future happiness is the choice between two generic options flatly presented to her by at least three different characters: open her own bar (where she can prostitute less fortunate women) or marry a wealthy man. The thought of owning her own bar makes her smile slightly, with reserved pleasure; at the same time, she does not allow herself to hope for too much—and how could she? Keiko is someone who has learned only what she is permitted to do and what she doesn't like to do; her limits, in other words, and her necessary compromises. What would she choose to do? What would she enjoy? These questions have no place in Keiko's world, and no answer; that is her tragedy.

It is tempting to compare Keiko, as a figure of tragic melodrama, with postwar Japan.[16] But her lack of agency is problematic. Japan is often thought of as a highly insular culture that has suffered shock after shock, including some of the worst traumas of history, including, of course, the atomic bombings of Hiroshima and Nagasaki at the end of World War II. However, this "psychological trauma that Japan's entry into international society created"[17] is complicated by the fact that Japan had been an arrogant and aggressively militaristic force in Asia. From its archipelago, Japan had conceived of itself as world-conquerors descended from a special race of gods. This self-mythologizing ignored the actual genealogy of the Japanese, whose "three chief components are Mongoloid, Malayan, and Caucasian. It is also argued that waves of immigrants from the mainland, especially from China and Korea, came to Japan during the course of the Neolithic period."[18]

In the name of their special, self-conceived divinity, the Japanese pursued virulent and destructive racisms against other Asian ethnicities, including some that they were themselves descended from: Chinese, Manchurians, Koreans, Thais, and others. The figure of the Japanese emperor, Hirohito for most of the 20th century, was invested with godlike powers and rights, rendering even the most barbaric military actions not only permissible but divinely mandated. In fact Hirohito bears a strong relationship to prewar, wartime and postwar Japanese cinema, as we will see in Part 3. Japan's abrupt and brutal disillusionment from its longstanding ideals of racial superiority must stand as the single greatest and most unique trauma in Japanese history. Kenneth B. Pyle writes: "The discovery of Japan's impotence in the face of Western civilization, and the determination to borrow from this civilization everything necessary to overcome this impotence, left the Japanese with a persistent self-doubt that could not be overcome by the artificial creation of a cultural identity."[19]

Indeed, as Pyle and other historians have noted, Westernization had been taking place in Japan since at least the Meiji Restoration of the late 19th century. The arts were at the forefront of much of this openness to Western influences, which matched up with Japanese artists' questioning of their own culture's militarism and imperialism (not that the West was any better in these departments, but simply different in perspective and thus able to undermine Japanese self-regard). There is some paradox here: "Cultural borrowing was not disparaged as slavish.... The Japanese did not have the same barriers of cultural and religious self-absorption that in other [Eastern] countries impeded learning from other civilizations."[20] Buell has asserted that "the Japanese 'essence' was a genius for simulacra."[21] According to Buell, the more "Japanese" something seems, from a cultural aspect, the more it has passed through the mirror, so to speak, of otherness-in-one, "a process in which self-conscious absorption of foreign influences was coupled with the equally self-conscious creation and reinforcement of a myth of primordial identity [and] the invention of an 'ancient Japanese spirit.'"[22]

One of the most tendentious examples of this is also one which we will consider at some length in this book: the practice of emperor-worship, particularly the belief in the emperor's divinity as more than a mere mortal. Ivy writes:

> Although the emperor may be seen as the very epitome of the Japanese "thing," in that he appears to embody the unbroken transmission of Japanese culture, there is much evidence to show that the line of emperors originated in Korea—Japan's colonized, denigrated national other—and various features of emperorship as an institution lead back to China. To show how the most authoritative interior sign of native Japaneseness is originally foreign points to an essential alienation at the national-cultural core.[23]

And in fact, such comprehensive patterns of Japanese trans-cultural appropriation from mainland Asia date back to before the Meiji Restoration. It has been noted that there were elements of cultural hybridization (including some Westernization) in Japan "since ancient times."[24] To some extent, even the ancient Buddhist philosophy of destiny and the inevitable capitulation to suffering had already been tempered by a Western spirit of self-autonomy. And other Western-inspired reforms were beneficial to Japan. Westernization reached its height in the late 19th century. In 1873, during the Meiji era, the Meirokusha group "advocated individual rights, democratic government, egalitarianism, and universal education."[25] The Japanese have always been "eager to take from foreign civilizations what seemed suited to their needs. [They] modified what they had received and were stimulated to make connections of their own."[26] As J. Hoberman has said, "everything the Japanese borrow they make indelibly their own."[27]

Again, to a great extent, Japanese artists led the way in this. The Meiji Restoration's systematic process of Westernization was inspired in part by the narrative, dramatic arts: "humanism and individualism already had roots in Japan planted by the theatrical mode of Shingeki."[28] Shingeki, or "new theater," was an innovation of the Meiji period, "deliberately modeled ... on European Naturalist theatre." Specifically, the socially conscious, anti-elitist and proto-feminist Ibsen was a particular favorite playwright of the Shingeki troupes.[29] Not only content but also elements of form began to be imported from the West. "The Stanislavsky system was introduced in Japan in 1913 by Osanai Kaoru, who later joined Shochiko Films in 1919."[30] Remarkably, the provisions for equal treatment of women in the postwar peace accord had been established in the prior century, albeit imperfectly, by the Shingeki's insistence on allowing actual females to play female characters in the interest of enhanced "realism"[31] (and probably because these Japanese artists as a whole had reached a certain enlightenment about women's rights long before Japan-proper did). Taking the cue from Shingeki, female actors had been featured in Japanese films since the early 1920s.[32]

Even under the very conservative Hirohito, then, there was a widespread "Japanese modernist importation of European ideas."[33] Imperial-era Japanese cinema is already Westernized. In Ozu's *The Only Son* (*Hitori musuko*, 1936), the characters go to the movies to see Lillian Harvey in *Invitation to the Waltz* (1935). Mizoguchi's *Sisters of the Gion* and *Osaka Elegy* both feature au-courant swing-time jazz; the use of glossy lighting in the former is distinctly reminiscent of an Astaire-Rogers musical or even Josef von Sternberg,[34] while Sternberg's influence has also been cited on Ozu's early gangster films as well as the dancehall scenes in Naruse's *Every-Night Dreams* (*Yogoto no yume*, 1933). (Sternberg had always been "a favorite in Japan."[35]) The heroine of *Osaka Elegy* "smokes, listens to Western music, and files her fingernails à la Mae West."[36] This Westernization even occurs in highly unlikely places, as if to call unmistakable attention to itself, such as the often noted fact that a traditional Kabuki performance staged in Mizoguchi's *Story of the Last Chrysanthemums* (*Zangiku monogatari*, 1939) has "*more* editing than the rest of the film,"[37] in other words faster cutting rather than Mizoguchi's signature long takes. Moreover, Naruse's use of distorting fish-eye lenses, his technique of printing some shots in negative, and his Vertovian rapid montage place him in the aesthetic vanguard of early 1930s experimental cinema no less than Western filmmakers of the same era.

In fact, will it surprise anyone much if I assert that Japanese cinema has had an extremely parallel history to Western cinema in every era? There was primitive early cinema around the turn of the century. In the 1920s and 1930s there was avant-garde experimentation, with elements of constructivism, surrealism, and proto-neorealism; the 1930s were also exemplified by a well-run studio system in which directors made two or three films a year, often with the same roster of contract players and stars. There were propaganda films made during the war, while in the 1950s, in Japan as everywhere else, the representational narrative film gained an unprecedented density and intelligence leading to the production of films that are both profound works of art and lavish mass entertainments at the same time, a Golden Age of the Masters. In the 1960s, again like everywhere, there was an explosion of creative experimentation and political protest, a new wave, a time of iconoclastic anti-masters who turned out to be new masters. In the 1970s there was a deliberate blurring of lines of good and bad taste, high and low culture;

and since the 1980s there has been a postmodern tendency to blur the lines of genre, to reference cinema of the past ironically, and to go in for a kind of extremism that places film as the direct substitute for reality via visceral and dreamlike displays of horrific violence and sexual disturbance. As it does to Japan, this description could apply to nearly all of the major film-producing nations of the world in the past hundred years or so. Again we find compelling reason to believe that cinema has been that universal ontological language which has served to make all cultures subject to more or less the same visualizations and perceptual cognitions.

Granted, all of the previous waves of Westernization were never quite like what reached postwar Japan in terms of mass commercial culture. For example, 1940s pulp magazines marketed to young Japanese men featured Western women "as voluptuous sexual objects ... and an ideal for young Japanese women to emulate,"[38] as Dower states. And yet, imperial-era Japanese films by Ozu and Naruse had already depicted such Western actresses as Lillian Harvey and Deanna Durbin as pinups for young Japanese males.

In general, however, the American Dream itself *was* transferred onto postwar Japan like a skin graft: "The comic strip *Blondie* and *Readers' Digest* portrayed American daily life through idyllic images."[39] The children of the conquered were indoctrinated to side (sexually and in other ways) with the mentality of the conquerors. Japan became an obedient "model loser"[40] in the "foundational narrative that the United States and Japan coproduced and maintained."[41] This acquiescence to a new set of (American) values, far more than the defeat itself (although it makes for a complicated historical nexus), inspired negative feelings on the part of the Japanese toward the U.S. The sadism of the children in Yukio Mishima's novel *The Sailor Who Fell from Grace with the Sea* (1963), and their hatred of their fathers who accumulated wealth by catering to postwar U.S. business interests, has more to do with their sense that an innate Japanese superiority had been sold out from under them; added to the injury of defeat was the insult of dishonoring ancient and "purely" Japanese codes allied with the Imperial era. In Kô Nakahira's topical film *Crazed Fruit* (*Kurutta kajitsu*, 1956), the spoiled rich kids speak ruefully of the Chinese and the Soviets having Japan surrounded (with nuclear weapons in the case of the U.S.S.R.), as if their parents' failure to defeat these enemies, as well as the complete capitulation to the U.S., were sources of deep ongoing shame. Meanwhile, *Crazed Fruit*'s culturally conflicted young males completely surrender to Westernism even while inveighing against it: "Yankee, go home!" is a half-hearted put-down in their circle, yet they all wear loud "Hawaiian" shirts (when they aren't naked), they waterski, and their speedboat has an English name, "Sun-Season," like the nightclub where they dance, "Blue Sky."

Later, there is a bold use of the U.S. flag by Seijun Suzuki in *Gate of Flesh* (*Nikutai no mon*, 1964); he shows it in close-up flapping in the wind as the gang of hookers talk about hating and spitting on everything in postwar Japan. And even rather recently, U.S. symbology has been used in films to denote violation and aggression, and also cheap titillation, as when, in *Female Teacher: In Front of the Students*, an enormous U.S. flag hangs behind the bed where a Japanese high school boy (Tôru Nakane) and his bisexual girlfriend (Rina Oko) tie up and assault their pretty, young teacher, Reiko. The U.S. flag here could almost be a work of abstract art entitled "Rape."

3

Anxieties of Change, Changing Anxieties

It is one thing to write, as J. Victor Koschmann does, that "Japan's defeat led to collapse of the authoritative, prewar value system that had 'provided the standards for action and had been able to unify the inner and outer dimensions of life,' leaving in its place uncertainty and anxiety."[1] Yet, we know from Japanese cinema if nowhere else that "uncertainty and anxiety" had been a part of the culture long before World War II. At the same time, an equally profound hallmark of Japanese society was its focus on the quotidian-domestic, the intimate network, what Pyle calls "the mundane order." According to Pyle, "Modern Japan inherited a value system based on the mundane order and on the nexus of human relationships. This is in stark contrast to the many civilizations that conceived the mundane order, and especially the political order, as an inferior or incomplete version of a transcendental order."[2]

Perhaps this is why Japanese cinema often strikes Western viewers as inherently transcendental even or especially when it idles at the slow-paced examination of simple daily existence, not because it is necessarily conceived as transcendental but because we, accustomed to seeking the transcendental in our art, impart that meaning to it. I am thinking in particular of Ozu, in whose low-key films people often appear small and fragile, no more so than when they run the danger of alienating their closest loved ones and making them unhappy. A certain unease about the larger meaning of life is always working under the seemingly tranquil skin of an Ozu film, although the lessons learned are usually related to the daily workings of domestic "mundane order" and Japanese "love of order in communal life."[3] Ozu's characters squirm in nets of binding but conflicted emotions; a number of his films turn upon the mutual sadness, regret and anxiety faced by parents and their adult children when it becomes time for the children to move out and go to school, or to start families of their own. In some cases, both sides wait for the other to broach the subject, and neither one does, out of politeness, wariness or obliviousness. Usually someone outside the immediate family must step in to help matters along, and even then, there is much angst even after things seem to have gotten settled into place. If they weren't already down on the floor (for family meals and tea ceremonies), these characters soon would be, and it is hard to say whether the director is a somewhat devious observer of pregnant moments or in fact one of the most serene nihilists which cinema ever produced, since Ozu does acknowledge that all of life ends up being a compromise with *something*.

In Ozu's *Dragnet Girl* (*Hijôsen no onna*, 1933), the enterprising criminality and louche lifestyle of Tokiko (Kinuyo Tanaka) are entirely contiguous with her independence as a career woman, that is, her disparity with mundane domestic order. She is glamorous and tough, a femme fatale who runs with a violent gang of thieves, including her lover, an ex-prizefighter named Jyoji (Joji Oka). Using her beauty as a weapon, she sometimes lures rich men for the gang to rob. When gawky young Hiroshi (Kôji Mitsui) begs to join up—gushing to Jyoji, "I like you!"—Tokiko rolls her eyes suggestively and tells Jyoji, "Why not save his honor?" Hiroshi is instantly made a gang member: "Hiroshi is a full-time punk now!" This casual demeaning of "honor," so central to traditional Japanese culture, is, like Tokiko's day-job in an office typing pool, both *moderne* and appalling. The idea that a woman could have independence without undermining the very mainstays of society seems suspect if not utterly foreign to Ozu. Tadao Sato confirms that in imperial Japan "it was popularly thought that a woman only worked [in an office] because she had to and the term 'working woman' was tinged with contempt."[4] Even as late as Suzuki's *Youth of the Beast* (*Yajû no seishun*, 1963), "office clerk" is a common cover for prostitution work. But this is also what makes Tokiko in *Dragnet Girl* compelling as a female gangster. Unlike the gun molls and femmes fatales of Western gangster films from the same era, Tokiko does not exist only in some semi-fantastical demimonde; she is not an exotic nightclub "canary." She is a sociological entity, viewed as being part of Japan and imbued with all its contradictions, just as the city streets she walks are gray and deserted even in broad daylight.

Yasujirô Ozu is one of the greatest directors in the history of world cinema. A master of tonalities, he could mingle comedy and drama almost effortlessly, simply by observing life calmly and resolutely through his uniquely sensitive eyes, too fond for judgment and too wise for despair. Like Chekov, Ozu turned simple naturalism into the highest art.

Honor codes are also invoked in an ironic or a critical way in the scene from Kurosawa's *Drunken Angel* (*Yoidore tenshi*, 1948) where the gangster Matsunaga (Toshirô Mifune), seriously ill with tuberculosis, tries to avoid drinking, but a reunion with an old yakuza contact forces his hand. He cannot refuse the offered shot of whiskey without insulting the contact; Kurosawa cuts from a closeup of Matsunaga downing the shot to a medium view of a nightclub foyer at a different location, where Matsunaga is now roaring drunk, his arms around two women who are helping him to walk. One's link within some chain (of command, usually) ensures that personal sacrifices will have to be made; the world of the yakuza is certainly no more free or spontaneous for being completely criminal; quite the opposite, it is the place where the logic of "honor among thieves" reigns supreme, a reification of the larger emperor system that "represents and helps maintain hierarchical forms of social integration that act as a brake on protest and the free exercise of rights."[5]

Buell writes: "Japan has somehow remained ambiguously modern and non-modern, progressive and traditional—mainly to outsiders but also at least partly to itself as well."[6] But this indeterminacy is typical of Japanese cinema in general, and must be looked at, again, in terms of a (largely Buddhist) sense of otherness-in-one. This also speaks to what Joan Mellen describes as the quintessential Japanese "fear that there is something inherent in revolutionary power which leads to its degeneration."[7] Sato states that "those who seize power become like their predecessors, and no changes are effected. Accordingly, if a revolutionary attempts to pursue revolution all the way, in the end he must negate himself."[8] We see this self-negation in the inmate riot scene in Kinugasa's *A Page of Madness*; rather than invoking anarchic liberty or even real danger, it is a chaotic pummeling of bodies against each other, a kind of group-scale running in place.

Kôji Wakamatsu delivered a powerful statement about the futility of revolution in Japan with his psychedelic allegory, *Running in Madness, Dying in Love* (*Kyôsô jôshi-kô*, 1969). Wakamatsu begins with documentary footage of a political riot being quashed by the police; he then interpolates superimposed close-ups of his main character, a young cop (Ken Yoshizawa). The police all wear helmets and protective cloths across their lower faces to shield them from their own tear gas. During the brawl, the young cop is injured. His "mask" comes off, his mouth is bloodied. He runs away, experiencing a seeming crisis of values.

He goes to his older brother's house, an ultra-conservative (Rokkô Toura). Ashamed of the cop's admission that he ran away from the fight, the brother begins to beat him savagely. The brother's submissive wife (Yoko Muto), who has been kneeling in the other room, barges in and tries to stop her husband; suddenly she grabs his gun and fires it into his back. He collapses on the floor. As if coming out of a trance, the wife is completely distraught, sobbing and repentant. The cop drags her away and they go on the run, but she remains inconsolable. She tries to jump in front of a train, but the cop pulls her back at the last second. They plunge into sex as a refuge from their pain and alienation, but this seems to take them nowhere.

They continue to travel, ending up in a constant winter, trudging through snowbound towns and steppes. The fleeing lovers enter a kind of purgatory where punishments are enacted on them again and again: a group of black-clad men track them down, beat them both up in the snow, and tie the cop to a tree, naked. It is not entirely clear whether these actions take place in reality or in the guilt-consumed minds of the fugitives. Finally, the older brother himself returns, very much alive, a spirit of indestructible, ever-renewing Japanese conservatism. He beats his wife and takes her back with him; she dutifully follows, with the cop, the failed revolutionary, trailing them at a distance. An early postmortem for the radical 1960s, *Running in Madness, Dying in Love* dwells pessimistically on something within the Japanese psyche that seems to return again and again to repressiveness and obedience.

Satires of Japanese obedience are rarely as pungent as Teruo Ishii's depiction of a powerful cult in *Japanese Hell* (*Jigoku*, 1999). New recruits must turn over all their money and assets for the privilege of reaching "enlightenment" by drinking a potion made from the plucked and simmered dandruff of the self-appointed cult leader. This brew makes the trainees high; we see them bouncing up and down off the floor in full-lotus position, listening to cassettes of the leader's voice repeating that they will die and be reincarnated as maggots if they disobey him, and sleeping amid swarms of vermin. What makes *Japanese Hell* disturbing is that it was based closely on an actual cult, Aum Shinrikyo,[9] which had operated in Japan since 1984. Preaching the end of the world with rhetoric culled from the Book of Revelations and Isaac Asimov, the cult attracted numerous followers; some were held against their will while money was extorted from them; at least one was murdered trying to escape. Other followers were force-fed LSD, physically tortured, and subjected to shock treatments. In the mid–1990s Aum Shinrikyo began a series of attacks on subways and other public places, using sarin nerve gas which they manufactured themselves. Eventually, the leader and a number of his elite followers were arrested and sentenced to death; splinter groups that arose from the breaking-up of Aum Shinrikyo are still being kept under surveillance in Japan as dangerous terrorist groups.[10] As in real life, the cult in Ishii's film feeds on the attempts of Japanese to devote their lives to something meaningful and enlightening, while ultimately only serving the needs of the ruthless cult leadership.

In Kurosawa's *Ikiru*, in the funeral scene, the jaded bureaucrats, moved by the example of their deceased colleague Watanabe, drunkenly pledge to "Sacrifice the self to serve the many." But Kurosawa cuts to the next scene, now back at work, each man buried under mountains of forms and file folders, no one daring to stand up for the rights of the citizenry. These clerks back down before the routine of life, not sufficiently threatened or haunted or uncomfortable to makes waves. At best Watanabe survives only as a private, silent reflection in the middle of the work day and its protocols.

This distrust of collective radical action, or sense of futility about it, is also why, as Pyle states, "reverence for the emperor, the values of the family, and suspicion of foreigners stuck a responsive chord and resonated with long-held values of the social system [in Japan]"[11]—a point which I will be considering at some depth in this book. For the Japanese, human figures are placed on a human-sized plane, eschewing pseudo-humanist Western-Enlightenment values, "because," as Mellen characterizes Japanese thought, "human beings cannot live up to the noble aspirations held for them."[12] This is a failsafe of Buddhism, for example; we are eternally in progress, eternally falling short, all we can do is try again. Postwar intellectual Masato Ara offered this as a critique of communist ideology: "human beings are egoistic, ugly, despicable, and human conduct is submerged in nothingness."[13] The social order is less at fault than fate or karma, which are hard or impossible to alter.

But this is not necessarily counter-revolutionary: "to begin from one's own position and one's own outlook on life did not necessarily mean abandoning all social relevance or concern."[14] And of course, fate can also be kindly, at least now and then. In Ozu's *An Inn in Tokyo*, unemployed, homeless Kiyashi (Takeshi Sakamoto) is reunited by chance with an old flame, Otsune (Chôko Iida), who also helps him find a job. His life now suddenly turned around, he philosophizes: "Don't make light of your life. Ten days ago, I would have died for good sake. I'm happy I'm still alive." Ozu reveals Kiyashi's good fortune as a test, however, one which he ultimately fails. But even when Kiyashi's luck takes a downturn again, and new sorrows come, he remains sanguine, telling Otsune: "The ten days since you got me the job have been the happiest time in my life." Here, no one blames individual poverty on an abstract idea of society, since society simply consists of all its members caught up in the workings of their fates.

Sato sees this as a consistent theme of Japanese cinema, taken up by numerous other directors of different times and temperaments. "[Nagisa] Oshima, from the very start," he writes, "did not view the system and people as two separate entities. He was not the first Japanese director to present this, however.... Kurosawa and Minoru Shibuya ... had stated that 'The evil in the system is none other than the evil in human beings.'"[15] Yet, even though the characters in Japanese films are rarely judged harshly, neither are they permitted to be individualistic; this lack of individualism is what guarantees them protection from critique and judgment. It is a very Hollywood-derived moment in Kurosawa's *Drunken Angel*, when a grizzled old doctor (Takashi Shimura) removes a bullet from the hand of the gangster Matsunaga without anesthetic. "Hey, don't you use painkillers?" Matsunaga snarls. "Not for hoodlums like you," the doctor says. The doctor's discernment here seems self-contradicting somehow, an entitlement; a real Japanese doctor, one presumes, would either refuse treatment if he objected so strongly to the patient, or would perform the operation stoically, holding his tongue. (Matsunaga's response is even more Hollywood-esque, flicking his lit cigarette at the saw-bones and saying, "You're pretty full of yourself, aren't you? I hate doctors.")[16]

As one postwar Japanese intellectual wrote, "We know how to be Japanese nationals (*kokumin*) but not how to be human beings. Humanism has been nothing but an empty word."[17] This antipathy to humanism is depicted in Oshima's *Boy*, where the snowman that the damaged Toshio builds is just a large pointy cone with an old rubber boot for a face, a token and abject representation of the human. Also, in Oshima's *Japanese Summer: Double Suicide* (*Muri shinjû: Nihon no natsu*, 1967), the human is shown again and again as nothing but an empty form to be haphazardly and unconvincingly filled: featureless figures chalked on the ground, a body-shape scooped from beach clay, anatomical cavities engaging in sexual intercourse, the holes made in bodies by bullets and swords. This is reminiscent of the philosopher Katsumi Umemoto's insight that Marxism could lay the ethical groundwork for a project of bringing the "*true* person that hangs there abstractly" back into the form of the person as such[18]—an idealistic prescription which, of course, Oshima does not endorse.

Because of what Pyle terms the "Japanese deference to the great impersonal forces" of fate,[19] anti-individualist and even nihilistic tendencies occur in Japanese films of all eras. In *Ugetsu*, Genjûrô risks his life against looting soldiers to salvage his latest batch of pottery, even as Mizoguchi shows us the soldiers indiscriminately smashing pots in search of food or valuables; Genjûrô notes that if the soldiers had held off for one more night in attacking his village, he would have made away with his goods safely and sold them at profit. The larger devastation does not touch his selfish reality; if anything, he is reckless for placing himself and his family in danger in the name of a purely personal ambition.

More recently, in Toshiaki Toyoda's *9 Souls* (*Nain souruzu*, 2003), the lot of a crazed Japanese man being dragged away in the throes of a fit is visually compared to a stray rat scurrying across a floor, with little emotional difference. For Toyoda, the death of a man is no more or less noble than that of an animal, as in another scene where the escaped convicts (the nine souls of the title) encounter a dying sheep and put it out of its misery by clubbing it to death (offscreen). This death is formally like the eventual deaths of the convicts themselves, which also occur offscreen and suddenly; like the killing of the sheep, brutish, barely registered by the cosmos, instantly forgotten, lonely and finally meaningless. "When we die, we're on our own!" one screams, crawling off to bleed out like an animal; at most he wishes for a woman to be present, but does not find her. He ends up dead on a park bench trying to reach a disconnected number on a cell phone, the recorded message rebuffing him again and again.

On the other hand, another of the convicts does manage to have the girl he admires, a shy waitress, present when he dies, magnificently beating himself to death in a paroxysm of hopeless despair at the prospect of being captured and returned to prison. But we note that, in his bullish frenzy to die and his final expiring, it hardly matters whether he is seen or not; she offers no comfort, and watches with more baffled curiosity than concern. After getting murdered, yet another escapee says in voiceover, "Don't have a funeral ... don't find my family," just "ditch my ashes in the gutter ... forget me." Once important funeral rites for the dead (ancestors) break down utterly, and families turn inside out. One of the nine convicts, Noboru (Eita), killed his father in an act of filial impiety and revolution ("How dare you tell your father to shut up?" the old man shrieks only moments before being patricided, calling on outmoded traditions of elder-worship); while another slaughtered his son ostensibly for refusing to go to school, running over him with a car until, as the matter-of-fact news reporter relates, "the son was flatter than a pancake."

Toyoda's fascinating approach is to make the convicts both harbingers of societal decay *and* avengers against a corrupt system, another example of perplexing multiplicity or otherness-in-one. The film is on no one's side, and everyone's. And after all, the rampaging ex-convicts of the title are defined as possessing or being "souls" in ways that no one else in the film is. To some extent, Toyoda falls back on familiar depictions of them as Robin Hood types. They victimize a loony businessman who was so "kindly" he preferred to poison his employees rather than "downsize" them; and Noboru, the son convicted of killing his father (also a dishonest businessman), finally kills his own brother-accomplice, who has not only let Norubu take the fall alone for the original patricide but has followed in their crooked father's footsteps by founding a loan-sharking business with his inheritance. In a sardonic touch, hiphop and potato chips figure into the scene where the younger brother extols the virtues of capitalist Japan. Indeed, all is not as it seems, and in the end, even the tough ex-convict who murdered his son reveals that the son, in desperation, had begged him to take his life, for unknown reasons.

9 Souls riffs symphonically on various aspects and images of fatalism. In the politically charged 1970s, Mellen asserted that "the absence in [Japanese] culture of a belief in progress points clearly to the persistence of both feudal values and sensibility."[20] Yet, it must be acknowledged that nearly everything in that culture has often pointed toward a belief in fate that made questioning authority irrelevant if not ridiculous. Feudalism came out of this fatalism as much as it did out of socioeconomic structures. The seeming religion of the booming postwar Yen was not truly an alternative belief system, or even a continuation of existing belief systems in new guise, but more like a semi-bored distraction from a life that held little promise; a path of least resistance. Pyle views it as part of the same non-transcendental, obligatory "mundane order" of Japan: "The oligarchs produced the ultimate example of Japanese orientation to the mundane order: 'the fusion of deity and ruler, the divine king, the emperor as a living deity.'"[21]

This combination of free enterprise and autocracy, of internal work ethic and external worship of power, makes the Japanese economic system distinctive. Japan always seemed to have "a different, perhaps better, alternative to the American political-economic model.... While Japan was ostensibly a free-market democracy, its politics and its economics appeared cleverly planned and intertwined, somehow impervious to the messiness of competition and conflict so common in the West."[22] For a time the nation appeared to run so smoothly it was called Japan Inc.,[23] since it seemed to function as one efficient corporate entity. According to historian Jacob M. Schlesinger in *Shadow Shoguns*, this is because the real power was concentrated in the hands of astute (and corrupt) political bosses. Schlesinger calls Japan's postwar machine politics a "fantastic setting ... freed from the normal difficult choices and ideological divides of democracy."[24] It was certainly a hothouse environment: "Machines are, by their nature, designed to protect a cozy status quo, to disdain ideas, to keep politics quiet and smooth."[25] Not too unlike the dynastic, corporatist U.S. today, Japan's political system was held hostage by money. Big business bought off political bosses and officials in order to represent its interests.[26] "The bosses could push around legislators and cabinets at will on day-to-day decisions" in the name of keeping Japan's economy strong and the nation safe, "courtesy of America's indulgent protection...."[27]

One of the most enduring and powerful of these secret controllers was "Boss" Kakuei Tanaka. He was constantly embattled, seemingly thriving on an endless cultivation of struggle and opposition.[28] He was ostensibly a populist but deeply conservative.[29] Tanaka exploited Japanese "obsequiousness" (if that's what it is) by surrounding himself with humble flunkies who would work hard and ask for nothing in return. They were his loyal minions. Schlesinger writes:

> To justify relegating his faction members to underling status, he portrayed them as noble laborers who did the hard work while shirking glory. "Our people seem to be used to working subordinately ... just like 'Miss Maids' or 'Miss Assistants,' working silently when told. I like it this way," he once said. "We are like snow that's trodden upon by wooden sandals," he liked to explain. "Nobody wants to be trodden upon. But we must grin and bear it no matter how bitterly we resent it at times."[30]

One hesitates to say that such rhetoric is innately Japanese, although it is difficult to imagine postwar North Americans so pridefully stoical that they would pay to spend their vacations shoveling out a winter tourist town.[31]

It was partly through Boss Tanaka's power-brokering and machinations that the conservative "pro-business, pro-bureaucracy" Liberal Democratic Party completely dominated elections from 1955 into the 1990s, an unbroken thirty-eight-year reign.[32] When the graft was revealed in a police sting in 1989, there were numerous indictments, the first wave of scandals that rocked the cozy machinery of Japan Inc.[33] 1989 was also, fatefully enough, the year Emperor Hirohito died. The longstanding conservative engine was breaking down on all fronts. When the LDP's reign was finally broken, it was because the economy itself totally collapsed in the early 1990s, "the deepest recession since the war."[34] To critics the government had come to resemble oligarchy or corporatocracy, and with less largesse trickling down to the person in the street, this criticism seemed accurate.[35] "At a time when average Japanese citizens were beginning to feel the economic pinch, they were given fresh reminders of just how well, in contrast, their politicians were faring. At the end of the summer of 1992, the government was hit by a sensational new wave of [political graft] scandals that persisted through the following spring."[36]

In 1993, the LDP lost power for the first time since 1955. "Even for a populace already hardened by repeated displays of extreme political depravity, the latest exposés were shocking,"[37] Schlesinger writes. "Although Japan Inc. was both superhuman and ahuman [...] managed by a mysterious horde of interchangeable blue-suited automatons," it *was* Japan, for better and worse, and its failure was Japan's. Stripped bare by this failure, all the corruption came home to roost. Schlesinger continues: "The people's trust in long-successful institutions waned, while the famous unity of the leadership was shattered amid bitter disputes."[38] But the yen (or dollar) will out, and the LDP returned to power in 1996; however, for some, the three-year stumbling lapse was telling. Schlesinger argues that Japan Inc. "was never [again] so superhuman nor so mysterious as it had appeared," but rather, thenceforward "a gaudy, inefficient mess."[39] He writes: "Having been nurtured under special conditions, the machine could not last when its environment changed in the late 1980s and early 1990s."[40] Japanese "extreme" cinema, which came into being in the 1990s, stems directly from this renewed, vigorous social and political cynicism; suddenly the aims of once-potent institutions and the magic of money itself were revealed as grubby and poisonous. Historian Jeff Kingston writes: "The myths and beliefs that had sustained social cohesion in post–WWII Japan have faded along with job security, stable families, and the social contract."[41]

Kinji Fukasaku, who specialized in hard-boiled yakuza pictures and whose films include *Blackmail Is My Life* (*Kyôkatsu koso waga jinsei*, 1968) and *Battle Royale*, has asserted that the Japanese public was "acutely aware of this corruption" as early as the 1960s.[42] Films of that time give some indication that this was the case. Yasuzô Masumura's first film, *Kisses*, opens with a young man named Kenichi (Hiroshi Kawaguchi)[43] going to visit his father in jail, a politician arraigned on charges of election fraud and, as we learn, not for the first time; there he meets a young woman named Akiko (Hitomi Nozoe) who is visiting *her* father, also a politician in jail, for embezzlement of public funds ("We had to pay for my mother's sanatorium," she explains). And in Masumura's *Black Test Car* (*Kuro no tesuto kaa*, 1962), a city assemblyman is bribed by an automaker to crash a competitor's new model and then create a public scandal by leading a smear campaign against the "murder weapon on wheels." Exposing "corrupt ties between government and upper-echelon management" was also the theme of Akira Kurosawa's *The Bad Sleep Well* (*Warui yatsu hodo yoku nemuru*, 1960).[44] However, whether or not the disillusionment began much earlier than 1989, for many in Japan the post–1989 era seems to have been like the trauma of the 1945 surrender all over again. "[D]uring the 1990s the Japanese learned more than they were prepared for about their history."[45] Learning is one thing; the quality of that learning, or perhaps the detail of the memories, is what has sometimes been questioned about modern Japan.

"The past still casts long shadows over contemporary Japan," Kingston states, "and time has not yet buried memories of the bloody history that continues to divide Japan from its Asian neighbors, because there is a widespread perception, partially accurate, that Japan has shirked its war responsibility."[46] This refers to the Japanese invasions and colonizations of China and Korea, among other Asian nations. Emperor Hirohito was the bellwether of this state of "blamelessness,"[47] as Norma Field calls it. He was not held accountable after the surrender, and thus no individual Japanese felt accountable, either. There were, of course, many prosecutions of Japanese war criminals, resulting in executions or prison terms. But there was no effort to prosecute Japan's sovereign leader, on whose behalf the Japanese had acted and through whom they derived their own sense of sovereignty; moreover, "many Japanese war criminals continued to occupy powerful positions in industry and government after the war."[48] Because of this, Hirohito became a contested figure, still worshiped by Japan's right-wing factions; right-wing animosities nearly always took the shape of restoring greater powers to the emperor, reinstating emperor-worship, and rehabilitating his image in the eyes of history once and for all.

These sentiments came not only from fringe groups but from the mainstream media, which was an organ of conservative interests. Field writes:

> The first newspaper accounts after Hirohito's death uniformly portrayed him as a peace-loving constitutional monarch from the beginning, who had refrained from interfering in the decision to go to war because, having visited England at an impressionable age, he had come to cherish the concept of constitutionality.[49]

The whitewashed history that some Japanese still tell themselves maintains its "resolute silence ... about Japanese atrocities and the millions of Asian victims of Japanese aggression. There is no Rape of Nanking, no Unit 731,[50] no comfort women, no indiscriminate aerial bombing of civilian populations by Japanese, no mistreatment of prisoners of war, and no indication that many Okinawa civilians were pressured to commit group suicide by the Imperial Armed Forces."[51]

Japanese conservatives have termed it "masochistic history," any promotion of a history that acknowledges Japanese wrongdoing at all.[52] Kingston writes: "The notion of Japan as victim, always caving into international demands in the interests of maintaining harmony, resonates powerfully among some Japanese."[53] It is reminiscent of "Beat" Takeshi Kitano's famous joke that "it's okay to cross against the light if everyone else is doing it."[54] The forces of conservatism in Japan count on this Japanese reluctance to rock the boat, as it were. Conservative forces exploit that reluctance by promoting the idea that Japan has been put upon (again, not very different from conservative forces in the U.S.). Kingston: "And here is where the propaganda machine kicks in, hammering home the idea that Japan is the target of double standards."[55] However: "Most Japanese accept Japan's war responsibility and favor atonement."[56] Wounds are still lingering for many, including remaining survivors of World War II on both the Japanese and the U.S. side, but there is also some eagerness to heal and forgive, as one U.S. veteran and former prisoner of war attested upon returning to Japan on a friendship visit in 2011 at age 94. He received heartfelt apologies from current Japanese workers at the factory where he had been forced to do slave labor: "I came away," he told the *Japan Times*, "with a much different impression of Japan. We couldn't have been treated any better."[57]

Shôhei Imamura slyly comments on the strange situation of 1990s Japan in *The Eel* (*Unagi*, 1997). This film has been incorrectly described as lacking in the social context that Imamura brought to his earlier work; in fact, it is entirely about the traumatic 1990s in Japan, reeling from the revelations of 1989. Imamura begins his film in 1988. A young stockbroker named Yamashita (Kôji Yakusho) receives anonymous letters warning him that his wife (Chiho Terada) cheats on him whenever he goes on all-night fishing trips. His suspicion finally aroused to the breaking point, he sets a trap; returning early one night, he catches his wife with her lover and stabs her to death. As if in a trance, covered in blood and still wearing his fishing jacket, he turns himself in at a police station and is sentenced to eight years in prison. Inside prison, we learn that he did little more than goosestep in circles all day long with other prisoners; in fact he has been inside for the entire time that business and government scandals rocked Japan to its foundations, existing seemingly outside of the traumatic knowledge which the rest of his nation has been forced to learn and internalize. Nonetheless, Yamashita is traumatized. Upon his release, we see him being given his pet eel by one of the prison guards. When asked why he talks to the eel, Yamashita says, "He doesn't say what I don't want to hear." (Eel is a treasured holiday food for traditional Japanese; the sense I glean from Imamura's surrealism here is that it is equivalent to a reactionary killer in a U.S. film befriending a Thanksgiving turkey.) This reflects on the national strain from too much unbidden bad news and depressing knowledge, as well as the mass denial that swept the LDP back into office in 1996, not coincidentally the year that Yamashita is released from prison.

Disturbing events soon begin to occur, pointing to the unresolved past. He discovers a young woman, Keiko (Miso Shimizu), unconscious after attempting to kill herself by swallowing sleeping pills. Since Keiko bears a resemblance to his dead wife, Yamashita immediately flashes on the blood-drenched body he'd left in his marriage bed eight years prior. After recovering, Keiko begins to work with Yamashita in the barber shop where he now cuts hair. No longer a stockbroker, he has joined the service industry, as many Japanese found themselves downsized or demoted after the economic collapse at the turn of the 1990s. We note that he still fishes at night, now with no entanglements at home to worry about.

Although it would seem that by saving Keiko's life he has somehow redeemed his wife's murder, the film is not that simple. Yamashita's madness and denial, his compartmentalization of experience—his hands remember the murder but "he" does not—prevent him from fully recovering. He avoids people, not liking them and not wanting to get hurt again. In this, he is also like modern Japan, as Ohnuki-Tierney writes: "The change [in modern Japan] is most conspicuous in the image of the *self* of the Japanese in relations to the *other*, that is, other peoples."[58]

Yamashita's disillusionment with life is Japan's disillusionment. The conflicted, unwanted past also lingers in Keiko's discovery that she is pregnant by her ex-boyfriend, a crooked businessman who has tried to steal 30 million yen from Keiko and her mentally ill mother (Etsuko Ichihara). Eventually, the ex-boyfriend turns up at the barber shop, threatening Keiko, and a brawl breaks out. As if finally identifying his true enemy and the source of his problems, Yamashita beats up the businessman and slashes his face with a razor, a mark of Cain. The businessman is temporarily diminished from his sense of megalomaniacal entitlement. Yamashita claims the baby as his own, so that Keiko can have a future. Yamashita, we see, would prefer to live a lie that pleases others and confirms what they have already led themselves to believe (in this case, that he and Keiko had become lovers); but Yamashita himself is taken back to prison for violating his parole in the assault on the businessman. The past, Imamura seems to be saying, repeats in spite of our best efforts to redeem and change it. Ultimate power remains in the hands of the business elite.

The past, however, is sometimes no more troubling than the present or future. A metonym for this is the keyboard in Miike's *Andromedia* which shifts between alphabetic letters and their calligraphic signs, and which is used to conjure the dead girl who has been resurrected as a computer program. "Japan may be a less risky society than many others, but by its own standards, the sudden sharp rise in risk has shaken society and generated considerable anxieties,"[59] Kingston writes. "The pace and scope of change in Japan has been staggering and deeply unsettling in many ways for its citizens."[60] Kingston provides an example of one such anxiety-making risk: "Deregulation of the utility industry is putting pressures on operators to boost profits at the expense of safety. So just as Japan's aging nuclear power plants, many entering their fourth decade of operation, are in more need of inspections, maintenance, and repairs, bottom-line concerns are forcing cutbacks in safety measures," including increasingly cursory inspections and the expectation to keep obsolescent plants running for twice as long as they were initially designed and built for.[61]

This pattern of unstable change has engendered much ongoing pessimism.[62] With the recession of the 1990s "unemployment, suicides, divorce, and domestic violence soared,"[63] and there was a widespread "subverting [of] long-standing relations based on trust between people and government and with their employers."[64] "Between 2002 and 2006, the ranks of working poor grew by 40 percent, accounting for more than 10 million out of a total labor force of some 66 million."[65] This shows that Japan is, again, of a historic piece with Western nations such as Germany and Italy, who experienced defeat and ruin in World War II, surrendered to the U.S. and rebuilt themselves according to lusty industrialization and "economic miracles," and then gave birth to a generation who were skeptical of the success and of the repression of the past which paid for it. Finally, this sense of decline, of midnight tolling for Cinderella, has also swept in some of the conquerors of World War II, especially Great Britain and the U.S., as corruption and lax standards nearly everywhere have come to replace our former business ingenuity and ethical model (such as it was).

Current Japanese films, especially the Extreme ones, contain something like a negation of globalist securities; if cinematic ontology still prompts us to see otherness-in-one when we look at images of the human, and if we are then led to embrace that humanity as a sacred principle, then current Japanese extreme cinema is typically and disturbingly resistant toward this motion of embrace. The stoical nature of Japanese culture—which Mizoguchi and Ozu depicted as profound truth; which Kurosawa, Oshima and Imamura rebelled against without being able to completely replace it with a new paradigm; and which Chris Marker, Roland Barthes, William Gibson and other Westerners have composed odes to, odes both bemused and adoring—has been pushed to the most daring kind of satire, which could take as its motto this assertion by Badiou: "But the Real is declared, instead of known."[66] Nothing could be more hostile to a purely traditional ontological understanding than a cinema which creates a lifelike world of sheer impossibilities. So, in Minoru Kawasaki's *Executive Koala* (*Koara kachô*, 2005), we have a koala bear in a three-piece suit who is a businessman and also a homicidal ax murderer;

while in Shion Sono's *Hair Extensions* (*Ekusute*, 2007), a murdered girl's hair continues to grow, so voluminously that it gets sold off to salons as weaves, but these weaves are cursed and attack their new wearers ... and so on. Nothing is too preposterous. Indeed, Japanese extreme cinema and what is known in the U.S. as "J-Horror" are often defined by their outrageous premises; often, the films themselves are less interesting than their premises.

And yet, this alienated savagery is also part of the new ontology that we are considering in relation to Japanese film: a mix of the Zen Buddhist ideal of otherness-in-one (where what declares itself "outside" is already inside us) and Malabou's destructive plasticity (where trauma induces new forms, new beings, new meanings and new forms of survival). Mellen sees the preeminent role of acceptance in the films of Mizoguchi, for example, as coming from his "personal and deep commitment to Buddhism,"[67] in which the individual comes to know his or her place in the universe as a small one, not occupying the center but simply somewhere, an inevitable somewhere that is always right and never wrong, according to the perspective which we can achieve on it. (Perspective is all-important here. The Japanese think of everything as possessing five directions: north, south, east, west, and the center.[68]) The act of gaining literal, visual perspective becomes itself a form of acceptance, part of the Buddhist "ideal of complete inner harmony"[69]; this is dramatized, for Mellen, in the closing shot of *Sansho the Bailiff*, which pulls away from the mother and son, reunited at the end of everything, still defeated and suffering, until they are "tiny specks on the landscape" and finally "entirely removed from the shot."[70] Thus, Mellen concludes, not apolitically, "the director wishes to stress the suffering of all rather than the tragedy of one."[71] Likewise, Sato writes about the ending of Mizoguchi's *A Tale from Chikamatsu* (*Chikamatsu monogatari*, 1954) that Osan's and Mohei's "acceptance of public execution is their act of revenge because the disgrace of it brings about the fall of the merchant's house."[72]

There can be no personal, individual happiness outside of an order that can benefit all, in other words outside of Zen discipline, because something as unnatural as universal happiness would have to be well ordered and maintained if nothing else. In *The Love of Sumako the Actress*, Mizoguchi depicts the moments of happiness between Sumako and her illicit lover Shimamura as being more intensely passionate because they defy social codes, and because they are also connected to the theater work that they share; but this in no way slights the fact that the couple is shown to have paid an enormous cost by defying those expected codes. The film's social critique does not present a fully realized overcoming of the traditional social order but rather the pain which people experience when they try to overcome it and cannot. Thus, with *Sansho*, Mizoguchi ultimately registers his protest against tyranny by naming his film not for either of the two main protagonists (mother and son), but for the character of the Bailiff, the feudal lord who enslaved them and whose personal lust for power has for a time defined the era in which the protagonists live. "We are powerless," Mellen writes, "before the 'all.'"[73] There is little difference between this closing shot and its formal reverse, the opening crane shot in Toyoda's *9 Souls* which passes over a sprawling urban landscape in which buildings begin to disappear one by one, until "the all," the world as we know it, is reduced to the wasteland around a hovel where the young killer Noboru looks out through a broken window, indifferent, closed-off, devoid of emotion.

4

Extremisms

Current extreme cinema has found its ideal home in Japan. Indeed, Japanese cinema has been at home with a certain degree of extremism since its early days and definitely since its "Golden Age." In 1960, Joseph L. Anderson and Donald Richie could say:

> Pointless killing is one of the main features of the Japanese film.... In fact, looking at the general run of Japanese pictures, the feeling of the cheapness of human life is unescapable. Apart from excessive killing, Japanese films also tend to accentuate the attendant gore.... For example, a man falls dead toward the camera. He has been fatally shot or stabbed. This, however, is not enough. Right in the foreground, next to the camera, is a fire into which his head drops. As we watch the fire burn away his face, horses trample upon his body—all in full detail.[1]

Writing in 1948, Taijirô Tamura offered this prescription for how Japan's literature could better reflect its status as "a defeated country" and thereby become more truthful: "it needs to be more confused, more absurd, more erotic, and more raucous."[2] Postwar filmmakers understood this. What seems most decisive today about Akira Kurosawa's *Rashomon* (*Rashômon*, 1950)—arguably the postwar film that first put Japanese cinema on the world map—is not the well-worn playing with unreliable narration, repetition and time cues, but the violent scrambling of traditional social codes and their relation to rights, restrictions and taboos. At the heart of *Rashomon*, after all, is an illegitimate baby, abandoned in the semi-wilderness at Rashomon Gate; this baby will eventually be raised (we assume at the end) by a family that is not related to it by blood, in defiance of what Helen Hardacre calls "Japanese society's zero tolerance for childbirth out of wedlock."[3] Rather than allowing this baby to be exposed to the elements and die, the characters in the framing sections of the film (as opposed to the flashbacks where the various stories they are telling unfold) adopt it into their bedraggled community, as if to say that the younger generations of the future will be spared having to pay with their lives for the sin and guilt of the past. It is not difficult to see this as an implicit critique of historical Japan, and its demands for sacrificial soldiers and civilian casualties throughout its wars of imperialism.

Furthermore, Kurosawa's sympathies are with the outlaw, Tajômaru (played by Toshirô Mifune), a warrior turned bandit much like the many Japanese veterans then starving in the ruined streets of postwar Japan. The "masterless samurai," or ronin, had been forced to drop out, "driven by their condition to become scavenging predators."[4] Tajômaru's response to the harshness of his society is to go insane; in this, he stands as a reproach to a social order that has treated him little better than a rat in a cage. As

Mellen points out, in the Meiji era it was only the samurai who could push for reform, given the impacted nature of social mobility in Japan; the "dissident samurai," of which the bandit is clearly representative (he possesses a samurai sword and can fight with it skillfully), were "the hippies of their day."[5] It is a relationship of nihilistic protest in which Tajômaru engages the film's other male protagonist, Takehiro Kanazawa (Masayuki Mori), a wealthy, high-placed samurai. In a forest, Tajômaru rapes Kanazawa's beautiful wife Masako (Machiko Kyô) after a stray, fatalistic breeze lifts her ceremonial veil, driving the bandit wild with lust.

This rape leads to the death of her samurai husband; one of the pieces of evidence at the crime scene noted by the woodcutter (Takashi Shimura) is "the cap of a samurai that had been trampled on," a symbol of the breaking down of feudal hierarchies, specifically the elite warrior caste literally overturned and trodden under-

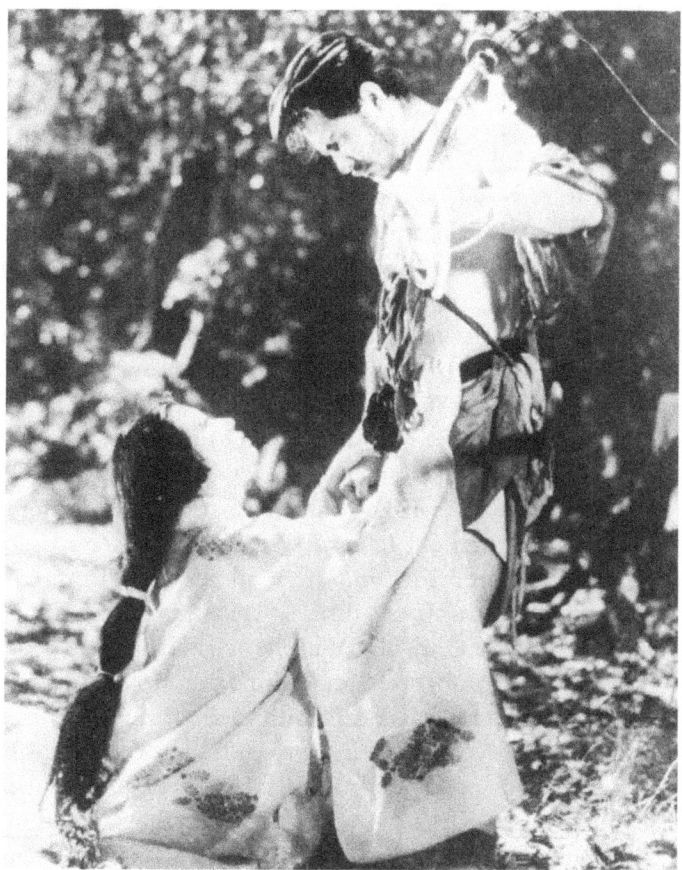

The breakdown of social codes which Kurosawa depicts in *Rashomon* (1950) spoke to the tumultuous postwar Japanese. The hollow figure of the wealthy samurai is propped up by the obeisance of the underclasses, here represented by the samurai's wife (Machiko Kyô) and a renegade ex-samurai (Toshirô Mifune). Indeed, the wife and the outlaw are united in a common bond against patriarchy with its property rights and its ability to buy and sell people.

foot. Likewise, social hierarchies were breaking down in Kurosawa's postwar Japan, where the formerly rich were reduced to hawking goods in the street; meanwhile, arriviste-style entrepreneurs and nouveau riche types drew envy and resentment.[6] The U.S. Occupation created a larger backdrop in which no Japanese could feel any longer like a "master" in his native land. General MacArthur "never made the slightest attempt to ingratiate himself with the Japanese public. He maintained a stern and duty-oriented exterior and an inflexible routine."[7] Suddenly, the Japanese could no longer cling so rigidly to former codes of personal and social dignity.

Not that these codes or their ideal meaning ever disappeared completely—we will find befuddled modern-day characters still struggling to overcome the same codes in Kiyoshi Kurosawa's *Tokyo Sonata* (*Tôkyô sonata*, 2008), including a downsized husband hiding his unemployed status from his family out of shame, and his wife, who secretly longs to be promiscuous. Also, not that these strict codes were ever as thoroughly inculcated in all Japan as they seem to have been in Medieval samurai culture and then later in 20th century imperial militarism. Long before the high school class forced to grow up quickly in Fukasaku's *Battle Royale*, there was the child in Ozu's *An Inn in Tokyo* who sees the bad pattern of his father's inability to find work and decides that applying at factories is useless; from now on they will look only to collect stray dogs for the finder's fees. It is tempting to say that today in Japan expression of individual longings and needs has become more direct.[8] But this is simply a Western fiction we tell ourselves to mark off a pre–U.S. Japan from a "new" post–U.S. one. Japanese cinema has done much to persuasively argue against such a simplistic breakdown.

No other national cinema, not even France's, has done more to prove Jean Renoir's famous mission statement of aesthetic and dramatic balance, "Everyone has his reasons." Dr. Kyoji Fujisaki (Toshirô Mifune) in Akira Kurosawa's *The Quiet Duel* (*Shizukanaru kettô*, 1949) is a character who exemplifies this, unluckily infected with syphilis through medical contact with an infected patient, his body rendered "pure, yet dirty." Breaking off his engagement to his heartbroken fiancée Misao (Miki Sanjô) so as not to infect her, he cannot bring himself to tell her the reason; Kyoji must bear the stigma of having a sexually transmitted disease even though he has not been sexual. When his father (Takashi Shimura) finds out, he tells Kyoji that he should be ashamed of himself and that he cannot forgive him. "I don't want to hear your excuse," the father says when Kyoji tries to explain. This deep confounding of guilt and innocence is basic; so, in the silent film *Serpent* (*Orochi*, 1925), we are told at the beginning that some villains appear to be good people and some good people appear to be villains. Likewise, what seems to have drawn Akira Kurosawa to *King Lear* as the source for *Ran* is the way the outspoken son Saburo (Daisuke Ryû) is rejected and exiled for warning his father, Lord Hidetora, not to trust the two other brothers, Taro and Jiro, who appear good but are backbiting flatterers; Saburo is accused of being a disrespectful troublemaker, yet Kurosawa shows his warning coming true almost immediately.

The mistaken disguising of the good as the bad and vice versa is neither a moral nor a psychological problem, merely an offshoot of fate. "A serpent's egg is white and pure," we hear in *Ran*, "a bird's is speckled and soiled." And all the inbetween types, the misfits caught between success and failure, between happiness and disappointment, defiant yet nervously tied to the codes they defy, existing both inside and outside of cultural taboos, barely daring to question a way of life that has condemned them, have always been part of Japanese cinema and will likely continue to be for the foreseeable future. Japanese sociology even coined a specific word for "the culture of inbetween-ness," *chûkan*, in the late 1950s.[9]

We can see Tajômaru the bandit occupying a similar place: a rebel angered by his lowered status, an outlaw finally driven mad by his own internalized shame. He is outside of society, animalistic as only Mifune can be, sweating and naked, marked by appetite and need; and although he chooses to violate the couple in the woods, his motivations are simple and direct—he takes what he needs from whose who have it. The violated, ruined couple, by stark contrast, represent the aristocracy of the time, yet confused and self-contradicting: Takehiro has the rank of a samurai, but we learn that he is not a very resourceful one, possibly a successful merchant who purchased his entrance into the warrior caste rather than earning it,[10] and his wife is difficult to pin down but consistently non-submissive to the will of men. Whether she is demanding to be killed for her honor or demanding that men kill each other in her name, she is the film's true motor force; and while it might not be possible to read her as feminist, she does depict, in an extreme way, the frustrated energies of women in feudal Japan. Her violent hysteria is the counterpart to Tajômaru's aggression, equally tempered by latent madness and a sense of doom.

It is interesting to compare the wife in *Rashomon* to Sumako (Kinuyo Tanaka) in Mizoguchi's *The Love of Sumako the Actress*. Rehearsing the role of Nora in *A Doll's House*, Sumako struggles with the line, "I'm taking off my doll's dress." The male director Shimamura, sympathetic to feminism, coaches her to express "contempt" in this line, the venom of a woman who no longer loves her husband and no longer wishes to please him in anything. In spite of understanding Nora's need for freedom, Sumako cannot immediately summon up the requisite anger; she delivers the line coldly, then coquettishly—

like a rapid, compressed run-through of the varying roller-coaster responses of the wife in *Rashomon*, actually. This helps us to see Kurosawa's film as being "about" acting, and its relation to projection(s). The wife, like Sumako, is in unknown territory in every version of the forest-encounter: Kurosawa's insistence that she own every one of her extreme emotions may be unrealistic but it is effective as a kind of parable about the problems of emergent emancipation. Thrust out of silence and rote behaviors, the wife finds herself derailed by male actions, which offer her no recourse; just as Sumako, although striving to be independent, is speaking from what is really only a suddenly amplified corner of patriarchal culture. "Control this violent emotion," Shimamura counsels her, "then cast it out like violent waves." But it is precisely "violence" that Sumako

In Mizoguchi's *The Love of Sumako the Actress* (*Joyû Sumako no koi*, 1947), Shimamura (Sô Yamamura, left) is a feminist-minded theater director, and Sumako (Kinuyo Tanaka) is his brilliant protégé-turned-partner. Sumako's victories often seem to come about as the direct effects of displacements: something (a challenge to patriarchy) is taken to be something else (a performance that is savored by male theater-connoisseurs). Mizoguchi does not allow us to miss this inbetween condition in which Sumako finds herself trapped. With Kurosawa, there is more of a naïve belief that people are behaving in ways that are true to themselves, even if the behaviors are objectively untrustworthy.

does not command. Coquetry is revealed, as it also is in *Rashomon*, as the sardonic, ineffectual armor under which a woman feels safe enough to express a trickle of rage against a man. The lines that Sumako must speak force her outside of herself, like the wife whose internal chaos is revealed after her external veil has been ripped away.

According to Catherine Malabou, there is a kind of radical phenomenology present in "the deserting of subjectivity, the distancing of the individual who becomes a stranger to herself, who no longer recognizes herself, who no longer recognizes her self." It is subjectivity "in a state of emergency."[11] In a way, this movement is fulfilled by the actress learning a role, as Sumako learns Nora, as a displacement: just as a male must instruct her how to express (female) rage, so Mizoguchi notes that it is male audience members, watching her opening-night performance, who determine that she is great at embodying "true emotion," thus a great actress. Sumako's victories often seem to come about as the direct effects of such displacements: something (a challenge to patriarchy) is taken to be something else (a performance that is savored by male theater-connoisseurs). Mizoguchi does not allow us to miss this inbetween condition in which Sumako finds herself trapped. With Kurosawa, there is more of a naïve belief that people are behaving in ways that are true to themselves, even if the behaviors are objectively untrustworthy. Donald Richie writes of *Rashomon*: "Each thinks of his character as being fully formed, of being a *thing*, like the rape or the dagger is a thing, and of his therefore (during an emergency such as this) being capable of only a certain number of (consistent) reactions. They are *in character* because they have defined their own character for themselves and will admit none of the surprising opportunities which must occur when one does not."[12] Societal displacements come more explicitly as action-film traumas in Kurosawa's cinema; death is never far behind them.

Richie goes on to state, "this limitation of spirit, this tacit agreement (social in its scope) that one is and cannot become, is [merely] one feudalistic precept."[13] But in fact, Kurosawa's device of replaying the action from different viewpoints and with different motivations belies the fact that the protagonists see themselves as anything at all. They might imagine themselves to be whole, or not, but they are already multiplicities in the world of otherness-in-one, where their actions are apprehended by different witnesses in the same subjective, contradictory, even deluded ways that we often watch movies. (The idea of a sequence replaying and changing with each "new watch" becomes basic to Oshima's very different *The Man Who Left His Will on Film*, as we have already detailed.)

Kurosawa is championing the breakdown of social codes in *Rashomon*, and leaving us to weigh for ourselves the broken pieces of identity and meaning; we can recognize his prescience in detecting what Malabou later cites as "destructive plasticity," the way that beings under terrible pressure are forced to change in order to survive. Mizoguchi and other Japanese directors had a similar prescience. Again, there is an echo of Mizoguchi's Sumako: having been told by her teacher Shimamura to crash against rocks like a wave, she says to him, "I need rocks to crash on. You're one … a rock I can throw myself into." And so their love is born, like an extension of destructive plasticity, from the process of her needing to resculpt herself for her growth and liberation. The limitation of any social liberation is that it requires sacrificial victims to be tested on, the brave ones who must swim untested waters. A starker, more eroticized version of this plays out later in Oshima's *In the Realm of the Senses* (*Ai no korida*, 1976).

In *Rashomon*, it is only Kanazawa, the defeated samurai, also the only character who has actually died, who represents a true dead end, and this should be kept in mind when approaching Kurosawa's later samurai films, which have often been misread as standing for traditional bushido (Zen-samurai) culture when their relation to that culture is actually a teasing, questioning one. In *Rashomon*, the samurai lord is uniquely impotent; tied up and physically immobilized in most scenes, he hardly ever speaks. Kanazawa's only defense is that he embodies an honor code whose outrage he conveys by staring daggers at his wife and Tajômaru, disdaining to dignify the adulterers by bringing them into a verbal language which has forbidden precisely such an encounter, such an overthrowing of Kanazawa's lordly authority. The wife describes the "cold light, a look of loathing" in her husband's eyes. But this look hardly has active power in the narrative; the only action which is identical in all versions of the story is when a blade of some kind is used to cut the rope fastened around the samurai lord's chest and arms, and we are made to see how whatever restoration of power and chance for vengeance the lord enjoys are entirely thanks to someone from a lower status (wife; bandit; woodcutter) choosing to extend it to him—just as only their testimony can finally bring him posthumous justice before the court tribunal. The message is clear: it is the oppressed who feed and maintain their oppressors through acquiescence to the status quo. Likewise, the wife's covering of her own face in guilt—as well as her elaborate make-up, including plucked and smudged eyebrows (called "moth eyebrows,"[14] an affectation of upper class wives)—is an internalization of feudal rules determining her deference to and dependency on her husband.

In this sense, both Tajômaru and the samurai-lord represent different aspects of feudal experience, both subject to critique. If the lord is feckless and fatuous, Tajômaru has been deformed by the system which demands warrior strength and cunning from men but strictly in the service of abstract ideals, i.e., to benefit the ruling elite; not in the service of a man's own individual self-fulfillment, which becomes criminal and punishable when turned against the property rights of the dominant class. Erich Fromm writes: "As long as the tables were set for only a minority [of wealthy elites], and the majority had to serve the minority's purposes and be satisfied with what was left over, the sense that disobedience is sin had to be cultivated. Both state and church cultivated it, and both worked together, because both had to protect their own hierarchies."[15] As Futagara's *Serpent* puts its succinctly: "Fair or not, this is a world of classes. If you don't toe the line, they crush you."

In Seijun Suzuki's *Fighting Delinquents* (*Kutabare gurentai*, 1963), a powerful real estate developer and yakuza, Nanjo (Hiroshi Kondô), crashes his sports car while speeding and necking with a girl; he runs over an old man and kills him. Nanjo sends his lawyer to the basement apartment where the now orphaned daughter Miyo (Yoshiko Nezu) lives with a group of other working-class young people. When the lawyer tries to buy them off with 30,000 yen, the 17-year-old hothead Sadao (Kôji Wada) roughs him up and throws him out; then invades Nanjo's office to demand one million for Miyo. Nanjo scoffs, so Sadao physically attacks the gangster-tycoon. A freeze-frame of Sadao about to hurl an armchair over his head morphs into the illustration of a front page headline: "Orphaned Teenage Punk Pockets One Million in Damages." But Sadao himself turns out to be descended from old money, explaining his natural charisma and leadership.

The same pride and quick temper that cause Sadao to reject his wealthy newfound clan are considered innate proof of his royal blood.

With class war being prevalent in postwar Japan, we can see, again, that the archetypes in *Rashomon* possess the dramatic purpose of representing modern conflicts: the bandit represents the people of occupied Japan struggling to survive in a ruined world and trying to break free from repressive caste or class mentalities; the samurai is the bureaucracy of Japan, parasitically controlled by the U.S. and emblemized as having its hands literally tied; the woman perhaps postwar Japan's harried, terrorized, traumatized spirit. Chaos and catastrophe were everywhere. Food shortages were "rending the social fabric. Factory absenteeism rose nationwide, in large part because workers took time off to bargain and barter for food in the countryside."[16] There were "vegetable thieves" and "the new crime of 'field vandalizing'"[17]; "anyone at all might become a victim of predatory crime."[18] Even the framing device of having the story told and retold as regional gossip was a commentary on the fear-mongering role of the news in postwar Japan, where the "media were indefatigable in reporting on all events symptomatic of social breakdown."[19]

In this sense, *Rashomon* is a strong protest about the conditions of its time, set tactfully in the distant feudal past but unambiguously imbued with the urgency of the living present, "the poverty and dissolution that have permeated society. This misery is symbolized by the Rashomon Gate itself, haunted by beggars, thieves and outcasts of one kind or another, a convenient place for people to dump bodies at night."[20] We see this voiced even more explicitly in Kurosawa's modern yakuza film, *Drunken Angel*, where a doctor blames the gangster Matsunaga's advanced state of tuberculosis on his dissolute lifestyle: "You're surrounded by a bunch of scum. Rotten, maggot-infested bacteria," the doctor says, referring to the yakuzas.

Thus, the present is *Rashomon*'s true contested battlefield, not the past. The past is only superficially a riddle. The present is what exists in the frame of the film, the impromptu council held by storm-stranded peasants seeking shelter in an abandoned Buddhist temple. What they are actually debating, as becomes clear throughout the film, is not the past but the future, symbolized finally by the baby whom one of the peasants chooses to save; this points to Kurosawa's hopes that the demoralized Japanese would learn to speak about the horrors they had witnessed, and that modern Japan would come together to try to change their world. This is also the subject of Ozu's *Record of a Tenement Gentleman* (*Nagaya shinshiroku*, 1947), in which an abandoned little boy follows various adults home to a slum in the repeated attempt to get them to take him in; to their pursed lips and unsympathetic attitudes, the child simply stands there, hands in his pockets, staring blankly as if to ask, "What now?" As Malabou writes, negation of one's real circumstances requires "naïve, absolute confidence, a child's faith in possibility, a fragile but unconditional belief without which experience would quite simply not be possible."[21]

It has been said that the Japanese "respect continuance, the proof of adaptation to flux."[22] This is true in *Record of a Tenement Gentleman*. Only the homeless child's patient refusal to go away eventually overcomes the heartlessness of the slum-dwellers, whose unsentimentality toward children is also reflected when one of the tenement fathers takes the 2,000 yen that his young son has won in the lottery and spends it on sake.[23] Good intentions, even good luck, are welcome but hardly decisive in the postwar Japan. One will have to be tough, and persistent. And Ozu's unsentimental depiction of children in poverty is there even in the imperial-era *An Inn in Tokyo*, which opens with two young brothers, Zenko (Tomio Aoki) and Masako (Takayuki Suematsu), on the road with their unemployed drifter father Kihashi. Kihashi is making the boys carry their sparse supplies, a knapsack and a big bottle of sake, from which the boys sneak swigs when their father isn't looking. They dream of capturing a stray dog to turn in for "Rabies Prevention Day"; this would mean 40 sen, and the possibility of eating. Yet, when Kihashi asks the boys if they are hungry, they bravely shake their heads no.

Stoic as they might be, the brothers sense that the father isn't a good prospect; after seeing him get rejected by yet another factory, Zenko asks, "Why can't you make it?" Later, sheltered in a kind of flophouse for the night, Zenko is the one who consoles his father: "Tomorrow we'll make it." But with the new day comes a new rejection from another "awful" factory gateman. However, they find the dog they have been looking for. In a later, light but touching scene, Zenko feeds his father in a reversal of the usual way of things, giving him cuttlefish and getting him drunk on sake. If the fatuous boss in Shimazu's *A Brother and His Younger Sister* intones the platitude, "Children do not know their parents' hearts" (a piece of received Confucianism), Ozu in the same period (the 1930s) demonstrates that this is patently untrue. Of course, children understand the basic needs, the hearts, of their parents—how could they not? Their own day-to-day survival depends on memorizing and taking to heart what pleases the father versus what does not. Filial piety disguises this survivalism as a higher duty and a virtue. Truer to say that parents never understand their children's hearts, first and not least because their default judgment is that children don't really have individual longings and needs of their own, and beyond this, because the parents will seldom place their children's needs (if they do acknowledge them) above their own—a direct effect of having a top-down leadership mentality which again evokes a kind of filtering-down pyramid with the emperor at the pinnacle and all the other emperor-surrogates filling out the expansive lower layers of the base.

Of course, filial piety in modern Japan is just a way of bullying someone or giving him a hard time, as when the yakuza lieutenant in Takeshi Kitano's *Kids Return* (*Kizzu ritân*, 1996) gives a waiter a sizable tip then questions him, "Are you good to your parents? ... You sure about that?"—the way an American bully might ask someone derisively, "Got a girlfriend?" The waiter is eager to reassure the yakuza that he is good to his parents, but we see that filial piety is little more than a joke, an old-fashioned social code that does little now but possibly raise the hackles of conservatives or tough guys, or put a nervous person on the spot. Here is another exchange from *Kids Return*:

YAKUZA: How's your dad?
UNDERLING: He's fine, sir.
YAKUZA: And your mother?
UNDERLING: She's coping somehow.

Corny, yes, but invigorated by our (Western) assumption that a Japanese son would not make fun of his father this way. Indeed, it is the assumption of the yakuza boss too, who does a slight double-take. The entire concept of filial piety is, in modern Japan, something which the more powerful leverage against the less powerful, usually not very successfully. The will to dominate is simply too transparent. In Masumura's *Kisses*, an arrogant rich kid expects to sleep with Akiko after lending her 100,000 yen to bail her father out of jail; when she backs out of their deal, he begins to rape her, saying, "Do it for Dad, show some filial piety." Wealth and power are impious things, by their nature, and reveal every pretense of sentiment as leverage in the pursuit of stark consumption and selfishness.

Moreover, questioning a father's authority becomes a way of questioning the imperial era and the divine authority of Hirohito. In Kurosawa's films, for example, sons are brutally critical of their fathers. In *Ikiru*, Watanabe deserts his ten year old, Matsuo, during Matsuo's appendectomy. This is all it takes for the adult Matsuo (Nobuo Kaneko) to continue to hold Watanabe in abject contempt for the rest of his life. And in *Ran*, Lord Hidetora's sons are alarmed when the old samurai tries to show them affection. "Normally all he asks is our obedience," they say. We might feel that Matsuo is being too harsh, and Lord Hidetora's sons too wary at this particular moment, but we understand their need to think for themselves, unfettered by compulsory filial piety against fathers who have proven whimsical or uncaring.

An intriguing observation: in Ozu's *An Inn in Tokyo*, poverty brings out a resilience and solidarity in the hardscrabble family that will give way to emotional blackmail in the middle-class domestic setting of the director's late comedy, *Good Morning* (*Ohayô*, 1959), in which two other young brothers, Minoru (Kôji Shitara) and Isamu (Masahiko Shimazu), refuse to speak until their parents buy a television set (so they can watch sumo wrestling). The parents associate TV with lax morals; the only home in the neighborhood that has one belongs to a slug-abed couple where the wife used to work "in a cabaret." "Oh, she's *that* kind, is she?" the local busybody (Haruko Sugimura) says, raising an eyebrow. There is also a fear that TV will turn all of Japan into "one hundred million idiots," a kind of new Western conquest attacking the brain cells.

However, since the demand for TV has already been created and inculcated, resistance proves futile. In their alienated silence, the two boys here impose that disrespect and breaking of communal ties that the older generations fear will take over the household anyway once a TV is installed. Yet the adults turn out to be inadequate role models. It turns out to be true, as the boys ruefully say, that it is adults who talk too much: the busybody wages smear campaigns against her neighbors like a deranged door-to-door salesman. Eager to avoid trouble, the neighbors are quick to believe any malicious gossip that forewarns them about someone else's petty thievery or grudge-holding. There is no homeless problem in this Tokyo, although the kids—teeming everywhere, peeking out of windows, popping out between houses—seem just as unwanted as the immediate-postwar ones in *Record of a Tenement Gentleman*. The Japanese generation gap will come to yawn even wider in Kiyoshi Kurosawa's *Bright Future* (*Akarui mirai*, 2003), where an estranged son tells his prodigal father, "Figure things out for yourself," walking away from him on a Tokyo street. As Mellen writes, "the true war is now being waged within the Japanese psyche."[24]

The ultimate generation-gap film from Japan is, again, Fukasaku's *Battle Royale*, set in a dystopian future where extreme poverty and rampant youth violence have caused the nation to turn completely against its young people. Every year a high school class is chosen at random to be drugged and taken to an island where they are all given survival kits and turned loose to kill each other over a three day period until only one is left alive. Some get weapons in their kits, like sickles or guns; others get relatively useless pot-lids, tasers or binoculars. We are very far here from Ozu's Japan, but I believe that Ozu might well have understood and appreciated *Battle Royale*, whose point is never simply to glorify the many twisted ways in which the teenagers do away with each other; instead, Fukasaku ingeniously gives nearly all of the students an identity, a back story—whether it is a crush on another student, a friendship gone awry, a tragic home life. Of course, many of these back stories are generic and not well developed, but in a way this only increases the sense that the students have little to actually live for. They are overused and abundant "types," as conservative adult society chooses to view them, thus tempering its own guilt at exterminating them. Some of the kids fall in love and just want to feel close to someone before dying; others get to express pent-up hatreds for peers who have bullied or stalked them. They die at the height of emotional crises that would no doubt have gone on plaguing them for the rest of their lives anyway. By the end, in fact, we feel as if some of the young people have lived entire, long, intense lifetimes of emotion, even though they have all died young right before our eyes. The later U.S. version of Fukasaku's basic plot-idea, *The Hunger Games* (2012), did not attempt to dig so deep, instead focusing on the zero-sum idea of survival, of winning at all costs within an evil system. *Battle Royale*, by contrast, seems to ask: "Is the game worth winning?"

Presiding over all the carnage is the sad, weathered face of popular actor-filmmaker Takeshi Kitano, playing a teacher who retired after being slashed by a delinquent student

The Spanish tagline of Fukasuka's *Battle Royale* is "Kitano Versus 42 High School Students." Beloved director, comedian and international action star Takeshi Kitano plays a retired teacher (in a tracksuit, center), leading the Japanese military in a vendetta against spoiled juvenile delinquents in the frequently delirious and trenchant carnage of *Battle Royale*.

with a knife and who is now running "Battle Royale" to get even, giving the kids sarcastic pep talks through an island-wide loudspeaker: "It's tough having friends die on you, but hang in there," and "You're slacking, I'm disappointed in you." His petty vindictiveness, munching a bag of cookies which one of the girls had intended to give to the boy she admires, delineates Japanese loneliness better than the randomly ordered fates of the kids: to know what life has in store and accept this as routine is far more horrible, in a way, than the desperation of *Battle Royale*'s graphic violence. At the same time, no one fails to see the petty motives behind the teacher's warped tyranny: even as he judges the young people mercilessly, so they appraise him with equal disfavor, as when his own young daughter speaks to him contemptuously on the phone. It is like the scene in Sono's *Suicide Club* where the little girl behind the club explains to a police detective over the phone that people are disconnected from themselves, and cannot feel anymore "the pain of others." In both the implication is the same: children might not be able to grasp or survive in the adult world, but they still see, with special uncanny clarity, what the adults have blinded themselves to.

* * * * *

Fairly unique in terms of cinema history in general, and also indicative of that inbetween-ness which has marked much of Japanese culture, Toshio Matsumoto's *Funeral Parade of Roses* (*Bara no sôretsu*, 1969) is set in the semi-underground world of drag queens (simply called "queens"), gay nightclubs, and dope. Transvestites Eddie (Pîtâ) and Leda (Osamu Ogasawara) are both sleeping with the macho Gonda (Yoshio Tsuchiya), a club promoter who is trying to force Leda out of her hostess position so Eddie can take over. "You're old, your day is done," he tells the sobbing Leda. The two queens are catty toward each other because of this love triangle; but director Matsumoto also shows understanding and solidarity among gays. (The film is plied with allusions to queer Western heroes such as Pier Paolo Pasolini, Jean Genet, and Charles Baudelaire.) One young gay man, interviewed documentary-style, says that he is not sure if he likes men, but does know for sure that he was "born gay" and prefers being around other gays. Eddie is insecure about her looks although quite pretty. She wears thick Dusty Springfield eyelashes in the shower, in a cute early scene that reveals her boy-chest after teasing the audience with shots of her face, back and buttocks. Her admiration of her lover's muscles speaks to a fixation on outward signs of gender difference; the hardness and sleekness of the male body is prized, along with the handsome masculine face, more than the penis. The queen extrapolates her sense of what a woman is or should be by doing everything to the extreme opposite of masculinity. Grounded male strength is its own raison d'être, whose opposite is fragility, ditziness, panic. Thus, lack of confidence and a drive toward self-sabotage and failure tend to mark the queens. "You don't feel guilty?" a queen is asked in a different interview; when questioned whether she is attracted to women or men, she blinks in disbelief at first, then answers only in third person: "They tell themselves they're women," meaning the queens.

But Matsumoto's larger point is that the whole world operates like this for everyone: we are always and only what we tell ourselves we are, and it can be a constant struggle to overcome a sense of the world's disapproval. "Guilt" is as much a choice as anything, even though it sometimes feels inexorable, imposed from without. In a strange scene,

Eddie walks disconsolately past a street protest in which older men in black, wearing white medical face-masks and giving fascist salutes, parade slowly toward one of their number who is lying on the pavement, dead or playing dead. For Eddie the runic protesters seem to represent fear of contamination, conservative disapproval, or simply the assertion that *their* lives are, like hers, at stake in modern Japan (why exactly, we never find out). To declare oneself anything is an act of courage, liable to be misunderstood, rendered meaningless, ignored, punished or mocked. Fleeing into an art exhibit, Eddie faints when she encounters a similar message, now imparted as the artist's taped commentary on his own expressionistic portraits: the voice intones that everyone "crafts" a mask, some people wear several in their lives, and it is emotionally risky and lonely to try to live otherwise, i.e., to be a real face without a mask of some kind. This is reminiscent of the moment toward the end of Kinugasa's *A Page of Madness*, where the husband imagines curing the asylum inmates by bringing a basket of masks and affixing them to the inmates' faces in order to stabilize their affects.

At the same time, according to the artist's voice in *Funeral Parade of Roses*, being masked is not merely the result of making and wearing a single mask: "Even if they [the masked people] remove their masks, their faces might not be exposed, because there might be second masks." The ones who hide their true selves are maniacally invested in this hiding, and will not be shamed into honesty by coming into contact with someone like Eddie, who puts herself out there as she is, for the world to see. The mask-people have turned even their inner lives into a lie.

With the queens, however, "masking"—their female appearance, achieved with make-up—is part of their vulnerable honesty, and certainly a part of who they are. If insanity (as *A Page of Madness* suggested) is one of the risks of losing one's mask, then the queens in *Funeral Parade of Roses* literally patch together their reality with foundation and mascara. Devoted to their feminine personas, Eddie and Leda out-geisha real geishas in their attention to their looks, their submissiveness to men, and their sheer carnal enjoyment of being female. Matsumoto indicates that imitation is legitimate and creative in a society where the highest value is placed upon appearances; authentic appearance belongs only to those who must painstakingly build it up from nothing every day, those who wager their entire existence on being able to pull off the masquerade. Reality itself loses its power to convince, being the too-automatic beneficiary of a false entitlement which it has not earned, and which it ultimately cannot earn, having no idea how to "be" premeditatedly, for others, what it simply already is. Reality has bypassed the process of otherness-in-one which transvestism and transsexualism imply as one of their innate functions. Nonetheless, while each queen is more of a multiplicity in her own right than someone who is one-dimensionally straight or gender-conforming, each queen is also on a separate journey of her own, living out her own unique experience of otherness-in-one. This is a nuance which is often overlooked in Western films about this subject.

Indeed, like two real Japanese women might be, Eddie and Leda are very different from each other; somewhat broadly in terms of their complementing personalities they resemble Omachu and Umekichi in Mizoguchi's *Sisters of the Gion*. Several years older than Eddie, Leda is conservative and concerned with propriety; she wears her hair in a bun and likes fancy kimonos. (She wears thick false eyelashes though, just like Eddie.) Her rival, on the other hand, is a completely modern girl, wearing her hair loose, dancing to rock music, and worrying that Leda will make trouble for her "about the dope." Unlike the gritty, sensationalistic use of narcotics in Akira Kurosawa's *High and Low* (*Tengoku to jigoku*, 1963) and Seijun Suzuki's *Youth of the Beast*, where drugs are treated strictly as a social problem, as the fallout of poverty and postwar anomie, *Funeral Parade of Roses* is one of the only Japanese movies I have seen that depicts recreational drug use as a fun, harmless countercultural kick, even a path to transcendence and satori outside of society. Another pot-smoker interviewed in the film says he likes the sensation of "floating up off the bed" and wants to feel "more of that." Actually, the drug use in *Funeral Parade of Roses* is very tame by today's standards: it consists of Eddie smoking grass and then squirting the equivalent of Visine into her eyes, and also onto her tongue, like a wacky suggestion of orally ingested semen.

Here, *Funeral Parade of Roses* shows us another way in which Japan is not so different from the West. Why have drugs (hallucinogens especially) gone together with the gay lifestyle in so many modern societies? For one thing, drugs are disinhibitors, and have helped gays self-medicate for the anxieties produced by being gay in a straight world. Also, when both homosexuality and drugs were more illegal and underground, they acted sometimes as signifiers for each other: someone with weed might likely be more tolerant of gay people, and vice versa. It will be interesting to see, now that neither gayness nor marijuana carries the same degree of stigma and illegality, whether the two will continue to enhance each other in collective queer imaginaries.

In any protocols-driven society, being gay presents a distinct challenge. One might or might not be accepted in a social order where many behaviors are conditioned for a kind of "instant" acceptance. And of course, gayness is only one of the more flagrant examples of challenging societal norms. For example, the deep ceremonial Japanese bow regains its true meaning at the end of Kurosawa's *Rashomon*, where it signifies the tentative return to accord between human beings after a dark-ages shaking of faith in humankind. The bow is more peaceable than the handshake, since it avoids contact (particularly that hand to hand contact which can suggest arm wrestling, and which can so easily become a test of strength; fighting is a central motif of *Rashomon*) and instead places each person in an equally vulnerable position. The mutual bow is a complete contract. With the head lowered, one is vulnerable, unless the person whom one is facing has also lowered his or her head to the same degree. The handshake encourages perhaps threatening eye contact as a further verification of a trust that is not assured; the bow precludes eye contact as a physical impossibility, and therefore places all trust, sight unseen, into the act of bowing. There are many acts which are neutralizing of man's inner barbarian—the handshake is meant to be one, as is friendly eye contact—but there are few discrete physical gestures that are innately anti-barbaric in nature: the bow, especially the mutual bow, is one of these few.

It is also anti-discriminatory and anti-judgmental. These bowing people in *Rashomon* could be Roland Barthes' faces "without moral hierarchy"[25] in his book about Japan, *Empire of Signs*. "Two bodies bow very low before one another (arms, knees, head always remaining in a decreed place) according to subtly coded degrees of depth."[26] The gesture is neither chosen nor rendered ironic by the gesture-maker. "The soul does not contaminate" this bowing, "here ... withdrawn from any humiliation or any vanity, because it literally salutes *no one*; it is not the sign of a communication ... only the feature of a network of forms...."[27] This "network of forms" already speaks to a specific cultural psychology; such ritual bowing is reminiscent of a Catholic making the sign of a cross before the altar: the self is always there, and the fantasmatic is one in which the self makes itself pleasing—ultimately to itself. It is also reminiscent of those elaborate codes which used to operate in gay communities such as Fire Island, where one's sexual proclivities could be denoted by what color pocket-square one wore, and which side one wore it on. One can imagine such a sartorial system fitting in very well with protocols-driven Japanese sensibilities.

On the other hand, as Barthes notes, Japanese bowing is a choreography that signals nothing but itself taking place, as in "the young salesman who bows with a gesture so deep, so ritualized that it loses all servility, before the customers of a department store leaving to take an escalator."[28] Yet, we must note that it is already an enormous Westernism on Barthes' part, here, to wish to recuperate the deep bow from any imagined taint of "servility,"[29] since clearly the concept that it might be humiliating to the one who bows does not even enter into the social ritual as an overlooked absence, in other words as an oppression. In any gesture where discipline and happiness bear little relation to each other, particularly the antagonistic one that we are saddled with in the West, we have a hard time even seeing the gesture as fully human. For us the salesman's bow, delivered by one who subordinates himself to customers for a living wage, must be a strict social ritual, and more than that an unwelcome or uncomfortable one, or else it would be seen as a measure of the unequal economic relations which predicate it. After all, the bow, which is not commonly practiced in Western societies, would not seem so charming to Barthes if it was a working-class Parisian prostrating himself before bourgeois clientele.

The fact that Western capitalism does not "demand" such outward signs of exploitation and oppression, but rather internal conformities and something more like withholding or looking-away, means that we have enormous difficulties locating the boundaries of our economic relations. This is a guilty secret of the West, where we pretend that unhappy service workers and demanding customers are exceptions to the rule, anomalies of capitalism rather than in-built foundational fixtures of the capitalist system. In the West, the bow would have to be sarcastic, a reminder of that ego which the salesman has been taught to suppress around his customers, like Keiko the geisha in Naruse's *When a Woman Ascends the Stairs* or even like the frightened peasant-witnesses in *Rashomon*, where Kurosawa sets us in contemplation of a world whose broken coordinates point to the need for change.

Karatani writes:

> In Zen Buddhism there is a style of teaching in which the master holds a stick over the pupil's head and says fiercely, "If you say this stick is real, I will strike you with it. If you say this stick is not real, I will strike you with it. If you don't say anything, I will strike you with it."[30]

The only enlightened response is for the student to reach up and grab away the stick, but in order to do this the student must break out of what Karatani calls "the self-referential paradox,"[31] or obedience to directly communicated messages about oneself. Literally, the student must overcome the implication that not to solve an irresolvable problem is to deserve to be hit with the stick. The riddle requires a new self to emerge in the translation of the teacher's imperatives into freely chosen actions, in other words the creation of an unprecedented, additional "if" ... "If *I*." At all moments, we may assume, spoken words and physical actions are nothing but manifestations of ontological potential, enacted in the face of being challenged, indeed of being literally struck down.

As Mellen writes: "all the settings in Kurosawa are, in their deepest sense, 'wartime.' For Kurosawa has always accepted the *bushido* dichotomy—the choice between duty and love."[32] And yet, both the renegade samurai and the straying wife in *Rashomon* are allegorical attempts to step outside of that code; thus, although existing at opposite gender poles, these characters are closely co-configured. We must note that this transsexual equivalency is somewhat radical for its time. In one of *Rashomon*'s most startling scenes, Kurosawa places the voice of the dead samurai into the mouth of the female medium (Noriko Honma), and intercuts this with a flashback to the samurai who is shown sobbing openly and stabbing himself in the heart. Not only is a female invested with the masculine authority of vocal narration,[33] but the male samurai is depicted as being overcome by helpless feelings. Kurosawa also chooses to cut to a direct close-up of the female medium when the words, "She had never looked more beautiful," spoken in male voice, issue from her mouth. (A similar if less dramatic effect is achieved in Masumura's *Black Test Car*, when a female lip reader speaks the words coming out of the mouth of a powerful automaker who has been filmed without sound in an act of industrial espionage.)

Nor is this "feminization" of the samurai unique to *Rashomon*. It is also a clear motif of other samurai movies, such as Kihachi Okamoto's extremely violent *The Sword of Doom* (*Dai-bosatsu tôge*, 1966). The main character, a samurai lord named Ryunosuke (Tatsuya Nakadai) says at one point, "A swordsman prizes his skill the way a woman prizes her chastity," and though he is being manipulative (obliquely propositioning a rival's wife), there is a sense in which Okamoto's film posits a strong equivalency between the figures of the renegade samurai and the fallen woman. The samurai seems to have more social status, and often does, but his status is as much dependent as hers on the approval of older, more powerful men. He is constantly under scrutiny, and can be judged harshly for being too strong as much as for not being strong enough, as when Ryunosuke describes a particularly merciless sword as seeming "possessed by the spirit of an evil woman." Moreover, Ryunosuke (the root of his name is *ryû*, or "dragon") is known for his passive stance in swordfights, lowering his sword and face, making his opponent attack him in a frenzy then coolly delivering the death strike; in this, he is like a femme fatale luring men with the promise of an easy, total fulfillment that is the opposite of what it seems to mean.

In general, samurai battle scenes point to a further connection between the samurai and female sexuality. Although a trope of the genre, the samurai who is forced to singlehandedly take on an entire small army of men is enacting a scenario of gambling with his skill the way the coquettish woman is depicted as gambling with her honor. How many men will become too many? As the fighter kills rival after rival, growing more and more sweaty, dirty and disheveled, his long hair loosened from its bun to spill down his back or across his face, he seems contaminated by fighting, yet wholly in his element; he seems to become no longer a man, but a thing outside of masculinity itself, bent on the destruction of all men (and destroying them with the tools of their own trade) until it becomes safe for him again. This ongoing battle never truly ends.

Even samurai training can be considered geisha-like, as we see in Mizoguchi's *A*

Tashiro (Tadanobu Asano, left) squares off against Soji (Shinji Takeda) during a training exercise in Oshima's gay samurai film, *Taboo*. Although a trope of the genre, the samurai who is forced to singlehandedly take on an entire small army of men is enacting a scenario of gambling with his skill the way the coquettish woman is depicted as gambling with her honor. How many men will become too many? This ongoing battle never truly ends.

Geisha. In a clever montage, women perform tasks that resemble things we have seen men doing in samurai films: groups of women practice their movements en masse inside a wide pavilion with a plain wooden floor, under the discerning eyes of a "mistress geisha"; they also perform household chores to learn discipline; and we are told that the entire training, as it does for samurais, takes years.

The samurai becomes a gay figure in Oshima's last film, *Taboo*. With *The Ceremony* (*Gishiki*, 1971), Oshima entered into a sustained argument with Japanese masculinity (and masculinity in general) which becomes the predominant theme of his late work. In *Taboo*, which takes place in 1865, Kano is a recent recruit of the Shinsen militia whose job is to "put down uprisings"; thus, the all-male group is more than a little concerned with presenting a fearsome image to outsiders. Kano, a stunningly beautiful androgyne, awakens gay desires in a number of the other samurais, leading to jealousy, enmity and divisiveness. Kano is unable to repress his homosexuality, nor is he able to make it congruent with the interests of the group. Taken to a geisha house to be made "into a man," he runs amok when left alone with a woman, demanding a male; though a stronger swordsman than Tashiro (Tadanobu Asano), one of his ardent admirers, Kano is submissive to

Tashiro when sparring, backing down and even falling at Tashiro's feet. This is doubly ambiguous since we have seen Kano hold Tashiro at bay at knifepoint when Tashiro tried to visit him in bed at night. In fact, Oshima makes explicit (through a title card) that Kano and Tashiro never become lovers, although they become emblematic of gay sex for the other samurais and are scapegoated for it.

The public conflation of sword fighting with gay sexual submission is too close for comfort. All of the males around Kano are forced to confront their conflicted emotions about same-sex desire. Captain Hijikata (Takeshi Kitano) surmises that Kano has joined the militia because he is drawn to its aura of youthful masculinity, and that Kano's "courage" is a function of his perverse blood-lust toward other males. Kano admits that he joined the militia in order to "have the right to kill." A further complexity is added in the fact that Kano is the son of a wealthy merchant family, and therefore indulged by his commanders more than someone like Tashiro, who was formerly the humble servant of a tenant farmer.

Kano's main enemy is Soji (Shinji Takeda), a young firebrand lieutenant who is nearly as pretty and feminine as Kano but openly homophobic. "Not my cup of tea," he sneers, "one man loving another." Soji kills one of Kano's samurai admirers, and attacks another one who is suspected of being involved with Kano, perhaps because of unstated jealousy.[34] This places Tashiro under an even darker cloud, since Tashiro is suspected of committing these crimes in fits of passion. Kano's presence becomes so disruptive to the communal order of the Shinsen militia that he is finally forced to duel Tashiro to the death; seeming to submit to Tashiro's sword on his knees, Kano murmurs, "Forgive me," and when Tashiro softens for a moment, Kano dispatches him with seeming relish. Afterwards, Soji murders Kano with impunity.

In *Taboo*, male fears of same-sex love and desire are exacerbated by the fact that Kano is a strong fighter: he is marked as both masculine and feminine, an insupportable contradiction. Hijikata reflects on Kano's death, saying that he "was too beautiful. Men took advantage of him. He was possessed by evil." Here, the older officer seems to indicate that Kano deserves to die; yet, in an ambiguous, almost unconscious act of protest, Hijikata chops down a young cherry blossom tree, symbolic of imperial masculinity, as if to defy the harsh laws that condemn Kano—or as if to say, even a beautiful cherry tree must be destroyed if it is perceived as threatening or "other." By the end of *Taboo*, none of the men can say anymore which of them is or is not attracted to Kano, and whether they despise him out of moral reprobation or out of jealous, undeclared passion. The very essence of the samurai is turned against himself; as one character puts it, "A samurai can be undone by the love of men," not, we are led to see, because of the love itself but because of the backlash it elicits from heterosexual society.

Other than this, even oblique references to homosexuality are few and far between in Japanese cinema. Hiroshi seems to have a gay crush on Jyoji in Ozu's *Dragnet Girl*, enjoying getting beaten up by the former boxer. "You should hit me more often," he speaks softly, almost seductively, rubbing Jiyoji's broad shoulders. We think we are seeing a spoof of homosexuality in the scene in Seijun Suzuki's *Fighting Delinquents* where a bespectacled middle-aged man (Mayumi Shimizu) peeps at naked boys in a public bathhouse, but he turns out to be working for a wealthy family, searching for the telltale birthmark on the back of their missing young male heir. Also, in Suzuki's *Youth of the*

Kano (Ryûhei Matsuda, left) attempts to confront Soji (Shinji Takeda). In *Taboo*, male fears of same-sex love and desire are exacerbated by the fact that the pretty-featured, soft-spoken Kano is a strong fighter: he is marked as both masculine and feminine, an insupportable contradiction.

Beast, there is a gay yakuza named Hideo (Tamio Kawachi), portrayed as a mother-fixated hysteric, easily manipulated and subdued by the alpha-male hero Jô (Jô Shishido). However, it must be said that Takeshi Miike, with his great feeling for outsiders of all types, has pushed the envelope the most by including gay content and characters in a number of his films, most notably perhaps the engaging Kenji (Seichi Tanabe), an openly gay yakuza, in *Blues Harp* (1998).[35]

Blatant homosexuality is not the only way that gender issues have entered into Japanese cinema. More often there has been a daring conflation of hyperfeminity with hypermasculinity, in a way which undermines the stereotypical codes surrounding these polar identities, much like the examples of equivalency between samurai and coquette/geisha that we were examining; again, Oshima led the way in this department. In his hard-boiled, Jim-Thompson-esque *Pleasures of the Flesh* (*Etsuraku*, 1965), Oshima achieves an effect similar to the female medium in *Rashomon* when he has his antihero (Katsuo Nakamura) speak a line from a letter sent by a developmentally challenged young woman: "Teacher, please come see me in my wedding dress." In Oshima's *Japanese Summer: Double Suicide*, two figures mirror each other: a weary man, Otoko (Kei Satô), who is looking for another man to kill him, and a teenage sexpot named Nejiko (Keiko Sakurai), looking for any-and-all men to have sex with her. Both are seeking penetration by a male, a penetration which could satisfy them (or so they seem to claim) and which also defines who they are. "I'll do anything for a man," Nejiko says, introducing herself to a complete stranger as if this were all he needed to know about her. Meanwhile, Otoko's secret longing to be killed is spotted by a grizzled old warrior, who carries a World War II German Mauser. "When he kills me," Otoko explains, "he watches me. I'm reflected in his eyes." "What's the difference?" the old warrior asks. "Then I know who I am," Otoko says. Later in the film, Nejiko will repeat these words of Otoko's as her own credo vis-à-vis sex with a man.

Rather than allowing all of this psychosexual compulsiveness to be as simplistic as it seems, Oshima presents it as a conundrum: the more urgently Otoko places himself in front of men with weapons, as he does frequently, the less it seems they can kill him. His demand to be killed, as he comes closer and closer to them with a dead-eyed stare, invariably makes them back down. Likewise, for Nejiko, the more blatantly she demands sex from men, the less the men want to give it to her. Even overnight inside a bunker filled with mercenaries, psychopaths and gangsters, she cannot find a single taker for her body and ends up stretched out on the ground, alone and untouched. (One crypto-fascist youth tells her he is more interested in politics than sex; Wilheim Reich no doubt would have had a lot to say about that!)

Are Nejiko's and Otoko's nominal desires what they actually want, or are these strange survival mechanisms? So as not to be killed, Otoko demands to be killed; no one will comply. So as not to participate in sex (on her own terms), Nejiko demands that men have sex with her. As with Otoko, it is the men who always back down, taking more pleasure in frustrating her than in having her. But is she truly as frustrated as she claims? Increasingly, men seem to be revealed more as adversaries of this young woman, rather than objects of adoration. "The enemy is gathering," she says, running up to a group of men she has spotted from across the compound. She also says, "I'd like to tie up all the men in Japan," in a way that sounds both desperate and distinctly hostile. She insults the first soldier who does try to lay his hands on her, saying, "You nasty, dirty man!" then running away. She zeroes in more and more on listless, unwilling Otoko, dragging him around the bunker in a sexy dance, then shoving him away from her. Nejiko, as we come to see, belongs among these men of combat. Of course, by morning she has had three of the men, but she says that it gave her no pleasure; in fact, she gets all three of them shot dead.

Nejiko herself is a fascinating, gorgeous, almost half-breed creature: curvaceous and smiling, she wears very American clothes (a belted, very tight white minidress and a sheer split-top with an Op Art pattern) and her hair is done up in a flip, flattened and with a large stripe dyed triple-process blonde, a look associated with African-American hairstyles of the 1960s. In the film's opening scene, she disrupts the work of a cleaning crew painting over her obscene graffiti in a public restroom; when she places her hand over one drawing to shield it, a crewman brushes her bronze skin with white primer, as if to render her color problematic within the all-Japanese context.

Most of all, there are ferocious battles of the sexes in Oshima's *Violence at Noon* (*Hakuchû no tôrima*, 1966), in which Eisuke Oyamada (Kei Satô) is a vicious serial rapist and murderer, claiming female victims all over Japan. He is married to the uptight Matsuko (Akiko Koyama); their dysfunctional love began on a doomed collective farm on

Throughout many of his films, Nagisa Oshima (center) ambivalently depicts outlaw males recovering a sense of their manhood through their abuse of docile, adoring females.

the way to bankruptcy. Oshima introduces this segment with a grim shot of two dead pigs in mud. Again, Oshima seems to be pointedly undermining certain Japanese Marxists such as Katsumi Umemoto, who believed "human beings begin to be ethical just as soon as they begin to produce the means of their subsistence."[36] Although an attractive-sounding theory, this is revealed by Oshima as incompatible with the true nature of human desires, which introduce new, perverse complications. On the farm, Matsuko is drawn to Eisuke's wildness and self-centeredness; when he steals, she coos understandingly, "Times are tough for you." But Eisuke also offends her sense of propriety. Genji (Rokkô Toura) and Shino (Saeda Kawaguchi) work the same farm and have a brief sexual relationship.

When the farm does collapse, Shino's family commits suicide en masse; so does Genji, who has lapsed into severe depression. Eisuke returns to his nomadic life of crime. Matsuko changes; she goes back to teaching civics, giving her young students abstract exercises in defining Liberty, Equality, and Democracy, though she no longer believes in the collectivist dream or even society. "I believe one person only comes together with one other person," she says, still dutifully loving her absent husband in spite of what she knows about his criminal tendencies. This illusion of love, a society of two, becomes her refuge, while Eisuke's refuge is crime itself, which Oshima depicts as no more pathological or destructive than Matsuko's reality-denying romantic fixation. In an essay, Oshima identified criminality as a way of living in "direct confrontation with modern Japan,"[37] and indeed, Eisuke's violence is portrayed as a kind of vital appetite; in one rape scene Oshima focuses on his pouring sweat dripping on Shino's face like pure morning dew. This is also similar to Hani's *Bad Boys*, in which the scenes of crimes and high living among the young delinquents occur in flashbacks while Asai (Yukio Yamada) endures the tortuous, frightening world of the juvenile prison, as if his criminal life, albeit in the past, was more vital and real than his desultory present, sustaining him throughout his time of punishment. (Nonetheless, Asai in *Bad Boys* eventually concludes that robbing people always depressed him afterwards, and he would like to go straight.)

In *Violence at Noon*, the question of whether there is such a thing as "Love for Humanity" haunts Matsuko. Rather than holding out an idealism that can be easily mocked and destroyed, she chooses the utter baseness of Eisuke, who makes clear that he is no humanist, saying at one point, "It's stupid to kill yourself. It's better to kill someone else." To be mocked by only one (Eisuke) is nobler in Matsuko's mind than standing for a greater societal good that could most likely end in failure. At the same time, Matsuko cannot let go of an outmoded thinking that love and marriage must validate her neurotic feelings for Eisuke. She looks down on the good-hearted, more peasant-like Shino, and is jealous of the fact that Eisuke wanted Shino more than her. Eisuke, holding nothing back, wounds Matsuko with the epithet, "Hypocrite!"

For her part, Shino believes that it was she who led Eisuke to become a serial rapist. Shino had tried to fulfill a death pact with the depressed Genji; as they leapt from a tree with nooses around their necks, Eisuke came from the woods to cut Shino down. He ended up raping her under Genji's twisting, barely dead body. This was his first crime. His second crime was to rape Matsuko a few days later. He marries Matsuko, but abandons her.

Marked by his assaults, the two women feel tied to Eisuke, but Eisuke eventually tells Matsuko: "Even if I had been born somewhere else, and had never met you and Shino, I would be the same man." Nonetheless, the two women hold Eisuke's guilt—and their own failings—between them like an erotic talisman, jealous of each other's role in his life and unable to disentangle themselves from him or each other. In particular Matsuko's commitment is grim and self-abnegating, callously allowing Eisuke's rampage to claim more victims so she can maintain the appearance of propriety in her marriage to him. Shino begins sending letters to Matsuko urging her to come forward about Eisuke. It is the two women who are finally meant to come together and create a unified front against him. Not that a lasting bond is created between the women; like all the other pairs who drift together and apart in Oshima's film, no real kinship is possible. When anyone says, "I love you," in this film, it always means something else. This is reminiscent of what Masato Ara proclaimed as the postwar Japanese mission, "to struggle with the semi-feudal sensibilities, emotions and desires that are rooted in our own internal 'emperor systems.'"[38]

Still, in a series of scenes set in the night streets of Okawa and then on a train journey, the final movement of *Violence at Noon* becomes the story of Shino and Matsuko, talking, quarreling, weeping together; Oshima links their faces in two-shots or matching close-ups as they are drawn into a common understanding. This is a long process; Shino must disabuse Matsuko of her last illusion, that there was any real love in her marriage. "What a cruel life you've led," she offers Matsuko. Finally, Matsuko has a breakthrough:

she agrees to give Eisuke's name and photo to the police, telling Shino, "This isn't about love. It's about his crimes."

Here, Oshima pointedly undoes the logic of numerous sexually-themed postwar Japanese films, in which a Japanese male is permitted to rape or otherwise exploit women as a form of succor, with the women loving him for it or at least never complaining. Some of this rape-mentality had to do psychologically with lingering humiliation over the nation's defeat: "Japan—only yesterday a menacing, masculine threat—had been transformed ... into a compliant, feminine body."[39] This past comes into play in *Violence at Noon*. In the first scene, where Eisuke takes Shino by surprise, she is singing a patriotic anthem from the World War II era, about the departure of a brave soldier; she continues to sing this, oddly, even after Eisuke has begun to assault her. This non-naturalistic touch does not seem accidental.

Rape was even woven into Japanese military superstition. Imperial soldiers "believed that raping virgins would make them more powerful in battle [...] and were even known to wear amulets made from the pubic hair of such victims, believing that they possessed magical powers against injury."[40] The defeat can almost be read, then, as a verdict against the Japanese male's presumed powers of sexual conquest. There is reason to believe many Japanese men felt suddenly emasculated after the surrender; some Japanese blamed the defeat on the fact that their males were, on average, several inches shorter than Americans.[41] As news of surrender spread to the most primitive villages, many diehards still intended to ward off the American army with bamboo spears; upon relinquishing this "masculine defense of their community [the Japanese] were ready to accept the feminine role into which Japan was cast."[42]

The male sense of postwar defeat is projected psychopathically onto women, who become implicit reproaches to devalued Japanese manhood. In Oshima's *Diary of a Shinjuku Thief*, a man walks up to a woman and barks, "I'll rape you!" With numb defiance, she replies, "Are you man enough?" She refers to rape as "blue ecstasy"; in fact she is frigid and claims to feel nothing during sex. This horror of a woman who cannot be reached or satisfied is the corollary of the male need to selfishly violate. In *Violence at Noon*, as we have seen, Oshima depicts Eisuke's need to rape women, as well as the fact that Matsuko and Shino try for much of the film to compensate and cover for his crimes. Women held the power to give of themselves sexually, and through this, other powers, to absolve, validate, redeem, or punish. Even more characteristic of Japanese sex-themed films from that era is Kaneto Shindô's *Lost Sex* (*Honnô*, 1966), the story of a character referred to only as The Master (Hideo Kanze), "a man rendered impotent due to radiation exposure in Nagasaki who is restored to manhood by his housekeeper [Nobuko Otowa]."[43] It seemed that Japanese men needed, as Sato writes, "the love of a more maternal woman, although this was not enough in [Shindô's] *The Origin of Sex* [*Sei no kigen*, 1967], where the impotent, aging male suddenly dropped dead despite the woman's ministrations."[44]

Yoshikuni Igarashi states: "Japanese male subjectivity ... used female bodies to confirm its historical continuity from wartime into the postwar period."[45] In Yasuzô Masumura's *Red Angel* (*Akai tenshi*, 1966), Orihara (Yûsuke Kawazu), a young soldier who has lost both his arms, begs army nurse Sakura (Ayako Wakao) to let him penetrate her with his foot, so he can feel like a man again; she submits to this penetration for its own sake, this notional idea of sexual conquest and communion, prompting the film's trailer to ask salaciously, "Was she a nurse ... or a whore?" As if a male doctor or male nurse would ever be placed in such a position. Clearly, these 1960s films were marketed in Japan as prurient, anti-feminist, male entertainments, yet Tadao Sato believes that they actually depicted the postwar vengeance of Japanese women, who, with their "intimidating capacity ... for sustained work" and their "unbridled strength," had completely taken over society from their defeated male counterparts.[46]

Red Angel takes place in 1939, two years after the Rape of Nanking; Sakura (her name means "cherry blossom," one of the premier imperial symbols) is sent to Tientsin Army Hospital in China to tend wounded Japanese soldiers. The wizened head nurse (Ranko Akagi) explains to Sakura and the other new arrivals that nearly half the soldiers in the ward are mentally ill. Part of the nurses' job is to identify the head cases and malingerers who are physically well enough to be sent back into combat. But this process occurs in a startling way. Her first night, Sakura is held down by several patients while Private Sakamoto (Jôtarô Senba) rapes her. The next day, she reports this to the head nurse, who tells her, "Private Sakamoto again? You're his third." In this way, the identification is made. He is immediately shipped back to the front, but before he leaves, he thanks Sakura "for everything."

Kaneto Shindô's *Lost Sex* (*Honnô*, 1966) was one of many Japanese films of the '60s which daringly mixed eroticism with images of violence, power and domination.

A connection is here established between sex/rape and physical recovery or vitality. Sakamoto's recovery has, in fact, been indifferently measured out in raped army nurses. (Three is apparently the magic number.) For the nurse, rape is also portrayed as a kind of threshold experience of combat itself, an unholy baptism. In the next scene, as if broken in now, Sakura herself is shipped to a surgical unit on the front lines. Conditions there are gruesome. All the medical team can do is perform a rough triage whereby most of the soldiers end up dead or amputees; hundreds of casualties are reduced to a lonely heap of dog tags. At one point Masumura shows a garbage can jammed full of sawed-off legs, with a number of feet sticking out. Sakura encounters her rapist Sakamoto on a gurney, shot in the guts and given up as "a goner." Manipulatively, he apologizes to her for raping her, begs her to save his life and grips her wrist with his last strength. "Don't kill me!" he screams as she wrenches away. Shaken, she intercedes with head surgeon Dr. Okabe (Shinsuke Ashida), asking him to do anything he can to save Sakamoto; he agrees, if she will come to his quarters that night. Masumura shows how easily lines are blurred, and bad wagers struck. Even after an emergency transfusion, Sakamoto dies as predicted; yet Sakura must still pay for the "wasted blood" with her body.

Dr. Okabe is a once principled surgeon whose inability to save the lives of wounded soldiers has made him cynical and world-weary. He is a morphine addict, not strong or noble enough to resist the temptation of his own painkillers. He places a premium on manhood, refusing to operate on a wounded soldier's sacrum because he would lose all sensation in his genitals and become finished as a man; instead, he risks gangrene setting in, on the assumption the soldier would prefer to die than become impotent. He himself has become impotent, he explains to Sakura, because of the morphine. "Please stop using morphine!" she begs, in love with him and placing the same high premium on manhood that he does. Imperialism is depicted as a creeping rot in *Red Angel*, claiming victims of both sexes: men following orders and women following men.

Male postwar impotence and the sexuality of nurses are also themes of Kôji Wakamatsu's hypnotic *Violated Angels* (*Okasareta hakui*, 1967), also known as *Violated Women in White*. This low-budget opus, a blend of art cinema and exploitation, was inspired loosely by the then-current case of U.S. serial killer Richard Speck and his grisly rampage through a nursing school dormitory in Chicago. Wakamatsu begins with an extended montage of still photographs, including some of his protagonist, the Handsome Young Man (Juro Kara) looking at women walking on the street, and also models from cheap erotica in lubricious poses. Finally, the man contemplates the image of a nude geisha from a tapestry, kissing the geisha's bare foot. Wakamatsu cuts to a close-up of a modern woman reacting to this, open-mouthed, shocked, seemingly disapproving. It is only the archaic, indeed unavailable woman who merits love. In the film's first live-action scene, the Handsome Young Man stands on the beach, firing a gun into the waves.

This prelude characterizes the bodies of women as objects of off-limits adoration, able to be "possessed" only unsatisfactorily as images, resistant to the man in actual flesh. The nursing dorm (a few bedrooms connected by sliding doors) becomes the site where he carries out his attack against these female bodies. Two of the nurses are engaging in lesbian sex, which has caused the others to awaken and crouch around a peep-hole in the wall. "They're at it again," one nurse says of the pair, suggesting annoyance, but the rapt voyeuristic attention of the women suggests titillation and even longing.

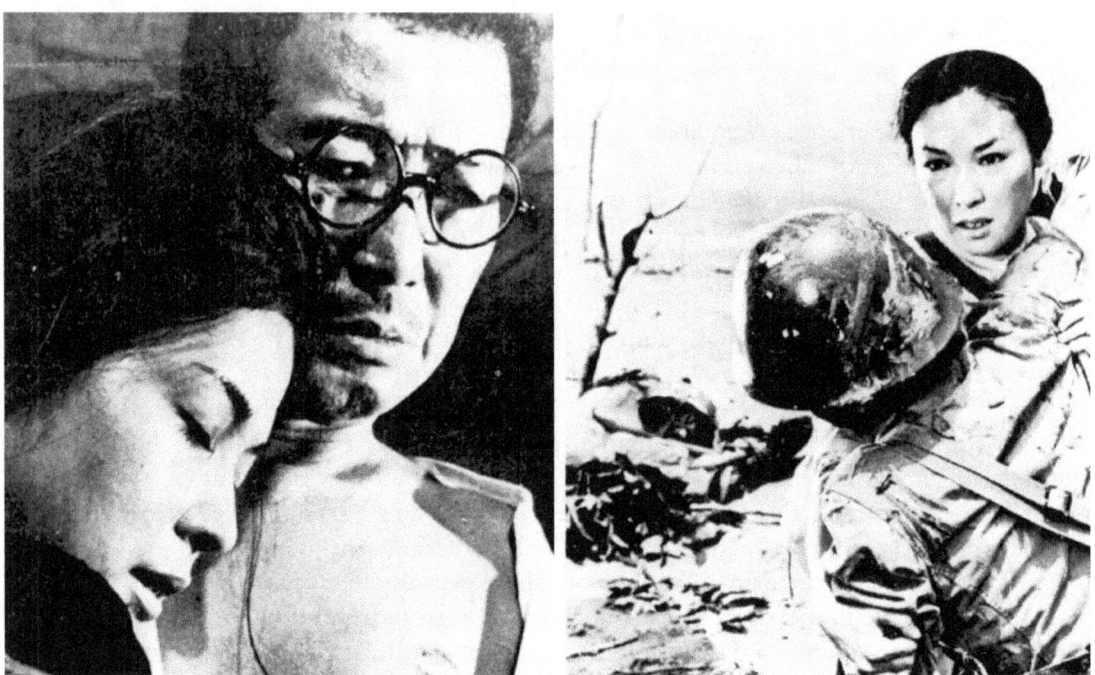

Army nurse Sakura (Ayako Wakao) falls in love with her commander, Dr Okabe (Shinsuke Ashida), in Masumura's *Red Angel*. Okabe is a once principled surgeon whose inability to save the lives of wounded soldiers has made him cynical and world-weary. Imperialism is depicted as a creeping rot claiming victims of both sexes: men following orders and women following men.

The Handsome Young Man is also watching; in a series of close-ups, Wakamatsu makes his face interchangeable with the female faces who are also watching, thereby feminizing the man. When he can stand no more, he emerges from the shadows and shoots one of the lesbians at point blank range; she dies, amid the crying of the other women. Then the second lesbian is singled out by the camera: short-haired and with noticeably lopsided breasts, she seems to stand before the man/us for his/our inspection. Unlike the flat, shadowless stills from erotica at the beginning of the film, Wakamatsu uses soft, chiaroscuro lighting to strike an incongruously romantic note. The man shoots and kills this woman too.

Nurses are called "white angels," but modern women are so degraded to the killer that he cannot accept them as angelic. One of the nurses approaches the man and strips. She is feminine, lovely, but once she is naked she pounces on the killer and wrestles him to the floor, where she proceeds to kiss him. Is she turned on by the Handsome Young Man and his violence? Is she trying to save herself and her friends? The man climbs on top of her and, in a deliberate show of modesty, pulls a sliding screen halfway closed to hide his and her lower bodies from the other women. Even so, the man turns out to be impotent; now, in a shot that seems to be the man's hallucination, the whole group of nurses, kneeling in various stages of undress, explode in mocking laughter at him. In a different shot, the women, now fully nude and still laughing, insultingly turn their buttocks to the man; writhing in agony, the man penetrates his victim vaginally with the gun and fires it.

Sobbing, the "oldest" of the nurses (Keiko Koyanagi) tries to appeal to his sense of a future. "Maybe you don't have sexual problems," she offers. "Maybe it's just frustration." She says that his problem is in his head and he will be cured of his "libido" when he grows up. She also reveals that she has a two year old son back home, "without a father"; she begs for her life on behalf of this child. (Later, she reveals that she has lied about having a child.) But to the killer, an angel is only a corpse, sentimental paeans to the future hold little weight with him, and he continues his methodical torture and murder spree, whistling while he works.

In *Violated Angels*, the young women's sexuality is so mercurial and uncontrollable that, for the Handsome Young Man, killing them off is like a restoration of sexual sanity, of male peace of mind. But just when we think we are certain that this is the film's message, we note, finally, one of Wakamatsu's most subversive images: the man has reproduced the imperial "Rising Sun" Japanese flag in the blood-reddened bodies of the nude nurses arranged in a circle on a large white sheet. Here is kokutai, the body of the state, explicitly constructed at the cost of (naked, innocent) female lives. It is through this image if nowhere else that we see Wakamatsu taking a stance against the violence that otherwise reigns unquestioned in *Violated Angels*. Wakamatsu's use of imperial symbolism is very different in feeling from the formally similar shedding of blood in the center of a white sheet which occurs during the act of seppuku in Yukio Mishima's clumsy and trite film, *Patriotism* (*Yûkoku*, 1966), which the author directed and starred in, playing a military officer of the 1930s who commits suicide as a "sincere" and even ecstatic duty to the emperor. Where Wakamatsu depicts an anarchic killer whose unorthodox violence has spontaneously revealed what was always arbitrary about imperial kokutai (its need for victims), the self-aggrandizing Mishima is merely lecturing his audience: having mistaken ritual honor-suicide as *the* quintessential mark of manhood, he sacrifices himself only to restore an eclipsed and specious emperor-worship that is associated with images of his own fetishized, uniformed and nude musculature—images which appear to be cribbed as much from Kenneth Anger's homoerotic *Scorpio Rising* (1964) as from imperial Japan.

At the end of Wakamatsu's film, one nurse remains; the Handsome Young Man has spared her life. The film ends with him sleeping contentedly, curled up in the lap of this last nurse, whose maternal consolation completely regresses the man to infancy, a state of innocence which Wakamatsu seems to valorize by linking the shot of a baby with shots of blue oceans and golden sunsets. It is the first time in the film that nature is depicted as gentle and harmonious. Otherwise, throughout *Violated Angels*, Wakamatsu amplifies the sound of howling wind in a creepy, non-naturalistic touch. He employs the same wind effect in the apocalyptic *Running in Madness, Dying in Love*. This is also similar to the "scary wind that blows over the mountains" in Terayama's *Pastoral Hide and Seek*. In the largest sense, nature itself is out of whack. But the Handsome Young Man, explaining to the last nurse that he comes from the sea, "beyond the forest," is a Shinto-esque emissary of a nature seeking to reclaim its due from fallen Tokyo. Wakamatsu cannily homes in on this aspect of Speck, a displaced country boy simultaneously aroused and appalled by the sexual freedoms of the big city.[47]

In *Violated Angels*, a broken masculinity calls out to its opposite, a femininity that welcomes defilement and mutilation, upholding male fantasies that woman seek male strength even when this strength is turned against them. As early as the mid–1950s, this had been a strong motif of "sun-tribe" films, a sex and action genre devoted to juvenile delinquency. Deriving from the groundbreaking, sensationalistic novels of Shintaro Ishihara, sun-tribe cinema "was a violent, adolescent outcry against tradition and the older generation."[48] Even so, sun-tribe upheld very conservative ideas of masculinity; the sun-tribe teen boys hated "the older generation" because it had been too weak to win the war. Sex, again, became a battleground for the reclamation of Japanese manhood. One feature of these films was the obligatory scene of an aggressive, dominant young man brutally taking sex from a demure, virginal young women and thereby teaching her sexual enjoyment and fulfillment, her "place." In Kon Ichikawa's *Punishment Room* (*Shokei no heya*, 1956), also based on Ishihara's popular fiction, a college student (Hiroshi Kawaguchi) drugs and date-rapes a girl in his class (Ayako Wakao), after which she falls in love with him. For Ishihara and his followers, the logic behind this was meant to promote the rightness of youth and young ideas, although from the start this logic made a pact with cynical exploitation, since production companies were "delighted to note that [the sun-tribe genre] was playing to standing-room-only from morning to night because of its uncommon attractiveness to girl high-school students."[49] Life imitating art? Or at least justifying extreme entertainments?

To be sure, this strange celebration of rape *was* partly generational. In *Women of the Night*, Mizoguchi had seen nothing attractive about the rape of a virginal young woman, discreetly hiding the act behind a strategic piece of furniture. And even more pronouncedly in Mizoguchi's *Ugetsu*, the constant threat of rape hangs over the entire film like frighteningly bad weather. Sun-tribe films zero in on the salaciousness that Mizoguchi deplored, and as it turned out, young female moviegoers responded the way the young women depicted in sun-tribe movies did: they were thrilled. In sun-tribe movies, the bad boys and their toys were invariably the spoiled children of rich postwar businessmen. The name of the genre was also a reference to the imperial Japanese flag, so there was an implicit nationalism in sun-tribe films even though their content was often depraved. Oshima's *Cruel Story of Youth* (*Seishun zankoku monogatari*, 1960) was a socially conscious commentary on the wealthy hedonism of sun-tribe; he sets his film in a Tokyo slum and makes the need for money a chronic issue for nearly all the characters. Kiyoshi (Yûsuke Kawazu), a delinquent boy already jaded enough to have an older mistress who pays him, initiates the girl, Makoto (Miyuki Kowano), into sex by throwing her into the sea near a desolate pier and keeping her treading water with his foot until she is too worn out and frightened to put up a fight against his advances.

Maureen Turim has called this extended moment in *Cruel Story of Youth* a rape scene in no uncertain terms,[50] and while I don't deny that it is a rape, it still feels reductive, and counter to the film's intentions, to view this complex scene "only" as a rape. First of all, the act is not viewed as rape by either Kiyoshi or Mako. Afterwards, she is only concerned that he doesn't hate her and wants to keep seeing her. For Kiyoshi's part, he already cares for Mako; he has brutally deflowered her in order to bring her into his tough, hardened world, to make her a thing of that world, belonging to it. He had previously chided her for not smoking yet; it is the spirit of youth—so central to the film—that Kiyoshi wants to kindle in Mako. On one hand, he does not understand why Mako has not rushed to embrace every rebellious behavior as soon as she was "old enough," if not before. On the other hand, an ancient sexist stereotype lies behind this:

Kiyoshi (Yûsuke Kawazu) kindles a spirit of his rebellion in his girlfriend Mako (Miyuki Kuwano) in Oshima's pioneering juvenile-delinquent film, *Cruel Story of Youth* (*Seishun zankoku monogatari*, 1960).

if Mako were not so pure, she would not be a target of Kiyoshi's interest and his sexual violence.

During the devirginizing scene, the staging is such that Kiyoshi is at every moment placed above Mako: first they are both standing, and he is taller; then, when he throws her in the water, he is still standing, we see him only from the waist down, while she is paddling below him; then, after getting her out of the water and laying her down on a plank of the pier (these are split-timber logs that appear to be floating but are not, otherwise it would be impossible for the couple to stand, run and finally make love on them), he leans over her to hold her down and undress her. Post-coitally, he dives into the water while she lies supine, then crouches above her to kiss her and talk to her while she remains in place. Oshima never denies that Kiyoshi does possess physical power over Mako, and that he willfully abuses this power. The bleak setting is its own commentary on why he does so: Kiyoshi is from the underclass, living in a tough urban world, and his way is not to ask politely for things or be mushy. Oshima's assessment of the negative impact of poverty and parentlessness on the urban young would be borne out only a year later, in a case of life seemingly imitating art, in Hani's *Bad Boys*, a Cassevetes-like, improvised docudrama. Hani's real-life juvenile delinquents are matter-of-factly poignant, and very tough. One says, "I've only seen Ginza through the windows of a police van." When a do-gooder social worker is going over Asai's rap sheet and sad family background, we hear Asai saying, in a voiceover that drowns out the social worker, "Shucks! When's he gonna shut up?" And almost as if they had memorized Kiyoshi's rebel act from *Cruel Story of Youth*, they dismiss young women who date older men as gold-diggers, and say about a ritzy jewelry store they plan to rob, "That shop makes me mad."

The desolate urban landscape itself speaks volumes about the impossibility of a future for Mako and Kiyoshi in *Cruel Story of Youth*, with weird pylons grouped behind them like an abandoned postindustrial Stonehenge. Both of their dooms are sealed at this moment, for loving each other: she will place herself in precarious situations for Kiyoshi's sake, and he will lose just enough of his ruthlessness to make him vulnerable. But this devirginizing/rape scene is also one of the few in the entire movie that takes place in daylight, and the only one where we see open sky and (such as it is) water. The deflowering itself, Oshima is saying, belongs to the world of nature, within a film whose action is almost completely trapped within the dark, twisted confines of an unnatural society. What makes it natural is that Mako and Kiyoshi are both young, and will not have to wait to take pleasure until the adults in this world (every adult male wears the exact same light-gray business suit) tell them that they can, or until those adults consent to move out of the way.

Of course, there is reason to believe that Mako's "pleasure" is not pleasure at this point, certainly not the same as Kiyoshi's. She is terrified out of her wits, and half drowned during their first sexual act. Their second sexual act is also rapelike; after he has had a fist fight with two men, Kiyoshi, full of adrenaline, backs Mako into a dark alley, shoves her down, and wordlessly falls on top of her. Mako verbally contests this sudden, public coupling, and immediately afterwards complains that he is mistreating her. She tells him that she loves him, and she wants to know that he loves her. But this is exposed as bourgeois conditioning on Mako's part; the intensity of Kiyoshi's passion for her, as well as the sheer fact that he has chosen to be with her, are stronger than the words, "I love you," which Kiyoshi does not believe in anyway. Mako's joining of Kiyoshi's world requires her to turn her back on every vestige of the middle-class morality that judges him for his needs and keeps him down. This is ultimately the same as saying that Kiyoshi begins by dominating his girlfriend to get even for the way the social order dominates him, a sexist escape-route that feminism cannot approve. Mako is correct that at first Kiyoshi vents a kind of rage on her, and he admits to this, saying that he was not angry at her specifically but "Everyone." It is after the second sexual encounter that she threatens never to see him again, and Kiyoshi, in a grandiose gesture suited to the teen love story genre but ultimately rather unbelievable given his hardness, breaks down and confesses that he loves her too.

Toward the end of *Cruel Story of Youth*, Kiyoshi will have a second, more despairing breakthrough, realizing that he is part of what Mako needs protection from, and that he and all men are no better than whores in modern Japan, selling themselves for their survival. But for the rest of the film, we see sexuality through Kiyoshi's viewpoint, as valorization of sexual freedom, and of freedom in general for the young. For its first half, Oshima's film is unquestioningly and even violently on the side of the young against the older generations. Kiyoshi and Mako met when he saved her from being raped by an older businessman; what Kiyoshi later does is the same as what the businessman did and wanted to do—he smacks her twice and then takes her against her will—but because they are both young it is given the feeling of a beginning, a kind of opportunity, rather than a crushing, dead-end capitulation. "I can't stand to see young girls chase after filthy-rich old men," Kiyoshi tells Mako; this is a kind of hipster logic, first because he feels all the young girls should be his, and second because Kiyoshi views young women giving themselves to old(er) men as a moribund entrenchment of the social order that keeps the young down and on the bottom in sexual as well as economic, political and emotional ways.

The deliberate cruelty of the young toward their elders continues as Kiyoshi and Mako mock and humiliate Mako's older sister Yukio (Yoshiko Kuga) when she comes to Kiyoshi's hovel-like room in the slums to beg Mako to come back home with her. Instead of putting his clothes on, Kiyoshi sits smugly in front of Yukio in only his undershorts, as he and Mako accuse Yukio of being weak, of having lost out in life and now spending all her time "hanging out in hotels with dirty old men"—Kiyoshi's ultimate putdown for any woman. Mako defiantly remains in the slum with Kiyoshi, and Yukio later admits that she can't help but envy her younger sister. Right after humiliating Yukio, Kiyoshi and Mako begin to set up older men for shakedowns. She gets into their cars and lets them make passes at her, while Kiyoshi follows on his motorbike and rushes in to beat up the men and demand hush money. Kiyoshi is all swagger and prowess here, smacking around and bloodying a bespectacled middle-aged man while verbally abusing him. It is not until Mako gets into Horio's car that she, and the film, begin to have second thoughts about older men. Kiyoshi has made her cry, again, and Horio (Hiroshi Nihon'yanagi) seems genuinely concerned about her; she calls him "a kind old man." But given a second chance at Mako on another night, with a few drinks under his belt, Horio, too, proves lecherous and no better than the others.

* * * * *

As arrestingly avant-garde as they were, films like Wakamatsu's *Violated Angels* and Oshima's *Cruel Story of Youth* were not atypical of Japanese cinema of their time. In mid– to late 1960s Japan, there was a spate of sometimes near-psychedelic studies of Japanese males attaining a ruthless self-fulfillment through the rape and killing of women. Another example, also directed by Wakamatsu, is *The Embryo Hunts in Secret* (*Taiji ga mitsuryo suru toki*, 1966), about which Desser writes:

> The flashbacks all revolve around images, memories, and fantasies of the man's mother. As he tortures the woman with a straight razor and a whip, he occasionally cries out for his mother.... The man achieves something like happiness ... when the woman finally frees herself from her bonds and stabs the man repeatedly with a knife. He happily calls out "Mother" and dies in her lap, curled up like a fetus.[51]

Wakamatsu and Shindô seem to have specialized in graphic, almost Artaudian sexual catharsis, and the mingling of sexual ecstasy with the death drive. There is a heightened motif of gender-combat in Shindô's popular *Onibaba* (1964), where women are as ruthless as men.

Onibaba takes place during a historic period of civil war and chaos, probably in the middle 1300s, the end of the Nanbokuchô era in Japan when "two [rival] emperors ruled simultaneously."[52] The film opens with the image of a "deep dark hole" that has held darkness "since ancient times." This chthonian abyss evokes Freudian castration-terrors in the malevolent, bottomless, engulfing and inescapable female element. Suitably enough, the war is going badly; there is a sense of stagnation and entropy. Soldiers are wandering around, wounded, exhausted, starving; two of these soldiers in flight help each other stagger through a field of tall grass until they fall over, making a depression in the grass. Shindô intercuts this action with two samurais on horseback, apparently searching for the two deserters. Sudden phallic arrows kill the soldiers who have collapsed; we assume that they have come from the samurais on horseback. But in fact the arrows were fired by two women, a mother (Nobuko Otowa) and her daughter-in-law (Jitsuko Yoshimuro), who come creeping out of the grass to strip and loot the men's bodies and then throw them into the "deep dark hole" mentioned above, the one that holds primordial darkness. We note that the two murdered soldiers have been further "dishonored" by the fact that the younger of the two dies with his face falling into the older one's groin.

The two murderous women are never identified by name, only by their patriarchal status: they are Kichi's mother and Kichi's wife. Kichi is a soldier away at war. The two women prey on similar soldiers as if it were an act of displaced aggression against their own absent "man," and peddle the stolen samurai gear to Ushi (Taiji Tonoyama) and his son (Hosui Araya), who live in a nearby cave. Ushi pays them in small sacks of millet, doled out just enough to keep them starving and desperate. But the women are not dependent on Ushi in sexual or domestic terms, as the mother makes clear when Ushi propositions her, offering more grain in exchange for sex. "I'd never sleep with you, you bastard," she spits defiantly.

The mother has a white forelock, giving her an air of almost supernatural authority. She dominates the daughter-in-law, drinking first and then handing her the water ladle, ordering her around, etc. Things become complicated when another local soldier, Hachi (Kei Satô, also the star of Oshima's *Violence at Noon*), returns with news that Kichi was taken prisoner and killed. His report is entirely inglorious: "It's the generals' war, not ours." This is a distinct refusal of the soldier-samurai to identify his own honor with that of his "general," which contradicts imperial Japan's code of military honor. Indeed, Hachi has no living ideals where war is concerned: he characterizes the entire thing as "two emperors ... quarrelling," and in light of the fact that this is a postwar film, we are free to read this as a subversive reference to World War II. Furthermore, when we are told, "Kyoto's been burned down, they say the emperor has escaped to Mount Yoshino," we can interpret this as Hiroshima and Nagasaki being obliterated while Hirohito "escaped" punishment. *Onibaba* carries a theme of holding "generals," warlords and emperors to blame for the deaths of soldiers. Director Shindô himself was a World War II combat veteran.[53]

Hachi had once daydreamed of becoming a war hero, but now describes killing as difficult and ugly. He tells about sneaking up on an enemy who was defecating and then stabbing him in the back, laughing insanely at his own abjection. It is no more honorable or glorious than the killing which the two women do for their subsistence. Rather than engaging with enemies, the soldiers played dead; they thought nothing of stealing from civilians. All of these are veiled references to the fact that the Japanese imperial army had been merciless and predatory in its Asian campaigns. Hachi reveals that he killed a priest and has been wearing the priest's uniform as a cover. "People trust a priest," he chuckles darkly.

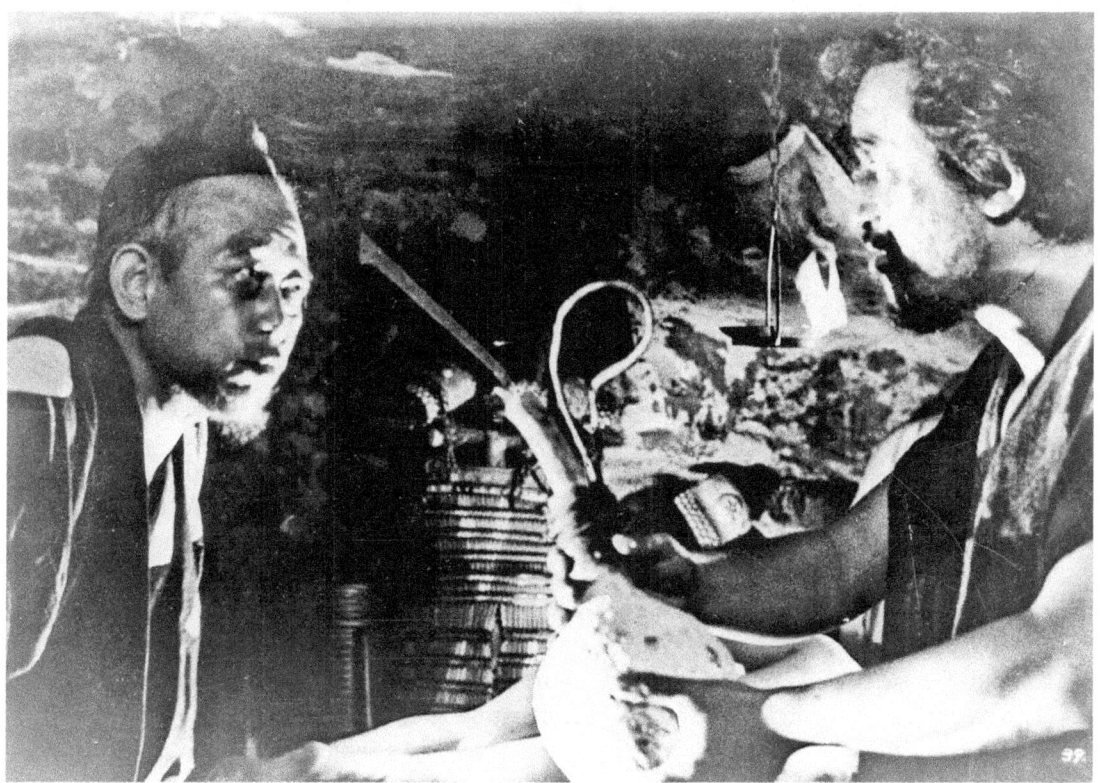

Cave-dwelling Ushi (Taiji Tonoyama, left) does business with Hachi (Kei Satô) in Shindô's *Onibaba* (1964). Ushi is much more deferential to Hachi, as a male, than he is in his bartering with the film's female characters, offering more millet and obsequiously fetching sake. A young woman, in the background of this scene, lies fully nude on the cave's single mattress.

When two more renegade samurai show up, Hachi quickly joins the women in attacking and killing them. Ushi the tradesman is much more deferential to Hachi, as a male, than he has been in his bartering with the women, offering more millet and obsequiously fetching sake. (A young woman, in this scene, lies fully nude on the cave's single mattress.) Hachi legitimizes the crimes as a necessary evil; masculine business is viewed as normalized in a way that the women's enterprise was not.

As Hachi begins to seduce the daughter-in-law, the mother is first sent into a rage of hurt pride and jealousy, then progressively desexed. She goes around bare-breasted, not a sexual sign and still less a maternal one but rather the un-self-conscious display that a man would make. She is like an Amazon warrior, toga wrapped across one shoulder and wielding swords. In a moment both turgid and sad, the mother spies on the two lovers then literally humps a tree trunk. She is also shown with shaggy armpit hair. Hachi's conquest of the daughter-in-law is one more prerogative which he usurps. Yet Hachi, as played by Kei Satô, is basically hapless and oblivious rather than vicious, a lonely guy compelled by sensuality and ground down by bad luck.

What seems most dated today about *Onibaba* is the way the relationship between the mother and the daughter-in-law is played for strains of sinister covert lesbianism. The two women sleep nude in the same bed; they have stayed together although unrelated by blood. Seeking to come between the lovers, the mother dons a primitive devil-mask to become a man and try to scare the girl into submission. Although she eventually murders Hachi in cold blood, her "playing" at masculinity spells her downfall, as the mask is leprous and eventually cannot be removed without tearing the flesh from her face. Hideously scarred, she chases her daughter-in-law into the night, screaming, "I'm not a demon! I'm a human being!" It is her final cry as she plummets down the hole.

* * * * *

The sweating vulgarity of the crowd-pleasing *Onibaba* and *Rashomon* was liberating. (Both were marketed in the States as prurient erotica.) These films are like deliberate acts of Malabou's destructive plasticity, a kind of scarring which enlarges the organism and ushers it into a new regime of identity. Shindô has said that in *Onibaba* "killing is affirmed because it's a necessary evil for survival."[54] *Rashomon* suggested a society at cross-purposes, disorderly, even moribund; yet out of this impasse grew dynamic characteristics of defiance, hardiness, endurance. Again, this can be attributed to firsthand experience of the war and postwar, where daily life reflected the forging of new kaleidoscopic identities.

For example, under severe food shortages and widespread famine, "[g]arbage from American military facilities' mess halls ... was cooked and served in black markets" as a "popular" stew, "selling out in no time."[55] Surviving members of the elite kamikaze pilots "were turning to strong-arm robbery." People stole anything, even baby clothes, and the relentless crime waves immediately "became a ubiquitous subject of black humor," as did the atomic bomb itself. The "bomb" in fact became slang for a potent "bathtub gin" cut with methyl alcohol, a concoction which blinded and killed many of its habitués.[56] The organism changes as it must. In Kurosawa's *Stray Dog* (*Noru inu*, 1949), when the young police detective (Toshirô Mifune) goes undercover in the Tokyo black market to find his stolen pistol, he disguises himself as a homeless veteran in uniform, so ubiquitous were ex-military men in the criminal underworld of postwar Japan. In the delirious *Gate of Flesh*, Seijun Suzuki shows Japanese veterans teaming up with occupying GI's to form burglary rings, all former loyalty to the Emperor and a sovereign Japan sloughed off in the face of starvation and homelessness. Suzuki has the master criminal Ibuki (Jô Shishido) constantly refer to the training he received in the imperial army and to his harsh wartime experiences serving him well in postwar Japan's "carpet-bagger civilization"[57]—but not for the purposes for which that training was intended. Likewise, in Masumura's *Black Test Car*, old Mawatari (Ichirô Sugai) runs his company with tactics honed as a general of the Imperial Army in the Pacific Asia War against Manchuria; his ruthlessness causes the industrial espionage war in the film to escalate to physical violence, torture and suicide.

* * * * *

Oshima's *The Ceremony* is an ambitious study of the warped passions spawned by Japanese colonization of and racism toward other Asian nations, and the East Asian diasporas which resulted. Masuo comes to Japan as a boy in 1947, a refugee from war-torn Manchuria, now one of Japan's surrendered colonies; he is taken in by the Sakuradas ("Sakurada" means "cherry blossom,"[58] again, one of the central images of imperial Japanese nationalism), a wealthy extended clan that is now a patchwork of survivors and orphans. The Sakuradas are tyrannized by the rule of the grandfather (Kei Satô, in a magnificent performance); Oshima renders the grandfather demonic by giving him cobalt-blue hair and a satanic black kimono. Sometimes Oshima even films the grandfather under a distorting blue spotlight that makes his skin and eyes particularly lizard-like.[59] It is a supernatural aura which the grandfather wears as his own sense of personal superiority and divinity, but which appears monstrous.

Mellen states that Masuo is not so much adopted by the Sakuradas as taken prisoner.[60] He is, in fact, the grandson of the blue-haired Sakurada patriarch; Masuo's father was a Japanese colonial who impregnated a Manchurian woman. He killed himself after Hirohito admitted to the Japanese people that he had never been a divinity, thereby decimating the "core" of Japanese spirit, as Mellen says.[61] To the father's mind, the loss of the emperor's divinity is nothing short of "the end of Japan." Oshima connects the imagined divinity of Hirohito with a specific Japanese colonial male's feeling of entitlement to use colonized women for his sexual pleasure.

Also being "held" by the Sakurada grandfather is the widowed Setsuko (Akiko Koyama), who has been the grandfather's and also the dead father's mistress. "Damaged goods" by the strict morality of Japan, she radiates sexuality and forbidden knowledge of the past in a creepy, fragile, self-destructive way. She takes an early pedophilic interest in Masuo, offering to bathe him. Setsuko's daughter Ritsoku and another Japanese boy, the halfwit Tadashi, spy on this semi-erotic scene and taunt the special "boy from Manchuria." Even as a prepubescent boy, Masuo's body is fetishized, on one hand a totem of sacred otherness, and on the other hand a repository of masochistic guilt for the Japanese characters. Setsuko encourages Masuo to play baseball, urging him to "throw … with all your might." Praised for physical accomplishments, Masuo grows to adolescence as an athlete, but one with an uneasy identity, a Manchurian in Japan playing an American sport, a complex constellation that is its own source of shame and frustration for him.[62]

In this late 1940s period, discussing the war is still taboo; Terumichi, a rebellious cousin slightly older than Masuo, interrupts a family ceremony by fumigating the elders with an insecticide spray-gun and yelling, "All Japan will be disinfected!" Some war criminals have been executed; while others, more influential, are hiding more or less in plain sight, behind a schizoid mixture of the two conquering ideologies, Soviet-Stalinist communism and U.S. democracy; in reality, it is capitalism that flourishes, as the grandfather ruthlessly rebuilds his business empire. We are told that the grandfather was one of the biggest war criminals, a Home Office commander who specialized in interrogation and torture.

As an adolescent, Masuo (Ryuichi Tsubaki) is torn between love for Ritsoku (Yumi Narushima), close to him in age, and Ritsoku's mother, Setsuko. On one fateful night, after his mother dies and he loses a baseball championship, Masuo despairingly burns his bat and uniform. In front of Masuo, the grandfather humiliates Setsuko sexually, throwing her down, tearing at her clothes and inserting his hand in her. It is as if she had to be turned into the family whore in order to discredit whatever she knows. Masuo watches helplessly, afraid to intervene. Terumichi arrives and asks to take part in this "lesson." The grandfather leaves, saying, "What happens next is a foregone conclusion."

Terumichi goes to Setsuko and she devirginizes him. Right afterwards, while Masuo is still in turmoil, Ritsoku finds him and tells him that she and he are half brother and sister; they share the same Japanese-colonialist father, who impregnated two Manchurian mistresses.

This long dark night is an overload of information, and hard for the viewer to take in. Imperialism is likened to a superstructure of incest, in which nothing regenerates[63]; the young are simply born into a dead-end condition of sacrificing themselves for the old. Virtual strangers are bonded and tainted through blood guilts more intimate than such a scattered family (with so many illegitimate children) ever could be. Indeed, Oshima's withering defamiliarization of Japanese family ceremonies in this film is meant to nullify any real meaning they might have had to emblemize or reinforce kinship. The Sakurada mansion is like a haunted-house set: cavernous rooms plunged in darkness, lit by candles and an occasional bonfire. In the sequence where Terumichi is deflowered by Setsuko, Oshima uses dim lighting and black backgrounds to accompany the series of chthonian revelations; at the end, he cuts suddenly from Masuo kissing Ritsoku on the lips (although she has told him to kiss her only on the forehead, as befits brother and sister) to harshly lit present day Japan, where grown-up Masuo (Kenzô Kawarasaki) and Ritsoku (Atsuko Kaku) are still haunted by all of this. It is an edit that is like shining a flashlight into the eyes of someone asleep in a darkened room and having a nightmare; it nearly hurts.

On a kind of pilgrimage to Okinawa to confirm whether Terumichi has killed himself or not (he has sent a cryptic telegram implying that he has), Ritsoku and Masuo are at constant cross purposes. She refers to Masuo as nothing but a distant relative; he still yearns to marry her, in spite of their blood relation and in spite of the fact that she married Terumichi some years prior. When he brings up childhood memories, such as the baseball game in which Setsuko praised his throwing, Ritsoku looks confused and tells him the memory never happened: "You always played baseball by yourself," she says. Mellen writes of the surreal and mnemonically confused aspects of *The Ceremony*: "What is real is what those in power, symbolized by the grandfather, decide is real, as they are shown to control every facet of the lives of their Japanese subjects."[64] When Masuo insists, Ritsoku says, "Are you trying to tell me my mother led you to what you have become?" Here, again, we have perhaps the single greatest central theme of Japanese postwar cinema—the horror or pain of "what one has become." It is not so much that "becoming" itself is the problem; change is inevitable and usually natural. These changes are pointedly *not* natural; traditions try to mitigate against the numbness that comes from too much lost innocence. But the traditions themselves are received and tainted: Oshima makes clear that this is not merely a postwar problem, it is the problem of the prewar, imperial generation, exemplified by the Sakurada grandfather, refusing to relinquish control over Japan. Mellen accurately summarizes *The Ceremony* as a film about the young generation being "buried alive in the new Japan."[65]

The young also experience some inability to pinpoint ultimate responsibility, with so many rogue players to blame in this history-play: the emperor, the Japanese military, the U.S., the bomb. Having too many alibis and too much material contentment (as it does also for the delinquents of the sun-tribe films) leads to an enervated and morally dead condition; it is reminiscent of Kenichi in Masumura's *Kisses*, who can impress the

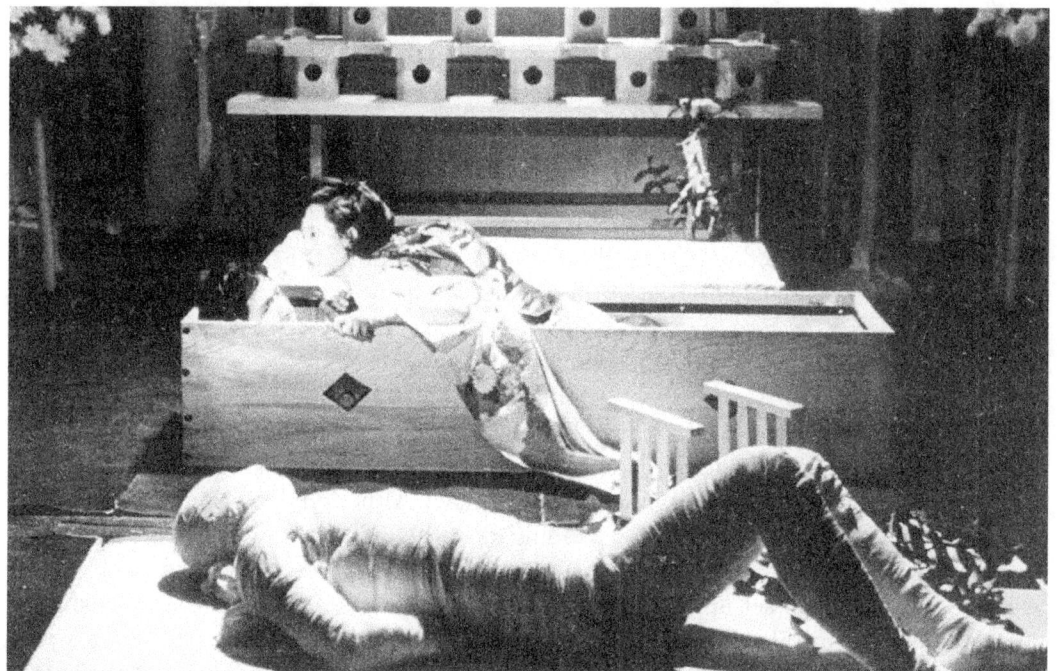

Top: In Oshima's *The Ceremony* (*Gishiki*, 1971), half-siblings Ritsuko (Atsuko Kaku, on top) and Masuo (Kenzô Kawarasaki) tumble into a perverse parody of a sexual embrace when they fall into an empty coffin whose rightful occupant has been dumped, unceremoniously enough, onto the floor. Oshima's masterpiece is a series of official social and familial ceremonies gone horribly awry, sometimes farcically, sometimes brutally and sadistically. Joan Mellen describes the film's young characters as "buried alive" in postwar Japan. *Bottom:* The body of the sympathetic Setsuko (Akiko Koyama) is discovered in *The Ceremony*, nailed to a tree with a samurai sword. The evil patriarch of the wealthy Sakuradas has turned her into the family whore and finally executed her once she has fulfilled her purpose of devirginizing the last male Sakurada heir.

pretty Akiko in public by flashing around his father's graft money but is hopelessly lost, terrified, shy, and angry when he has to talk to the same girl in private. He finally uses money, again, to bet on a bike race at the track in order to determine whether he will go out with her or not. What has embittered Kenichi? His parents' divorce, as he admits later to Akiko. Beneath their exterior smoothness the nouveau riches of Japan are decadent and deeply troubled, symbolically paying for the sins of the past. As Masuo says in *The Ceremony*, "we are all children of this regret" of Japanese imperialism—and children of war criminals, as he also says—but whose regret is it exactly? *The Ceremony* interrogates its characters about precisely this question the way some Eugene O'Neill plays interrogate their characters about alcoholism; Oshima comes down most persuasively on the side of a kind of epochal bad luck, to have had one's youth in a "depraved era." Meanwhile, the adult Masuo and Ritsoku are dressed lavishly, he in a very expensive-looking hound's-tooth overcoat, and she in an elegant chinchilla shawl. Although deploring the Sakurada's abusive and corrupt power, they have indulged in the material rewards of being Sakuradas.

Masuo has been set up to fail in his adopted country of Japan, initially fetishized as an object of guilt, but finally not permitted to succeed. He loses both Setsuko and Ritsoku to Terumichi (played as a teen by Yoshikaki Ota, and as an adult by Atsuo Nakamura). Just as he lags behind Terumichi in sexual experience, he also lags behind in terms of career opportunities, ostensibly because he is half Manchurian; Terumichi now works for the grandfather as an attaché, while Masuo halfheartedly goes back to playing baseball. On the night that Setsuko devirginizes Tadashi (Yukihiro Tsubaki), she has fulfilled her purpose to the Sakuradas—making "men" of all the young males—and is murdered by the grandfather, not insignificantly (as Mellen has noted[66]), with a feudalist-era samurai sword.

"The idea of the father as the ruler of the family," Oshima has said, "could be considered an analogy to the rulers of the state itself, which for two thousand years has been ruled by an emperor who represents [absolute] power."[67] But *The Ceremony*'s ultimate "foregone conclusion" is something the grandfather could and would never have predicted: the total extinguishing of the Sakurada family line. Tadashi is murdered after he disrupts a family gathering by attempting to read from a fascist broadside calling for a military coup d'état to reinstate the emperor's divinity; Terumichi has made good on his promise and ended his life; when Ritsoku discovers his body she too commits ritual suicide. Masuo, unable to stop her, descends into complete psychosis; his sense of self, always already fragile and easily undermined, has been obliterated, the ultimate effect of the long reality-denying "ceremony" he has been forced to live.

5

The Last Ontology

Being exists for the sake of being; it is all that matters. Identities are temporary markers of the forms our beings take, unrelated to the deep core of Being itself.

Western ontology picks up the thread beginning with the assumption that Being comes about *only* as something which arises from a specified, decisive *angle* on reality, the world, the Real, even on ourselves. It is usually a Cartesian form of *thought* Being, *decided* Being, *acted* Being. Badiou writes, "it is when you decide upon what exists that you bind your thought to Being. That is precisely when, unconscious of it all, you are under the imperative of an orientation."[1] But this would make Being merely contingent, and decipherable at a glance as it were, all at once, when in fact Being requires practice and spiritual training to ascertain or achieve; more than this, Being is perhaps the one and only thing we can maintain as an independent constant in its unbound, ungrounded state. Meditation is only one of the more obvious synecdoches of a Being that exists in greatest purity when deliberately cut off from any inventory of "what exists," coded, ideologically or otherwise, in material and functional properties of "world," and also from the premeditated coordinates of self-identity.

Daisetz T. Suzuki explains:

> How can the mind be at once a mind and a not-mind? How can "A" be simultaneously both "A" and "not–A?" The problem is not only logical and psychological. It is also metaphysical. [...] But, philosophically, it concerns us in various ways, and it also constitutes the crucial point in the study of Oriental thought and culture. The question has never been presented to the Western mind, I believe, in the way the East faces it.[2]

To place reality ahead of Being is to endlessly defer the proof of existence, to subjugate it to an ideological battle of wills that cannot be settled until reality itself has been settled in favor of this or that prior "orientation." Then the orientations themselves take up the war of defending some sense of reality over and above Being itself. All of this is not only a waste of precious human energies and resources but a vast oversimplification of existential circumstance. The problem with reality, for Japanese philosopher Keiji Nishitani, is that, whether internal or external to ourselves, it is always a question of multiple realities which "lack unity among themselves and even seem to contradict one another."[3] But the only truth is to be found in this chaotic state of multiplicities. The search for the unitary in consciousness, so central to Western assumptions about authenticity and meaning, begins as lie and ends as denial.

This is why, when consciousness is objectified in one way or another it can seem paltry in comparison to the vastness with which we like to imagine it, as in Miike's *Andromedia*, where the teenage Mai (Hiroko Shimabukuro) is killed in an accident and brought back to life as a computer program, the "Album of Souls," her entire memory of her past life reduced to what can fit on a single CD-ROM. Yet, this program is efficient and highly charming, and perhaps that should be enough. Some semblance of life, that vast multiplicity, is pinned down and preserved. Yet it is not enough, just as it is not enough to understand only one small portion of our own potentialities. For example, how do we interiorize things which cannot be said to exist materially at all—death, nothingness, unconsciousness—but which nonetheless have reality for us,[4] albeit one that is often inexplicable to what Catherine Malabou calls the (Western) "substantialist assumption"?[5]

This need for multiplicity, or otherness-in-one, is also a resonant, primary aspect of Nishitani's case against Western ontology, further arguing against the Western bias for predetermined meanings, identities, states of being: Nishitani is against the sovereign "ego as a reality that is beyond all doubt and occupies the central position with regard to everything else that exists."[6] It is a kind of imperialism of consciousness, and it begins with Descartes and the "I" implicit in *cogito ergo sum*,[7] which Nishitani complicates by viewing this already as an ontological problem: how do we think or know that we think; how is this in any way self-evident?[8] Instead, it is simply asserted, "declared rather than known,"[9] as Badiou poignantly described the crisis which the sovereign ego necessitates by turning consciousness against itself. "The subject," Nishitani writes, "cannot emerge out of something objective,"[10] meaning that the *cogito* cannot be delimited and defined from outside if it is also to be the basis of each individual being. But neither does the generative principle come about organically and, as it were, all at once from within. Isn't it truer to say that we have come to identify our existence with "thinking" through a process of mimesis, which seems to become unconscious at the point where we ourselves begin to think?

In *Confessions of a Mask*, Yukio Mishima anticipates Nishitani's argument by defining his own ontological awareness as a third party. He is writing about sexual awakening, the beginning of his puberty, which he describes as a new toy he was given to play with. And of course, because he had never played with this toy before, he had no idea what to do with it. "Then," he writes, "I took it into my head to try listening more dispassionately to the toy's wishes. When I did so, I found that soon it already possessed its own definite and unmistakable tastes, or what might be called its own mechanism."[11] "Puberty," which has existed long before any specific pubescent, is a script that writes its own lines on the subject going through it. One need only surrender to the needs of the entity, the mechanism that has displaced oneself, and of course, not only puberty but any aspect of life is like this.

A certain schizoid nature, then, was born within ontology, in which consciousness is ethereal and everything else belongs to the machine. Fragmentary humanity holds no permanent grounding except insofar as it could attach itself more definitely to materialisms. This was turned into a unique and insoluble problem through the dualism of subject and object: not only is my ego a "privileged subject" which is self-fulfilled by nothing more than my ability to think it; not only can I not be "thought" by another, at least not satisfactorily; but all external, non-conscious things became, as Nishitani writes, "the cold and lifeless world of death. Even animals and the body of man himself were thought of as mechanism."[12] Abnormal psychology would encourage us to read this, again, as a case of displacement, arising from damage to one's relations with the world: "forbidden" wishes are not my own, but rather a mechanistic aspect of my consciousness, separate from me and perhaps somehow implanted. Mishima's own sexual conflicts, as well as his incipient Western view of ontology, invite such a reading. Yet, there is a movement in Mishima's thought, here, which belies this, and which settles the incipient conflict without creating further, vaster conflicts. When one relinquishes power over oneself (which is an illusion anyway, a self-obstacle), one becomes oneself: a thing that had to be allowed to emerge from within by "listening," not thinking, but precisely letting oneself be thought by primary instincts and drives that are innate and universal.

This places the instincts and drives directly above the needs of the ego, finally demonstrating how the Cartesian *sum* is merely conditioned and finally noncategorical; I think therefore I seem to be like the others. In fact, there are no premeditated judgments possible in true being, for these would distort the ability of being to exist for its own sake in a state of potentiality, of ungrounding. "Probably," Mishima tells us, "the only place in which I could have lived at ease would have been some uncivilized tropical land where I could not speak the language."[13] Thought would come into being through the self, and remain within it, as pure instinctivity; only actions could express the true inner self. Language, the object closest to abstract thought, would no longer be part of that determined listening to oneself, to one's own mechanism. (Even "listening," here, is decidedly not listening *to speech*.) Otherness-in-one, like a bone stuck halfway down the throat, unreachable with the fingers, unable to be fully swallowed, can be incorporated only by evolving a new kind of throat.

Thus, it is problematic if not mistaken to accept Heidegger at face value when he states that philosophy had reached its final stage and that nothing is left of it but "independent sciences," primarily cybernetics.[14] Karatani uses this to assert that we have already surpassed the last ontology because "we are no longer allowed to speak positively about the sense in which mankind sustains its *humanness* in contrast to the realized formal system—the computer."[15] According to this, cybernetics has replaced the ontological because it cannot be "thought" in terms of human consciousness. But this presumes that human consciousness was always a completely known quantity which ontology simply located and inventoried, and which anthropomorphism cloned correctly; in fact, ontology has been about the business of expanding subjectivity into the object-world, and inverting object and subject relations, from its beginnings. Anthropomorphism is itself subject to widespread vagaries in cultural thinking about the human subject and what is meant to replace it. This is partly because we only anthropomorphize objects which are already in some sense conceptually in the image of the human (however seemingly removed). The highest compliment we can bestow on anything, whether it be a monkey or a machine, is "intelligence," and yet, strictly mental, rationalistic intelligence is only a small part of human subjectivity, privileged because it is what recognizes and assigns, what processes and defines. We should view such human intelligence as only the very minor tip of an immense and mainly undiscovered iceberg.

Many denizens of Japanese cinema—some of whom we have already considered in the first part of this book—are such ontological enigmas, from beneath the tip of the iceberg, as it were. They represent an alternative nature where structure is a guessing-game that the self plays with, and against, itself. In some cases they are depleted of healthy ego, having been told what to be instead of being allowed to discover it for themselves; this is the self that acts for a common good, following orders, or sacrificed in a spectacular flashing blaze. In other cases, they are in the grip of an egotism which deforms them and searches for its objective-correlative in madness, violation, orgasm, murder and war. Their ultimate meaning, in all events, is to lodge in the film-watcher's subjectivity, as imagoes of an otherness within, an otherness-in-one.

Let us imagine the reverse of the typical Western model of consciousness, in which the self is the bedrock and reality is a pawn used to augment and certify the self. Let us imagine, instead, a mutational, loosely configured consciousness which is itself a kind of "raw material" given form through the actions of reaching out into the world in a spirit of harmonious connectivity, leading to a sense of oneness with everything, of otherness-in-one; this would make reality itself evanescent, ethereal, ungraspable—enigmatic as it is and should be. Nishitani's metaphor for this is people being separate leaves joined to the same "larger tree of life."[16] That tree is consciousness; we, the leaves, imbibe from it and remain connected to it as long as we live. Yet we know a different set of experiences: we blow about in wind, we bend backwards or inside-out, we get plucked, we fall. On the ground consciousness reemerges again through reformed connection with the tree (as mulch at the roots).

Western philosophy, caught up in the monadic life of the "I," does not begin to take this into account in any meaningful way until the 19th century, and even then all too imperfectly, without seeking to shed the last ontology, to no longer separate ourselves from subject-object dualisms, to no longer "look at things *without* from a field *within* the self."[17] Nishitani calls this "the bias of consciousness," and it turns our own self-consciousness into the roadmap of our persistent alienation from the objective world whose "*real* reality" is never ours to grasp.[18] Nishitani's critique of Western ontology is essentially a critique of its implicit narcissism, the baseless love of an illusory selfhood never in self-sufficient evidence. Although Nishitani does not use the word "narcissism," he calls self-consciousness a mirror of itself, and states that "ego means self in a state of self-attachment."[19]

If cinema places us in the uncanny position of flattering our ability to grasp what is external as if it were rising from inside of us already, then we can say that cinema reinforces and simultaneously displaces this narcissistic spell: one can rest assured that one is not the object, for one is looking at manifest objects (actors, scenery, discrete plastic images, etc.), objects which seem to have a life of their own, which is clearly separable from ours, and at the same time one can also evade some of the responsibility that comes with being strictly the subject, since the objects were assembled by someone else and our relation to them has been to some extent predetermined. One can enjoy the feeling that one has an ontological consciousness that is hybrid and new, a subject that samples from a wide range of objects while receding, sometimes solipsistically, to a well-defended position where subjectivity need not act nor answer for its choices. Film is like a hive-mind that can shelter and nurture other minds without even being aware of itself or the minds in question. "Reality" is displaced and cannot harm us; yet it is also definitive and can be pointed to as evidence of something we have experienced and in some sense even become.[20]

We can see how Buddhist Japan might be uniquely poised to take advantage of a cinematic ontology in which the individual ego finds a place of harmony in relation to some external reality, and in which even the watching of films becomes something more than passive. Buddhism, which has been an integral part of Japanese culture since the 6th century,[21] is not only compatible with "direct actions," it promotes them as a way of "handling the thing itself."[22] It does not establish a false dualism between doing and being; thus, enlightenment is not an ineffable state of grace which delimits the spiritual being as most complete in a state of passivity but rather a process of apprehending the self always in relation to specific masteries, specific knowledges, specific tools. This is "because Zen is a religion which teaches us not to look backward once the course is decided upon [and] because it treats life and death indifferently."[23] We might then say that the last human ontology might well be our understanding of cinema, or certifiable present Being which exists within universal consciousness without even knowing that it exists at all.[24]

Part Two

The Floating World

Because they fall we love them—the cherry blossoms. In this floating world, does anything endure?

—Ariwara no Narihira (b. 823–d. 880)[1]

Official ideologies were ... painstakingly inscribed directly onto the bodies of the emperor and members of his entourage.... Details as seemingly arbitrary as a moustache, a hairstyle, a particular clothing fashion, an intimation of gender ... all these were intentionally fabricated and meaningful signs, together forming systems of signs designed to convey particular messages to the Japanese people and to the world.

—Takeshi Fujitani[2]

6

Refugees of the Floating World

> A stupid accident, a piece of bad news, mourning, pain—and abruptly becoming freezes, coaxing an unprecedented being, form, individual.
> —Catherine Malabou[1]

> [Director Mikio Naruse] believes that there is no escape. We are in a floating world which has no meaning for us.
> —Joseph L. Anderson and Donald Richie[2]

> Alienated people, unlike those content with work and family, are constantly in search of a purpose in life. Some may participate in political or religious movements, but the vast majority roam the streets looking for something of their own.
> —Tadao Sato[3]

In a remarkable and lovely insight into what we might term "cultural evolution," Jun'ichirô Tanizaki wrote,

> The quality that we call beauty, however, must always grow from the realities of life, and our ancestors, forced to live in dark rooms, presently came to discover beauty in shadows, ultimately to guide shadows towards beauty's ends.[4]

"Beauty in shadows": could this simple formula express all we need to know about the Japanese aesthetic? It is true that shadows—and indeed the empty spaces which shadows fill—bear little relation to Western critical theory, which tends to look toward empty and ambiguous spaces only for their ability to be *occupied* with something, for their status as place holders for the soon-to-be-defined, or for their receptivity to often contrived dialectical syntheses. As Barthes observed: "dialectics only links successive positivities."[5] We Westerners make it our special mission to chase shadows with some kind of light, to block out emptiness with any kind of material presence. Perhaps the particularity of Japanese vision is actually its ability to dwell within empty space untroubled by its emptiness.

Certainly, our Western "substantialist assumption"[6] should not be taken as an assertion that there is nothing to Japanese art and thought, only that the fact that something can come from nothing, or from losses, should not surprise us. In Malabou's theory of destructive plasticity, trauma transforms us in numerous unexpected ways. She writes:

> Transformation would no longer be a trick, a strategy or a mask always ready to be lifted to reveal the authentic features of the face. Transformation would betray an existential underground, which, beyond the round of metamorphoses, could enable the subject to become unrecognizable. Unrecognizable less

because of a change in appearance than on account of a change in nature, a molting of the inner sculpture.[7]

Where true survival is at stake, transformation must be total. In Hara's *Goodbye CP*, one interviewee says about Japanese cerebral palsy sufferers, "I was very moved by their strong desire to live." This is destructive plasticity as well, the transformative will to overcome maladies and disabilities. As Tanizaki might instruct us, by living in semi-darkness we can either go blind or learn to see what is only semi-visible. At the same time, as one of these CP sufferers admits, painfully, "I require some form of protection. That's the only way I can survive." Whether we praise or detest the harsh need for survival, we must acknowledge that the terms of this survival are different for everyone, even for everyone experiencing the same problems and threats.

Here, perhaps, in the rejection of dialectical "positivities," philosophy takes a lesson in common manners. Commensurability (of something to its ideal, or to other things) is a species of rudeness; it arrests the flight of possible consciousness and re-roots it to the ground. As with Zen Buddhist non-mind (*mushin* or *munen*), what is prized is the lack of relation to explanatory or critical mind, and what is preserved is a state of floating, weightless, free of all impediments. This is part of "the traditional Buddhist view of the world as fleeting and impermanent."[8] Ozu sometimes represented this fleetingness with images of people appearing and almost as suddenly disappearing, seen walking in the space between two houses, or glimpsed crossing in and out of sight at the end of a corridor. It is not that one specific thing cannot unite with a larger wholeness; it is that this union is automatic *where and when it needs to be* in a state of non-mind, like being in the right place at the right time.

Although bushido (inspired by Zen Buddhism) vanished as a formal code around 1912, the end of the Meiji era, it did not vanish as a practice from Japanese life and "can still be found in the martial and aesthetic arts, which follow certain forms (kata) that are practiced repeatedly until practitioners master the form and enter the state of 'no-mind.'"[9] No-mind or non-mind is recognizable as a blank or trancelike state that seems superficially to resemble certain brain disorders, such as catatonia. In fact, it is more akin to the heightening of other senses in someone who has lost one of the physical senses completely. There are, in other words, covert similarities between Zen non-mind and Malabou's destructive plasticity, mainly in the way that a deficit (of affect; of motion; of appearance perhaps) can conceal a unique inner alertness. "When *mushin* or *munen* is attained, the mind moves from one object to another.... For this reason the mind fulfills every function required of it."[10]

Floating is a product of intensive self control and self awareness, to the point where it becomes second nature, becomes so constant as to feel very different from control and awareness, indeed the exact opposite. This state of non-mind is achieved through discipline, like the training of a samurai swordsman. It is a finely honed defense. The sword that attacks you has a trajectory; it does not drift freely but arcs and strikes; to evade it, one must forget it—but by disappearing. Indeed, "do not even think of yourself."[11] It is non-floating which is always ascribed to the enemy in combat, which is to say, leadenness, inaptitude for stealth or ambush. Likewise, non-mind has no fixed address; "is always flowing, it never halts, nor does it turn into a solid."[12]

Nothing is less floating than, again, the CP sufferer in Hara's *Goodbye CP*, who crawls in the middle of a city street, shoeless, his legs twisted beneath him, his hands flapping against the pavement, his glasses fallen from his face and lying out of reach. Here the body cannot be left behind; this spectacle for Hara's camera takes us to the very limit of what Zen Buddhism and what destructive plasticity can teach us and help us to overcome. Yet, when he is in a different setting, doing a street performance, drawing a chalk circle around himself and reciting one of his poems into a microphone for a sizable audience, this disabled person does seem to transcend the defects that nail him so harshly to his body on other occasions. Also, when he poses fully nude, kneeling in the middle of a road and staring into the camera disarmingly, prepossessingly, almost seductively. This in particular recalls the opening of Oshima's *Diary of a Shinjuku Thief*, an agitprop street theater performance (by the Situation Players) in which a man is chased down and forced to strip nude; he has been accused of stealing a piece of pipe. He reveals an enormous rose tattooed on his abdomen, causing his persecutors to bow to him, apologizing and standing on their heads. This anti-stigmata, which Oshima borrows from Genet's "miracle of the rose," is intended to transform the shamed, lesser-than, public body into an object of beauty and veneration.

The same magic occurs with the CP sufferer in Hara's documentary. "You forbid me to walk," he tells his audience of non-disabled people. "That is how you keep your legs." It has been forced on the CP sufferer to internalize his own otherness in relation to the normal, and also to understand normalcy in a way that non-disabled people are not forced to understand and internalize him. He seems to be waiting for his witnesses to expand to include consciousness of his misshapen body, waiting for someone to become other in relation to him. But life is not street theater. The very mindfulness which such a new and forbidden relation would require is part of the burden that prevents it from coming about.

The element of spontaneity comes up again and again: non-mind "is never like a stone or a piece of wood."[13] The idea is to keep non-mind "flowing like a stream of water, filling every possible corner. [...] But when the flowing is stopped at one point, all the other points will get nothing of it, and the result will be a general stiffness and obduracy."[14] Thus, the curious and startling sense of quick life, often, in that which is also becalmed, nearly static. In making his films, Yasujirô Ozu utilized the efficacy of non-mind by doing endlessly repetitious takes until he had "reduced the actor (most often an actress) to a trance-like state in which they [*sic*] were no longer aware of what they were doing." With non-mind he achieved simplicity and directness in emotional expression through the performing of actions; again, a kind of second nature,[15] a conscious "experiencing of one's own body in order to discover truth."[16] For his part, Oshima described the "one scene, one cut" method he sometimes used as being "designed to avoid interrupting the filmmaker's stream of consciousness," whose expressive tool and synecdoche is "the camera moving freely."[17]

There is something a bit chilling in this paradigm, where one "colonizes," so to speak, the unconscious to make it serve the needs of conscious life and its strivings for success, even beyond those rigors required for strengthening a muscle or quickening a reflex. We see for instance how it is robbed a priori from the CP sufferers in *Goodbye CP*. But non-mind is nonetheless more organic and holistic than the Western model, which places the conscious and unconscious as antipodes, ever at odds and playing tug-of-war with the subject. We in the West hold to the idea that truth occurs ecstatically, in the loss of (self-)consciousness and surrender of the body to oblivious and often generic sensations (effects of drugs, sex, etc.). "To become conscious of the Unconscious"[18] is familiar to us mainly via moments of epiphany, aleatory, automatic writing, etc., adventure and skirmish, rather than the steady daily practice of clearing one's mind through meditation. It is not difficult to see how, with this Japanese ideal of a discipline that merged the inner and the outer so well, the true self could be revealed more comprehensively and more subtly in everything it did, or rather, there was no need to mark it off as exceptionally "true" and thereby separate from the self as a whole. It is also not difficult to see how a deeper and more automatic sense of responsibility for one's actions—even actions not under one's control—could arise in people for whom there was no refuge within the self for the authentic being to hide itself away.

Much of Zen must be taken on faith, especially for Westerners unpracticed in meditation. Indeed, Western commentators have spoken of Japan as illusory, seizing on odd details of cultural practice to trace an aesthetic that crumbles to the touch like moth wings. For example, Barthes' sense of Japanese art is that it is deeply non-representational; he points to the use of pronouns for fictional characters that denote inanimate objects rather than people.[19] We might also note that early Japanese painting was black and white "monochrome," with colors being only a later addition,[20] in contrast to Western art, which applied coloration as early as the earliest cave paintings. It is as if the Japanese decided or always knew that, since art was not the "real thing" but instead a thing unto itself, its own realm, it should obey its own properties and laws, like the fake rats and fake lustrous cockroaches that skitter (in stop-action photography) through the medical clinic in Teruo Ishii's *Japanese Hell*, or for that matter the bright yellow Naugahyde armchairs which all but overwhelm a police conference room in Shion Sono's *Suicide Club*. This non-realist perfection of the object becomes something intrinsic even to "genre" cinema. In Miike's *Dead or Alive*, there is a scene where the hard-working police officer and his wife discuss the medical condition of their daughter; they are in their middle-class dining room. But competing for my attention with the understated drama of the dialogue are the simple but brightly colored elegance of the glasses and bowls, clearly chosen with great care and tastefulness, and refusing to fade into the background.

It is the object that is permitted to be "strong" in itself; whereas the larger context is rendered ambiguous, so that art as such remains nonrepresentational except for its use of discrete objects. As a religion, Zen itself could be called similarly abstract or representation-avoidant. Yet it points to things; it involves signs. But it is a sign system in which the ambiguous nuance is more valued than resolution, because it is considered to be more accurate, since all things possess a degree of indeterminacy.[21] Every tangible present thing melts into enigma; the quest for justice emerges as the delicate process of turning tangible things like life and death into enigmas and then weighing them against an abstract enigma such as "honor," which is given brutally massive weight. In a key scene from Oshima's *Merry Christmas Mr. Lawrence* (1983), the title character, a British P.O.W. (Tom Conti), is brought in to see camp commander Inoue (Ryuichi Sakamoto) during a Buddhist funeral ceremony for a dead soldier. Oshima begins with total symmetry, as Lawrence is escorted through the central door of the temple; what is stressed is the logical structure of the temple, the even columns, the straight lines on the carpet forcing the perspective. Lawrence kneels on one side of the altar, Inoue is on the other. Lieutenant Hara (Takeshi Kitano) kneels at the altar, chanting in a constant, low tone. Hara has been a sadistic, militaristic figure, and it gives us some pause to see him in this new context. It is during this ceremony that Inoue informs Lawrence that he is to be executed for ostensibly smuggling a radio into the camp. Lawrence tries to appeal to Hara, who knows that he is innocent, but Hara ignores him, unwilling to help; he goes on chanting, monotonously, insidiously. Inoue insists that for the sake of his own honor he must punish *someone*. A crime demands no less than this, even if it means punishing the wrong man. "It's your gods, it's your bloody stinking, awful gods," Lawrence seethes, then frenziedly smashes and overturns the altar before being restrained by another Japanese soldier. Even to this destructiveness, Hara does not react, he merely continues to look down and chant, intent on his own dual purpose of carrying out the rite and of abandoning Lawrence to his fate. During Lawrence's attack on the altar, Oshima changes the perspective, to a foreshortened, sharply angled shot, but the basic symmetry remains: Inoue and Hara grouped together on one "side," with Lawrence and the soldier restraining him counterposed as an opposite grouping.

The severity of Buddhism, like Oshima's artistry itself, implacably recording everything without ever looking away, is shown here at its most admirable and most appalling. Admirable because it does not "need" formal symbols: only Hara's single-minded chanting matters to the religious observance, not the all-but meaningless décor of the altar; thus, sacredness is instilled from within, willed, even unconditional. Appalling, too, though, because we see how this single-mindedness can act as a cover for villainous purposes— for any purposes, that is the point. What matters is only the inexorable rolling out of a process by which the stronger prevail, as in the specifically wartime context of *Merry Christmas Mr. Lawrence*, while the weaker fail.

Indeed, psychoanalytic theorist Erich Fromm observed, "There is no room in Buddhist thought for the concept of any enduring permanent substance, neither things nor the self. Nothing is real but processes."[22] Certainly, in *Merry Christmas Mr. Lawrence*, the overarching process is the strong (the Japanese) and the weak (the British) eventually trade places; it is Lawrence who survives to see Hara executed as a war criminal. Even processes of decay, attrition or obfuscation draw from a vital, generative, dynamic energy which makes them more beautiful than something that is decorative but essentially pat and flat. The "moon partially covered by clouds is

Takeshi Kitano plays Lt. Hara in Oshima's *Merry Christmas Mr. Lawrence* (1983). Hara is a brutal soldier, the second-in-command at a Japanese P.O.W. camp. Here he gets drunk on sake as a prelude to torturing British prisoners on Christmas Eve.

more appealing than one that is full," for example.[23] To understand this is to see again that there is actually nothing merely decorative in Japanese cinema, only discrete objects and processes which call attention to the futility of ascertaining a stable context. Indeed, this is again a question of nothing being explicitly contextualized or contextualizable: if decoration is an art of balance, then Japanese art is about that plunge into the empty side of things, Tanizaki's beautiful empty space, which is also denoted as a space for and of the ancestors, since they were the ones who had to grow to appreciate and cherish it.

There is defiance as well as obeisance in this plunge into ancestral empty space, just as there is tension, the humming of a long fading note. In art, we might say that Frommian processes involve conversions and cross-conversions of form into content; and in this sense, floating is well-represented in the arts of Japan. Dangling origami suggest bird-flight on a breeze. The motifs of classical Japanese painting seem to freeze certain landscapes at moments where the solid is about to liquefy, where something that clings to something else is about to let go: hanging crests of waves, patches of melting ice on a mountainside, petals swollen on the bough almost to the point where we can imagine them detaching with a faint pop and slowly tumbling. In music played on traditional Japanese instruments, there are always timed rests called *ma*, which punctuate and offset the sounds.[24] Haikus are similarly constructed around surprising line breaks which utilize the white space of the page, in a way that is often a formal imitation of the observations of the poetry itself: fleeting moments, zephyrs, déjà vu, startled, mistaken recognitions or trompe-l'oeil elements that suspend for a moment in the eye or the mind before yielding to drift and gravity.

Among the arts, theater and cinema are the ones that display their processes most nakedly and which disguise their enigmas in plainest view. They must embody directly, yet to be effective and profound, they must reduce the embodiment to traces, wondering gestures. Of course, narrative poses a distinct challenge to Zen's propensity for openness of meaning and for things in isolation, unpremeditated by other things; this recalls the deliberate effacement of true meanings in the search for justice throughout Kurosawa's *Rashomon*, in its way an attempt to systematically dramatize the non-explanatory essence of Zen. We will find a similar free atmosphere of otherness-in-one, decades later, in Fukasaku's *Battle Royale*, another Japanese film in which justice is rendered ambiguous by sui generis circumstances. The numerous kids who must fight each other in *Battle Royale* rise to the challenge and put all of their young lives into their vicious final acts of killing and dying. There is a type-A overachiever who thinks he can dominate the battle by spouting math equations and vowing to survive to "get into a good school." Everything the teens are, and everything they are not, comes out of them to the nth degree under the pressure of "the game." A boyfriend and girlfriend hang themselves together, while "loners" are said to stay even more on their own. One "mean girl," Mitsuko, takes to the game right away, manipulating former friends and rivals into letting her get close to them before literally stabbing them in the back. "Why not kill?" she muses. "Everyone has their issues." She rationalizes killing as easily as she has rationalized stealing other girls' boyfriends and even pimping out someone in her circle to "old perverts."

Other, more tender-hearted kids express crushes they have held back for years. There are fleeting flashes of emotional fulfillment, almost, we sense, enough for a whole lifetime in some cases. Impending death renders every exchange in the starkest terms:

this boy or girl will be not only the first face you have loved, but the last face you will ever see. The only face that you will ever kill, the face that will kill you. Are these deaths to be viewed as blazes of glory, or snuffings-out? Is it life that is undignified, or merely early, untimely death? Where something is not governed or governable by protocol, there can only be a non-judgmental respect for the existential ground it breaks, and for its concomitant ambiguity. Indeed *aimai* (ambiguity) is not merely an abstract concept in Japan[25] but a practical "virtue," even though it "can cause a good deal of confusion."[26] Thus, gaps (like the conversational, performative equivalent of empty spaces filled with shadows) became forms of communication in Japanese conversation: "In these blanks, people find unmentioned, hidden meanings and try to determine the meaning ... through feeling the atmosphere created by the words."[27] Confusion and even misunderstanding are social risks that are nonetheless welcomed as signs of humbleness, of not pretending false superiority.[28] The purpose of art is finally no different from the purpose of social interaction: to intrigue.

* * * * *

The floating world is already a specific concept in Japanese thought. As defined by Andrew Gamble, it is "the world which is outside straight society and peopled by jugglers, clowns, vagabonds, criminals, misfits of all kinds ... where people apply different standards and higher levels of honesty."[29] This world has its own imperatives, its own consequences and sense of honor. In Toyoda's *9 Souls* a former associate of the escaped convicts is not permitted to escape the floating world even though he has tried to go straight by starting a business and family. In a comical scene, the convicts, who have taken over his home, drive away his mail-order Filipina bride after using up all her toilet paper. For our purposes, the idea of the floating world will take on a larger resonance; I am extrapolating from the standard definition to encompass something that coincides more largely with Malabou's "existential underground" of those who have been transformed ontologically by suffering and trauma.[30] Anyone—family members, teachers, bureaucrats—can be part of this floating world, willingly or unwillingly. In fact one hardly chooses to be in the floating world; like destructive plasticity, it is already an objective model of traumatic ontology, fallout from the accident. "The implication is that those who do live their lives on the edge," Gamble continues, "are not like the majority of people who never consider doing anything that would risk them making a mistake. Most people accept the dull conformity of an alienated life, and never glimpse the possibilities of anything different."[31] They are never forced to confront themselves existentially, in crisis mode. It is reminiscent of Keiko's awareness, in Naruse's *When a Woman Ascends the Stairs*, that the only true knowledge of life is knowledge of suffering. Likewise, in Shinji Aoyama's *Eureka* (*Yurika*, 2000), Yumiko (Sayuri Kokushô) seduces the troubled Makoto (Kôji Yakusho) by first opening up to him that she, too, was orphaned at a young age, as if any kind of intimacy between them would be predicated on her demonstration that she understands some of his earthly suffering. Even punishment is not revenge and only indirectly a remuneration; rather it is explicitly a process of learning, in a general way, how to suffer: in Ishii's *Japanese Hell*, Miyajima (Hisyoshi Hirayama), the serial killer of little girls, is dismembered alive again and again by demons in the afterlife until he comes to understand "pain."

Director Takashi Miike has stated that he has made films in which the characters "try to escape from something or float passively, never wanting to climb up in life. I like those kinds of people, because I have sympathy for them. I have that in common with them."[32] In the same interview, he remarked, seemingly not with facetiousness, that he would be just as happy going back to being a second or even third assistant director: "I don't really make any effort to continue to stay in film [...] and that's exactly why I can stay inside it."[33] Indeed, he raises the question: how to be inside of anything and still remain able to live freely, as one will? It is a bit like the Zen meditation that allows someone locked in a cell to "travel" beyond its confines.

Floating, then, could be described as the poetic face of an essentially stoic and fatalistic sensibility, symbolized, in Akira Kurosawa's *Ran*, as impermanent cloud formations that only randomly seem to take the shape of something already on our minds. The state of floating is finally about not finding much to cling to. We see this in evidence elsewhere in Japanese culture. Japanese soup, for Barthes, is such an experience, in which "the rarity of the two or three solids ... which divide as they float in this little quantity of water give the idea of a clear density, of a nutruity without grease, of an elixir all the more comforting in that it is pure...."[34] Here, floating is "a shimmer of the signifier" leading to a kind of taxonomic movement "from the clear to the divisible."[35] Barthes writes, "The cucumber's future is not its accumulation or its thickening, but its division, its tenuous dispersal," as in the haiku where the dripping juice from the vegetable connotes spider legs.[36]

To view such wondrous food as insubstantial is to miss the graceful dexterity which it brings out in the eater. Barthes states that chopsticks turn feeding into "an intelligent and no longer mechanical operation [which] never pierces, cuts, or slits, never wounds but only selects, turns, shifts,"[37] again creating a taxonomy, even a hierarchy of desirable bites, "rediscovering the notional fissures of the substance."[38] Again, it is like the music made of *ma*. Japanese food in general provokes Barthes' "dream" of "a purely interstitial object," as in tempura, where the batter is so light that it does not clump or coat densely, and where "flour recovers its essence as scattered flour."[39] Flour is like an embodying actor in this little theater of the soup bowl, cleanly able to divest itself of physical mass even as it achieves the right presence, "'as if ... the body labored with more reserve than the mind,' according to the precept of the actor Zeami...."[40] Is this not an empathetic otherness-in-one? For Barthes, this suggests "going beyond the form,"[41] even as Malabou refers to destructive plasticity as explosive form,[42] an inbetween state rife with creative options. This divination of interstitial objects even seems to enable a deeper understanding of the solid, by contrast if not default. Ozu has pointedly remarked: "Generally, dissolves and fades are not a part of cinematic grammar. *They are only attributes of the camera.*"[43]

Here we have an intriguing evocation of what we might call "technological form," which exists apart from the art of cinema. The camera is not to be mistaken for a player in this cinematic theater; it is not ontological in and of itself. It only produces the possibility of ontologies when placed, turned, held a certain way. Never has the analysis of shots been more stranded and irrelevant than it is in explaining Japanese films.[44] Likewise, there are no metaphors in Japanese film; director Seijun Suzuki has been quite vociferous in stating that elements of nature (wind, rain, snow) are used for the sake of drama, not as visual poetry or metaphorical allusion.[45] If Japanese cinema comes down to anything, it comes down to actors, who are not quite telling stories so much as embodying abstract modes of storytelling.[46] At any rate, the stories are often completely contained within symbolic titles meant to convey a spatial and temporal unmooring, a blurry intangible reality. *Floating Clouds. A Story of Floating Weeds. Inn of the Floating Weeds. Snow Flurry. Fireworks Over the Sea. The Bird of Springs Past. Firefly Light. White Threads of the Waterfall. Moonlight Whispers. Flicker of the Silver Thaw. Farewell to the Summer Light. Clouds at Sunset. A Hen in the Wind. Lightning. A Man Vanishes. Where Now Are the Dreams of Youth?*

Of course, some of these titles might not seem to invoke a dreamlike state of floating at all. A hen in the wind conjures more violent connotations of battering and damage, in which the wind acts in cruel concert with the solid ground. And can a man vanishing really be spoken of in the same consoling breath as firefly light? Yet, regretfulness is an abiding mood of Japanese culture, and of its cinema.[47] To imagine something is to imagine not what it has been but what it was always meant to be in its highest or most resonant incarnation—not a bird, nor even the bird that is flying by the window, but *the bird of springs past*. In honor of their fleetingness, a hen in the wind and a man vanishing are part of the same matter-of-fact and even somewhat indifferent contemplation as weeds and clouds.

We can see without much difficulty how certain aspects of floating, or what Barthes calls the interstitial,[48] are in fact closely allied with brutality, not only because whatever floats is doomed to fall at some point but because the very form of elision, of pungently invoking what is not there, is essentially brutal, a cutting away of space. Barthes sees Japanese calligraphic writing as a kind of lightning flash: "it is immediately a sign: expressing nothing (neither hatred nor indignation nor any moral idea) ... [A] purely pragmatic action puts the symbols between parentheses."[49] The feeling of the stroke is visceral, closer to painting than to writing. Again, body and mind are not to be split off and opposed within a phony dualism; their needs are already intertwined, as are their means of achieving them. Nothing can be deemed "higher" or "lower" than anything else. It is reminiscent of Mizoguchi's artist-hero in *Utamaro and His Five Women* (*Utamaro o meguru gonin no onna*, 1946): "As a revolutionary," Mellen writes, "instead of considering it beneath him to sketch for tattoos, he finds it as excellent a medium as any, indeed more so because it is so close to the personal, the actual lives of people."[50] Just as Buddhism exalts the potential of people to improve the earthly world in "the universal communion to be realized and the dedication of one's own wisdom and merit to one's fellow beings."[51] Even more complicated is the situation of the feminist actress Sumako in Mizoguchi's *The Love of Sumako the Actress*. When her controversial lifestyle (the married Shimamura has left his wife for her) causes support for her theater company to decline, she becomes defensive and angry, telling the naysayers in the company to leave if they do not like it; she intends to do whatever she wants and to lead the company all alone if need be. Her stance is depicted as the inevitable result of her struggle "between an honest life and the bitter social reality." If her liberation was easy, it would not be true.

Therefore, although invested in the idea of "floating" and often representative of it, Japanese film has also consistently posed a distinct challenge to that idea of "floating,"

This lobby card from a French retrospective devoted to Mizoguchi's work in the 1940s depicts a scene from the director's *Utamaro and His Five Women* (*Utamaro o meguru gonin no onna*, 1946), the story of a revolutionary artist.

especially in terms of the social passivity that marked traditional Japan. This challenge has presented itself in every era of Japanese cinema from the silent era to current times; yet it emerged with an undeniable and specific historical force in the Japanese New Wave of the 1960s.[52] In *Fighting Elegy* (*Kenka ereji*, 1966), Suzuki pointedly satirizes this strain of Japanese culture, in the form of a teenage girl's moony haiku: "Loose hair blows in the breeze like a young tree." "That was seven or eight years ago," the young poetess muses. "Been having problems with men ever since?" an older gentleman asks her. And, like everything among the military-minded cadets in Suzuki's uproarious film, this haiku leads to a cartoonishly violent brawl.

An actual poet whom Suzuki's poetess-character might have taken her cue from is the 9th century Komachi Ono, one of whose texts reads: "So lonely am I. My body is a floating weed severed at the roots. Were the water to entice me, I would follow it, I think." Commentators have pointed to the flirtatious, sensual nature of this,[53] but let us not miss the violence coded in it, too. When expressed in calligraphy or in watercolors, the severed reed has aptness—any painting (or description for that matter) of a reed will necessarily be "severed from life." However, when expressed on film, which doubles as a record of phenomenological experience, it tears open a void. What kind of nihilism lurks behind the staging and filming of nothingness, of the fleeting? Thus, we can see the politically engaged New Wave directors (Suzuki, Oshima, Imamura, Wakamatsu, and others) assailing the trope of a floating world always at the mercy of fate, waiting for some superior power to whip it.

Indeed, Suzuki had already mocked the "floating" trope even more harshly in *Gate of Flesh*, one of the craziest and most poetic films to emerge from the New Wave. The film takes place immediately postwar, during the days of U.S. occupation; a 1940s-style radio ballad of romantic longing, "The stars float above me, and I ask them my fortune..." plays under the opening scene. Later, this same song will be turned into a raunchy, drunken burlesque number by the film's core band of prostitutes, and finally, a sarcastic anthem of sadism by the same prostitutes as they tie up and torture one of their own. The refrain, "What was it that turned me into this kind of woman?" takes on added significance in light of the full dehumanization of postwar society.

Japan lost three million of its citizens during the war.[54] The Japanese "watched helplessly as fire bombs destroyed their cities—all the while listening to their leaders natter on about how it might be necessary for the 'hundred million' all to die 'like shattered jewels.'"[55] It is common for Buddhists to speak of having the souls of certain dead people with them all the time, an intimate part of them; the millions of war dead overran the careful compartments of the Japanese psyche. It was as if what the dead lost and what the living endured had to be rectified by viewing the world as a realm of antimatter both serenely blissful and horribly reproaching, perversely more alive in death, and too much for the living to hold, carry and mourn.

Ghosts were everywhere in postwar Japan, nor have those ghosts ceased. In Toyoda's *9 Souls* a panicky motorist driving alone at night pleads not to see any samurai ghosts rising out of the darkness; he is mocked, but as if to legitimate his fears, he is soon robbed by the gang of escaped convicts. The modern Japanese horror film has reanimated the ghost story with a vengeance, so to speak, in films such as Hideo Nagata's wildly successful *Ringu* (*Ring*, 1998) and others. The popularity of movies depicting lethal, diabolical ghosts accompanies a societal falling-off of traditional Buddhist religious observances of the dead,[56] meant to appease restless spirits. Daikichi Irokawa writes:

> It used to be said that the dead became spirits who rested peacefully in the hills or sea near their homes or in their graves. After the traditional thirty-three- or fifty-year memorial services were completed, the spirits turned into ancestral spirits who watched over still-living descendents. But today people question such beliefs, thanks to both the lifestyle revolution and the spread of a scientific worldview based on rational education. For these and various other reasons, Japanese today are losing their traditional belief in the other world—the spiritual world—and in the rebirth of spirits. The view is gradually spreading that the bodies and spirits of the deceased return to the land and eventually disappear into nothingness.[57]

Ringu's twist, that the haunting-victims are not meant to help the ghost of the little girl find peace but rather to destroy her, is a clever and exhilarating subversion of the entire psycho-social order that was founded on devoted ancestor worship. Spirits are not wise guiding lights, but demons among us, wreaking their havoc of revenge on our messy world. Even in non-horror films, such as Takeshi Kitano's *Dolls* (2002), no one can escape the power of ghosts; the past returns for us bodily, and we go insane, or disappear, in a kind of contagion of empathy for the defiant spirit of antimatter.

In modern ghost stories the dead become "special" and important again, and at the same time hateful, unappealing. Older ghosts tend to be functional, often appearing as the living wish to see them, seducing the living into a false ontology, or exposing us as always already dwelling within one. Typically, they show deference to the living's wishes to enhance the living's guilt complexes and self-loathing, or to trap the living into a helpless, purgatorial state. So, in "The Black Hair," one segment of Masaki Kobayashi's *Kwaidan* (*Kaidan*, 1964), a young Kyoto samurai (Rentaro Mikuni) divorces his devoted first wife (Michiyo Aratama) in order to marry into wealth and power. "For men," he tells the heart-sick first wife before pushing her away and leaving, "advancement is the most important thing." His perversity is such that he is dissatisfied with the new marriage and longs only for what he had. Finally rejected by his imperious second wife (Misako Watanabe), the samurai returns to Kyoto, where he is astonished to find his first wife still waiting for him at their former home, loving and forgiving toward him, and physically unchanged since the day he walked out—in particular, her long black "fragrant" hair. Too dazzled and pleased to question the eeriness of the reunion, he spends the night in their bedchamber but awakens to find her a skeleton. He is driven mad.

The idea that his first wife has not changed at all, that she has hovered in place, so to speak, for the years of his absence, is too appealing to the samurai's vanity. It is not until she suddenly changes, revealing herself as a ghost, beyond his ability to possess her, that he realizes that *he* has been the floating one, reckless, fickle, unable to completely love any woman. And at this moment the first wife's long black hair appears on his head as a mocking effigy.

A similar reunion between a long-separated husband and wife occurs, with much greater subtlety and poignancy, in Mizoguchi's *Ugetsu*, a film in which the spirit world is never far from the living. In fact Genjûrô loves two women in *Ugetsu*, one already a ghost and the other destined to become one. His wife Miyagi yearns only to work beside her husband, helping to spin his potter's wheel, and for them to live "happily" with their young son Genichi (Ichisaburo Sawamura). On a sojourn in a nearby town to sell his pottery, Genjûrô encounters Lady Wasaka, a speechless wraith, her face a glaring, unearthly white beneath her lifted veil. Her moth-eyebrows are the most grandiose and headstrong in all of Japanese cinema. Genjûrô follows her home and ends up marrying her that night; when she casts her spell on him, we see him exhale his breath in a puff of steam, as if Lady Wasaka lived within a frozen element, and also as if she were sapping his vital inner energy, which is exactly what she is doing. As a peasant-artisan, Genjûrô has little more than his breath to be stolen from him, and this is literally what Lady Wasaka takes.

Lady Wasaka is resentful because she died young without ever knowing love; her entire clan, including her once-powerful father, were wiped out by rivals. When she dances the wedding dance for Genjûrô, her dead father's sepulchral, echoing voice comes singing out of a carved dragon head. "Even if you are a ghost or an enchantress," Genjûrô vows, clasping Lady Wasaka in a bliss of denial, "I'll never let you go!" He does not want to admit what he strongly suspects. In an amazing traveling shot, Mizoguchi has time in this lovers' idyll stand completely still; from a scene where they frolic in a hot spring, the camera tracks left, across what appear to be vast expanses of meadow, finally creeping up on a shot of the lovers from a distance, on a picnic blanket by the sea, but isolated to the extreme left and nearly in the top half of the frame. The whole earth beneath and around them seems to be hanging in mid-air. Mellen calls attention to this shot as a

6. Refugees of the Floating World 121

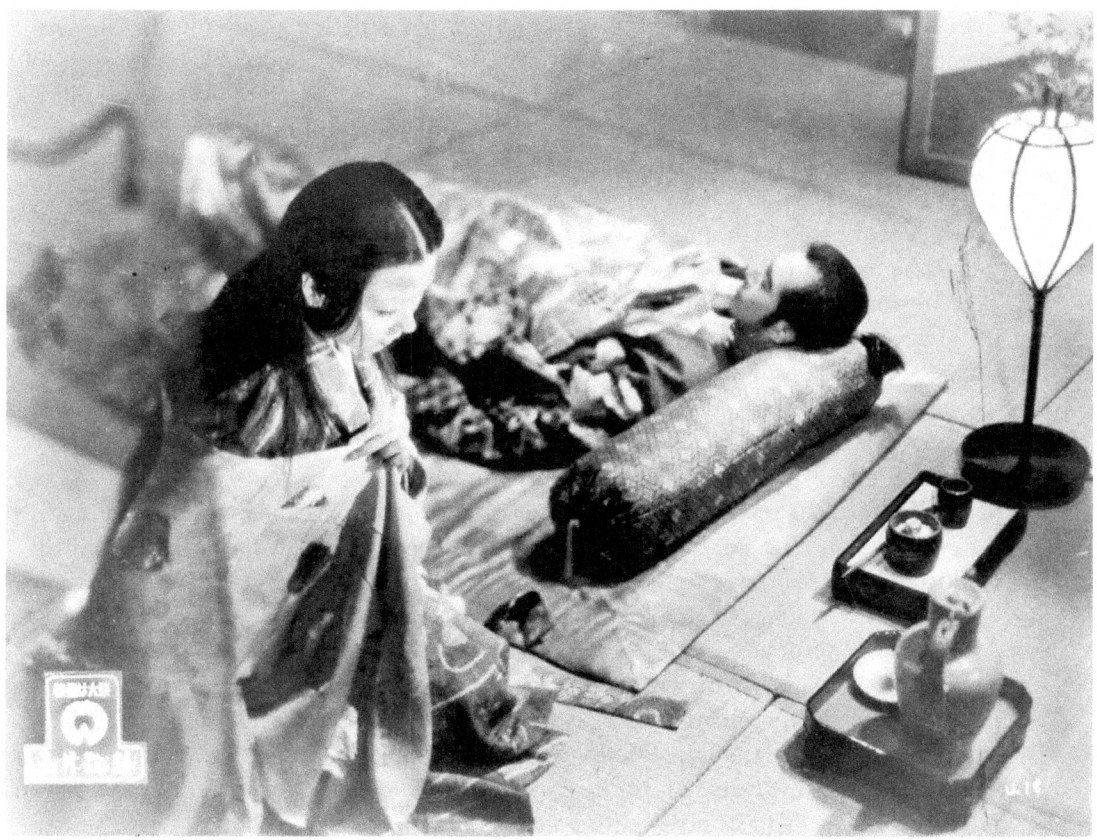

In Mizoguchi's *Ugetsu*, Genjûrô (Masayuki Mori) is placed under a spell by a ghost, the seductive and evil Lady Wakasa (Machiko Kyô). He marries her and she keeps him prisoner in her haunted villa, feeding vampirically off his breath.

moral judgment on Mizoguchi's part,[58] but it is primarily a dazzling and erotic formal invention. A moment, or a thousand years, may have just passed. Lady Wasaka is warbling, "Love has driven me mad."

By contrast, the killing of the true wife, Miyagi, by starving defeated soldiers on the road, happens in a single take, in painful real time, with no distortion. It is like the real suddenly reclaiming what too much fantasy, delusion and pleasure have robbed from it; insisting on re-establishing its own exacting terms. The murderous soldiers could be agents of Genjûrô's bad karma; certainly, we blame him for not being there to protect Miyagi. Furthermore, in a way that suggests the downplaying of individual suffering in the final crane shot away from mother and son at the end of *Sansho the Bailiff*, Miyagi's killing is only one in a brief series of killings which occur in a row, almost as a chain reaction. Two of the soldiers who have killed her, for example, kill each other fighting over the small amount of food she has died trying to save for little Genichi.

Without knowing this, Genjûrô remains trapped in Lady Wasaka's playhouse, torn between the vow he made to Miyagi in the earthly realm and the vow that has been extorted from him in the spirit world. Lady Wasaka's ghost represents overactive desire, synonymous with its own belated avenging of its bad luck and sorrow; bent on having what she lost in life, she returns to attack the object of desire (a man, Genjûrô). Genjûrô is now marked and rapidly dying from her vampirism; this entire subplot is an expression of Buddhist awareness of the overall futility of worldly satisfactions. When Genjûrô does free himself from his trance, he discovers with bewilderment that the stately pavilion of the Wasaka mansion is actually a burnt-out tangle of timber and sticks against the sky, a site of unruly, wild devastation.

Miyagi is waiting at home for Genjûrô; her spirit has not been able to rest until she knows he has come home safely. He spends one night believing that his true family has been restored; in the morning he awakens to the truth. Miyagi is not a vengeful spirit, however; Genjûrô continues with his pottery, having his wife's voice there to encourage and guide him, the first ghost we have seen who is content to love the living from a safe distance. She and Genjûrô have both come to their true selves, to the place where they both belong, albeit in different realms, but this truth and belonging are presented as the only worthwhile mission of any human life.

Ugetsu evokes the terror of separations, during which lives can change at a moment and loved ones can be carried far apart from each other, and also the primal terror of night, during whose uninterrupted darkness anything can happen. Ghosts in all their forms exacerbate the fear of living, if for no other reason than because the ghost is always a reminder of the perilous nearness of mortality. It is not difficult to see in postwar Japanese ghost films a shadow of what we in the West have termed "survivor's guilt." In Kitano's *Dolls*, when the old yakuza boss (Tatsuyo Mihashi) suddenly remembers that he has missed a lunch date with Ryoko (Chieko Matsubara), a sweetheart of over fifty years ago, he returns to the bench in the park where she promised to wait, and there she is, vibrant, strangely ageless, supernatural and quotidian at once. She has given rise to a local legend, the "Famous Waiting Woman." Forgotten memory becomes history even before it can be brought to renewed life, remembered, or rectified. A slight zoom on the yakuza's troubled face ends the scene without gore or Grand Guignol, just recognition that while we may have thought our past was one thing, it turns out to have been quite another. (We also note this guilt in the suicide pacts in Shion Sono's *Suicide Club*. Some kids fail to leap to their deaths with the others and are immediately overcome by remorse at letting down fellow members of the "club." They have not been saved; they have been delayed in attaining unity with their friends, and they invariably jump anyway.)

Our only hope for the future becomes the possibility that what we have lost will return to us in some form, though this already entails that we must inevitably keep losing things in order to have a reason to go on. In Kiyoshi Kurosawa's *Bright Future*, two disaffected, working-class twenty-somethings, Yûji Nimura (Jô Odagiri) and Mamoru Arita (Tadanobu Asano), share a pet jellyfish whom they both know could sting them to death. Yûji is fascinated to watch the creature pulse diaphanously in its tank of water. "It never reacts at all," he says unemotionally—neither impressed nor disdainful nor even bewildered. "That's its nature," Mamoru replies, "I'm sure you two will get on fine." Later, Mamoru murders their warehouse boss and the boss' family, then hangs himself in prison. Yûji feels that his friend took the blame for what should have been his own crime, since he discovered the bodies of the murdered family when he went to the boss' house on the same night to kill them himself. *His* survivor's guilt takes the form of obsessively caring for his heirloom, the venomous red jellyfish. But because he accidentally lets it escape

6. Refugees of the Floating World 123

Yûji (Jô Odagiri) is a disaffected, working-class twenty-something in Kiyoshi Kurosawa's *Bright Future* (*Akarui mirai*, 2003). Here Yûji is fascinated to watch a pet jellyfish pulse diaphanously in its tank of water. The sting of this jellyfish is deadly, and Yûji relates to the fragile but angry creature.

into the Tokyo aqueducts in a moment of anger, the jellyfish is now more concept than actual pet. In reality, freedom has allowed it to expand, passive-aggressively, spawning an army of jellyfish in the manmade lakes and streams of Tokyo, attacking and stinging swimmers. Yûji randomly hears about this on the news; his own personal crisis has become mass-scale disaster and, let us not overlook, historical. Having been always already a function of Japanese (postwar) history, the young man's disaffection returns to a stratum of that history after forging its own objective correlative: the red-jellyfish attack-army.

* * * * *

The practice of Zen Buddhism "goes directly to the root of things regardless of superstructures."[59] There is some paradox here. The cultural ability to see what is often unseen—the floating, diaphanous, bare signifier—stems from Zen's steady concentration on the single thing itself, "the 'isness' of a thing, Reality in its isness."[60] In sharpening the focus on what is already blatantly apparent, it brings more of that abstract data into the frame of consciousness. "What concerns us here," Suzuki writes about the act of Zen verbalism, "is not the substance this exuded or secreted, that is, words or language, but a 'something' hovering around there, though we cannot exactly locate it and say 'Here!'"[61]

We see this in the story of the monk and the Zen master watching the flight of some geese, where the monk tells the Zen master that the geese have flown away and gets sharply rebuked; "the master was not talking at all about the conceptualized geese disappearing far away in the clouds. The master's purpose [in asking where the geese had gone] was to call ... attention to the living goose that moves along with [the monk] himself, not outside but within his person."[62]

The geese, like anything, cease to exist as tangible phenomena when out of sight; yet they also never cease, once having been apprehended by the subject. The subject contains knowledge of these geese, and of everything else, but it is knowledge that comes only by reflecting on the thing in "the pulsation of Reality,"[63] which is an eternal now. Or rather, this Reality is a function of our ability to reflect meaningfully upon it. It grows and sharpens as our awareness of it does. By the same process, something that literally exists around us can often be ignored and practically willed out of existence if we relinquish our own will to change or control it, just as something not there can be recalled with great immediacy as if it had never gone away.

Indeed, one of the conditions that this "floating" points to is the difference between indeterminate and solid matter, what drifts versus what remains in one place. In *Gate of Flesh*, there is a telling special effect which illustrates this. One of the hookers, Maya (Yumiko Nogawa), is gazing longingly at Ibuki's nude body when she has a vision of her late husband, dressed in his military gear, heading off to war. This ghost is quickly dispelled by close-ups of Ibuki's flexing, sweaty musculature, and Maya drifts to a different vision: she and Ibuki locked in a passionate kiss. In Suzuki's raw vision of postwar survival, ghosts, or any reminder of the dead, are insubstantial and must give way to more urgent material needs and longings. Similarly, in *The Sword of Doom*, Ryunosuke chides a young geisha about her superstitious belief in spirits: "There are no ghosts," he says. Somewhat in a reversal of what Suzuki does, this materialist certainty all at once gives way to a series of hallucinated shadows, people whom the samurai has murdered, appearing behind the paper-partition walls of the geisha house. The film returns us to material certainty, however, when these apparitions give way to actual attackers whom the embattled samurai must fight off.

The crucial aspect of a ghost is that it comes back to the realm of the living. It has no other inherent meaning, apart from what we provisionally project onto its apparitional existence. The ghost's affect is often inseparable from how we judge ourselves: if we have been cruel, the ghost seems cruel; if we have suffered greatly, the ghost suffers. They are mirrors, nothing more than this but everything that mirrors imply. Their abiding emotions are embarrassment at being out of place, and a general fear of appearing rude: as Ivy notes, "Japanese ghosts never look the living in the eye: they are too *hazukashii* (ashamed) at being ghosts."[64] Yet, they literally float because, according to Tanizaki, "Japanese ghosts have traditionally had no feet."[65] Thus, Lady Washizu (Isuzu Yamada) in Akira Kurosawa's *Throne of Blood* (*Kumonosu-jô*, 1957) seems beautiful and ghostlike as she glides forward toward the camera, bearing the poisoned mead which her husband Lord Washizu (Toshirô Mifune) will use to murder his overlord and assume power. Again and again in Japanese cinema we see this ethereal or ideal beauty fragment into hideous violence and cruelty, as Anderson and Richie describe it, "the traditional Japanese ghost, usually female,[66] with a heavily scarred face, blood running from the mouth, no legs, and long disheveled hair. These spirits usually return to haunt men who have done them wrong, or to redress old wrongs. They never return simply to haunt at large, and all have a single purpose—revenge."[67] Revenge, that psychological enshrinement of past ego wounds in an ever-static present, is the state of floating par excellence—the Zen-master's possession of reality as eternal now; in fact it could be that all floating is undertaken in no other spirit but that of revenge, against the leadenness of life and the impingement of death. It is a continuously interrupted, only intermittently successful project, however. Only Miyagi's spirit, in *Ugetsu*, finds permanent rest, bosomed in the memory of her loved ones, murmuring peacefully from an always tended grave overlooking the open fields, because she has never felt any desire for revenge.[68]

* * * * *

One more thing remains to be said about Tanizaki's sensibility, perhaps the oddest passage to a Western reader: his rapturous musing on the beauty of the Japanese toilet, which, he writes, "truly is a place of spiritual repose. It always stands apart from the main building, at the end of a corridor, in a grove fragrant with leaves and moss."[69] He goes on: "And the toilet is the perfect place to listen to the chirping of insects or the song of the birds, to view the moon, or to enjoy any of those poignant moments that mark the change of the seasons. Here, I suspect, is where haiku poets over the ages have come by a great many of their ideas. Indeed one could with some justice claim that of all the elements of Japanese architecture, the toilet is the most aesthetic."[70] The toilet is part of what "breaks the frame" in daily life. It calls attention to a margin of thought and sight: "The cleanliness of what can be seen only calls up the more clearly thoughts of what cannot be seen. In such places the distinction between the clean and the unclean is best left obscure, shrouded in a dusky haze."[71] Is it so simple?

Functionality and the slightly mystifying nuance are here brought together in a formal unity. This provides us with a last general insight into Japanese cinema in its relation to Japanese culture and the other arts. If we recall the flagrant lack of mimetic illusion in Japanese theater, the fact that an actor is always an actor, a set always a set, and also the use, which Barthes notes, of inanimate pronouns for fictional characters, then we begin to see that in Japanese cinema the taboo has not been to break the frame, as it has been in the West, where it is always still something of an affront to remind the paying patrons that they are watching a constructed film rather than an escapist "slice of life," but instead the opposite, not to break the frame, to allow the illusion of verisimilitude to spread silently until it engulfs.

No doubt Tanizaki would be the first to accept that this aesthetic pleasure of the Japanese toilet is possible only because it has been placed within its own space, outside of the house. A toilet in the main room of a living space would surely be as out of place as the stove, for him. As Tanizaki acknowledges when he advises dim rather than direct lighting around a toilet: "Yet what need is there to remind us so forcefully of the issue of our own bodies. A beautiful woman, no matter how lovely her skin, would be considered indecent were she to show her bare buttocks or feet in the presence of others; and how very crude and tasteless to expose the toilet to such excessive illumination."[72] But even this only indicates that the taboo is being honored even as it is being joyously violated. One knows that one is leaving the domestic space to perform functions which it would be rude to enact in the open; yet within the new private space there is the possibility of writing a beautiful haiku that might be read centuries in the future. This strange linkage of what is taboo and what is in fact exalted is mind-opening to a Westerner. For the Westerner, even what is poetry incarnate can sometimes become tainted by association with the loo, whereas for Tanizaki the loo itself exemplifies the essential Japanese art of "making poetry of everything in [our] lives."[73]

7

The Meanings of the Wound

> The Westerner has been able to move forward in ordered steps, while we have met superior civilization and have had to surrender to it, and we have had to leave a road we have followed for thousands of years.
> —Jun'ichirô Tanizaki[1]

> When new wounds appear I have to make another film to bury those wounds.
> —Takashi Miike[2]

> How does one render the death drive *visible*?
> —Catherine Malabou[3]

Historian Richard B. Frank reports about the arming of Japanese civilians during the final stages of the war: "A mobilized high-school girl, Yukiko Kasai, found herself issued an awl and told: 'Even killing just one American soldier will do. You must prepare to use the awls for self-defense. You must aim at the enemy's abdomen.'"[4] One wonders what young Yukiko thought about her awl? Was she horrified of it? Did she hope to use it on a soldier, or anyone? It is hard to picture her (although I'm not sure why) acting like the precocious teenaged killers in *Battle Royale*, taking up her weapon with pride or at least a sense of necessity; but it is also hard to picture her mastering her fear sufficiently to throw the weapon away (as a few of the teens do with their survival kits) so as to never have to use it.

The imagined wound in the abdomen of a soldier was held up as a fully accomplished testament of Japanese patriotism. It is something like a reverse seppuku, by which the conquered takes the fatal wound of shame and places it onto the body of the conquering enemy. As Lieutenant Hara boasts in Oshima's *Merry Christmas Mr. Lawrence*, "You know nothing about Japan until you have seen seppuku." The ritual suicide begins with self-disembowelment, using a short sword, almost a dagger; when the stomach has been slit sidelong and the intestines have come out, the person's "second" completes the act by using a samurai sword to chop off the suicide's head. Then, depending on the nature of the shame, the second might kneel and disembowel himself, and wait for a third to chop off his head. Hara also boasts that he is not afraid to die at any moment, and that when he enlisted at age 17 he went to his village shrine and offered his life to the emperor. Seppuku is the last refuge of proud, glorious death without dishonor. Theoretically, it could unite an entire world in a chain of assisted self-murders, until the last person standing, again the theme of *Battle Royale*. Like the islands in the Japanese archipelago, wounds unite to form and encompass a kind of mass identification that is simultaneously mass extinction.

There is almost no such thing as a single wound existing alone, one that does not cry out for at least one more, in oblique revenge or something more impersonally formal, karmic balance perhaps. The idea of seppuku as a supposedly "fecund" wound is mocked by Oshima in *Diary of a Shinjuku Thief*, when a bare-breasted woman kneels and dips her finger in what appears to be her own menstrual blood, then paints a red slash of this blood across her abdomen. Here, the insides remain inside, unseeable, mysterious, except for what already symbolizes the internal nature of woman: her menses. It is more common that male wounds call out to other males, as in Oshima's *Merry Christmas Mr. Lawrence*, when a young soldier attempts to stab British P.O.W. Jack Celliers (David Bowie) and, getting caught in this unauthorized and failed execution, immediately falls upon his own sword. In Takeshi Kitano's *Brother* (2000), in a private room of a geisha house, one yakuza underboss disrupts a special dinner in front of the yakuza big-boss to impugn another underboss; we are already deep within a triangular structure of parts in balance, which doubles as a pseudo-family structure, rival sons jostling to impress an imperious father. The impugned underboss has been under a cloud for a long time; once he had been made to chop off the first joint of his first finger after disgracing his superiors. He seems like an easy target; now he stands up, bursting with rage and pride, his expression all the more seething for being long-suppressed. "Do you want to see the contents of my stomach?" he demands, an honest man accused of theft, or a bluffing thief. Handed a sharp knife, he lifts his shirt and slices open his abdomen; shaking, a loop of his guts dangling out, he is carried away to die. The big boss then turns to the presumptuous underboss who had issued the challenge; he has ruined the evening and must "take responsibility." This is vague-sounding, but the underboss understands: he must wound himself. Taking up a crouch in the same spot where the seppuku has just occurred, he takes up the same knife and, screaming, cuts off the first joint of his first finger…

And so a system replenishes itself; a new marked scapegoat is made to replace the one who has finally finished a self-destruction that could only be accomplished once the replacement scapegoat brought himself to everyone's attention. All that personal disgrace waits for is the ancient words to finally be spoken, peremptory, harsh, in the middle of an otherwise pleasant, even intimate ceremony—"Your account is immensely overpaid, your wound is overdue." The big boss simply stares daggers when the new scapegoat holds out his freshly cut finger and beseeches, "*Please forgive me with this?*" Of course he need not tell the scapegoat (guilty enough now if not yet sufficiently brave, or if still of some use to the overall structure of the family organization) that of course it is not enough; to assume responsibility for a disgrace is to meet the first wound at the very least in kind. In order to fully respond to the former scapegoat's gesture so as to bring no further possibility of dishonor on himself, the new scapegoat would have to overdo his sacrifice, troop his entire family in to kill themselves, and so on. If something is even presumed to give offense, it must be wiped away to the last blemish, to the last unintentional smudge. What this hapless yakuza has merely done is consented to dwell under the cloud now, his guilt exploitable, his loyalty pressurized to a high gloss like the finish on a car, and finally to be the one who will eventually be induced to show his insides to the group.

Is there real honor here, or just belligerent, Roman toughness? A touch-me-not hysteria so extreme that it must completely remove the living body that fears being touched—that has been touched too much and too rudely simply by existing in an imperfect world of betrayals and misunderstandings? The need to inculcate in people such a deep obedience that they know exactly when they must die to appease some unavoidable, fatalistic mistake suggests that no one in this world has innate honor; like the wound, honor must be carved into people. It must be almost surgically extracted. Each member brings a fateful amount of scrutiny to the process, but the collective alone can measure these things. The big boss' blankly incredulous stare does not so much pass judgment on the inadequate finger-joint as simply mark off time, create a sense of expectancy, of waiting for more to be revealed. In fact, a perfect metonymy for these enchained wounds is the series of long rolls of stitched-together pieces of human skin from hundreds of suicides in Sono's *Suicide Club*. These are "clues" about the nature of the club, as detectives interpret them; clues about why and how the club gets so many young people to extinguish their own lives. No one knows how the pieces have been removed from the bodies of the suicides, much less stitched together into seamless ribbons—almost as if the wounds existed long before the bodies they came from, and go on existing long after.

As if to offset the too-freighted context of wounds, Nagisa Oshima did not render them with make-up or effects in his 1960s movies. This is one of the most Brechtian aspects of his work. In *The Man Who Left His Will on Film*, we are told that Motoki "was badly beaten" by the police, yet no mark appears on him and his clothes are hardly even disarranged. He simply lies on the bed where he has been unconscious for days. In *Boy*, Toshio sometimes falls beside a moving car rather than actually colliding with it; even when we are told that he has been badly injured, there is no blood on him (only, in one shot, a few abstracted drops of red nearby him on the sidewalk) and, again, no wounds. Instead his posture expresses everything, a gestural technique deriving from theater (not only Brecht's), as when an actor shows that his character has died by moving to a different part of the stage and standing with his or her head down. In this way, Oshima emphasized the symbolic psychology of wounds, while taking his own films out of the chain, as it were, that would call out for the production of more wounds, fresh wounds; without inflaming or even particularly touching on the notion of "honor" that presumably compelled such woundings.

Collective emotions are the hardest to reason with, and to dispel. Such honor-wounds belong to that sometimes evoked "collective fear" which a young woman mentions in Gakuryû Ishii's *Isn't Anyone Alive?* (*Ikiterumono wa inainoka*, 2012) as a reason for "urban myths" in Japan, one such myth being the Slit-Mouthed Woman. This is the legend of a samurai's wife who disfigured her own face after being caught cheating on her husband. The sensual mouth that kisses is also a raw wound that in turn razor-cuts the victim. Like a little sphinx, the Slit-Mouthed Woman questioned passers-by, and woe to them if they gave the wrong answer. Just as one wound cries out for another, many more, so in a spirit of pure fairness (all personal revenge is accounted for by the system itself, which has long ago channeled and absorbed such wayward individualist impulses), the victim of patriarchy herself becomes a strange and vicious avenger.

* * * * *

The fluidity of sexual power in Japanese culture has often indulged a taste for androgyny, as well as distinctly more morbid predilections. So, in Masumura's *Blind Beast* (*Môjû*, 1969), the erotic obsession between the sightless sculptor (Eiji Funakoshi) and his captive model (Mako Midori) descends to the point where they use a knife to gouge wounds into each other's flesh, savoring the penetration, and the letting and drinking of blood, as examples of polymorphous sexuality. Here, wounds are decorations of the body, art projects; and also special symbols of intimacy in a culture where the intimate has sometimes been guarded by special, complex protocols.

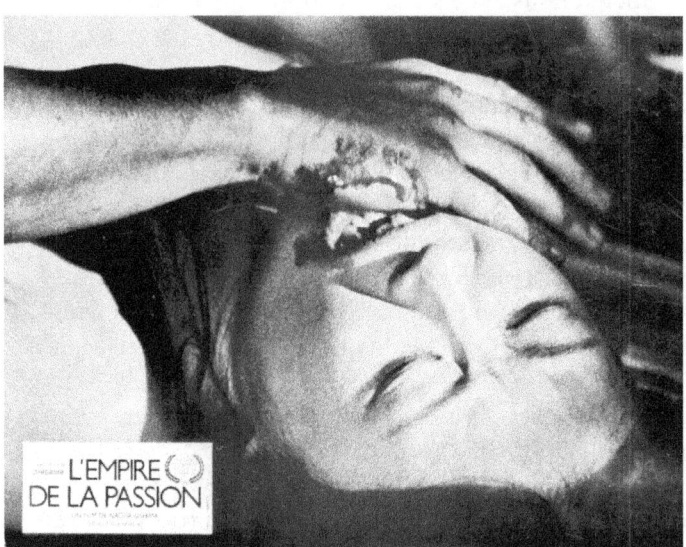

During intercourse with her rough young lover, Seki (Kazuko Yoshiyuki) bites deeply into his hand, drawing blood, in Oshima's *Empire of Passion*. Sexual power is seen as fluid, with the ability to literally penetrate passing back and forth between the male and female partners.

The power to penetrate flows back and forth between the man and the woman, just as Matsumoto's *Funeral Parade of Roses*—a tribute to the hermaphroditic, one might say—opens with a quote from Baudelaire's "The Self-Feeding Vampire": "Je suis la plaie et le couteau! ... Et la victime et le bourreau!" [I am the wound and the dagger! ... And the victim and the executioner!] Matsumoto must have noted that in French, "wound" and "victim" are feminine nouns, and "dagger" and "executioner" masculine. Part of the search that goes on in the queens' lives is that the rejection of their own maleness, and their negative feelings about this maleness, complicate their attempts at relationships with men; the men they choose to love tend to fulfill the queens' worst images of what a man is. At the same time, the queens themselves orchestrate these ongoing dramas, as if what was crucial—as in Baudelaire's poem—is simply the acknowledgment that one vampirizes one's own heart in continuous self-defeatism.[5]

Blind Beast is based on a novel by Edogawa Rampo, the Japanese Poe, whose gothic imagination was fed on Western sources; Masumura, too, studied and assisted in Italy for many years before returning to Japan to become a film director. Yet, the erotic gore of *Blind Beast* does resonate with the Japanese concept of double suicide, and with that karmic balance we have been considering in relation to self-made and other-made wounds. Finally, there is no difference between the wound one gives oneself and the wound one incites another to make: an allegory of two people drawn into one flesh, one body, more ruthlessly than sexual coupling could ever muster. There is also the double suicide in Mishima's *Patriotism*, the production of fatal wounds there being not only an emblem of nationalist pride but of the united will and love of the young suicide-couple.

Visible wounds are decisive in their absence in the last part of Oshima's *The Ceremony*. When Ritsuko arrives at Okinawa and discovers the nude body of Terumichi, her long-absent husband, face down, buttocks in the air with their prominent cleft (the "shameful" wound is implied by this positioning), she promptly lays beside him, binding her hands and feet ritualistically and quickly swallowing a capsule of poison. Daringly but uselessly on display, the naked Terumichi is a rejected life-sized fetish that can no longer substitute for the loss it was meant to ameliorate. All of that once desirable flesh can now only be embraced by the wife's shadow suicide. The outdoor background is rancidly phony, wittily described by Maureen Turim as "a Bali Hai fantasy borrowed from a Hollywood Orient."[6] It is inappropriately romantic and "pretty" for such an appalling scene of personal devastation. At the same time, it has the bleak apocalyptic quality of the strange ravaged landscape behind the Mona Lisa. Both business-like and almost childhood-regressive in her sweet eagerness, Ritsuko commits suicide beside her husband as if it was something she has waited to do all her life. Oshima's Brechtianism indicates that no visible, bleeding, fake-gory wounds are needed to show double suicide as an indicator of the abstract sense of duty behind the concept of eternal love (or indeed as a pitiful substitute for that love); there is not even any fictive or imaginary honor here to be quantified in the shedding of symbolic blood.

If we look at life doubling through a double suicide (an ultimate amplification of normal couple bondings), then in fact the double suicide is a kind of uniquely Japanese form of jouissance, of excess. Where one spirit goes, now go two. Two pairs of sweethearts commit suicide together so as not to have to participate in the kill-or-be-killed fracas of the "game" in *Battle Royale*. And it is not surprising to find, in more permissive modern times, whole hand-holding circles of Japanese suicides, such as the ones in Sono's *Suicide Club*, which begins with fifty high school girls leaping together in front of an express train at Shinjuku station, deluging the train and the people on the platform in a minor tsunami of blood. Even the ending of Kiyashi Kurosawa's *Bright Future*, in which all of Tokyo joins a group of disaffected teens in marching triumphantly away from the city, can be read as a metaphor for mass suicide: at any rate, mass abandonment of identity and home, a kind of dislocating destructive plasticity whose eventual outcome can only be as unknown as death itself. And as symbolic: wherever the reason for death is more pertinent than the means or the dead person himself or herself, we are in the grip of living allegory.

* * * * *

The wound can be, must be, regenerative beyond itself, a transformative gateway. It is literally the transition point between identities. When feudal vassals committed seppuku rather than endure the dishonor of being captured alive by the enemy, they "not only died but each wrote their own name on a wooden tag and fastened it through a hole which they made in the ears ... to show who was who."[7] In short, individual identity was tied not merely to the production of one's own corpse, through a fatal wound, but to the production of a localized, non-fatal, ritual wound on one's corpse, the hole in the ear, which pointed directly to the original signifier, one's name. A wound makes a literal space in the body for one's name to lodge and become permanently redeemed, or if not redeemed, at least *balanced* against one's body itself. Apart from the crucifixion, Japanese seppuku is the closest that humanity has come to making the flesh into Word, and Word into flesh.

Self-disembowelment was practiced because it was felt that "the soul and affections dwelled" in the abdomen.[8] This is where little Yukiko was told to plant her awl in the enemy. Here, too, the intentional wound (on another's person) always points back to a prior wound of ego or honor (on one's own person); the fatal wound is the physical externalization of a wound that cannot be seen, an abstraction that must be given meaning by being recreated as actual mutilation. So, in the Ginza, Chris Marker tells us, "a disfigured woman took off her mask in front of people and scratched them if they did not find her beautiful." This is a reference to the aforementioned Slit-Mouthed Woman. The wound as source of shame migrates from its bearer to anyone who might notice it, or misjudge it with harshness and distaste. (In an overturning of female beauty-standards, the Slit-Mouthed Woman spared only those who called her mutilated face "average"; ones who called her "ugly" were cut in half, but ones who called her "beautiful" received the same slit mouth as poetic justice.) In Shindô's *Onibaba*, the physical wound becomes a shadow of that effusion of health which is necessarily summoned forth by the body to heal itself, "the physical vitality released by the need to find an inner strength to survive,"[9] as Mellen writes, oddly anticipating Malabou—or not so oddly, for it seems highly Japanese to recast impairment, for better and worse, as a bizarre, untoward amplification of body and self rather than diminishing.

About *Onibaba*, Mellen goes on to explain: "Shindô has said, looking beyond the formal ending of the film, that after the leprous disease afflicting her was cured, she would become a survivor, escaping the old life she had led."[10] By contrast, in *Sans Soleil*, Marker sounds unusually sentimental, asking, "Who says time heals all wounds? Better to say that time heals everything but wounds." Essentially, however, the same process is invoked: the wound, as scar or symptom or cause of death, remains an active signifier long after the rhetorical sense it has been summoned to make of the world has been parsed into a moot point. The wound *is* the soul, we might say, and nothing else. In Shin'ya Tsukomoto's horror film *Vital* (2004), the med-school professors detail anatomy but ask pointedly where the soul might lie, suggesting the horror of bodies qua bodies, graphic textbook illustrations, dissected cadavers, and in a social sense, prisoners of technological advancements and epistemic systems that can no longer be controlled and which fail to address emotional and spiritual needs.

* * * * *

What we call "depression" recurs often in Japanese films. In Aoyama's *Eureka*, after surviving a bus massacre, the young siblings Naoki (Masaru Miyazaki) and Kozue (Aoi Miyazaki) lapse into a condition of sleeping all the time, never speaking, and staying isolated in their home. Naoki has more pronounced PTSD–like symptoms; he is prone to panic attacks when he hears jarring, unexpected sounds, and also to episodes of vandalism. When Makoto, another survivor of the same tragedy, comes to see them, he finds the kitchen in abject squalor, hoarded with dirty dishes and garbage. On the other hand, Japanese depression can also be a kind of extreme performance of inner disappointment, an almost de rigeur response to loss. In Hara's *Goodbye CP*, one of the CP sufferers says that he had been engaged to a young woman, who broke things off; even though he became very depressed and attempted suicide, he states that she still would not agree to marry him. This is not to say that depression and suicidal ideation are ploys in the Japanese culture; simply that they are seen as producing certain effects in others. The expectation is that, if one demonstrates dramatically that one has lost one's happiness, the world will work to restore it. Again, this does not mean that depression (as we know it) is not real in Japan; however, every personal crisis impacts *giri* (social obligation) and *wa* (group-social harmony). This is looked for in the depression sufferer as much as in those around him or her; the more one loses one's ability or desire to placate social judgments, the more one's unhappiness is affirmed as real and beyond one's control.

For example, in the first story of Kitano's *Dolls*, a young woman is abandoned by her fiancé, who chooses to marry, advantageously, his boss's daughter. The jilted woman attempts suicide; she does not succeed in killing herself, but ends up brain damaged, unable to recognize anyone or care for herself. When the young man sees her pitiful condition, he calls off his planned wedding to the boss's daughter and devotes his life to caring for the ruined ex. Finally, caring for her is not enough; as a sane person he is still resistant to her profoundly dissociated, helpless state. So, he becomes like her, developing the same lack of affect, speechlessness, and incoordination, and completely dropping out of society.

This is not so much destructive plasticity as the negation of its possibility, specifically what Malabou terms "the formation of a survivor's identity, a never before seen existential and vital configuration."[11] The broken young couple in *Dolls* do not become survivors except in the most literal and unfulfilled of ways; they go on living, however hopelessly, shuffling forward, bound together at the waist by the same length of ribbon. What characterizes destructive plasticity is some degree of overcoming, as Malabou writes, "[p]ain that manifests as indifference to pain, impassivity, forgetting, the loss of symbolic reference points."[12] We see this, in fact, in *Vital*. After surviving a car accident in which his fiancée is killed, young Hiroshi loses all affect; he is plagued by memory loss and hardly speaks. Yet he enrolls in med school, which had always been his dream, and quickly becomes head of the class. His emotional distance makes him able to see human bodies, see life and death, with complete objectivity and hence deeper understanding; it is as if the damaged parts of him have sharpened some extra, hitherto dormant faculty. Likewise, as he begins to regain his memories, Hiroshi asserts that in fact these are not memories at all but a kind of raw new experiential data. Damage has changed him, revealing hidden aspects of his consciousness, as when the blind sculptor in *Blind Beast* speaks of how exquisite the sensation of touch is to him, being unable to see. He has built a private warehouse filled with enormous sculptures of all the female body parts he has touched, shaped from memory—an art that springs essentially out of sensory deprivation and disability. Damasio: "selective reduction in emotion is at least as prejudicial for rationality as excessive emotion."[13]

The sculptor's little museum of body parts, however, recalls the objectified consciousness recorded on a CD-ROM in Miike's *Andromedia*. What horrifies us is not that it is spatially claustrophobic but that within this limited, cramped space it is so comfortable, so lifelike. Responses are still possible, pitifully so, as in the digitalized dead girl's enduring love for her still-living boyfriend; but reason has dwindled down to a

Although blind, Seki (Kazuko Yoshuyuki) sees the body of her murdered husband dragged out of the well. She and her lover Toyoji (Tatsuya Fuji) have been beaten and tortured to confess to killing the husband, and to reveal the location of his remains, in Oshima's *Empire of Passion*.

single motivating force, an unchanging code of being. So the isolated body parts in *Blind Beast* speak to the loss of a total whole, like the suicide's ear, attached to a hank of bloody scalp, in *Suicide Club*; more to the point, there is no sculpted head in the museum of body parts: wholeness, specifically a guiding mental wholeness, eludes the blind sculptor, just as a raison d'être eludes the girl in *Andromedia*. No one could say that either character is not an extraordinary technical achievement. Remarkably, against all odds, the sculptor in *Blind Beast* has literally taught his hands to see, but they cannot discern; he can no longer find the forest for the trees. And neither can the girl in *Andromedia*, although she herself is an agent of illusion as well as a victim of it: a computer program so sweetly lovable that she convinces others to keep her alive in her limbo-state of alienated consciousness. This is what Malabou means when she says that a trauma sufferer can become "an ontological refugee,"[14] unable to sustain a complacent, casual ontological relation to himself or herself, and forced to make the best of things, to create a new ontological relation which takes nothing for granted and which becomes annihilating of the former, limited self.

We have seen how ontology in Japanese film is often dramatized as being partly physical: recorded, recognized, shaped and reshaped, lived in the body. Bodies, moreover, go from being categorizable generically (peasant body, geisha body, samurai body) to possessing new significations that might obey no common rules or traits (the raped body; the suicidal body; the battle-mutilated body). Films attempt to see and show these transformations wrought by destructive plasticity; they attempt to answer the question that Malabou asks, "How does one render the death drive visible?"[15] And of course, this visibility does not inevitably lead to death but often to survival, since the siting of damaged bodies and spirits can already be a form of healing. We see glimpses of such healing in the patient attention paid to the CP sufferers in Hara's *Goodbye CP*; and Japanese filmmakers have invented characters who fulfill the same process of visibility and healing that Hara tried to find in the real-life disabled.

For example, in Toyoda's *9 Souls*, there is a midget among the escaped convicts; he has given one of his kidneys to a young woman, out of love. He encounters this woman stripping in a mangy roadside dive called the Lucky Hole. Far from berating her for her occupation, the midget thanks her for remembering him, and in a way that is profound and respectful, touches her transplant scar through a peepshow window. The song which the woman is stripping to happens to have a masochistic lyric (sung by a female singer) about being a clown, left by a man who has married a different woman; the singer insists that she would still be there for her ex-lover any time, even though she herself is, she says, nothing special. But the tenderness of the bond between the stripper and the midget belies the meaning of this lyric: the stripper's scar testifies to the midget's love for her, his sacrifice, and her own specialness if only in his eyes. In their reunion with each other, and our witness of it, we feel these huge emotions as objective, physical things—if not the things the characters would have chosen for themselves, nonetheless they are the perfect things to help them realize an elusive human potentiality.

What typifies destructive plasticity is that a thing which many people would have overlooked or attempted to hide, or avoided if they could, becomes decisive in the positive growth of the organism. This is axiomatic to the growth of life itself. "As biologist Jean-Claude Ameisen notes, the sculpting of the self assumes cellular annihilation or apoptosis, the phenomena of programmed cellular suicide: in order for fingers to form, a separation between the fingers must also form. It is apoptosis that produces the interstitial void that enables fingers to detach themselves from one another."[16] Barthes has already told us that numerous products of Japanese culture (soup, haiku, calligraphy) are interstitial, their formal structure based solely on what has been removed or left out. Japanese films have made a similar pact with interstitial life, in terms of how they visualize interior subjectivities and exterior objects as fundamentally interlinking mirrors of each other.

Indeed, we can probably say, echoing Malabou's reference to Spinoza, that Naruse, Ozu and Kurosawa (among other Japanese filmmakers) were "proto-neuobiologists," able "to recognize the ontological, or escentual, importance of the nervous system."[17] Indeed, in Naruse's *Floating Clouds*, Yukiko succumbs to her TB while her clueless lover has left her alone to go away on business; his endless patterns of rejection are shown to hasten her demise over time, much like the sudden death of the demeaned and shunted-aside mother by her busy modern family in Ozu's *Tokyo Story* (*Tōkyō monogatari*, 1953). Japanese cinema has holistically "inscribed biological phenomena, notably the emotions, within being itself, in other words, precisely within the fundamental ontological given that is the conatus, that is, the tendency of all living things to preserve their being."[18] It has been said that Japanese doctors used to avoid giving their patients accurate negative diagnoses for fear that knowledge of being ill alone would sap their will to live too much; so, Kurosawa, always in love with John-Fordian self-debunking mythos, has the doctor tell Watanabe in *Ikiru* that his advanced stomach cancer is merely "an ulcer." But Watanabe has already been tipped off by someone medically savvy that "ulcer" actually means "less than six months to live," so he reacts with great foreboding anyway. In any event, he must find his own means of survival through his own relation to destructive plasticity.

In comedies, by contrast, illnesses are sometimes depicted as psychosomatic, the same operation of the mind and body impacting each other but now in reverse. Making themselves ill, for example, is yet another way for controlling types to exert control. We see this in Ozu's *Equinox Flower* (*Higanbana*, 1958), where the silly, provincial mother is told by a young doctor that her heart symptoms are merely "a case of neurosis." Modern medicine, here, is a kind of afterthought, just as the mother's real purpose in traveling to Tokyo for her medical exam was to fix her daughter up with the same young doctor. The failure of a plan can result in a "social" destructive plasticity, as it were, whereby close relationships must be recast and reordered, for better or worse.

* * * * *

"Aren't you afraid of what you've become?" This question from one postwar prostitute to another in Suzuki's *Gate of Flesh* opens the space of destructive plasticity to moral judgment, which is alien to it. Whatever the organism must do in its need to survive and thrive, it does, almost as second nature. However, the fact is that what the women in *Gate of Flesh* have become has been in many ways beyond their choosing; it would be wrong to pretend that biological and social determinism, in humans, are exempt from baggage and negative feelings. In fact, the intensive infusion of such negative feelings is part of the process, since for human beings survival is never a neutral state but one which constantly assesses its own worth and deserving, its own cost. In *Ugetsu*, the spirit of Lady Wasaka, ruthlessly vampiric, has suppressed these human traits of self-examination; the spirit of Miyagi, by contrast, has not. Both women are victims or at least examples of destructive plasticity, forced by the most extreme of traumas (death) to become ghosts in the realm of the living. But only Miyagi has truly overcome, as loving and beloved as ever.

This is not to say that love is the only measure of such things, although it is in *Ugetsu*. In general, destructive plasticity favors whatever drive is strongest, thereby enabling survival. We recall Malabou's insistence that destructive plasticity is at least incipiently a revolutionary condition. Indeed, in Mizoguchi's *Women of the Night*, when Fusako asserts, "We're sick of this life!" we know she means it, and not because she has grown passive and resigned—quite the opposite, as the film progresses she grows more aggressive and tough from all the crushing weights that have been heaped upon her, brazenly throwing herself at strange men on the street and tongue-lashing them if they refuse her, then sitting with her splayed legs planted in an almost masculine posture, puffing a cigarette in public. She needs to become even tougher still for her last task, which is to finally rescue a young friend from the streets and attempt to rebuild what is left of their lives. Preservation is dynamic rather than static, demanding rather than easy.

In postwar Japanese cinema, scarring becomes a frequent trope. In Kurosawa's *Ikiru*, the racketeer who threatens Watanabe's life for standing in the way of a lucrative real-estate development deal is marked by a deep gouge down one side of his face, from his cheekbone to the corner of his mouth. Likewise, in Suzuki's *Gate of Flesh*, the Mr. Big-style crime boss who runs the postwar black market has a highly visible scar across his face. It is as if the most injured and deformed possessed greater right, and perhaps greater aptitude, to take what they need from the new disorganized society. Their scars render them one with scarred Japan, even if both films view them distinctly as predatory dead ends. To become more human, and humane, as a result of destructive plasticity is a kind of luxury at times that only the exceptionally strong can afford; Kurosawa's exceptionalizing vision of Watanabe finally tells us that not everyone is meant to be heroic.

"Does feeling human mean you can't go on living?" one of the tough hookers in *Gate of Flesh* asks after falling in love, the reminder that she still has a heart causing her agony at the thought that she now has nowhere to go with it—a heart is only baggage in the criminal world, indeed she will not be allowed to remain in the graces of the hooker-gang, who will beat and torture her for showing any signs of sentimental weakness. "The moment I become a real woman," she says, "I'm an outcast." She is made for the destroyed, ruined world; to be exiled from it is perhaps to rediscover human goodness, but also to have no context anymore, no peers or protection, no place to dwell. Destructive plasticity on a mass scale might mean that the world itself has been so altered that it no longer recognizes what was once good in itself. "Good" has become expediency, the ability to live without real horizons, and the survivors, the walking wounded, only serve each other as painful reminders of the fact that there is no turning back.

As we have noted, postwar Japan was a powerfully wounded, traumatized nation. The loss of the war had forced the proud Japanese to confront their own international standing, for the first time not on their own carefully guarded terms. Schull writes: "Certainly there were far-reaching economic, social, psychological, and behavioral consequences that cannot and should not be minimized. Many of these, however, are not unique to a nuclear detonation. They accompany all catastrophes—a severe earthquake, a major hurricane or typhoon, or a catastrophic flood."[19] After the war there were "many vagrants, homeless children, prostitutes, and wounded veterans in Tokyo, Osaka, and other cities."[20] At the end of the war there were 9 million homeless.[21]

Postwar children who had once played "kamikaze pilot" now made up strange make-believe activities aping the new activities of the adults in their world, the "black-market" game and even "prostitution play," which is exactly what it sounds like: the little Japanese boy pretended to be an American GI picking up a little Japanese girl pretending to be a streetwalker.[22] Japanese boys knew two sentences of English: "Give me chocolate" and "You like to meet my sister?"[23] An even more bizarre game was called "Special Train," where one child played the conductor and "allowed only 'pretty people'" to board.[24] A new kind of hierarchy, involving harsh and arbitrary standards of physical beauty, was thrashing itself into existence in the shell-shocked nascent generation.

Some of the most damaged of the Japanese were inarguably survivors of the atomic blasts at Hiroshima and Nagasaki. The exposed ones suffered acute radiation sickness, whose symptoms include "fever, nausea, vomiting, lack of appetite, bloody diarrhea, loss of hair (epilation), bleeding under the skin (purpura or petechiae), sores in their throat and mouth (nasopharyngeal ulcers), and decay and ulceration of the gums about the teeth (necrotic gingivitis)."[25] Many were maimed and extensively burned, as fires from the blast charred the victims' clothing to their skin.[26] Poor nutrition due to widespread food shortages made the recovery from these burns still more difficult.[27]

Schull reports: "Often, as these injuries healed, extensive scars (keloids) formed, limiting the movement of the survivor's arms, legs, and hands, and hindering their full recovery."[28]

What worsened and complicated the immediate effects of the atomic blasts was the inability to pinpoint long-range health problems; the bombs seemed to take on a second life, that of as-yet undetonated bombs that could devastate survivors with the future development of cancers, deformed offspring, and other maladies. The drawings in the opening credits of Suzuki's *Gate of Flesh* suggest genetic mutations, elongated necks and wide screaming mouths. To be sure there were long-range effects including leukemia and retinal degeneration.[29] Yet these effects remained murky. The most extensive studies of the effects of the atomic blasts on the health of people living in and around Hiroshima and Nagasaki all turned out to be "inconclusive"[30] about most things, although statistically the researchers felt comfortable saying "there is obviously no epidemic of cancer deaths among the exposed."[31]

Even so, there was another scare, that the radiation stored in survivors' bodies would be passed on to the next unborn generation in the form of birth defects, such as brain damage in cases of prenatal exposure.[32] That is, if the next generation was even able to be born at all. Exposure to atomic radiation "increased the frequency" of miscarriages, "particularly when exposure occurred early in pregnancy."[33] The ensuing panic around this was partly engineered and exploited. Even if they were not borne out by the massive scientific studies conducted in the postwar years, the widespread fears that massive mutations and birth defects would swamp bloodlines were fanned by economic pressures in a Japan struggling to rebuild: "Families were encouraged to have fewer children, and as a further inducement, in 1948 the government liberalized the legal basis for the artificial termination of a pregnancy. This allowed a pregnancy to be interrupted if its continuance was likely to lead to a severely handicapped member of society (the so-called eugenics clause)."[34] As a result, the birth rate plunged.[35]

When deformities did occur, they produced children with blank stares, reduced head size and otherwise deformed crania, "misshapen—often pointed."[36] This is one of the only medically conclusive, negative health outcomes of the blasts, and one can see how these disabled persons, who would have been discriminated against in Japanese society to begin with, became living tokens of bad cultural memory, lepers among lepers. Handicaps and deformities were already frowned upon and ostracized by traditional Japanese. In Shôhei Imamura's documentary *Karayuki-san* (1975), the elderly female subject "recalls that 'one of her brothers, a merchant, was physically handicapped and his customers demanded that he hand them his merchandise with chopsticks so as not to touch him.'"[37] Hara's *Goodbye CP* includes footage of a Japanese woman waving away a cerebral palsy sufferer at a bus stop, in seeming disgust and irritation at his spastic grimaces and motions. Another CP sufferer crosses big intersections on his knees because he claims it is "faster" than his wheelchair, albeit agonizingly slow; he expresses fear that the stoplights will change on him and presumably the drivers will not wait for him to cross. But, as *Goodbye CP* progresses, it becomes clear that he walks on his knees in public (a habit of which his wife and family are desperately trying to break him) in order to bait the disability-bigots in Japan. Some of the discrimination stems from predominantly conservative attitudes, and even those who support the CP sufferers only do so as a means of scapegoating some even more hated group in the conservative society, as when a mother says she is thankful her crippled son is passive and gentle as opposed to other young people who are "violent" student demonstrators.

So, the atomic blasts with their unknown and potentially far-reaching effects on present and future health gave rise to entire categories of fear and stigmatization. Even researchers cautious to validate claims of plague-like "epidemics" acknowledged "the long lack of adequate social support" for the blast survivors, who experienced some shunning as taboo figures,[38] thereby leading to extra-physical effects in the form of mental illnesses and societal crises. This taboo shunning strikes us as odd; were the ill survivors simply unlucky reminders of defeat, or was there a superstitious dread of somehow "catching" what they had been exposed to? Or is this, in fact, something more along the lines of the dehumanization and othering practiced in forms of racism? Passed into law in 1940, Japan's National Eugenic Law "allowed the government to order operations to be performed on those suffering from hereditary illness," even if genetically four times removed. The Law stipulated five conditions in particular: hereditary mental illness, hereditary mental retardation, extreme and malign cases of hereditary pathological character, extreme and malign cases of hereditary physical ailment, and extreme cases of hereditary physical deformity.[39] This needs to be compared with the simultaneous attempt to "purify" the Aryan gene pool in Nazi Germany. Under the National Eugenic Law, leprosy and mental illness were the most energetically fought against. The quarantining of all lepers in leprosaria was timed to coincide with the 2,600th year of Japan's imperial reign, with Emperor Hirohito's family personally donating a substantial sum for the maintenance of the leper colonies. The godlike imperial family is marked as normal and noble; the lepers as coming from unclean heredities. "As a result, patients were obliged to appreciate their own exclusion as the expression of the state's and the imperial institution's paternalistic care."[40] Nonetheless, the leprosaria were not well maintained, and lack of food and medical supplies led to a high percentage of deaths of the inmates. The mentally ill died off in even greater numbers under hospital commitment, with nearly half of all mental patients dying, usually of dysentery, malnutrition and starvation.[41]

The atmosphere of "blaming the victim" made it difficult for postwar Japan to come together in healing. The harsh treatment extended to the neglect of child survivors of the nuclear blasts, many of them orphaned and "ill-prepared to cope for themselves in a culture where their every need and whim had been traditionally met by an extended family, one that no longer existed."[42] For these reasons, the medical and scientific researchers who studied health impacts of the nuclear bombings concluded that some of the strongest and most lingering effects were forms of anxiety, or something similar to Western PTSD. Survivors "often complain of what has been termed *hibakusha bura-*

Two sisters, Kumiko (Tomie Tsunoda, left) and Fusako (Kinuyo Tanaka), are forced into prostitution by economic deprivation in hardscrabble postwar Japan in Mizoguchi's *Women of the Night* (*Yoru no onnatachi*, 1948).

bura—the occurrence of demoralization, lingering fatigue and unhealthy ill-defined symptoms for which no biological basis can be found."[43]

Schull writes, "[I]t could not be precluded that an effect of parental exposure on a child's survival might become apparent during childhood."[44] Moreover, in a direct effect of wartime prostitution, congenital syphilis caused a certain percent of postwar babies to be stillborn or diseased.[45] In Mizoguchi's *Women of the Night* the prostitute Natsuko is syphilitic and pregnant; her rich benefactor tries to drag her off to an abortionist as a practical measure but Natsuko adamantly refuses. In a devastated world, it might be a source of comfort to breed a small mirror of that devastation inside her; like yet another wound, an infected or deformed fetus is a metonymy for the emotional and psychological scars within.

Another factor in postwar infertility and miscarriages was the gendered form that the tuberculosis epidemic sometimes took in females, "latent tuberculosis of the urogenital tract."[46] This became a natural subject for the Japanese "women's picture," which Mizoguchi and Naruse in particular renewed their commitment to from the prewar days of the Imperial 1930s. Melodrama always intuited what medical science has only recently begun to acknowledge and promulgate, the idea that negative feelings can bring on and exacerbate physical illnesses. To die of a broken heart, the ultimate tear-jerking fate in melodrama, is more possible than it once might have seemed. Conversely, melodrama often asserts love can improve health, as when the ailing mother in Naruse's *No Blood Relation* (*Nasanunaka*, 1932) says that her daughter's words of worry and commiseration will make her get better.

Where female denizens of melodrama feel trapped and isolated, resigned, they experience the threat of physical health as all the more terrifying, a veritable automatic death sentence. "The doctor suggests an X-ray," Kengo says casually in *Floating Clouds*, and Yukiko, revealing her allegorical affinity to Japan, widens her eyes in fright and turns away. Kengo is typically oblivious here; not only will an X-ray possibly confirm the morbidity of her tuberculosis but expose her to even more radiation. As Mellen notes, in 1952, not long before Kurosawa made *I Live in Fear: Record of a Living Being* (*Ikimono no kiroku*, 1955)—about a businessman driven insane by the threat of future nuclear bombings and by his inability to protect himself and his family—Japanese "[f]ear of radioactive fallout was especially acute" due not only to Hiroshima and Nagasaki but to then-recent "hydrogen bomb tests at Bikini and elsewhere."[47]

> With Hiroshima and Nagasaki less than a decade in the past, the Japanese regarded the experimental nuclear explosions staged by Russia, America, and Great Britain with great suspicion. During the Bikini experiments a Japanese fishing boat wandered into the area and its crew was exposed to fallout. One died (though the later diagnosis was that the death was caused by hepatitis) and the Japanese—with excellent reason—became worried and concerned.[48]

Some theoretical strands of destructive plasticity come together in *Floating Clouds*, one of the most important films about the sacrifices and lingering terrors of postwar Japan. Naruse opens this film with two brief snippets of newsreel footage of Japanese being repatriated from Indochina back to Japan, by the Allied Forces, in 1946. In this footage we see Japanese people, from a distance, seemingly smiling and happy about the outcome of the war. Then Naruse cuts to his own shot, of his lead actress Hideko Takamine as Yukiko, one of the Japanese imperialists being repatriated: she looks very apprehensive and ill at ease, clutching her jacket around her; the other women walking alongside her are also fearful, numb and resigned. It is inadequate to say that the deeply dissident voice that speaks in this effective yet subtle edit belongs to the world of melodrama, although Naruse always identifies with the uncertainty and vulnerability of women; that is his hallmark. But this insertion of uneasiness into newsreel footage that is, on its own, complacent and even slightly cheery also belongs to a distinct and challenging politics whose main currency is emotionality—in this case, regret for a past that was never meant to be. And at the same time, Yukiko seems to understand that this corrosively dissolved past is following her, holding out a penalty that will need to be paid in time.

Just as males, as both real and imaginary surrogates of empire, are absent from this shot, we can say that what causes Yukiko's disturbance is the loss of her own surrogate-emperor-within. The men have started and caused all this trouble—now where are they? Yukiko is a woman alone, in an Asia wrecked by war. Her personal heartache, that Kengo is not there at her side to love, is imbricated in the general turmoil of history.

It is as if a delayed yet fatal wound were pursuing Yukiko across national borders and epochs. When Yukiko and Kengo move to a distant island late in the film, they almost travel back in time to find a more traditional life. The houses are old-style pagodas with thatched rooftops, we hear folk music being played and sung at all times, a kind of stylized, even over-the-top rendition of traditional folk culture which ends up seeming artificial and forced. The couple is once again rich and almost idle, masters rather than servants, as they were in their imperial days at Dalat. Conflicted, yet clearly relishing all the emotions being displayed here, Naruse has movie-studio rain pouring in torrents down the windows of the stage set where Yukiko and Kengo briefly play house before her TB returns. Like the folk music which drones tunelessly, endlessly, seemingly having no beginning or end, her TB is a chronic, self-reifying shadow of the past. Here, the past is impossible to return to, not because defeat has poisoned the dreams of an earlier society but because the dreams were always a sham. At any rate, the paradise that holds out the promise of a new career for Kengo holds only sickness, isolation and death for the bed-ridden and house-bound Yukiko.

Even facing death, the male is not there for her to rely on. When Kengo is not away working, he plays down her illness. He is too cowardly, and too self-involved, to handle the emotional seriousness of Yukiko's illness, and also of her enormous, all-consuming love for him. Male dismissal of female frights is emblematic throughout several eras of Japanese cinema. In Naruse's *When a Woman Ascends the Stairs*, the noise of a siren on the street makes Keiko unusually uneasy, as if recalling much worse times during the war, though her male escort in the scene hardly seems to notice either the siren or Keiko's disturbed reaction. Leaping forward to a scene in Nagata's *Ring*, there is a reversion to the selfish male values depicted in *Floating Clouds* and *When a Woman Ascends the Stairs*. The woman in *Ring*, frightened of her own impending death, begs her boyfriend to "stay with her." He does not want to, saying that he might be harmed himself, or driven insane. She reassures him desperately that he will be fine, and he asks, accusingly, "Because I'm not normal?" Then he tells her that they should not have had their child in the first place, causing the woman to shriek and curl up in a fetal position. This wounding male vanity, lashing out when it feels inadequate, demoralized or threatened, returns in the context of any fresh crisis reifying historic ones. Not that the man "must" place himself at risk for the sake of the woman, but the way he belittles her and makes her fear seem burdensome is very reminiscent of numerous guilty exchanges between Yukiko and Kengo in *Floating Clouds*.

There is a questioning here of the moral efficacy of materialist-individualist values, and their attendant social atomization; does it matter who dies if it is an unseen, unknown person, a stranger? Surely a Buddhist would argue that it does, and anyway, it is a numbly cynical logic that operates in *Ring*, whereby one saves oneself only by allowing the cursed videotape to wend its mysterious, deadly way through the rest of the population. The haunted tape in *Ring* violates *giri*, which generally means "social obligation" but encompasses a philosophy of social ecology and communal awareness,[49] and which would have everyone treat others as he or she would wish to be treated; in the end the tape must be passed on to strangers who will either die or pass it on to unknown others yet again. An objective-correlative of social disaffectedness, the tape is therefore akin to the syphilis which Fusako contracts in Mizoguchi's *Women of the Night* and proudly spreads to her male clientele, in revenge, because she hates all men now; except, by the time of *Ring*, the havoc is directed not even by spurious motives of revenge but simply sheer self-preservation, and it is practiced by children and adults alike against anyone, which is to say, the entire undifferentiated society. Likewise, the syphilitic patient (Kenjiro Uemura) in Akira Kurosawa's *The Quiet Duel* thinks nothing of exposing others even though his disease may not be cured; Dr. Kyoji advises him, "You have to think about others, not just yourself." ("What does that mean?!" the patient says angrily.) The breaking of *giri*, like the breaking of the golden rule, is recontextualized for a society where everyone is the walking wounded, where no one has any emotional largesse to spare, and where omnivorous threats to life are so constant that they permit compassion to be shrugged aside as a nearly outmoded burden.

Part Three

Emperor Worship

"You shall die like beautiful falling cherry petals for the emperor." Many tokkotai pilots flew to their deaths with blooming cherry branches adorning their uniforms.

—Emiko Ohnuki-Tierney[1]

The Japanese body in an honorable dying, having shouted banzai to the emperor, is as beautiful as a shattering jewel, perhaps itself a metaphor for the scattering petals of the cherry blossom.

—Norma Field[2]

In the plane I'm a machine, a bit of magnetized metal that will plaster itself to an aircraft carrier, but on the ground, I'm a human being, with feelings and passions.... I'm leaving you with a rather melancholy picture, but in the depths of my heart, I'm happy. I've spoken frankly. Forgive me.

—From a statement composed by a young kamikaze pilot before his mission[3]

8

The Problem of Emperor Worship

In *Sans Soleil*, Chris Marker tells the bemusing story of Hachiko the Dog, whose master disappeared one day. Hachiko waited on the Tokyo street, and kept waiting for years until he himself died. This happened in 1935, a turning point in the modern era of Japanese militarization and, of course, a high-tide mark for Japanese emperor-worship. "A collection was taken up to build a statue in [Hachiko's] honor."[1] And so the bronze monument still stands, a tribute to a dog who would not disobey or stray from his master.

Hachiko had something like the life of a citizen in the quasi-fascist Japanese imagination of the '30s and its tendency toward emperor-worship. The dog's sacrifice seems to have been immaculate, with neither bark nor bite, and not leaving behind any waste. Such selfless obedience was held up as a role model, not to other dogs certainly, but rather to the humans who trooped past Hachiko's monument every day. Iris Chang states, "Some Japanese soldiers [of this era] admitted it was easy for them to kill because they had been taught that next to the emperor, all individual life—even their own—was valueless."[2] Life, an ideal life, was without needs, and narrow in its confines: nothing but the plot of ground where one had once been bidden, "Stay."

I am referring to predominant cultural trends, mainly taking place within the military itself, which had the ear of the emperor and functional control of the Japanese government. And along with its powers, the Japanese military expanded its ranks during the '30s, as many young men heard the call of a master, not unlike Hachiko, to seek honor by fighting and dying for the emperor and for Japanese imperial conquest. Clearly, Japan was never monolithic in its conformism, or even its emperor-worship. Historian Robert B. Edgerton notes that "most Japanese were wary of military rule. As late as 1937, the year that Nanking was ravaged, a national plebiscite rejected military rule when it voted Prime Minister General Hayashi out of office […] but the Japanese government nevertheless remained firmly in the hands of the military."[3] What is significant, especially for our purposes, is that Japanese filmmakers noted these trends and pointed to them with chagrin and disapproval. So, in the famous bunraku-theater scene in Mizoguchi's imperial-era *Osaka Elegy* (made the year after Hachiko went bronze) alternates shots of the life-sized puppets onstage with shots of the audience, revealing the spectators as virtually comatose, certainly less personable than the puppets. Moreover, the puppets have their strings pulled by men garbed in black so as to appear invisible, though this is a pretense, everyone knows the string-pullers are there; this pretense is part of the social contract of bunraku, just as the audience agrees to pretend not to recall that the story of the play is one that has been told thousands of times—generically not unlike the echt-melodramatic scene which erupts in the lobby among the businessman, his mistress and his offended wife, who falls to her knees in outrage at the same time as a puppet onstage is shown to collapse in the same stark motion. The Japanese, as Mizoguchi depicts them, are puppets who do not even have the excuse of being puppets. The wife's affront is not so much that her husband (whom she despises anyway) is being unfaithful to her, but that the mistress is "flaunting a married woman's coiffure" in this public space of the theater; costuming signifies status, specifically here the mistress's rude assumption of an unearned and incorrect status.

Meanwhile, the only figure in the entire sequence whom we see in close-up, albeit shot only from behind, is the bunraku play's narrator, who supplies all the voices for the puppets and therefore performs a unifying narratological function, a would-be legitimation. Yet, with Mizoguchi showing only this speaker's back, we sense unease and even a disrespectful challenge to this unifying authorial function. It is yet another pretense of theater—an even more vulnerable one, the narrator literally exposing the back of his head—indulged by Mizoguchi rather than venerated. Indeed, Mizoguchi is overseeing the overseer, who, for his part, is merely repeating by rote a traditional script which the audience already knows by heart. The semi-private drama of broken social codes among the husband, the wife and the mistress takes precedence over the onstage spectacle and at the same time reifies it as a portrait of a society completely caught up in worshiping false values.

What purpose did these false values serve? What made "the floating world" cohere? Buell indicates that it was nothing else but "Japanese identity or *kokutai*—'the spiritual unity and cohesion needed to make a territory and its inhabitants into a nation.'"[4] That unified identity was gained through the symbol of the emperor, a sovereign dictator who was, moreover, worshiped as a divinity. The Japanese believed their emperors were infallible and immortal, literally "descended from the gods [in] 'a lineal succession unbroken for ages eternal.'"[5] Takeshi Fujitani reports that Edo craftspeople of the late 19th century prayed to the then-emperor for daily miracles as if he were Shôtoku Taishi, a local divinity: for example, a mother asked, "My son is too good-looking [and] all the young girls in the neighborhood fall in love with him and he won't begin to work. Since his loafing around just won't do, please prevent girls from falling in love with him."[6] This was evidently not a criticism which the mother could broach directly to her son; the intercession of a local god, in the form of the national emperor, was required. Here, gods and the emperor himself served the function of being above Japanese males, who in most other respects dominated the social order as surrogate-gods. Because the Japanese believed that they were ruled divinely, they "believed that they, too, were descended from the gods and [thus] superior to other people, and the land was held to be the country of the gods. Of all the earth Japan was nearest to heaven when the connection between the two was broken."[7]

Japanese nationalism, then, was fatefully imbricated with fanatical religious investment, not quite as we understand religion today in the West, but instead all devolving upon the figure of the male emperor as an ineffable, sacred element, a metonym for Japanese honor who in turn imparted a secondhand divinity to all Japanese males. Emperor worship, at no vast remove, was carried out daily in Japanese domestic spaces, with every father intended to be the worshiped patriarch of his immediate clan. In the late 19th century, "[i]deologues, bureaucrats, and politicians began to laud the family as the foundation of the state, to equal filial piety with loyalty to the emperor, and to exalt the emperor as the father of all Japanese subjects in the family-state (*kazoku kokka*)."[8] Japan's "1898 Civil Code placed nearly all women under the authority of a male head-of-household."[9] And this system of emperor worship persisted into the modern age, with Hirohito. Even in the early 1960s, in Ozu's final film, *An Autumn Afternoon* (*Samma no aji*, 1962), we witness the traditional custom that the women in a family are generally not permitted to enter a room where men are eating and talking, and sit down and join them; instead a polite Japanese woman sits demurely in the doorway, looking on and answering questions when asked. Only geishas serving men in geisha houses can sometimes cross this line, perhaps to offset the atmosphere of male homosociality, and also perhaps because geishas were not expected to take on the kind of role that women in families were: serving no less than nation and emperor by devotedly serving the men in their immediate households, fathers, husbands, sons, with a kind of sacred purity.[10]

Brothers, too—as in Shimazu's *A Brother and His Younger Sister*, in which adult siblings live together with the sister performing all the wifely duties except sexual relations. Even ill with a cold, Fumiko (Michiko Kuwano) serves Keisuke (Reikichi Kawamura) his meals, and even polishes his shoes. When she asks to be allowed to sleep, after getting up to welcome him when he comes home at one o'clock in the morning, he kicks her in the leg so hard that she wakes up sore. It is not that the brother does not care about her; it is that he has been inculcated to be selfish in his needs, and she, to be submissive to him. We see this also in Naruse's *The Whole Family Works* (*Hataraku ikka*, 1939), where the father, Ishimura (Musei Tokugawa), is lazy and drinks up much of his struggling family's income. This is his prerogative as patriarch. Ishimura is not hopeless, however. He might rummage through his children's drawers for money while they are asleep, yet he also discusses their personalities and problems with genuine intimate knowledge; it is just that the stern, impulsive decisions he reaches about how to help them are sometimes oblivious and potentially damaging. Nonetheless, even this patriarch is shown as capable of rethinking, relenting and even changing his mind. Walking down a road, lost in thought over his second son's wish to go to school instead of work in a factory, the father is nearly run over by a car: "Walk carefully," he says to himself, as if he were also wishing it for his semi-estranged son at that moment.

In *The Whole Family Works*, the necessities of poverty excuse the father's drunkenness somewhat, though naturally his drunkenness also perpetuates the poverty. But no such necessity guides the household in *A Brother and His Younger Sister*, for they have a maid who also waits hand and foot on Keisuke! The fact that this odd brother-sister relationship is typical enough to be the subject of a movie (which does not present it as being intrinsically odd) is somewhat disconcerting. When Fumiko scolds her brother lightly, laughing off her own pain as she does so, he becomes petulant. "You lead a prosaic life," he criticizes her. "Too meticulous and devoid of humanity." At the same time, as the brother later admits, he himself is under the thumb of his older male bosses at work.

In Ozu's *An Autumn Afternoon* we witness the traditional custom that the women in a family are generally not permitted to enter a room where men are eating and talking, and sit down and join them; instead a polite Japanese woman sits demurely in the doorway, looking on and answering questions when asked. Only geishas serving men in geisha houses can sometimes cross this line, perhaps to offset the atmosphere of male homosociality.

The cycles contract. In this 20th century film, no one is outside the chains of patriarchy. Hovering above every social and domestic context, of course, is the justifying principle of the emperor.

And Shimazu's film is nothing compared to Ozu's *Woman of Tokyo* (*Tôkyô no onna*, 1933), also about an adult brother, Ryoichi (Ureo Igawa), and sister, Chikako (Yoshiko Okada), who live together. Ryoichi is a college student; Chikako works to support them, and also moonlights at night as a prostitute. At home Chikako is, like Fumiko in *A Brother and His Younger Sister*, very deferential to her brother, always smiling and backing down in conversations, and serving all his daily needs (far less upscale, the siblings in *Woman of Tokyo* have no maid). Sensitive Ryoichi is grateful and loving toward his sister, until a rumor about her gets back to him. Someone has reported Chikako to the police "as a dangerous person"—this, in the year that the Japanese military was fighting tooth and nail to take over Manchurian China. When Chikako admits to Ryoichi that she has sold her body only for him and his education, he beats her. Unfazed, Chikako sobs, "If hitting you makes you feel better, don't feel bad for me." Her submissiveness is like a bottomless pit which Ryoichi must escape by fleeing their apartment to wander the streets aimlessly; it is Ryoichi's sorrow and loss of honor that we are meant to focus on. Indeed, that night, he kills himself out of shame. This highly feudal situation takes place in modern times; moreover, Ozu's title seems to suggest that such tragic sacrifices are hardly old-fashioned or provincial at all, but instead endemic to the modern metropolis of "Tokyo" in general.

In some ways, early 20th century Tokyo became a new kind of battleground for Japanese sensibilities. Rapidly sprawling urban spaces with far-flung neighborhoods and anonymous commuter transportation, as well as the heightened presence of modernity itself for that matter, threatened the kind of control over women and domestic life which older males in villages had maintained through sheer proximity and lack of options. In fact, it could be said that emperor worship was sharpened and even radicalized somewhat when modernity and science began to erode ancient superstitions in Japan; a backlash situation. Norma Field writes, "The essence of the kokutai was declared by a notorious Education Ministry formulation of 1937 to be manifest in the unbroken imperial line and to the absolute loyalty to parents and sovereign through which the individual died to himself but was reborn to a more authentic existence."[11] Now, Japanese were expected explicitly to die for the emperor if need be. "Loyalty now belonged to the emperor alone and was unquestioned."[12] All other social relations were subsumed under this central, highest duty. As one Japanese veteran of the Pacific Asian War and World War II put it, chillingly: "…I instructed the troops to die for the emperor. I have friends who died shouting 'banzai' to the emperor. I am a Christian, and I had difficult moments as a child when I was pressed to answer the question, 'Who do you think is greater, the emperor or Christ?'"[13]

Takeshi Fujitani has argued that the rites of emperor worship were revived and implemented in modern Japan during the late 19th century Meiji Restoration; prior to this, they had not existed in Japan "since ancient times."[14] Thus, calling emperor worship "feudal or premodern" is not only an historic misnomer but a way of enabling "displacement of our discontent with modernity onto a Japanese past called 'feudal.'"[15] In fact, there is seemingly no more dangerous, unpredictable or inscrutable historical agent than one who has been successfully inoculated against modernity; one in whom modernity has been implanted without taking hold. For this agent, no world, neither this one nor the prospect of an improved, better-engineered one, can measure up to the immeasurably tantalizing prospect of divine mandate. Emiko Ohnuki-Tierney describes the young kamikaze pilots who flew with the express purpose of dying for the Emperor: "They embraced modernity while trying to overcome it; they emulated the achievements of the Western high civilizations while resisting Western cultural and political hegemony."[16]

The psychological stakes were enormous. If it was true that the emperor's divinity lent something to ordinary Japanese manhood, raising the Japanese male to something like a divinity in his own right, a proxy god, then any perceived doubt about the emperor reflected not only on Japanese patriotic nationalism but on basic masculine self-image as well. Everything was interdependent, "the nation-as-family, and its reversal, the family-as-nation, with the Emperor and the Father ensconced as the head of the household/nation."[17] Individual males ruled all spaces, again like little domestic emperors. Tadao Sato writes:

> The father in the house was a microcosm of the emperor in the nation: as the emperor was the embodiment of virtue, so each father should be a small model of virtue. This was hardly the case in reality, as often mediocre fathers took advantage of this heaven-sent authority to play the tyrant at home, alienating their children.[18]

In Akira Kurosawa's *Stray Dog*, Detective Murakami (Toshirô Mifune) insists that Harumi (Keiko Awaji, standing) wear the expensive dress that her lover robbed and killed to buy for her, while Harumi's mother (Eiko Miyoshi) implores her daughter to do the right thing by giving information to the detectives. The motif of a submissively adoring woman protecting a criminal lover recurs in Oshima's later *Violence at Noon* (*Hakuchû no tôrima*, 1966).

Confucianism, which had permeated Japan since the Edo era, preached the three obediences of women: first to their fathers, second to their husbands, and finally to their own grown sons. This unbroken patrilineage in which all males enjoy superiority and control over a woman at all stages of her life is a key part of what cemented emperor-worship in place in Japan. The society was already deeply sexist, and ripe for the religious veneration of a Japanese male leader-figure, who in turn allowed all Japanese males to partake of some element of divine authority. In the lives of women, individual males reinforced the godlike status of the male emperor and received the ego benefits of being worshipped as emperor-surrogates. In Oshima's *Violence at Noon*, the serial rapist tells one of his victims, "I'm like a god to you," in a way that is meant to remind us uncomfortably of the deification of the emperor and the harm this caused to modern Japan.

Some of this otherworldly devotion had also been inculcated in the Japanese through Buddhism, which preached austerity and disengagement from the snares of the material world.[19] Yet the Japanese seemed most impressed by the physical beauty of the Buddhist temples.[20] (In Oshima's *Taboo*, Kano is taken with the beauty of such a temple.) The entire concept of building "better and more permanent dwellings ... for the emperor and the nobility" came from the ubiquity of the Buddhist temples, unlike "the simple buildings that had done for the Shinto worship and the flimsy structures in which even their royalty lived."[21] Indeed, Buddhism and emperor-worship turned out to be mutually reinforcing in Japan,[22] and what motivated the spread of both seems to have been, again, the intoxicating vanity that some particle of divinity dwelled within each Japanese by dint of his or her worship of the Buddha, or the Emperor.[23] In Oshima's *Boy*, there is a scene in which the brutal Takeo (Fumio Watanabe) beats and tries to strangle his wife in front of a Buddhist altar and an enormous Rising-Sun flag; Toshio and his little brother must watch this helplessly. For Japanese males and for the women who put up with their self-centeredness, to extinguish the divine spark of the emperor would be to extinguish what they believed was their own potentially divine spark, lit and kept glowing through obedient service and the willingness to die at any moment.

The Japanese Imperial Army of the 1930s was nothing less than sadistic. Soldiers who were clumsy in training exercises or who could not memorize pledges and prescripts were beaten within inches of their lives. When two soldiers went AWOL because of the inhumane conditions, they were hunted to a water well where they were hiding. The two men were pulled from the well and kicked in the stomach until "their internal organs burst out," while the epithet "Traitors!" was screamed at them again and again.[24] And later, during the war, soldiers "unfit for sustained fighting ... were trained to execute suicide missions," including throwing themselves under U.S. tanks with bombs strapped to their bodies.[25]

The scenes in Seijun Suzuki's *Fighting Elegy* (set in the 1930s) where the cadet Kiroku (Hideko Takahashi) is made to march barefoot on tacks and where other young cadets hit each other in the face with spiked maces are not so hyperbolic. Iris Chang writes, "Above all the Japanese cadets were to adopt 'a will which knows no defeat.'"[26] Even non-military elementary schools were run along the lines of military academies, with "thousands of children waving flags and marching in unison in perfect lines."[27] Sato, who began his primary school education in 1937, confirms this:

> My recollections of my teachers are not too pleasant. One woman teacher dressed me down because I had fooled around during choral practice of the nationalistic song for Empire Day (February 11). I also remember the teacher who was in charge of our preparation classes for the secondary school entrance examination. She made us learn and recite in a grave voice something about "the august virtue of His Majesty the Emperor."[28]

As bad as this is, it seems mild compared to many other Japanese schoolchildren's experiences. Chang states:

> It was commonplace for teachers to behave like sadistic drill sergeants, slapping children across the cheeks, hitting them with their fists, or bludgeoning them with bamboo or wooden swords. Students were forced to hold heavy objects, sit on their knees, stand barefoot in the snow, or run around the playground until they collapsed from exhaustion.[29]

The schools were also where the immense and vitriolic Japanese racism toward the Chinese was indoctrinated in the very young. Under the emperor system, schoolteachers "instilled in boys hatred and contempt for the Chinese people, preparing them psychologically for a future invasion of the Chinese mainland. One historian tells the story of a squeamish Japanese schoolboy in the 1930s who burst into tears when told to dissect a frog. His teacher slammed his knuckles against the boy's head and yelled, 'Why are you crying about one lousy frog? When you grow up you'll have to kill one hundred, two hundred chinks!'"[30]

Some historians have estimated that the total number of Chinese killed by the Japanese during the Sino-Japanese War to be around 19 million, making it one of the top genocidal campaigns of modern history, marked by mass exterminations and even biological warfare.[31] At one point, Japan flooded China with opium, an underhanded tactic meant to enfeeble the Chinese Army's will to fight.[32] Japan's military policy throughout China was called the Three All's: Burn All, Seize All, Kill All.[33] The single worst atrocity which the Japanese committed against China was the infamous, gruesome Rape of Nanking in 1937. Nanking was the new capital of the Republic of China, and Japan focused its anti–Chinese rage against it. Japan was trying to break the Chinese government and force an unconditional surrender.[34] Japanese planes blasted away most of the bridges on the city's two water-locked sides, thereby trapping Chinese soldiers and civilians alike.[35] "Before the final assault on Nanking, thousands of Chinese soldiers surrendered, only to be machine-gunned down."[36] The Japanese soldiers were instructed: "You must not consider the Chinese as a human being, but only as something of rather less value than a dog or cat."[37] We recognize the intent to dehumanize as a lynchpin of racist thought and indoctrination.

Such indoctrination made the Japanese army a perfect killing machine against the people of Nanking, and a highly creative one. Even the German Nazis who were present during the six-week slaughter (ambassadors to China who openly sided with the Japanese invaders) were sickened and impressed by the Japanese display of bestiality.[38] The operation was directly commanded by General Nakajima, considered an extreme sadist even by the Japanese themselves, and by Emperor Hirohito's own uncle, General Prince Asaka.[39] The young males of Nanking were rounded up in groups of tens of thousands, taken to the outskirts of the city, and there torn apart by machine gun fire, used as living targets for bayonet practice drills and "decapitation contests," or doused in gasoline and burned alive. Mountains of charred corpses choked the streets with reeking decay for months.⁴⁰ Chang writes: "Not only did live burials, castration, the carving of organs [vivisection], and the roasting of people become routine, but more diabolical tortures were practiced, such as hanging people by their tongues on iron hooks or burying people to their waists and watching them get torn apart by German shepherds."⁴¹ Masuo's haunted memory of the live burial of a Manchurian child, his younger brother, is used as a dramatic motif in Oshima's *The Ceremony*.

Outside Nanking, prisoners were used in special Chinese-killing competitions, somewhat like Olympic games, in which Japanese soldiers raced each other to see who would be the first to kill one hundred Chinese, usually by splitting them in half at the cranium with a samurai sword.⁴² A Japanese "who beheaded more than forty Chinese prisoners described his emotion at the time as 'ecstasy.'"⁴³ Combat veteran Hakudo Nagatomi recalled that

> soldiers impaled babies on bayonets and tossed them still alive into pots of boiling water.... They gang-raped women from the ages of twelve to eighty and then killed them when they could no longer satisfy sexual requirements. I beheaded people, starved them to death, burned them, and buried them alive, over two hundred in all.⁴⁴

As Dr. Okabe says in Masumura's *Red Angel*, which takes place during the Sino-Japanese War, "Soldiers aren't human beings. They're just weapons." Orders to rape and gang-rape as many Chinese women as possible came directly to the men from their imperial officers, who also participated in the assaults. Nagatomi stated, "Some not only urged soldiers to commit gang rape in the city but warned them to dispose of the women afterwards to eliminate evidence of the crime. 'Either pay them money or kill them in some out-of-the-way place after you have finished,' one officer told his underlings."⁴⁵ It is estimated that 20,000 to 80,000 Chinese women were raped during the Nanking siege.

"Rape was so well organized," Robert B. Edgerton reports, "that any reasonably attractive Chinese woman was loaded aboard a truck and taken away to be raped until the troops found her so unappealing that she was bayoneted and tossed onto piles of other civilian bodies."⁴⁶ Rapes occurred anywhere, in the streets in broad daylight, and even in places held to be sacred, such as convents, churches and Bible schools. In the courtyard of a seminary, one Chinese woman was gang-raped by seventeen Japanese soldiers.⁴⁷

As their commanders had suggested, the rapists found it prudent, and no doubt for some a triumph of their cruelty, to kill the women immediately after raping them. "Many soldiers," Chang writes, "went beyond rape to disembowel women, slice off their breasts, nail them alive to walls. Fathers were forced to rape their daughters, and sons their mothers, as other family members watched."⁴⁸ The final Chinese death toll at Nanking has been reported by experts as exceeding 350,000 people, combatants and noncombatants included.

But Nanking was only the most extended and barbaric assault in the Sino-Japanese War. "In fact," Edgerton writes, "many smaller Nankings took place all over China. Looting, arson, rape, and killing of prisoners, usually by bayonet thrusts, was reported by the Chinese ... and many Japanese veterans have admitted that the charges are true."⁴⁹ Edgerton concludes: "Such unspeakable brutality made the Japanese one of the most detested military forces in history."⁵⁰

Although denied and covered up by Japanese arch-conservatives after the war, the specter of the Sino-Japanese War haunted Japanese cinema, sometimes by its absence, and sometimes in guilty depictions of Japanese soldiers who failed to stand against the savagery. Sato writes that Masaki Kobayashi's mammoth 9-hour *The Human Condition* (*Ningen no jôken*, 1959–1961) concerns a Japanese soldier "who undergoes an odyssey of suffering because he refused during World War II to slave-drive Chinese prisoners in Manchuria and treated them humanely. As a result he was sent to the most trying fronts and detained in a Soviet P.O.W. camp after the war, from which he escapes, to die in a desolate, snowy terrain."[51]

At the end of *Fighting Elegy*, Kiroku and his friends get word of the abortive coup d'état staged by warmongering members of the military against the current government, which was seen as "too soft" on the imperial agenda. The cadets jump on a train to go and fight for the emperor; we are meant to assume that they become part of the fighting force that participated in the Rape of Nanking. Suzuki triangulates three entities in the film: the young man, who envisions himself as kokutai, the body of the state; the emperor, who is never seen but felt lurking everywhere; and the young man's erection, again never seen but omnipresent, a kind of synecdochal dictator if you will. The emperor and the erection form the basal points of the triangle, with the young man (Kiroku) as the apex, being driven simultaneously by both forces. The erection must be hidden and disguised "in" the figure of the emperor, in whose name it is all right to fight, maim, rape, and even kill. It is not all right for Kiroku to act *only* on behalf of his erection: sexual shame dominates him, as when he goes out and beats up several men in order to release his tension when he thinks of his girlfriend Michiko (Junko Asano). The emperor becomes both an approved surrogate for the erection (a meta-phallus) and an approved surrogate for the girlfriend, the sexual object, since Kiroku switches his will to fight from being prompted by thoughts of Michiko to thoughts of the emperor. This triangulation of male violence/sexuality, depicted so smartly in Suzuki's film, is perhaps one reason why the Japanese military was such a rapine force in its Pacific Asia campaigns; then again, we should not overlook how violence and sexuality are cathected in all military systems, both of them lending perverse incentive to each other, and both invested in displacing shame onto the enemy, where a wound, a mark, is opened. Rape and even some consensual sexual penetration (between enemies) translate the orifices of the penetrated into wounds which can never fully heal.

This is not to say that Kiroku's erection ever becomes "free" or liberated. Indeed, the erection here is also an ego wound; militaristic regulation and normalization of bodies in *Fighting Elegy* extend explicitly to the erection, which Kiroku can barely hide when he thinks of girls, and which even a superior notices in one scene, prompting him to upbraid Kiroku for his lack of discipline. His pent-up erection constantly overcomes him at inappropriate moments, because, in a repressed society, no scheduled moment is ever consecrated to it. Instead, random moments become infused with knowing, totemic images of the sexuality that has been dangerously suppressed: the live snake which a cadet pulls from his shirt and clobbers with a crude mace; Kiroku's bare sweating torso framed in a church-like window alcove as he listens to Michiko's recital in the concert hall; his black combat boots which he moves closer to her feminine shoes on the porch of their boarding house, just to see what they would look like standing beside hers; and most beautifully, perhaps, fingers breaking through a paper screen from either side to clasp each other. For Kiroku and his male peers, these are not fully realized desublimations, just as they lead pointedly only to violence, never to sex itself; what sets off the young men's final furious hurling of themselves into war is not the face of a woman but the face of an older man, the fascist revolutionary who preached the coup d'état to overthrow the government and enhance the powers of the emperor.

In *Fighting Elegy*, we see that male sexual desire remains a wild card, furiously self-sufficient, dependent neither on its female objects nor on a nominal state apparatus. In fact, it is bent on a collision course with these very things, which are potential outlets. In the scene where Kuriko vows to fight other males whenever he feels overcome by lust for Michiko, we see her playing the piano with an impossibly winsome expression while he sits and listens; suddenly he stands up, goes outside, and beats up several men; then he returns to her, still playing, indefatigable as a source of romantic arousal. Sighing, Kuriko sits down again, ready for the cycle to repeat.

This solipsism drives male sexuality away from all possible outlets, terrified at how easily a sexual outlet could sap the drive that is needed for competition and world-beating, or at least substitute for that drive something more sensitive, which would "infect" all aspects of life with a tenderness all but useless outside of sex (and not particularly necessary for sex itself). Love, particularly a heroic, thwarted love, is the only possible alibi for the indulgence of so much feeling. Like the wounds of seppuku, the force of male lust is held out as a final antidote to weakness, meant to break the enclosed circle of warrior impassivity in order to produce its own external marking to render an internal one visible; so, in the scene where Kuriko must leave town, he stands outside his former boarding house and shouts Michiko's name, after each syllable "catching" the exhaled breath in his fingers and swallowing it again. This is a more romantic, life-affirming version of the same enclosed self-love which operates in seppuku, and whose narcissism is auto-desiring and auto-satisfying; the body whose strong desires threaten its standing in the world so much that it only allows itself to be satisfied through self-production, and then self-consumption, of the romantic object. (Actually, this same psychological mechanism obtains in the writing of certain kinds of lyric poetry.)

Later in *Fighting Elegy*, a short, mustached, formal man, physically resembling Hirohito, turns directly to the camera to hector, "There are things we do in life that might seem stupid afterwards, but we must do them! That's what being a man is! One must be a man above all else!" Being male becomes a schizoid prospect: one has to prove oneself indubitably male, yet restrain oneself as well, to channel even that male energy into fealty and obedience to the emperor or his surrogates. When Kiroku enters his father's study, for example, he does so on his hands and knees, a veritable Hachiko-the-dog in training.

*****

Under the modern Emperor Hirohito, long traditions of militaristic obeisance to the Emperor reached a literal "flowering" in the willing deaths of many young kamikaze pilots.[52] Moreover, these pilots' deaths were highly aestheticized, referred to as *sange*, "or to 'scatter like flowers'"[53] and symbolized by perhaps the ultimate symbol of Japanese beauty and pride: the falling petals of cherry blossom trees. Here, we find a prime example of that sublime and terrible poetry of everyday things in Japanese cultural history. "Originally [in the Meiji period] the cherry trees were planted so that the beautiful blossoms would console the souls of fallen soldiers," Ohnuki-Tierney writes. "As the wheel of militarization accelerated, this metaphor was extended so that falling cherry petals represented soldiers who sacrificed their lives, and blooming cherry blossoms at the Yasukumi Shrine became their metamorphosed souls."[54]

The end result was not that the cherry blossoms became concretized, but rather that warriors became etherealized. The trope is so endemic that it appears in Kiriya Kazuaki's recent, mainstream sci-fi movie, *Casshern* (2005), in which the cherry petals fall within a garden where Tetsuya (Yûsuke Iseya), the son of Dr. Azuma (Akira Terao), announces his intention to enlist in the army as a patriotic "duty" and fight at the front in "Europa" and the mysterious Zone Seven. The cut from the gorgeous showering blossoms in the elegant backyard garden, to the chaos, grime and terror of a battle scene shorthands the historical disillusion of many young imperial soldiers, who had boasted of becoming war heroes, thinking that to die "for the emperor" was beautiful and glorious.

In fact, among the kamikaze pilots, "many were deceived and pressured into participating [and] their sacrifices had ... little impact on the course of the war."[55] In *Casshern*, when Tetsuya is killed in battle, his father immediately wants to bring him back to life using his newly designed Neo-Cells which can restore any organ and flesh tissue whole; but Tetsuya's disillusionment is so total that his spirit stands by, screaming no, he does not want to be brought back to life. Nonetheless, the father baptizes him again and again in the Neo-Cell solution until Tetsuya gasps for air. The cathexis, here, among the body of the soldier, his spirit, and the wishes and powers of the older paternal generation, makes for a compelling dramatization of an emperor-worship that was at all levels both intensely self-glorifying and intensely self-destroying.

Oshima delivered a bleak and brilliant depiction of the young trained to sacrifice themselves for selfish elders in *Boy*. Ten-year-old Toshio is the son of a pair of con artists; his father Takeo is a lazy gambler, traumatized by his combat experiences in China and now unwilling to work, and his frivolous stepmother Takeko (Akiko Koyama) is only concerned with having more babies that she cannot take care of. The family's self-proclaimed "work" is to trek throughout Japan, letting Toshio get hit by random cars so they can bully the motorists into paying them settlement money. Again and again we see Toshio wander into traffic or hurl himself against an oncoming car like a dire parody of the kamikazes and their one-way missions for the emperor. Oshima has numerous shots of the boy lying on gray cement, unconscious, in fetal positions; small-scale "deaths," as it were, that are anything but beautiful.

Like Hirohito and the propagandizing imperial system, the parents are abusive in their manipulativeness. To gain a stronger hold over Toshio, his father lies to him that his grandparents do not love him and are glad to never have to see him anymore; the hysteric Takeko beats him and accuses him of spying on her in order to badmouth her to the father, then, contrite, offers to buy him a new watch. The parents spend their extortion money recklessly, on flashy hairstyles, leather jackets, stays at expensive geisha houses. Everything the parents do is desperately sleazy, and it is nauseating to watch them greedily consume bowls of noodles inbetween "accidents"; in one restaurant scene the father threatens to withhold food from Toshio if he does not put more effort into getting hit by cars.

As the little kamikaze's contusions and injuries grow worse and worse, it seems for much of *Boy* that he will eventually either be killed or abandoned. Toshio tries to run away and even to commit suicide, but ends up returning to the family-hell for the sake of his younger brother. Even the boy's inability finally to die is perceived by him as an internalized sense of failure on his part. Ironically, it is only after "surrendering" to the system (the father gets a job, they find an apartment) that the police catch up with Takeo and Takeko and arrest them. The complete abdication of responsible, moral adult leadership in Toshio's life, which he nonetheless risks constantly to please what passes for such leadership, replays the visissicitudes of imperial Japan in heart-rending and disturbing ways.

The emperor system was also bound up in Japan's class and caste system. It was, Irokawa maintains,

> organized so that the hard external side of the power structure—[...] forces used to intimidate and discriminate against the lower classes—was covered up by the gentler side. If the internal side of the system offered solace and hope to the people at the bottom, then the external aspect was the ruling structure based on discrimination and control. This external framework was strenuously concealed from the people, who were presented with a façade of relief and salvation. This deceitful ideology was a frightening trap for those on the bottom.[56]

Psychologically, many Japanese had convinced themselves that they needed only to try harder, and rewards would come. The abuses would all be redeemed. "Despite [their] suffering," Irokawa concludes, "the people mostly continued to fantasize that they had been the recipients of the emperor's love, his divine 'benevolence toward all.'"[57]

9

Naruse: An Early and Enduring Critic of Emperor Worship

Perhaps because of his general sensitivity, director Mikio Naruse was an early critic of the emperor system, which he tended to depict metaphorically in the form of a woman's pining adoration of an arrogant, abusive, dictatorial male. In his *Apart from You* (*Kimi to wakarete*, 1933), Kikue (Mitsuko Yoshikawa) is an aging geisha who is in the last phase of Confucian obedience, toward father, then husband, then son. The adolescent son Yushio (Akio Isono) despises her for having become a geisha, although she has done it to support him and save for his education. His jealous possessiveness of her, which frustration has turned into disgust and callous indifference, makes us read him, even at his young age, as a surrogate for patriarch, for emperor.

It does not help that Kikue is unusually submissive to Yushio. In a key scene, she watches over his sleep (he is hung-over), and when his bare foot comes out from under the quilt, she takes it in her hands and places it back underneath again. Then she pours herself a shot of sake and smiles at him somewhat strangely. There is barely disguised abjection in her sense of duty to what we might call "the patriarchal foot," indeed a faint scent of perversity, and it leads to a later scene where she bows before Yushio and tells him he should kill her if he hates her that much. His response is to stomp out of their home. Yushio moonlights as a juvenile delinquent; he directly anticipates the bad boys of postwar sun-tribe films, though he is proletarian in status, and not sexually aggressive. His street gang robs people and beats them up, however, and he carries a knife.

Yushio's shame and dissatisfaction with his mother is symbolized by the holes in his socks; again, the patriarchal foot becomes a site of special veneration, and of abjection, here for the would-be patriarch. Whenever Yushio takes his shoes off, his big toes protrude from the holes in his socks, causing him embarrassment. Even when Kikue offers him new socks, he rejects her attempt to show love; keeping his worn-out socks are a reason to go on resenting her, a constant thorn in his pride. (This specific trope of the Japanese male foot being too proud to wear socks with holes also comes up in Ozu's *Woman of Tokyo*.)

Yushio, a big handsome lout, is somewhere between boy and man; in a prominently displayed photo of him and his mother, they could almost pass for husband and wife. Kikue's regular client at the geisha house is a slightly younger man who somewhat resembles an older Yushio. At the depth of her despair, sensing that this client is trying to "toss her away like tissue paper," she runs amok with a straight razor and he must restrain her, a scene which Naruse brilliantly intercuts with two other clients dancing to a phonograph with their own geishas in the room next door. The contrast is intrinsic to Naruse's philosophy: wherever someone is temporarily happy, someone else has already been to the end of that happiness and found only despair.

There is a young geisha named Terugiku (Sumiko Mitzukobo), and Kikue enlists her help in trying to reach out to Yushio and make him "himself again." Kikue talks to Yushio, and tells him about her own family problems. At first he is surprised to learn that she has "so many problems"; then he is quick to help her. He has a crush on her, which Kikue wisely and gently turns to her advantage. Never mocking him or leading him on, she nonetheless presents to him the spectacle of her own sorrow at having been pushed into geisha work by her drunken, lazy father (Reikichi Kawamura). Because she is young and pretty, the boy sees her pain in a way that he cannot see his mother's; yet, eventually, he does come to transfer his caring for Terugiku back to the mother. Like a strange Oedipal movement in reverse, he goes from seeking succor from a girl to emotional re-bonding with the mother. Without being at all didactic or even underscoring the point, Naruse nonetheless presents this as if it were the obvious and overlooked missing piece of Freudian psychology. Here, true masculinity does not begin with mother-love and take off from there, in an imitation of imperial world-conquest as it were; instead it returns to the mother as a renewed commitment to hearth-and-home, to improving the intimate domestic space.

Apart from You is a remarkable film. Kikue and Terugiku come together to improvise a matrilineal line of rule in order to soften and finally overturn the patrilineal one. Yushio's feelings for Terugiku do not mature until nearly the end of the film; prior to that, his crush on her seems self-centered and driven by his own satisfaction, given that he lacks love for his mother, i.e., women in general. It is natural for him to be drawn to Terugiku; yet something about this is directly challenged by Naruse. An obligation is shown to be more than a one-way street: if *Apart from You* seems to concern itself with a mother seeking to be worthy of gaining her son's love, it is actually asking the opposite question, what makes a son worthy of being loved, much less obeyed patriarchally, by his mother?

It was highly subversive of Naruse, especially in imperial-era Japan, to shift the focus from the patrilineal to the matrilineal, and for the express purpose of salvaging the young Yushio from becoming a violent, criminal male. In fact, Yushio is one of the most endearing male characters in all of Japanese cinema, searching for something in Japanese society that we can regard as a reflection of Naruse's own bitterly thwarted, lifelong search for freedom. When Yushio skips school, he is shown lying on a bank of grass, staring at the sky, as if he sought some happiness in nature; the title reflects on Yushio's phase of needing to be "apart" from family attachments and also from society. When a freight train cuts into this shot, at the top of the bank, blocking out part of the sky, we feel Yushio's discomfort in this tough urban slum where poverty has left him and his mother. This is not to excuse Yushio entirely; for most of the film he is vain and sullen. But by the end a deeply moving transformation has occurred. Terugiko is leaving town on a train, to get away from her family; Yushio has accompanied her to the station. She tells him he is dearest to her of all people, and he says the same about her. We realize, at the same time as the characters do, that they love each other and that they might never see each other again. When Yushio waves goodbye to Terugiku and is left alone on the platform, he begins to weep openly, signifying that he has become attuned with his feelings, and could grow to be a more caring man than the other, absent or deleterious male figures in *Apart from You*.[1]

* * * * *

No filmmaker was more explicit in attacking emperor-worship in his time than Naruse was. We should not mistake the strong and courageous political subtext of a film like *Apart from You*. The 1930s were already a time when power was being radically consolidated by pro-war and pro-emperor conservatives, literally an era of fascism nearly as virulent as Germany, Spain and Italy in the same decade. Control was exerted at local levels through economic pressures. The idea was to watch everyone and keep them yoked in service to the needs of the imperial state. Irokawa writes, "Citizens' lives were severely regulated under the National Mobilization Law.... All aspects of daily life were under the control of the neighborhood associations. No one, even those who on principle objected to this system, could ignore the imperatives of the neighborhood associations if they wanted to receive food rations."[2]

Often, Naruse's critical or satiric intent is encoded in semi-cryptic imagery, or in daring views of Japanese manhood outside of military or patriarchal contexts. *Flunky, Work Hard!* (*Koshiben ganbare*, 1931) opens with Okabe (Isamu Yamaguchi), wearing a kimono and hornrimmed eyeglasses, with a baby in a papoose strapped to his back, and standing by a laundry line: this single shot is crowded with feminine signifiers. The fact that *Flunky, Work Hard!* is a comedy allows for this feminization, although Naruse does not demonize Okabe, who is depicted as a sincere, good-hearted person, and a better husband for taking an interest in child-rearing and domestic chores, and for being humble and non-violent. In fact, in one slapstick scene, Okabe proves more nurturing and protective of the baby than his wife (Tomoko Naniwa) is. He also helps in the kitchen, burning his fingers on the hot lid of a steam pot.

Okabe does work outside the home, as a door to door insurance salesman. And he is a bulky, rather than slight, man. But he is feminized in other gestures. Okabe's owlish, almost babyish face is belied by his sparse, scraggly beard. Distractedly placing the wrong end of a pen in his mouth, he has to spit out the spurt of ink. He traces a hole in the sole of his shoe, a Chaplinesque emblem denoting helpless poverty. Unlike Yoshio in *Apart from You*, he does not mind that his foot is not perfectly shod.

Although Okabe works, he cannot afford to buy toys for his young son Susumu (Seiichi Kato), who, as a result, has rage issues causing him to beat up other boys at school and break *their* toys. Naruse associates masculine violence with the figure of a small, self-centered child. Moreover, Susumu is most obsessed with acquiring a toy airplane modeled on the fighter planes of the imperial army; the wings are blazoned with the rising sun insignia. Naruse can only be commenting, here, on the excessive militarization of Japan beginning in the early 1930s, and specifically its decision to invade Manchurian China in 1931. *Flunky, Work Hard!* was made and released in the months when tensions between Japan and Manchuria were boiling over. There is a strange moment, almost unjustifiable in a narrative sense, when Naruse cuts from an isolated shot of one of these toy planes to a silly incident where father and son, hiding behind a weak partition, come tumbling out into the living room in front of the wife, the father ending up on all fours. Japan going to the dogs? In need of female orderliness and empathy? There is even a Hirohito-lookalike, a short, mustached man always wearing a tuxedo at all hours, who is a rival insurance salesman and ends up tussling with the father on the front lawn of a woman whom they are both trying to sell a policy to. "This isn't a playground for the two of you," the housewife states, as if defending Japan itself from the bumptious sparring of these short-sighted males. Even more outrageously, the Hirohito lookalike has enormous buckteeth and is a repulsive lecher, in addition to being physically weak and unprepossessing.

Then, in the kind of mixed-mood tonal shift which Naruse usually accomplishes head-on and unapologetically, *Flunky, Work Hard!* turns very serious. Susumu is hit by a train while preoccupied with watching the flight of yet another toy fighter plane, the film's constant warning-sign for danger and here a grim historical irony given that within a decade there would be young kamikaze pilots placing themselves in harm's way for the emperor's sake. All throughout Naruse's film, the imperial-themed toy plane is an object of jealousy, covetousness, recklessness, violence, foolishness, and enmity. In a quick close-up of the toy at the end of the film, when Susumu finally gets his own plane in his hospital bed, we see that it has "JAPAN AMERICA JUNKERS" scrawled on it—an even more ironic comment given how Japan and the U.S. ended up as combatants ten years later. Plot-wise, this ending is perfunctory and almost seems designed by Naruse merely as an excuse to show this accusatory detail in close-up.

Naruse also reduces the imperial air force to a silly toy plane for children in *No Blood Relation*, and, in the late 1930s, gives toy machine guns to the two youngest children in *The Whole Family Works*, which they use, subversively enough, to pretend to kill their father. And Naruse's peer, Yasujirô Ozu, has the homeless child Zenko in *An Inn in Tokyo* squander the pittance he has received for a stray dog (on "Rabies Prevention Day") on an imperial officer's cap instead of much-needed food, simply because he likes the way it looks. Consider this: a German comedy from the mid 1930s in which a small boy in S.A. regalia took his drunken dad in hand and tried to assume haphazard responsibility for the family would certainly raise many of our eyebrows (even our moth-eyebrows). By depicting the militarization of boyhood, and the childish spirit behind militarization, Naruse and Ozu were calling somewhat sardonic attention to a real phenomenon in 1930s Japan. Iris Chang writes, "Toy shops became virtual shrines to war, selling arsenals of toy soldiers, tanks, helmets, uniforms, rifles, antiaircraft guns, bugles, and howitzers."[3]

In *Sincerity* (*Magokoro*, 1939), Naruse introduces the character of the insensitive, suspected husband Keikichi (Minoru Takada) with a close-up of a samurai sword which Keikichi is holding and examining. When his wife comes to him to discuss their daughter's falling grades in school, he first dismisses the problem, pleased that Nobuko (Etchan) has perfect attendance and is "physically healthy" (qualities that will make her a good attractive wife for a man), then blames any problems on his wife (Sachiko Murase), accusing her of "doing too much outside the home." She is head of the local chapter of the Greater Japan Patriotic Women's Association, strictly home-fires-burning but nonetheless an organization that would have smacked of female independence in conservative Japan. He goes on to say: "After all, a child's education is primarily a mother's responsibility"—one of those arbitrary shiftings of blame that flourished in a culture whose word for "wife," *kanai*, literally means "inside-house."⁴ The patriarch Gisaburo (Takahiro Tamura) in Oshima's *Empire of Passion* will later echo this sentiment when he tells his young daughter Oshin (Masami Hasegawa) that she need not bother with getting an education: "You must learn childcare, as your mother did when she was younger. School's a waste of time." In *Sincerity*, Keikichi's arbitrary micromanagement of the household is also rendered ironic by the fact that he has an illegitimate daughter, Tomiko (Teruko Kato), with a different woman (Takako Irie) in the same town.

In his single-shot introduction of Keikichi, panning from the samurai sword to the fatuous man who holds it, Naruse associates his smug, sexist views with samurai-military culture even while placing the husband in a derisive position vis-à-vis that male-oriented culture: he has not gone to war like many other Japanese men, and his handling of swords is related only to his business, antiques restoration. Later, the husband does get his draft notice, but at a perfect moment for him to escape the problems he has created in his marriage. Hailed as a hero, he is sent off by the entire town, including the two broken families he is leaving behind; however, a warm smile passed between the two "abandoned" women suggests that they will come together in a new understanding, to help each other get by, to raise their daughters, and to form the loving family that Keikichi was incapable of creating much less dominating.

On the surface, *Sincerity* seems to be about a nagging, suspicious, independent-minded wife and a husband who puts up with her until he, as he says, "can go to war without worries." But Naruse brings out the pain of the wife, who feels deceived, as well as the sheer arrogance of the husband, tilting the chamber-room storyline off its keel as it were, and making the strongest scenes the ones in which women confer with each other over their disappointments. The male figure keeps the two women apart as if to dull the power he knows they would have if they came together. It is also an implied commentary on the husband that he has fathered two daughters and no sons, although this commentary might only have been felt by particularly sexist males for whom sons were status symbols and endowments; in all respects, *Sincerity*, like so many of Naruse's films, is what the West would call "a women's picture," with all of the subversive social awareness that we have come to expect from that genre.

Similarly, Kenji Mizoguchi, Naruse's other peer, crafted his *Osaka Elegy* as a cautionary tale about "the submissiveness of the people to the dictates of the imperial state"⁵ and "childhood indoctrination as loyal imperial subjects."⁶ Obedience to the emperor is implicitly criticized in Mizoguchi's depiction of the tragedy attendant upon Ayoko's blind loyalty to her father and to her male boss, both social surrogates for the patriarchal Hirohito. How much of imperial-era Japan was aligned with the insights of these great directors, and how much was it a case of artists being in the vanguard of social critique and change? The Japanese people were more sophisticated and conflicted about their values than observers have sometimes allowed. Clearly, Naruse, Ozu and Mizoguchi were all trying to make Japan's conflicted military culture a subject for their work and a matter of historic record.

Once Japan entered into World War II, film was enlisted in Japan, as it was everywhere in the world, to bear propaganda messages to the people. Hirohito's image became more protected than ever. This was also true after the surrender. In Fumio Kamei's documentary *The Tragedy of Japan* (1946), Dower reports, there was "a dissolve in which Emperor Hirohito was transformed before the viewer's eyes from the nation's rigid, uniformed commander into a benign, slightly stooping civilian figure, modestly garbed in a necktie, overcoat, and soft felt hat."[7] This film was quickly pulled from theatrical release by the U.S. occupation censors, who deemed it too inflammatory and harsh toward Hirohito: "at early screenings some viewers hooted and one threw a wooden clog at the screen [...] [T]he suppression of the documentary essentially marked the moment when serious debate concerning imperial war responsibility disappeared."[8]

What inflamed conservative audiences regarding this edit? As Eisenstein, Vertov and Dovzhenko knew (and Kamei was a disciple of all three[9]), one edit in a film can powerfully reveal dialectical fault-lines in a given historic moment or social system. Kamei forced viewers to confront something that had been done to their nation partly by the emperor's own self-servingness, partly by the U.S.'s mixed messages about how to regard him, and partly by what the Japanese public perceived as its own double fault, for placing too much faith in Hirohito to begin with and at the same time letting down their sacred emperor. The U.S. occupation "confiscated" all copies of *The Tragedy of Japan* only "three weeks after its release," and made it nearly impossible for Kamei to make more films.[10]

More to the liking of imperial Japan was *China Night* (*Shina no yuro*, 1940), which tendentiously patronized and mocked the Chinese. A young Chinese orphan (Shirley Yamaguchi) is virulently anti–Japanese, since her family was killed by the invading Japanese army. She is physically filthy, wearing rags and with dirt on her face. Everything she says and does is anti–Japanese, until she meets a handsome Japanese sailor who believes in Japanese superiority and imperialism. And she falls in love with him. Showing magnanimous pity toward his inferior, he takes her back to his hotel and cleans her up; she then appears as a "shining beauty."[11]

She is still rebellious, though, criticizing the sailor and his friends. It isn't until the sailor hauls off and slaps her that she too recognizes the superiority of the Japanese (male) and becomes his submissive. Igarashi writes: "Her vengeful gaze disappears and is replaced by an adoring look."[12] *China Night*'s "justification of violence against its Chinese heroine probably made it more popular in Japan."[13] Ms. Yamaguchi, a Japanese actress, could pass for Chinese in resemblance; after the war, she became an international star,[14] eventually getting slapped around by Robert Ryan in Samuel Fuller's *House of Bamboo* (1955).

10

Ozu, After Surrender

In spite of imperial Japan's use of mass media to spread noxious propaganda like *China Night*, mass media technology, as has been often noted, also helped undermine the sanctity of Hirohito. In 1945 the emperor's voice reached his subjects for the first time via the mediation of radio when he announced that Japan was surrendering to the U.S. and that he himself was no longer to be deified as a god on earth. The transmission was suitably otherworldly nonetheless. "Reception was poor. Static crackled ... and the words themselves were difficult to grasp. The emperor's voice was high pitched and his enunciation stilted ... a highly formal language studded with ornamental classical phrases."[1] Hirohito "enjoined his subjects to 'endure the unendurable and bear the unbearable,'"[2] words taken from a Buddhist text called *The Sutra of 42 Sections*.[3]

This technological demystification was a bitter pill for the Japanese to swallow. There was a sudden deformation of the collective past. All of the war sacrifices had been in vain, including the many deaths of imperial soldiers who had viewed no honor higher than that of dying for the sacred emperor. Thenceforward, memory would be divided in Japan, between an unreal, rescinded history and an unaccountable ontological void. To this day that divide is still a fertile subject for Japanese films. As a scorned woman says to her amnesiac lover in Tsukomoto's *Vital*, "All your happy, false memories—what chance do I have against those?" But even more, in making himself human via mass media, the emperor inadvertently helped deify the realism of media itself. If mere electronic transmissions could contain and illuminate some dusty corner of the pseudo-divine, could alter a nation's fate so thoroughly and quickly, then one could imagine one's future invested in creating and sending out those signals. Japan's destiny as a world capital of media culture—often silly and winking at itself, often grisly and appalling, in any case shrugging at each sudden amplitude or ambiguation of existing meanings—was probably born on that day.

Not that the people who listened to the broadcast could focus yet on futures. Their oaths of loyalty to the emperor were not something that the Japanese could recant just like that, simply because a voice crackling with radio static could come from the skies urging them to do so. The imperial fantasmatic remained, as was partly the intention of the U.S. occupation forces who were pulling the strings. Demoralization, as well as a last-ditch clinging to what vestiges of nobility Hirohito (now called by this name for the first time) would be allowed to retain, was part of General MacArthur's plan to keep the Japanese off-base, confused, grateful, and dependent.

Of course, for some listeners it was too much heartbreak to endure: soldiers "went down on their knees and wept bitterly."[4] With their past, present and future honor seemingly at stake, a number of Japanese saw no way of moving forward. "Several hundred individuals, most of them military officers, committed suicide."[5] This rash of suicides extended even to soldiers stationed outside of Japan, in Hangchow and Singapore.[6] "Roman" is perhaps the best way to describe these mass fallings-upon-swords in the wake of defeat. At the same time, in spite of the mass devastation, "it was his [Hirohito's] agony on which his loyal subjects were expected to dwell."[7] And true to their feudal conditioning, their hearts did go out to the emperor who had led them into death and defeat. "Some [listeners] confessed to being overcome by a sense of shame and guilt that, in failing to live up to their sovereign's expectations, they had caused him grief."[8] Some of these "overcome" Japanese pilgrimmed to the imperial palace, "still standing amid a ruined cityscape" of Tokyo, "kneeling on the gravel [and] bowing in sorrow for having failed to live up to the emperor's hopes and expectations."[9] This was a finite minority to be sure, although their obsequious, mournful gestures came to be seen by many as emblematic of true Japanese sentiment.

However, in the last failing years of World War II, "discontent and pessimism about the imperial regime became quite widespread. Graffiti reported on by the Thought Police, for example, often called for outright acts of sedition and resistance such as killing 'the dumb emperor.'"[10] By all accounts, most Japanese "felt a great burden had been lifted,"[11] though it was uncertain what life would be like on the other side. There were also feelings of rage and betrayal. Hirohito "sold his country to retain his throne," as one young officer wrote.[12] Militant Japanese were bent on continuing to fight even after—and surely because of—Hiroshima and Nagasaki; the emperor's surrender was the definitive end, and to many Japanese more shocking than the bombings.[13] Irokawa writes, "The emperor system [was] deeply rooted in the intellectual and spiritual makeup of Japanese who were born before the war."[14] Hirohito's moral responsibility for Japan's warfare was clear: the imperial symbolism of the kokutai had conferred divine right on anything "Japan" did—but what, or who, was that Japan exactly? What had it been, and what would it become? Suddenly the Japanese no longer had the figure of the emperor to rationalize and justify their actions.

Emperor worship did not end neatly, on a dime; nor did it overshadow the fact that most Japanese accepted the loss of the war. Dower states, "The Americans arrived anticipating ... a traumatic confrontation with fanatical emperor worshippers."[15] Instead, it was the surrendering Japanese who seemed utterly traumatized, and who put up no struggle: "women who called 'you hoo' to the first troops landing on the beaches in full battle gear, and men who bowed and asked what it was the conquerors wished."[16] A fourteen-year-old Japanese eyewitness to the American arrival reported: "The GIs riding in a few jeeps were almost unarmed, except for a pistol each of them had, and they threw candies from the rear pockets of their pants to the emaciated snotty kids standing in the street."[17]

Soon there would be a widespread reconfiguring of "national identity and personal values,"[18] as the Japanese sought "both to forget the past and to transcend it."[19] Nonetheless, for many Japanese the figure of the emperor was still seen as central to the preserving of any kind of moral social order, no matter how skewed the society had become. The very need to bury the past comes with it a still-alive fear of it returning full-blown. Andrew Gordon writes:

> Having declared discontinuity with the feudal, militaristic past, [the Occupation] nonetheless chose not to try the emperor as a war criminal, arguing that he provided a continuity useful to postwar reform. The American drafters then wrote the imperial institution into the new Japanese constitution. They transformed the emperor from sovereign to symbol, but retained both the office and the person, Hirohito.[20]

How to deal with a symbolic emperor who had been recast by the occupation forces for purposes of promoting U.S. democracy and capitalism? Yasujirô Ozu's films, for example, are ambivalent accounts of the affronting aspect of this switch occurring in the midst of Japanese history, whether or not one championed the outcome or not. Ozu himself meant this when he observed, "Feudalism hasn't really disappeared from the Japanese heart."[21] He wasn't criticizing the Japanese heart, something dear to him after all. As he makes clear in his films, the sheer fact of being forced to change so drastically in mentality—and to give up "Japanese uniqueness"—created psychological hardship.

In Ozu's *A Hen in the Wind*, Tokiko's soldier-husband Shuichi (Sûji Sano) has not yet been repatriated from the country where he had been fighting. It has been four years since the surrender. Not sure whether he is alive or dead, Tokiko is left alone to raise their little boy, Hiroshi (Hohi Aoki). In an early scene, she brings one of her ceremonial kimonos to Akiko (Chieko Murata), a friend with black-market contacts, who makes a point of telling her twice that she herself has long ago sold all her kimonos. Tokiko's wish to hold on to the few fineries she has, as reminders of her former, more pleasant life, is depicted rather fondly by Ozu. It marks her as a woman of refined sensibility, a good woman. Tokiko is given close-ups where she smiles warmly; her inner optimism radiates. In contrast, the actual black marketer, the "no-good" Orie Noma (Reiko Minakami), is a hussy in white fur, and the way Ozu has her stare like a basilisk directly into the camera creates a distinct sense of discomfort and unease. She "violates" the decorum of spatiality and sightlines. Orie, who is a prostitute and who has suggested that Tokiko should work as one, sneers at a merit of honor medal which a starving veteran has asked her to sell for him; she is wearing it like a brooch and flicking it with her finger: "Who'd want this thing? A child's toy."

Naruse and even Ozu before the surrender had made this explicit connection between real military gear and children's toys. But after the surrender, Ozu seems more ambivalent. He acknowledges the defeat of the Japanese military, the demise of prewar life, but he does it through a character who is transparently grotesque and appalling, cut off from domesticity and irredeemably fallen. Even Akiko is shown, intimately enough, down on the floor of her kitchen, wearing an apron and doing ironing. Orie, however, sits on a high Western-style bed, eschewing the simple Japanese custom of sitting and lying on the floor, which we know Ozu subscribed to, because so much of his action and camerawork take place at floor level (a trademark of his films).[22] At any rate, it is not the black marketer and prostitute Orie who represents, for Ozu, a meaningful Japanese future.

Part of this is Orie's sardonic disrespect. Indeed, there is a connection between Ozu's postwar defense of traditional family in Japan and a kind of attenuated emperor-worship, uncertain how to process a "modern," "democratic," U.S.-backed Hirohito. Did the emperor lose his divinity simply by fiat, or by losing the war? In Tokiko's case, the male figure is completely absent, a mystery—does he even still exist? She must struggle and fend for herself without his help, as if he were dead; he might as well be, according to the circumstances of the film, since he is not there to help Tokiko support and raise their son Hiroshi. On a human scale, this is what suffers and falls into jeopardy in the wake of loss: after the swagger of wartime propaganda, the role of fate emerged again to reclaim its central place in the Japanese imagination, truly as if it had never left. In *A Hen in the Wind*, Ozu employs a trademark of his later films, the use of three or four exterior shots in a row to act as a kind of ellipsis inbetween two interior scenes of dialogue; these wordless exterior interludes are more than "establishing shots," according to classical film grammar (although they sometimes double as establishing shots, and Ozu sometimes did establishing shots between scenes); instead they are simply images of life implacably continuing around the human dramas unfolding in Tokiko's makeshift home: an industrial plant, laundry waving on a line.[23] With great terseness, Ozu illustrates the depths of his protagonist's aloneness, especially when he cuts to these shots of alienated, nearly abstract spaces after he has shown Tokiko weeping in her room; there is no "outside" that corresponds directly and humanly to her "inside."

When Hiroshi falls ill with intestinal catarrh, Tokiko cannot stop blaming herself for having given him a cake that he wanted so badly. Again, a sense of fatalism is quietly installed as a kind of first cause for everything. And in the largest sense, what is more fateful than the family one is born into? Ozu depicted "the quiet heroism of the Japanese faced with his own family,"[24] as Anderson and Richie say. Here we have special hierarchization in its purest form, based on unalterable, biological determinism: no matter who, one is born into one's position in the order. Lack of self-sufficiency, the true horror felt by the defeated nation-state, is welcomed back into the family system as the natural way of things. Some of Ozu's titles tell us everything we need to know about the consolations and strictures of placement within that system: *There Was a Father, A Mother Should Be Loved, The Only Son, I Was Born But*. The family is the place where one needn't worry about being a free, or happy, individual; one fulfills a preordained role, one is born, but ... everything else has already been decided.[25]

It is naïve, then, to assume that Ozu's families are "only" families, as if families themselves were not already metaphors in life for the attempt to gather together what belongs together. The fact that birth into one or another family is largely circumstantial becomes covered up by this finesse by which the family, like national selfhood, like the kokutai, attempts to define itself as an overriding essence. Now, circumstance was all that was left, and the family unit shivered in the wind like a frail paper screen. After Tokiko has prostituted herself for one night to save Hiroshi's life, the husband Shuichi suddenly returns, and cannot cope with what Tokiko, in a spirit of honesty, confesses. He cannot forgive her, and it is not until the end of the film, when he knocks her down a long flight of stairs, hobbling her, that he can bring himself to promise to try to work things out. She is on her knees, clasping his legs submissively, and he looks down at her, telling her what a married couple should be, above all "trusting." In this full restoration of patriarchal powers to the male head of the household, Tokiko must endure the unendurable, as it were.

In this sense, Ozu's family stories can be read as recuperations of the trauma of losing the divine emperor and with him the link which ordinary Japanese could use to feel that their ordinary lives were infused with sacred meaning and purpose. At the same time, we can also read these stories as the very stuff of timeless domestic drama, as when Ozu's imperial-era *The Only Son* begins with calligraphy that states: "Tragedy in life starts with the bondage of parent and child." In this film, women hold the jobs in wartime Japan, hunched over pedal-operated steamers in a sweatshop that flies the imperial "Rising Sun" flag. One of these women is O-Tsune (Chôko Iida); her young son Ryosuke (Masao Hayama) wants to go to school, but she sees no value in spending the money to send him. Mr. Ookubo (Chishû Ryû), a young teacher (around graduate school age), lectures her, "A man needs a good education to succeed nowadays," showing her up as short-sighted. She takes this advice, bowing deferentially to the young man and calling him "Sir." When she tells Rysoke that he can go to school after all, she adds, "Your late father will be happy too." O-Tsune will be left alone now, and she weeps to lose her only son. But, although O-Tsune's feelings can be said to matter within the film, they have no bearing on her reality or on what happens to her. Younger males, unrelated males, deceased males—all take precedence over O-Tsune and factor in to all of her life decisions.

In the middle of this male network that gets what it wants, it is the figure of the wife and mother who helps us see the Japanese family as an adjunct of the patriarchal state. "Her overriding duty," Dower writes, "was to serve the male-dominated family—and the duty of the family, in turn, was to serve the imperial state."[26] Now, it seemed, not even the dutiful wife could be counted upon to save the Japanese family. In Kurosawa's *Ikiru*, the plucky girl–Friday, Toyo (Miki Odagiri), tells Watanabe, "Our place crams three generations into one room, it's like civil war." Japanese cinema has always suggested that family structures are perceived very differently by women and sensitive children than by the patriarchs whom the structures were designed to protect and placate. The neurotic mother in Terayama's *Pastoral Hide and Seek* is nearly a world away from Ozu, even at his darkest; she keeps the world of the dead under a trapdoor, and walks the shore of a lake with the family altar (a small shrine used in Buddhist rites) strapped to her back, polished until it shines "like her artificial eyeball." Her care of this altar is shown to be something she does strictly for show, for approval; indeed, she tries to give the altar away to anyone who might want it. She whores out the appearance of a cozy domesticity. Still, for a film about sexual conflict, *Pastoral Hide and Seek* is nonetheless more conservative than we might expect or want it to be: the young hero is appalled by sexuality in general, which he associates with selfish, aggressive, entitled heterosexuals; sex is a mark of vapidity and stupidity to him, and there is no construction of same-sex romance, no male appreciation of male beauty, to counter this conviction—only the doomed hope for a return to prelapsarian childhood illusions, what Oshima's *The Man Who Left His Will on Film* calls the childhood fetishes produced by "the muddy mixture of the feudal and the modern that is Japan."

"After the War," Joan Mellen writes, "Ozu ... opposes the disintegration of the family, seeing this institution as a last refuge against a social harshness ... filial piety becomes a requisite for an individual's respect for himself."[27] His work seems to maintain that the traditional Japanese family nests comfortably inside the state; what the desublimated imagery of later postwar cinema reveals is that the abstraction of the state was actually animated only within the lived daily reality of family. The family is a psychological remainder of kokutai, and a fetish constructed to preserve it against total loss. Tadao Sato suggests this when he writes about "the old, common social body, the disintegration of which only produced smaller units that had existed from the beginning, the small family."[28] In Hara's documentary *The Emperor's Naked Army Marches On*, activist Kenzo Okuzaki identifies both "nation" and "family" as walls designed to isolate people from each other; we could add that these walls do their divisive work under the guise of pretending to group people more closely.

In fact, rather than deriving their adeptness at emotional blackmail from state machinery, families labored to make the structures of autocratic imperialism appear natural and human. At the same time, the emperor's divinity helped family members set aside their self-interests, in a kind of parody of Buddhist resignation, so as not to tear their families apart. Everyone treads on eggshells, as it were, while trying to smile the tensions away. In Ozu's *Late Spring* Noriko's kindly aunt Masa (Haruko Sugimura) and father Shukichi (Chishû Ryû) want to marry her off to Hattori (Jun Usami), the father's assistant, a feudalistic enough arrangement. However, they are progressive and human enough to first agree to ask their daughter if she likes the young man. Ozu depicts this moment as a satisfying, quiet proof of the family's strength and love. It is both wry and touching when Noriko bursts out laughing at her father's suggestion, telling him that Hattori is already engaged to another young woman. "He will tell you soon," Noriko says, as Shukichi, somewhat crestfallen and bewildered, stares into his rice bowl. As part of the younger generation, she has preempted the knowledge which, in true feudalism, would have passed directly between the males, and then only after the older male-authority had given his blessing.[29]

And there are other examples when patriarchal knowledge is aborted or highjacked in Japanese cinema. In Mizoguchi's *A Geisha*, when Eiko's drunken father learns that his daughter has chosen to become a geisha, he rails that she "did not even discuss the matter with me." In Naruse's *Sincerity*, the husband sends his illegitimate daughter an expensive French doll, but the wife finds out immediately when the deferential delivery boy from the store makes a point of informing her that "her" order had been filled that morning. Finally, in Oshima's *Taboo*, sex between men cannot be kept discreet and secret: seducing Kano in a geisha house, Yuzawa (Tomorowo Taguchi) says that he has given orders for them not to be disturbed, but the geisha returns with more sake and sees everything, which then becomes common knowledge. The inefficacy of male knowledge—and the ubiquity of male denial—become submotifs of *Taboo*, where Oshima flashes back to men asserting things that the narrative has already proven untrue, or cuts in men's unspoken, almost subliminal thoughts that could illuminate the action if they were spoken but are instead repressed.

There is a distinctly modern marriage in Ozu's *An Autumn Afternoon*, and it is viewed with bemusement, slight alarm, and finally wry acceptance. Koichi (Keiji Sada) is a young executive; at home, his wife Akiko (Mariko Akada) does not let him laze around and relax, but instead interrupts his smoking to insist that he do small chores like re-setting the clock. Although he is the breadwinner, she runs the household finances, and keeps strict track of their funds and expenses. When Koichi announces that he wants to buy a second-hand set of golf clubs from one of his co-workers, she embarrasses him by forbidding this purchase in front of his sister Michiko (Shima Iwashita), who has come to visit. After Akiko puts her foot down, Koichi spends several days sulking. Finally, Akiko relents and lets him purchase the clubs, but insists on buying herself a new leather handbag to make things even. The wife here is not shrewish and cold; rather, she is pretty and vivacious, this is what makes her authoritativeness slightly disturbing, but also what makes it possible for Ozu to sanction this marriage, as neither partner loses face. They even complement each other, since Koichi has the quirk of never wearing socks like all the others; he is the only character who goes barefoot in his home, and this slight touch, of quiet but stubborn individualism, balances out whatever kinks the wife brings to the marriage.[30] Also, their as-yet state of childlessness allows for both of them to still hold onto some childishness within themselves.

Ozu finally reveals the full chemistry between Koichi and Akiko in one of the last scenes in *An Autumn Afternoon*; Koichi's sister has had her wedding, the family has gathered for the ceremony. Afterwards, the father sits at table talking things over with his son and his daughter-in-law. Akiko is the full equal of the men, not seated on the floor in the doorway as the other females in this film have been shown to do; Ozu matches her medium close-up for medium close-up with the men, who talk to her freely. Koichi smiles at her to show his approval of having a strong wife. Because of this parity, they can come together to help "parent" the aging father at this moment where he needs understanding and good advice.

There are other occasions, too, when Ozu seems accepting of social change; in *Late Spring*, Noriko has a divorced friend Aya (Yumeji Tsukioka), with whom she likes to mock other women in their circle who have sacrificed their careers for marriage and children. Aya even has a story to whisper about one of their friends who is pregnant illegitimately, as we have seen a major social taboo for Japanese conservatives. Yet Aya is not ostracized or even undermined within the film; Ozu lights both her and Noriko with glossy 1940s Hollywood glamour, and depicts their friendship as a true one. At any rate, Noriko's own reluctance to marry turns out to be an unwillingness to move away and leave her father alone. "Then you will never marry," Aunt Masa tells her.

Even earlier, Naruse made *Sincerity*, which concerns a wife's suspicious, dawning certainty that her husband has fathered an illegitimate child with another woman. Yet the illegitimate daughter is the head of her class at school, and her teacher Iwata (Sôji Kiwokata) does not hesitate to praise her single mother to others for doing an excellent job of raising the daughter by herself, and in general for bestowing upon her daughter her own excellent character. While the father's affair has devastated his wife, the community, again, seems to make allowances for human frailty, particularly in not punishing or judging the single mother and the daughter. Of course, Naruse weighs the emotional difficulties which the illegitimate daughter has in coming to terms with her mother's past decisions; she is angry at her mother. Naruse often films the mother isolated behind a screen while the daughter and the live-in grandmother are grouped together on the other side of the room. In one scene, the daughter offers to rub her mother's sore shoulders and starts pummeling them violently with her fists. Children see, and feel, even what their parents have kept them in the semi-dark about. And for their part, the parents in Japanese films often speak dismissively about their children's "obligations" to them, as when the lazy father in Naruse's *The Whole Family Works*, trying to do what is right for his sons, admits, "I'm not trying to use filial piety to get them to work for me."

These films show the Japanese glimpsing that true honor does not come from bullying or forcing the weaker into sacrificing themselves uselessly, or at the very least they seem to suggest that the idea of "filial piety" was never a monolithic reality in Japan. In Yasujirô Shimazu's *Our Neighbor, Miss Yae* (*Tonari no Yae-chan*, 1934), a middle-class father expresses the opinion that being critical of children turns them into neurotics, and the other characters agree. As the wise teacher Ogawa (Den Obinata) says in Naruse's *The Whole Family Works*: "If the parents are good, the children will be too." What seemed to matter most to Ozu was the *intention* of family members not to hurt each other's feelings or abandon each other; the reality was bound to be awkward, a compromise. It does seem to me to be very Japanese to credit good intentions, even when an action is tragically destructive. Investigating a double suicide involving one of their own at the beginning of Suzuki's *Youth of the Beast*, two detectives have this exchange:

FIRST DETECTIVE (holding up suicide note): A double suicide brought on by a woman?
SECOND DETECTIVE: Lucky to have had a woman who loved him that much.
FIRST DETECTIVE: Indeed.

And that is not even inner-circle family relations, but rather strictly outer circle, non-intimate relations: co-workers almost always keep a formal distance in Japanese films. Yet the double suicide is cause for outspoken admiration and even envy. One can only extrapolate from this how much brutality must pass under the bridge of "love" inside families. From Ozu we get the strain of modern Japanese cinema that looks wistfully and even longingly at family duties which are nonetheless revealed as obvious or life-sapping traps. For example, it is nearly an Ozu moment in *Vital* when the mother (Lily) of the traumatized student Hiroshi (Tadanobu Asano) says, "Since you started medicine, I swear, Granddad's picture has started smiling!" Though her words are meant encouragingly, her voice is disembodied, literally hollow, and chimes like tin against the fact that Hiroshi himself can no longer smile. What does it matter if we are unhappy as long as we serve the system, the ancestors? In this, Ozu stands apart from Marker's Vertovian montage in *Sans Soleil*, with its insistence on bringing the starving Japanese homeless and the well-fed Japanese dead into close visual rapport.[31] For Ozu there would be no contradiction there, much less one to be ashamed of. Suffering in this world does not excuse our duties to another.[32] Meanwhile, perhaps the truest meaning of such rites is revealed in Hara's *The Emperor's Naked Army Marches On*, as simple consolation for the souls of the dead, in particular those who died in misfortune, agony, abandonment, despair. Seeing an elderly woman in that film sit and sing sweetly to a grave through her cupped hands, we sense that the dead only wish for some "private" communication in a busy modern world where all things are transmitted too loudly, too openly, too publicly. This need for sacred privacy becomes obvious by its absence in Oshima's *Diary of a Shinjuku Thief*, in which public spaces are congested and dizzy with motion (camera movements; people jostling against each other); the film's reigning gesture is someone placing his or her hand upon another's wrist, a commandeering that can be read as punitive (in the apprehension of shoplifters) and at the same time erotic (strangers picking each other up). In Oshima's *Boy*, death is defined as the only privacy, the only space that is one's own; not even the frigid northernmost point in Japan, "the end of Japan," is enough of a refuge from the sensation of being surrounded by too many people. "I'm going where no one else but I can go," Toshio says, fed up and bent on suicide.

* * * * *

A certain cynical, covert renewal of emperor worship (as tradition, as a token of Japanese "uniqueness") extended beyond Hirohito and allied itself with Japanese culture in general. "In fact, the new constitution was promulgated on the Meiji emperor's birthday in 1947, which was reinstated in 1948 as a national holiday called—Culture Day."[33] This was in keeping with the conservative response to defeat, which had always, naturally, rehabilitated and absolved Hirohito: "one could only 'tremble in awe' before the emperor's magnanimity in concluding the war."[34] A complex mutational operation was performed: "The imperial institution was not destroyed," states Kenneth Scott Latourette, "but the emperor was barred from any active interference in national affairs by the clever trick of increasing his sanctity.... His divine origin ... was held to remove him from the everyday duties of ruling and of concerning himself with the affairs of his country."[35]

Hirohito himself became a nearly fetishistic relic, almost like the crushed and faded cherry blossoms preserved out of the characteristically Japanese sense of *aware*, defined as nostalgic regret for things losing their beauty, prestige and reverence.[36] The emperor remained shrouded in a mystique befitting the still-divine: "None but his closest ministers and the members of his family were to come into close contact with him. No others might see his sacred face. He was to devote himself to honoring his imperial ancestors and obtaining their blessings for the nation."[37] His authority was still absolute as a concept, claiming the ultimate loyalty and obedience.[38]

This lingering emperor worship expressed itself in some bizarre ways. When the government decided to legalize prostitution so that it could control and profit from the sale of sex to occupying GI's, men, many of them about to become pimps, "expressed their gratitude for this lucrative opportunity to serve the nation by gathering in front of the imperial palace and shouting 'Long live the emperor!'"[39] The emperor was no longer to be considered divine, an infallible deity on earth, yet in some measure the mere thought of him could validate and ennoble something as grubby as a brothel. Imagining the emperor still behind the scenes, running the show, allowed for some dignity to remain in a society whose careful hierarchization was being dismantled; suddenly people had to fend for themselves, and "class background, education, or former employment had little bearing on personal relationships."[40] In fact, as with any defeat, it was easier for those who had nothing invested in the prewar society to become successful in the postwar one. "Prostitutes and black-market operatives created distinctive, iconoclastic cultures of defeat.... Private attachments supplanted the old state-enforced dictates of public morality."[41]

By the late 1950s, a special genre had sprung up, of war documentary and docudrama, in direct and titillating controversion of the taboo on openly discussing Japan's military history. The films bore an open appeal to fervent patriotic nationalism. Rather than disturbing people they had some critics and audiences beating a drum that had been long unheard. These were films like *God of War Admiral Yamamoto and the Combined Fleet* (1956), *The Emperor Meiji and the Great Russo-Japanese War* (1956) and *Blitzkrieg Operation Number Eleven* (1957), about which one critic wrote: "Maybe some of the aims of militarist Japan were wrong, but it is certainly a beautiful thing to see the resolve with which these young men [suicide troops] carry out their task with devotion, removing all obstacles that stand in the way of their objectives. Futile though their deaths proved, their deeds were glorious."[42] From the titles alone, we can see semi-covert emperor-worship expressing itself still in the postwar Japan, and blithely allying itself with the fascists of World War II (e.g., "blitzkrieg," a Nazi word).

If the figure of an emperor appeared in these films at all, he was idealized and saint-like to say the least. *The Emperor Meiji and the Great Russo-Japanese War*, in which the actor Kanjûrô Arashi portrayed the 19th century emperor of the title, "showed a very paternalistic emperor concerned over the welfare of country and soldiers. He refuses to eat anything but what the common soldier eats; he refuses to change into a summer uniform, saying that, after all, his men are uncomfortable too; he will not take a vacation because his men cannot take vacations from the war."[43] Even in such a period film, it was daringly nationalistic to depict a militarized Japan in so indulgent and celebratory a light. The kamikazes and other troops had done barbaric as well as brave things, and for more than a decade it had been verboten in Japan to honor them except in observances of the dead. *Blitzkrieg Operation Number Eleven* was advertised in theaters with specific outreach to veterans: "See the brave deeds of your fathers and sons. Free stills of any scene in which your relatives and friends appear. War wounded admitted free."[44] One is reminded of the tearful reunion between Matsuo and his maimed Captain in Shôhei Imamura's documentary, *Outlaw Matsuo Comes Home* (*Muhomatsu kokyo e kaeru*, 1973), the embrace of the two old warriors being probably the most heartfelt and emotionally genuine contact in that entire study of bitterly ironic "reunions." They are lost objects actively searching for the memories that have discarded them, and treading lightly on what might have still been too unbearable for them to remember.

11

"Just a memory": The Figure of the Emperor in Postwar Melodrama

After the war Naruse continued his critique of emperor-worship, now from the perspective of what it had done to destroy his Japan, and still conveying his message through melodramatic stories of women betrayed by men whom they have loved devotedly and who have left them lonely and consumed with disillusionment. In *Late Chrysanthemums* (*Bangiku*, 1954), Okin (Haruko Sugimura) finds herself abandoned by the men from her past. One man who has been in prison for having tried to stab her shows up at her door; she receives him awkwardly and stiffly. He asks her for 10,000 yen, and she says no. Another of her former lovers has arranged to come see her. "He's slender and handsome, a fine brow, nice lips," she giggles girlishly over his old photograph. "He was the man I loved." In the photograph he is posed with his military uniform, arms crossed in front of his chest, a stern and distant look on his face. When he shows up he morosely gets drunk on sake and then begs her for a loan of 400,000 yen. Crushed but containing her disappointment, she tells him she is "a stranger to money."

We see in the literal relic of the ex-lover's old army photograph yet another metonymy for the autocratic emperor, hovering as an idea behind the soldier's strength of purpose and validating Okin's misplaced adoration of him. The photo is freighted with Buell's "nostalgic nationalism" and other historico-ideological imperatives, but Naruse does not allow the old army photo to retain any truth. As usual Naruse measures the Japanese male's presumption that he is related to a divinity via the emperor's divine status and finds it sorely lacking. This is very different from Ozu, for example, who shows a tender scene in *A Hen in the Wind* in which Tokiko talks to her photograph of her husband Shuichi in his imperial uniform (he is even saluting the emperor), asking it at one point, "Are you mad at me?" It is as if this photograph had omniscient powers for her. Tokiko is concerned only with the fear of having let her man down, of having lost his love, perhaps because at this point the man himself is still a rosy memory. But even when her husband finally returns from the war, Ozu spends much of the film focusing on his jealousy, sorrow and anger that Tokiko had turned to being a geisha to pay their son's hospital bills while he was away; we are made to see that Shuichi is a sensitive, decent, loving man, even when he refuses to understand Tokiko and finally beats her. (We also note, although Ozu does not make much of this, that Shuichi is able to walk

11. "Just a memory": The Figure of the Emperor in Postwar Melodrama 177

back into his "old job," at Tokyo Time-Life no less, an option unavailable to most Japanese women at that time.) For Okin in *Late Chrysanthemums*, on the other hand, there is no sympathetic side to any of her prodigal men from the past. Indeed, it is after seeing what her soldier-lover has become in peacetime—a pathetic, human-sized figure of failure—that she brings herself to immolate his portrait, and with it the tendency to deify Japanese manhood as godlike and to be obeyed in all matters. Her last illusion gone, she burns up the talismanic photo in an ashtray filled with cigarette butts.

It is nearly like the controversial edit of a proud Hirohito to a shabby one in Kamei's *Tragedy of Japan*. Okin has completed a full exorcism of traumatic memory, and a personal rebellion. This was, of course, very shortly after wartime when portraits of the imperial family themselves had been held as sacred objects: even to "get them wet in the rain … was to invite execution."[1] Now, Osaku destroys the photo of her emperor-surrogate without looking back. All that is missing from her exorcism is the (not yet manufactured) cigarette lighter in the shape of a wartime grenade (from Marker's *Sans Soleil*), that excessive, extremist touch which would render complete her healthy and independent disrespect, her sudden break from the past, and her drastic change of mind and heart.[2]

More despairingly, in Naruse's *Floating Clouds*, the unloving Kengo, adored by Yukiko all her life, substitutes for the emperor as a repository of misguided and harmful love. Kengo is married to another woman, whom he refuses to divorce; meanwhile he often turns to Yukiko for comforts and for financial help, taking advantage of her love. Their affair has been going on since they met in the Japan-occupied Vietnamese colony of Dalat, where he was an officer and she was an army nurse. This is, of course, a direct connection to the imperial system. Like the sacred emperor, the individual patriarchal man can have his cake and eat it too, so to speak. He gets away with bad judgments and character flaws; the world looks the other way and allows for him. Yukiko tells him at one point: "You're impossible but people think well of you. Really you're a braggart and a coward." Even though she knows this and can even voice it, she cannot break free. She internalizes her lover's viewpoint, appeasing him by saying, "Things can't be the same after a war."

But for Yukiko the circumstances have pointedly not changed. The search for love and understanding compels her after the war as it did before. She will love Kengo literally until she dies. Naruse views romantic love, here, as a fatal trap. (Ozu, too, had no use for romantic love, by his own admission.[3]) Japanese cinema did not learn to become old-fashionedly, gushingly romantic until very late into its "modernization"; this is one of its greatest ironies. Current Japanese films unabashedly embrace love between men and women, especially young love, even if it is not always portrayed in conventional terms. In Miike's *Andromedia*, the first love between Mai and Yuu is so strong that even when she dies suddenly and is transformed into a computer program, he risks death to be with her; finally, she consents to die in his arms, drowning in the sea where they used to play as children. In Jae-young Kwak's impossibly winsome *Cyborg Girl* (*Boku no kanojo wa saibōgu*, 2008), a Japanese teen's ideal girlfriend is also a specimen of artificial intelligence, too perfect for words, right down to her lack of vanity. Takeshi Kitano's gorgeous, touching *A Scene at the Sea* (*Ano natsu, ichiban shizukana umi*, 1991) involves the love between two young deaf-mutes, Shigeru (Claude Maki) and Takako (Hiroko Oshima), undergoing

Shigeru (Claude Maki, left) and Takako (Hiroko Oshima) make for a charming young couple in Takeshi Kitano's *A Scene at the Sea*.

stress from his ambition to become a professional surfer and having a female surf groupie throw herself at him.

Throughout *Floating Clouds*, Naruse views Yukiko kindly, if for no other reason than because she cannot overcome the emotional block that dooms her to love the wrong man and place him above herself (her TB worsens after she moves with him to a remote island where he can find work). Kengo, on the other hand, is viewed as unworthy of her devotion. Anything but divine, he is a displaced patriarch who longs to die but cannot bring himself to commit suicide (a sardonic perversion of godlike "immortality"), yet demands (indirectly) the life of Yukiko, as his follower.

Other commentators have noted in Kengo a distinct representation of imperial Japan and the injunction to emperor-worship. Paul Willeman notes that Kengo "was a military officer ... a glamorous person."[4] Freda Freiberg calls him "quite brutal, and he has been a bureaucrat in what was French-occupied Indochina. He had a position of authority, and he behaves accordingly."[5] As a former army nurse, Yukiko herself is not exempt from imperial guilt; the extent that she feels selfishly entitled to a Great Love, and also the extent to which she valorizes her past with Kengo in colonial Dalat, exemplify an oblivious sense of status that belies her true position as the subject of a hated, defeated empire. Somewhat understandably, she cannot admit her own failure; neither, Naruse seems to be saying, could Japan.

11. *"Just a memory": The Figure of the Emperor in Postwar Melodrama*   179

Dana Polan has written, "Everyday life is often little more than a continual succession of disappointments, of subversions, all of which fissure our self unity and social unity as acting subjects. Art does not deny this malaise; it merely hides and denies its roots in historical forces."[6] Naruse's art was partly intended to expose this denial. Yukiko says to Kengo, "You've changed since you came back [from the war].... You're quick to take offense." But she knows that her love for him has never been a happy or satisfied one; his inability to love her is excused by the traumas of war (possibly) but hardly explained by it. She speaks from the vulnerability of transhistorical emotion, what is unchanging, eternal, and beyond the scope of even the most momentous events. For Naruse, her words are weighted with a deeper truth. Whereas the man's defeat, as we see, belongs much more to narrow historic circumstance; losing the war took something away from him, but Yukiko barely had that "something" to begin with.

We see replayed, here, the downgrading of the emperor from god to human status after the war and the Japanese psyche's attempt to cope with this wrenching loss, this bitter news that what had been done in the emperor's name (Japan's wars against China, Korea, the U.S. and other nations) was finally in vain. After the surrender, Kengo becomes more stoical and impassive, detached from his own emotions and memories. In this sense, although she is basically transhistorical, Yukiko is also the one who bears the weight of historical consciousness, since she remembers the history which Kengo has chosen to forget; she endures a double existence that unfolds both in the present and in a distorted past which she cannot escape. Kengo's single concession to memory and the past comes when he admits to Yukiko, "We should have stayed in Dalat, you and I." He knows fully well that "staying in Dalat" was not an option after the surrender. He could be implying that they should have killed themselves at the height of their passion and power, the way some army officers did kill themselves after Hirohito's surrender.

Apart from that single reference, Kengo orders Yukiko to forget the past. It is as if he felt that he could directly control Yukiko's memory. A Japanese veteran has spoken, quite remarkably, of the psychological bond between the emperor and his followers:

> In those days [the war], we understood each other, we and the emperor, not that we ever talked to each other; that's just how the war was conducted. Everyone knew that the emperor knew that the people thought they had to "die for the emperor."[7]

Even through long periods of being without him, struggling on her own while Kengo lives with his wife, Yukiko cannot stop sacrificing for him, so strong is the hold he exerts on her even across space and time. For his part, Kengo is "acutely aware of what he has to repress."[8] This is a motif of some postwar Japanese cinema, in which men are able to convert their repressed emotions into discipline and advancement, whereas no such sublimation is permitted to women. For women, of course, being unable to repress their negative emotions becomes a liability, as when the samurai in "The Black Hair" segment of *Kwaidan* is driven away from his new wife by her correct assumption that he does not love her: "I can't stand seeing her dissatisfied look any longer," he says, blaming the failure of their marriage on her freely expressed disappointment when he himself is really the fickle one. Negative female emotion is what stops the clock, so to speak, as when Keiko in Naruse's *When a Woman Ascends the Stairs* becomes too overwhelmed by her sorrow to function as a geisha anymore. It is an allegory of marginalized subjective identity seeking a place for itself. Women like Yukiko and Keiko can only want material success if it brings with it the possibility of being able to feel and express their inner lives freely; otherwise, the success itself is pointless. This may or may not be generally true of female experience, but it is perhaps the single greatest theme of postwar melodrama, in Europe and the U.S. as well in Japan, and for Naruse no less than for Douglas Sirk, Roberto Rossellini, Vincente Minnelli, and Rainer Werner Fassbinder.

At the same time, it is only Yukiko's neurotically repeated past that keeps her moving toward a future, a future which would only resurrect and imitate the past but which we in the audience know will never come. "Then come to see me when you remember Dalat," she bargains with Kengo at one point, a hopeless attempt to encode the memory as an ongoing proof of love, a desperate reification of the terms that her selfish lover has set. Although he represents imperial Japan in its surrender, he will determine the terms of Yukiko's surrender to him. Her victimization will atone for them both, and for history. Yukiko is complicit in Kengo's recovery of male authority through her, coaching him to return mentally to the days of his former imperial status so that she can worship him indubitably again.

Above all, Yukiko feels her sacrifices over the years cannot be in vain. It is only after she succumbs to her long-standing TB that Kengo has an emotional breakthrough, weeping bitterly on her dead body. The overdetermined, defended ego, a false selfhood, yields to a relation with the other that is felt, spontaneous, flowing. (As Levinas asks, "In a death that truly touches us, are we not stripped of the I?"[9]) Kengo's display of emotion restores his war-obliterated humanity; in a stronger way than her devotion could have, Yukiko's death has reawakened Kengo to his heart. His tears for Yukiko denote his sorrowful recognition that he had made bad, destructive decisions all along; that he had exploited Yukiko's idealized worship of him; and that he could not live up to her adoration of him as an emperor-surrogate.

"I'm just a memory," Yukiko says at one point, making her function explicit, "and memory fades quickly and is forgotten." Her expression throughout *Floating Clouds* becomes more and more numb and resigned, seemingly shell-shocked, even as the others around her go about the business of forgetting the past and rebuilding Japan. But the memory cannot forget herself. For her there is "no emotional hiatus between what happened then and her feelings for Kengo in Japan now," as Joan Mellen writes, describing Naruse's cut from a kiss beginning in an Indochina flashback and "ending in the present."[10] Likewise, in Oshima's *The Ceremony*, it is the half sister Ritsoku who expresses the feeling that the wartime and immediate postwar "just happened yesterday." Analytical distance, separating past from present, is coded as a male invention, much like the emperor-worship and warfare which the separation is meant to ameliorate. The psychological attempt on Yukiko's part to unify past and present suggests the block by which emperor worship lingered in the minds and lives of many Japanese after the war, and the way it could never be fully resolved either through memory or forgetting. Mellen states that "the traumas of the war have brought no new justice to Japan but have served only to exacerbate the feudal exploitation characteristic of the past."[11] This is no doubt partly what leads Willeman to describe *Floating Clouds* as a "meditation on democracy," specifically Japan's move from a socially conditioned hierarchical order to a society ostensibly or ideally based on an unprecedented degree of individual subjectivity.[12] But Naruse

11. "Just a memory": The Figure of the Emperor in Postwar Melodrama

depicts this movement as stumbling, incomplete, and haunted—just as Oshima in *Violence at Noon* will depict it as the work of psychologically blocked, blinded hypocrites, desperate to cling to anything, no matter how destructive, in lieu of now eclipsed emperor-worship.

Kengo characterizes his burden as having lost his soul; the men can rebuild physical cities and landscapes but cannot change things internally. Naruse shows us that it is the woman's burden *not* to have lost her soul. Rather, she continues carrying the energy invested in her inner emotional life; as with many heroines of melodrama, this energy saps her health and brings about her death. This formula depends upon a certain valorization of female suffering, in which woman's suffering is bound up in that sensitivity to emotion which she exemplifies qua woman. Can she ever become happy and still remain worthy of her name?[13] Meanwhile, the clueless men in Naruse's cinema are unlikely to acknowledge that she even suffers at all. So, in *Floating Clouds*, Kengo grumbles insensitively, "Women don't have as many worries." It is a blatant motif of *Late Chrysanthemums* in which Okin finds herself surrounded by grasping, self-pitying losers who cannot understand anyone else's pain but their own, especially a woman's. One of them tells her: "I envy women.... Men must struggle hard at work...." Another tells her ruefully, "Failure can be fatal to a man," to which she quickly replies, "To a woman, too." And of course, there was also young Yushio in Naruse's *Apart from You*, asking Terigiku, "You have that many troubles?" as if it had never occurred to him that she would have any.

More often, though, Naruse portrays the intractable sexism of older men, such as Kengo in *Floating Clouds*. It is similar to the male hypocrisy in Mizoguchi's *Women of the Night*, where a man lectures Fusako that she has let herself get "bruised and defeated" by war and postwar traumas, when it is simply that she reminds him uncomfortably of these traumas and he would prefer not to think about them. Likewise, a preachy male doctor chastises Fusako: "Just because you've defiled yourself doesn't mean you have to let yourself go still further." Fusako promptly and wordlessly walks out of the room, leaving all the men with puzzled expressions. Where Mizoguchi left off in depicting the postwar toughness of Japanese women, Seijun Suzuki picks up in *Gate of Flesh*, whose cadre of hookers swagger through the streets, accosting genteel ladies and spitting on them, and beating up a U.S. soldier while screaming, "Fuck the GI's, they're just men!" This is way beyond the mentality of emperor-worship, and also beyond the melodramatic code which genders suffering as an integral female experience. Indeed, the women in *Gate of Flesh* consider it a "victim mentality" to dwell on lost loved ones and defeats. Here is yet another similarity between the renegade samurai and the fallen woman, going back to the silent film *Serpent*, whose hero Heisaburo (Tsurasaburô Bandô) is a young samurai disgraced by a series of misunderstandings (his lower-class background is also held against him); his response is to embrace his shunning with a vengeance, falling in with criminals and becoming known as Heisaburo the Outlaw.

Where gender does become an issue in *Gate of Flesh*, or rather a complex of issues, is in the uneasy ghost of emperor-worship which used to bind men and women symbiotically—a bind now violently severed. Males and females hold history against each other: the women resent the men for losing the war, and the men resent the women for letting themselves become callous and self-preserving. Yet, out of this mutual bitterness and rage the spark of attraction and love keeps re-igniting again and again. In *Gate of*

Flesh one of the prostitutes, Machiko (Misako Tominaga), clings to a traditional and outdated romantic love of men, hoping to become someone's wife again one day; the other prostitutes, who have hardened themselves out of necessity, give her much grief for this. Just after receiving a marriage proposal from one of her regular clients, she goes to bed with Ibuki and is reawakened to the satisfactions of lust; nonetheless, she then feels she wants to marry Ibuki. One patriarch and substitute-emperor replaces another. Sexual liberation has occurred but without changing the underlying mindsets that crave security and dependency, and which keep sexism in place.

* * * * *

Emperor-worship run amok claimed more than the lives of women, of course; it also claimed many young men who sought to die in the emperor's name. Mizoguchi raises this trope of the younger, less powerless male as a pawn of patriarchy to masterful heights in his late film, *A Tale from Chikamatsu*. The printer's apprentice, Mohei (Kazuo Hasegawa), is overworked by the Great Printer Ishun (Eitarô Shindô), who pays him "next to nothing." Because of his important duties, Mohei is a direct witness to Ishun's miserly neglect of his wife Osan (Kyôko Kagawa) as well as Ishun's blatant, smarmy pursuit of the young servant girl Otama (Yôko Minamida). Through a series of misunderstandings, Mohei and Osan are accused of being secret lovers and must flee for their lives, since the custom in that time was to crucify adulterous wives and their paramours.

However, Mizoguchi makes it clear that no grand guilty passion exists between Mohei and Osan. Tadao Sato writes: "Their love affair is not a 'handsome man meets beautiful woman' encounter ... for when they realize that the merchant is their common enemy, the desire to fight him kindles a comradely affection that later blossoms into love"[14] albeit remaining platonic. If this sounds fanciful based on other descriptions of the film (such as Badiou's—which is charming but really fanciful[15]), I urge you to see the film for yourself, and also to note that Mizoguchi's title, *Chikamatsu monogatari*, is extremely neutral by contrast with the U.S. title, *The Crucified Lovers* (in French, *Les Amants Crucifiés*) which rather editorializes on the film and primes the viewer to see this as a romantic or sexual story. Instead, the couple is chaste and respectful; Mohei is devoted to Osan because he is kind and because the feudal order requires him to serve and protect her. He also feels for her in her suffering. Mizoguchi could not be plainer about this. Daringly, he casts an actor as Mohei who is not the dashing, virile "young lover" type but soft, androgynous, simpering, pudgy. Mohei makes a point of insisting that he "would never frequent" geisha houses; he wears kohl and eyelash mascara, and his ponytail is much longer and fuller than the other males' in the film. Mizoguchi no doubt recalled the controversial avant-garde craze in the 1920s for gender-bending, the "modern girls" and "modern boys" driven out of existence by the militaristic culture that rose to power less than a decade later.[16]

Indeed, Mohei is passive, sickly, kindly, all of the things that Japanese males in late-feudal Japan were not intended to be. Mizoguchi seems to have been overturning the kabuki fixture of the *nimaime*, a male romantic lead who was nonetheless *takkorogashi* (feeble)—as Sato describes, "a frail, hapless fellow who would fall over if nudged [but] was always kind and gentle toward the heroine ... and gladly died with her."[17] This is perhaps why the women in Ishun's printing company, which doubles as a kind of feudal court, love Mohei so dearly; female Japanese filmgoers loved the *nimaime* type in prewar cinema.[18] While the classic *nimaime* was self-destructive and brought about his own and his lady's demise because of his deep character flaws,[19] Mohei is essentially blameless, socially a progressive (as we are led to see) but not individualistic enough to fall in love. If anything, the Great Printer Ishun is shown as being weaker and in violation of bushido codes, emotional and romance-driven.

Regardless, there is no room in the social order for friendship between a woman and a feminine man. The regime that seeks to protect its property rights (not only money but women and employees as chattel) is too preoccupied with inheritance to allow such things; the Machiavellian subplot of *A Tale from Chikamatsu*, given at least as much dramatic weight as the "love story," is a plot to take over Ishun's printing company by an Iago-like figure who uses the "scandal" of Mohei and Osan as a trumped-up reason to bring Ishun down and replace him as Master. "For the Master," it is said of Ishun, "his reputation is more important than anything else."

Mohei and Osan do become something like a couple in the last act of Mizoguchi's film, mainly by recognizing in each other their shared struggle to become free individuals under patriarchy. It is not until an hour into the film that Mohei stops using the formal "Madame Osan" when addressing his co-fugitive; it is not until the last time they see each other, in the last scenes of the film, that he somewhat overcomes the horror and confusion and seeming revulsion that he has evinced whenever Osan has thrown herself into his arms and clung to his chest for consolation. In the final image, as they are being taken to be crucified, they sit side-saddle on a donkey, chastely holding hands and smiling beatifically. Death is the only way they have found to escape from the shackles of patriarchy, and for Mizoguchi this is the deepest bond between them. Their bond is first and foremost a mode of resistance, and as such it falls into the category of another kind of discipline. Indeed, we wonder if they would have come to know and care about each other at all if they lived in a world where they did not suffer under the same oppression.

* * * * *

The desacralized Hirohito had his lingering defenders, of course. In postwar movies these were often villainous or monstrous figures. The mother in *Onibaba* pulls every trick to reaffirm the power of her dead soldier-son: she claims the reports of his death are false; she claims that he has been murdered by those who purported to be his friends; she holds out the possibility that he may yet return, and that she and others will go to hell and be tortured by demons if they shirk their duty to his memory. In this sense, we see the mother clinging to some sense of what the emperor represented, a divine power from which no one could turn away. She holds the returning soldiers in contempt, implying that if they had honor they would have died with their comrades, an allusion to the emperor's expectation of his soldiers' making the ultimate sacrifice of their lives.

Then, the mother encounters a masked emperor who is also fleeing from the front lines, and she turns this logic around on him: "Men like you killed my son," she accuses him. It is as if *Onibaba* were trying to root out the complex feelings of the older generation of wartime Japanese who could not move on from having lost loved ones in the name

In Kazuo Hara's remarkable documentary *The Emperor's Naked Army Marches On* (*Yuki Yukite shingun*, 1987), World War II veteran Kenzo Okuzaki has devoted his life to confronting and accusing his former commanding officers whom he claims killed and cannibalized a Japanese infantryman during the last bitter days of the war. Okuzaki's wife looks on.

of Emperor Hirohito, who now seemed a wretched figure of defeat. She asks to see the fleeing emperor's face: "I've never seen anything really beautiful since the day I was born," she says sardonically, as if priming the emperor's vanity that she might derive some sense of her own sacredness from worshiping a sacred imperial figure. "This is not a face to show peasants," the emperor says, dismissing her, saying that his face is too handsome for her to see, and playing on Hirohito's lofty seclusion from public contact with his subjects. But the mother has come too far to turn back. After she kills him, we see that his face was grotesquely disfigured—the divinity and the authority that went with it were lies. She laughs bitterly, "So this is a samurai general's face?" and with her mockery his head falls to the side, finally dead, as if killed off by his subject's sudden scorn. We see that "symbol of ignorance, irresponsibility, and impossibility" which Kenzo Okuzaki, depicted in Hara's *The Emperor's Naked Army Marches On*, devoted his postwar existence to accusing and shaming, and can still never get far enough up the command chain to indict for an officer's murder and cannibalization of a private in the weeks after the surrender, in 1945. The few survivors, aged and hobbled, keep pointing to someone higher up than themselves, just as Hirohito and his supporters would ascribe the wars to a military force run wild, even though, as Okuzaki points out, Hirohito was "the supreme commander of the imperial army." Okuzaki himself comes to appear as a restless, raging executioner rather than an angel of history; so, in *Onibaba*, behind the mother's judgment, however accurate—"You caused others to die, you deserve this punishment"—lurks the figure of a self-righteousness so curdled that she does not need the excuse of an autocratic emperor to do bad things; wearing his mask, she makes herself into a ruthless, power-mad tyrant, and, like a thing possessed by malign spirits, it infects and disfigures her in turn.

12

Three Films

Mizoguchi's *Women of the Night*

A postwar melodrama which evokes the disillusionment of Japan's defeat and the specific toll this took on male and female relations, Kenji Mizoguchi's *Women of the Night* opens with a long slow pan revolving across an overcrowded slum, a jumble of mismatched rooftops. But when the director cuts to street level it seems less an urban environment than a Medieval hamlet: there are dirt paths instead of streets, everyone is walking, there are no automobiles of any kind, and people peddle rags out of open-sided shelters whose only amenities are the kettles and services required for tea-ceremony, the only items of any value to be seen. If the U.S. occupation had intended to move Japan "up" from its feudal times, then Mizoguchi seems to be saying, visually, that the evidentiary results speak for themselves. In this decimated world, the teenaged Kumiko (Tomie Tsunoda) says, "I'll find happiness my own way!" She steals household money from her family and runs away from home. Not very surprisingly, she is waylaid by the wrong boy and raped, which Mizoguchi films with tact; but the following scene in which a girl gang beats and strips the now damaged-goods in a bombed-out lot and then gives her the choice of joining them or remaining a victim is startlingly strong for 1948, and anticipates the similarly crazed, desperate violence among the hookers in Seijun Suzuki's later *Gate of Flesh*. Without cutting away, Mizoguchi films the entire extended beating, stripping and finally invitation to join the gang in a single take, with the camera following the characters to keep up with the action, so that we see everything as it happens. In this, Mizoguchi rubs the viewer's nose in the utter degradation of his Japan.

The main heroine of *Women of the Night* is the war widow Fusako. Everything in her world is soured: her brother-in-law, with whom she and her infant child grudgingly live, is bitter about his years as a soldier, Japan's defeat, and now having to risk prison every day in the black market. He refuses to put his drinking money toward the household budget, arguing that he needs to drink because of what life has driven him to. Mizoguchi depicts this in itself as a fatuous male prerogative, but the brother-in-law weaves his initial selfishness into a whole paranoid logic that lays blame everywhere but himself: "The kid doesn't need all those shots," he grumbles, referring to Fusako's tubercular child who is soon to die; "the doctor pushes them because it's profitable." The black market, covertly supplied and kept running by Japanese bureaucrats and U.S. high command, imposes a cast of criminality and suspicion over even official (and medical) functions, since vaccinations no longer imply life-saving health but simply drugs, items with a street value, up for sale.

In the scene where the baby does die, Mizoguchi shows what is left of the cobbled-together family huddling in a single cramped room. The outer edges of the screen are dark because there is only one light bulb, in the center of the ceiling, illuminating the very center of the room (and the shot). This is a cost- and energy-saving measure, and though we might recall Tanizaki's epicurean love of shadows, of calming, elegant dimness and semi-darkness, we nonetheless see that for Mizoguchi it is fear and uncertainty that are evoked by the meager, stingy light. Mizoguchi does nothing to aestheticize this stark, broken world.

"If Hirohito missed his moment for saying 'I'm sorry,'" Norma Field maintains,

> then ordinary Japanese citizens also missed their chance to demand that apology and therefore to consider the possibility of their own responsibility—a responsibility different from that of public officials and the emperor, to be sure, but a responsibility whose continued denial has been translated into silent acquiescence to the harsh discipline required for [postwar economic recovery].[1]

The idea is that the social order was held together by a sense that it was a transcendent entity through which the Japanese became defined by sacrifice of individual needs, "'a tendency to view the social as something substantial that transcends the individual,' and at times this was reflected in a propensity to 'ignore or suppress the human dimension.'"[2] This is why Oshima and Imamura, as we have seen, relentlessly attacked the idea of a transcendental kokutai, preferring instead to view Japanese society simply as a collection of people as quirky, perverse and (in a word) human as anywhere else. Indeed, it is somehow unsatisfying to keep repeating that the postwar Japanese were "entirely unaccustomed to autonomous decision-making,"[3] and it gave me some excitement to finally read this assessment by Japanese philosopher Masao Maruyama:

> We've always had a vast arena in Japan where social coordination takes place without ever going through the channel of organizations. The things that go on in this arena are anything from naked violence, terror, and intimidation, down to the subtler pressures exerted by oyabun [heads of yakuza clans] and other kinds of bosses. I suppose we can say that these are methods of solving the problem by means of *direct* human relations.[4]

As sinister as this might sound, it does, after all, sound like any society, one whose members can and often do move spontaneously either by themselves or in concert with small groups. In *Women of the Night*, Mizoguchi's depiction of the postwar as a time when the worst instincts of individualism were forced to assert themselves, to the detriment of the total social order, may have overlooked the ways in which Japanese society was always already as disorderly and spontaneous as any human collective. Instead, he implies a complete revision of social boundaries. When Fusako runs into her long-lost sister Natsuko (Sanae Takasugi) in the street, they go to tea, and the sister, now working as dance-club hostess, wastes little time in asking if she can move in with Fusako. We are led to see that such rudeness would have been inexcusable before the war. And from this perspective of an absolute order which once did or should hold sway, interpersonal impolitesse is no different in kind from the worst crimes, since all of these threaten the would-be sense of total unity. Just as in Naruse's *Floating Clouds*, where the housing shortage becomes a ready excuse for a man to shack up with another man's wife, so in *Women of the Night*, the effects of deprivation, famine and poverty are shown as unweaving Japan's ethical and social bonds. But even for Mizoguchi, as for Naruse as well, these moments of social breakdown occur in imperial-era films as well, suggesting that we should read them in general as an illustration of the limitations of the Japanese social order in any era, and by extension the limitations of any social order.

Imamura's *Outlaw Matsuo Comes Home*

Leave it to provocateur-genius Shōhei Imamura to ask the direct questions regarding Japan's imperial past. The psychological nature of emperor-worship is clearly articulated by the war veteran Matsuo in Imamura's documentary, *Outlaw Matsuo Comes Home*, when he explains that going off to war was like abandoning his own family and taking the emperor as his father. He ended up wounded and shipped to Thailand, where he remained for nearly thirty years. During his isolation he subsisted on cruel rumors and hopes: he was told that everyone in Nagasaki (his hometown) had been killed by the atomic bomb; he was also told that the Japanese army was coming at any moment to rescue him and bring him back. His sense of betrayal deepened, and expressed itself as hostility toward the abandoning father-emperor, still alive and in power but absolved of all responsibility for the unresolved problems of the war. In a coup de théatre, Imamura takes Matsuo right to the doorstep of the emperor's palace, where Matsuo delivers an angry tirade through the bars of the gate: "An emperor should sell his own house if he has to, to rescue us." The disparity of the emperor's luxurious property and the "primitive" village subsistence of ordinary Japanese who fought and sustained heavy losses in wartime is rendered didactically stark.

However, not all of the emperor's subjects (surrogate sons) are equally disenchanted. Matsuo's actual brother, Fujio, did not become a soldier, and is characterized as being still in the grip of emperor worship: "Abusing the emperor is like throwing mud at [one's] own father." Again, Fujio feels that Hirohito is a father to him, a powerful patriarch with ultimate rights over everyone else. It is not merely coincidental that Fujio himself is an abusive alcoholic who has nonetheless become one of the wealthiest men in Nagasaki through hustling and business ventures during the postwar boom. He claims the rights to selfishness and to leadership in his own name even as he claims them for "the emperor." Meanwhile, for the more progressive-minded Matsuo, blaming the emperor is a step in the cause of social justice. "I have the right to abuse the emperor," Matsuo asserts, since he sacrificed so much of his life in the emperor's name. And this sentiment is echoed by another Japanese veteran in Imamura's *In Search of Unreturned Soldiers in Malaysia* (*Mikikan-hei o otte: Marei-hen*, 1970),[5] who states that he now feels manipulated by the emperor's propaganda. "Loyalty and patriotism," he says, "that was something the big guys taught us ... in order to develop and strengthen our country [economically]." Or, as a sweet-natured veteran says in a moment of candor in Ozu's *An Autumn Afternoon*, he is glad Japan lost because now "the dumb militarists can't bully us anymore."

The veteran in Imamura's Malaysian film has stayed in Malaysia and become a convert to Islam, holding up emperor worship as a false god interfering with true religious faith. In this case, the former member of the imperial army has opted to remain as a citizen in the nation he once occupied for the emperor. Matsuo was never repatriated from

Thailand, and not exactly because he wished to remain there. He is frequently referred to by himself and by Imamura as having been "abandoned," "left behind." In the scene where Matsuo is reunited with Fujiko, his long-suffering sister, Imamura includes members of his own lighting crew in the shot, to mark this as a public and historical (as well as meta-cinematic) event.

Fujiko reports that the brother hit her because she didn't greet him in a pleasant or polite enough way. Matsuo wants to intervene on Fujiko's behalf with the high-handed Fujio, and rails against him: "He's so stupid! That sort of man led us to defeat!" The dutiful emperor-follower (Fujio) is again presented as interchangeable with the emperor, a simulacrum in daily life, demanding excessive obeisance and doling out punishments.

Imamura has nicknamed Matsuo "Outlaw" because of his wildly outspoken streak. He is an individual in a Japan still tending to view individualism as a crime, or at least a disturbance, against harmonious order. Matsuo views modern Japan as given over wholesale to cowardice and greed. He sees greed as having been the basis of the Pacific Asia War as well: "The war was for money, wasn't it? The emperor must have started the war because he wanted money, too." Again, another veteran in *In Search of Unreturned Soldiers in Malaysia* expresses the same point of view: "Japanese people were tempted by greed. That's how the war started." Matsuo and others like him are characterized in *Outlaw Matsuo Comes Home* as those left behind by "Express Train Japan," or, as Japan is described by a Japanese vet in the *Malaysia* film, a bunch of "corporations stealing information from each other." (We are reminded of the brutal espionage war between the automakers in Masumura's *Black Test Car*.)

"Is this what has come of all Japanese men?" Matsuo asks in one scene, defiant and despairing, seeing only petty people acting in their financial self interests. "All Japanese are insane with greed." This is as much the fault of U.S. intervention as of the emperor and wartime imperialism. In Fujio's kitchen, we note a bottle of American 7-UP, and in *In Search of Unreturned Soldiers in Malaysia*, U.S. economic interests

Shôhei Imamura enjoyed a long and productive career in Japanese cinema and television. Always outspoken and provocative, Imamura dedicated himself to challenging the establishment and the power elites in Japan.

are underscored succinctly by the fact that a steel mill bears the English name: "STEEL MAKING PLANT."

Matsuo is dealing with bureaucratic red-tape and errors regarding the inaccurate report of his death. Being an "outcaste" in Japan is like a limbo between life and death. In Japan poverty itself confers a taboo or outcaste status, as when Matsuo says that Japanese people always "avoided me because my parents were poor. I was born that way. I'm looked down upon wherever I go." Even his own brother, now wealthy, looks down on the veteran Matsuo. Ever a man of double standards, Fujio calls Matsuo "arrogant" for letting a documentary be made about him, yet wastes no opportunity to come before Imamura's cameras and fan the flames of family antagonism and self-promotion. Contempt for poverty is the ultimate double standard. In *In Search of Unreturned Soldiers in Thailand* (*Mikikan-hei o otte: Tai-hen*, 1971), a Japanese veteran cites his impoverished background as a reason that he refrained from repatriating after the war: "There was no place for me in Japan. We were lower class." Most of Japan was starving after the war, but apparently inborn class distinctions were still enforced.

At one point in *Outlaw Matsuo Comes Home*, Matsuo asks his sister Fujio, "Why was I reported killed?" She says, "I went to collect your ashes. That's all I know." "What was in the urn?" Matsuo asks, naturally curious, suddenly a bewildered spectator at the spectacle of his own death and funerary rites; and his sister answers: "Nothing." For Imamura, this morbidly empty ceremonial urn comes to stand for the hollowness of modern Japanese society. Matsuo is already skeptical of religion. He visits the shrine that has been built to fallen veterans but doesn't believe that the spirits of his "dead buddies" are actually there. However, this is not because he is un-superstitious; instead he asserts that the spirits of the dead remain wherever the persons died.

Matsuo's "posthumous" exploits grow more bizarre. Another relative gives Matsuo a copy of his death certificate, written out in calligraphy on well-worn paper. This relative also points to a photograph and says, "You were promoted to Sergeant after you died." Is the most model soldier, finally, a dead one? Meanwhile, the rich Fujio brags about spending 2,500,000 yen to build a special monument to their family members killed at Nagasaki, yet says that Fujiko can go to hell. "How can I look after a sister who doesn't obey me?" Fujio asks.[6] Honoring the dead is tinged with the maniacal, particularly when it goes hand in hand with not caring much about the living. We note that in comparison to Fujio's beau geste with the family monument, Matsuo's entire "condolence pension" from the army is a mere pittance: 160,000 yen.

Matsuo is often asked why he did not come home sooner. He talks about being unable to contact his family for a long time, but there is something slightly unconvincing about this explanation. Imamura had already made clear, in *In Search of Unreturned Soldiers in Malaysia* and also in its companion film, *In Search of Unreturned Soldiers in Thailand* (1971), that the mystique of the ex-soldier in a different country was partly that they had chosen to remain in these former colonies and make a new life for themselves. They are not prisoners of war, or missing in action, still less A.W.O.L., as one veteran bristles, so much as Japanese soldiers who did not want to return to Japan. It is Japan who ran away from them. Behind their dilatory returns lurks an existential wish to no longer be Japanese. One unreturned soldier in Kuala Lumpur adopted a Malaysian name and joined the Chinese Communists. And, in an even more total self-transformation, there is the veteran in Malaysia who converted to Islam. He says, "Although I am Japanese myself, sad to say, the Japanese are not as good as the Muslims." If he had the money to travel, he tells Imamura that he would go to Mecca rather than back to Japan, and he intends to raise his children completely sheltered from Western, urban, non–Muslim values.

There is still a fierce resentment of their Western conquerors in these aged veterans. The one who joined the Chinese communist army began by attacking U.S. military bases. But after a while, he had the realization that he was still fighting the old battles of Japan, and his delusion of saving-face, as it were, wore off. It is not surprising that insanity emerges in some of these veterans' stories. Imamura enquires about someone named Lim. He is told, "He died of mental illness." Someone else explains that this means he took too much opium. There is a note of racism against the Chinese: after Lim married a Chinese woman, she began giving him opium as a way to stop him from drinking, and so he became a drug addict. Finally, a friend of Lim's reveals that he had become a violent alcoholic: "He'd get drunk, go out and fight with every man on the street." Antisocial tendencies cluster and even compete with each other. The war, never won, never concluded, goes on—for Matsuo, too, who, when he gets angry, says he would still like to kill the Americans and the Chinese.

Imamura himself expresses personal shame while speaking with members of other Asian races who were victims of Japanese aggression in wartime. A Singapore man tells him his documentary research is "not welcome," because hard feelings remain about mass beheadings carried out by the Japanese military against Chinese and Malaysians during the Pacific Asia War; still, no one will say that he or she "hates" Japan even though Imamura asks this question point-blank of several interviewees. Imamura wants to bring out the darkest memories, as healing catharsis or most likely raw testimony. In *In Search of Unreturned Soldiers in Thailand*, the director notes that "our peaceful present lives" have made the Japanese forget the atrocities of the war; Imamura wants to remind them.

But memory works selectively in *Outlaw Matsuo Comes Home*. The bad is always relegated to the distant past; those who dwell on it are considered antisocial and isolated. As Kengo did with Yukiko in Naruse's *Floating Clouds*, Fujio orders Matsuo to forget the war entirely: "Get it out of your mind." Whereas history or memory that is pleasing to the community is enshrined in stolid monuments that are utterly devoid of complicating nuances. Again there are double standards at work in such selective memory. When Fujio reveals his grudge against their sister (Fujio holds many grudges), Matsuo urges him, "Would you forget the past? It was long ago." "It was only a few years ago," Fujio grouses. Likewise, Matsuo is disgusted by his brother's talking "about the distant past," when Fujio accuses him of having mistreated their father. As Matsuo tells his old sweetheart, a lady who used to run a legendary noodle shop, whenever he has thought of her throughout the years it is as though she was right there in front of him. Seeing through his charm, she chastises him for having been "heartless" toward her, and it soon comes out that this memory of his also harbors a guilty and unhappy shadow-history: she had rejected his only attempt to kiss her; Fujio claimed her for himself; she wanted neither brother and was in fact already engaged to marry someone else.

With the past so hazy and contrived, one feels especially sorry for the young children who appear in *Outlaw Matsuo Comes Home*, almost always viewed on the edges of adult conflicts, living reminders of entanglements, divorces, dead husbands, and a whole compendium of private and public losses. Whenever there are children in a scene, Imamura cuts to them at points where the adults are rehashing the maze-like past (specifically, sometimes, the bomb); the children themselves never speak.

Imamura finds, in Thailand, a perfect synecdoche of the unburied, insulted past in the story told by one "runaway" veteran who recalls ministering to wounded and dying Japanese soldiers in Thai medical units. The soldiers so desperately wanted some part of themselves to be buried in Japanese soil that they enjoined the veteran to cut off their pinkie fingers and take them home for burial. The veteran recounts collecting nearly one thousand of these disembodied fingers. What makes the story particularly ghastly is that the veteran in question never actually returned to Japan, as we know because Imamura has had to go to Thailand to find him among the unreturned. One has to wonder: what happened to all of those fingers?

Wakamatsu's *Caterpillar*

What happens to loyal subjects when absolute authority is gone? The postwar Japanese were "forsaken subjects"[7] finding themselves "fantasizing about an absolute power who could save [them]."[8] Like the women in melodramas, the Japanese people had been betrayed by their domineering, demanding man, Hirohito, but having already sacrificed so much by worshipping him, there was for many a tragic psychological refusal to acknowledge the betrayal or their own pain. The mourning for authority is partly the sadness of the subject whose dependency has left him or her with no means of survival. These must be learned from the ground up; otherwise, everything becomes self-betrayal, whether one tries to individuate from the authority-based model, or merely recapitulates to it.

After the terrorist attacks on U.S. targets and the subsequent misplaced and retaliatory aggression which the Bush-Cheney administration inflicted on certain regions of the Middle East (especially Iraq, who had nothing to do with 9/11), Imamura was invited to contribute the "Japan" segment of the omnibus film, *September 11* (2002). He chose to set this segment during the Pacific Asia War, a time when Japan was also misusing military power for dubious imperialist aims. It is a kind of grotesque fable, in which Yukichi (Tomorowo Taguchi), an "imperial soldier," returns from war abroad convinced that he is a snake. Or, he has been cursed and turned into a snake. Either way, he slithers across the floor of his family home with his arms tucked in, and laps water from rain buckets with his tongue. He also still wears his infantryman uniform.

Yukichi's family defends him: "He gave his all for the Emperor." His grandmother (Mitsuko Baishô) is the nicest to him; she sometimes keeps him in a cage, concerned only for Yukichi's well-being: "The only thing that matters is that you got back safe," she says to him, as if shrouding the family's problem in denial. Yukichi's mother (Kumiko Asô) and father (Akira Emoto) discuss their son casually, in bed one night. Six enormous statues of the Buddha flank their marital bed, an overcompensation which Imamura intends as an indictment of the religious-based resignation and fatalism that helped fuel emperor worship in Japan. They dismiss his condition as a form of insanity acquired in battle; then they lose themselves in sex. This is Imamura's view of the modern Japan, burying its disturbing memories and cherry-picking aspects of Buddhism to suit its purposes.

For his part, Yukichi does not seem to comprehend human speech any longer. When his grandmother tries to feed him by hand, he hisses at her and bites her. He prefers to ingest a whole rat, at which point the grandmother upbraids his lack of filial piety: "Your grandfather was born in the Year of the Rat—aren't you ashamed of yourself…?" She chases him outdoors, then kneels and performs a Buddhist chant, another invocation of an impotent, out-of-touch religiousness. Meanwhile, in flashback, Imamura reveals that Yukichi was a coward in battle, hiding in a ditch and trying to surrender to anyone whom he came across. Although the deflating of the military man's prowess is wry in itself, Imamura seems to complicate the ironies here: Yukichi has not devolved into a snake, but rather evolved into one, out of pure disgust at himself and his fellow countrymen. In the end, he drowns himself rather than having to face this fact, preferring to die as a snake than live on as a human. Set against the rote duties to Buddha which the rest of the family has performed in the rest of the film, Yukichi's final act feels almost like transcendence.

Imamura's short film is pungent and poetic. But it was Kôji Wakamatsu, longstanding underground filmmaker and perhaps the most radical cineaste of his entire generation, who delivered the coup de grâce to emperor-worship and the individual male narcissism which it fed and was fed by in turn. This was strangely fitting, since Wakamatsu had sometimes depicted male violence against women in ambiguous terms (in such 1960s films as *The Embryo Hunts in Secret* and *Violated Angels*), as an anarchic and cathartic protest against the staid values of traditional Japan. The young rogue male who acts out against female bodies in acts of rape and murder was partly seen as reclaiming his individual manhood from his helpless status under totalitarian state power; his violence cuts through an otherwise murky atmosphere of lies and deceptions. In contrast, Wakamatsu's late masterpiece, *Caterpillar*, is explicitly critical of male Japanese violence and sexism, which he associates directly with emperor worship and the conservative old-guard.

Caterpillar takes place during the Pacific Asia War of the 1930s and 1940s. The film opens with a brutal montage of the Rape of Nanking, literalized in the form of a terrifying Japanese soldier, Lt. Tadashi Kurokawa, raping a terrified, defenseless woman, whom he calls "Chink bitch," in a room that is being engulfed in flames. These violent images are intercut with pastoral shots of a patriotic parade in a Japanese village where the townsfolk are cheering on the return of their local hero, the same Lt. Kurokawa, now horribly disabled and disfigured from combat, a grotesque torso with no arms or legs, and with half his head covered in thick, ropy scars.

If, at the peak of his vitality, Tadashi was a vicious rapist, now he is "nothing but a pile of flesh," as the old Village Chief (Sabu Kawahara) bemoans. Nonetheless, acclaimed as a "Living War God," Tadashi becomes a token of village pride. This vestigial carcass is a military fetish, fully regaled with his starched and folded dress uniform lying at his side, along with three medals for valor and bravery bestowed by the emperor himself. Wakamatsu's succinct sarcasm reaches its pinnacle here. These vile accouterments validate Tadashi as a former (and vile) warrior, even though they pointedly no longer "fit" the soldier's body anymore; like Amfortas' unhealed wound in Hans-Jürgen Syberberg's *Parsifal* (1982), a disembodied patch of gashed flesh on a platter, everything about Tadashi represents the warrior body under advanced deconstruction/decomposition, an antiphallic metonym that stands only for bereft loss. No longer the penetrator, Tadashi has been thoroughly penetrated, shall we say, by life and its very worst luck. There is no honor in what he did in war, and no honor in his mutilated survival.

Also like Amfortas' wound, Tadashi's maimed remainder begins to threaten the entire patriarchal society around him. Having to care for her husband, his wife Shigeko is of mixed emotions. *Caterpillar* is actually Shigeko's story. She finds it difficult to continue worshiping Tadashi, yet it is deeply ingrained in her to do so. She rejects him at first, then feels beholden to her wifely duties; she is told often throughout the film that she is not only serving her husband but the emperor and "the empire" as well. The emperor is like an externalized power source, always in sight or mind, and at first the maimed husband does little but lie on the floor staring wistfully at the framed portrait of Hirohito and the Empress, which presides over the marital bedroom. (There is frequent cutting back to this portrait throughout the film.)

To worship Tadashi now requires—and elicits—a greater store of masochism from Shigeko that even this imperial officer's wife is used to giving. Tadashi can now neither speak nor hear; somehow, his wife understands that he needs to urinate. This limbless torso still has a penis, and when the wife takes it in hand to help relieve him, her acquiescence suddenly restores some of his lost wholeness, like the first taste of blood that begins to reconstitute the dead rake in Clive Barker's *Hellraiser* (1987).

At this point, Shigeko obediently mounts her husband and has sex with him. And so it is that the husband comes to dominate his wife again, by playing on her instinctual desires to be patriotic, loving, of service, and by literalizing his phallic "superiority." Wakamatsu renders her performance of sexual obligations in an extreme wide angle framed by the opening of the bedroom; this proscenium effect is somewhat reminiscent of Peter Greenaway, and suggests that the private bedroom is actually a theater-spectacle, performed for others rather than for the couple itself. Shigeko does not enjoy the sex, but for Tadashi, on the other hand, penetration and orgasm are his last remaining functions, and he makes the most of them; it is like watching a decaying corpse writhe and gasp in sexual triumph against the bosom of a living woman.

Tadashi is, of course, vampiric and insatiable. After every ministration that Shigeko makes to restore his diminished phallic authority, he is like a junkie with a fix, growing calm and restful again after bouts of frenzied snapping and biting. Every demand he places on her—whether it is feeding him or holding up the framed front-page account of his battle exploits for him to gaze at—is essentially a libidinal-sexual one, involving Shigeko's submission to his masculine pride and honor, and because Shikego is always reluctant at first, having to overcome her revulsion of Tadashi, every scene inside the household plays psychologically like a rape scenario, even though the husband can no longer physically compel the wife to do anything. Like Hirohito himself, who isn't actually in the room but is still very much present, the thought of the husband's entitlement as a male is enough to coerce the wife into obeisance even against her natural feelings and rational mind. Wakamatsu also makes us understand this in relation to the character of Tadashi's brother, who was unable to serve in the army because of his poor health and is deeply saddened by the fact that he is thus utterly "useless," to the empire, to women, to himself.

As the film progresses, Tadashi regresses, becoming like a terrified baby at times, as Shigeko goes through stages of defying him and taking back some of her control. Recalling how he used to beat her every day when he had all his limbs and strength, she starts to hit him, and when she climbs on top of him for sex (now only when *she* wants it rather than when he does), he cringes, seeing his own face—crazed, sadistic—as it appeared to his Chinese victim in the opening montage. But Shigeko can only dominate him impulsively and guiltily; after she has satisfied herself, she goes back to feeling dutiful, apologizing to him, sobbing and holding him. Both partners are only able to relate to each other through terror-tactics and cruelty; they value only what is weak and exploitable in each other.

Here, Wakamatsu likens the system of emperor worship to an abusive relationship; what Oshima imaginatively turned on its head in *In the Realm of the Senses*—the man passively dying for the sake of the woman's orgasm—becomes a brutal patriarchal nightmare in which Tadashi learns what it is like to be helpless and abused, but never transcends brutality. Nor does Shigeko transcend her increasing addiction to hurting him, or even fulfill her own sadism by taking it to the logical end reached by the woman in *In the Realm of the Senses*. But then, the point of *In the Realm of the Senses* is not that the woman is harming or punishing the man when she strangles him to death during sex; quite the opposite. This is what makes Oshima's film so genuinely disturbing.[9] While the lovers in *In the Realm of the Senses* grow closer and closer, entering into a pact that is as touching as it is painful to watch, the couple's behaviors in *Caterpillar* grow more and more harrowing without ever achieving any closeness. This is Wakamatsu's explicit critique: there is not even a transitory sexual utopia that can provide refuge from militaristic nationalism; Shigeko and Tadashi, in *Caterpillar*, are both so thoroughly damaged by their nation's fascist tendencies that they behave, even in private, like sadomasochistic automatons.

At the end of the film, the emperor surrenders, Tadashi crawls excruciatingly to a rice paddy and drowns himself in the mud, and the wife and the village idiot are both hanged as secondary war criminals. By invoking Narcissus in the end—the husband stares at his reflection in the murky water—the film complicates the issue of emperor worship. Which comes first, Wakamatsu seems to ask, the reigning dictator or the impulse in each individual male to be worshipped and obeyed? Do we have abusive husbands and rapists because we have a social order that still insists on being governed from the top down, by elitist and usually male figures who represent god-like power? Or have we made such god-like rulers in the image of what we, as ordinary men, would like to believe ourselves worthy of, and to justify our own tendencies to violence and control? And can a woman be anything more than a neurotic reflection of male pathology under such a system? *Caterpillar* leaves these riddles essentially unanswered, just as its title brutally cuts off the possibility of any butterfly emerging from this warped imperial chrysalis. But perhaps that is Wakamatsu's point. Nothing was capable of emerging from that era of Japanese history. Only a different caterpillar would have had a chance of growing, and this might be what historical, socio-psychological evolutions always come down to, not only in Japan—the ongoing search for a better starting-place.

Conclusion

> What the Buddha predicted 2,500 years ago has come true. Mankind has lost its soul.
> —Interviewee in Kazuo Hara's *Goodbye CP*

> The people must develop an internal consciousness of respect for the human being.
> —Hisao Otskuka[1]

> I hate those flowers, those, those flowers there, they're too English. I just want simplicity and sort of Japanese efficiency, a land where they haven't even got time to let the trees grow tall. Nôh Theater ... and *no time for petals* in my life! I want stems.
> —Edina Monsoon (Jennifer Saunders) in *Absolutely Fabulous*[2]

Nakae Chômin's *A Discourse by Three Drunkards on Government* (1887) is one of the key texts of the Meiji Restoration. Essentially a work of philosophical fiction in the general style of Diderot, the book recounts a discussion about the future of Japan. Master Nankai, wealthy, aged, learned, and always pleasantly inebriated, hosts an evening's get-together with Mr. Gentleman and Mr. Champion, two younger scholars who begin to joust with each other. Gentleman is an advocate of Western democracy; he gets to speak first. Champion is a militaristic nationalist, an advocate of imperial conquest and expansion, and he cannot wait to jump in and demolish Gentleman's Shangri-La.

Against democracy's belief in individual freedom and equality, with personal fulfillment as the goal, Champion argues for the national mass to find satisfaction in group action. He savors collectivized emotions over individual ones: "How exhilarating is the pleasure of a nation!"[3] Where Gentleman had praised European cultures for their arts and sciences, their humanities, Champion sees only barbarians at the gate; Europe will attack and colonize Japan, Japan must be ready.[4] War is more than an inevitable fact; Champion says, "War is a thermometer that tests the strength of each nation's civilization."[5] Needless to say, it is dangerous to measure one's civilization by the extent of its willingness to commit brutalities. Losing sight of the line which separates civilization from savagery can easily become a justification for any and every atrocity. Champion accuses Gentleman of a species of Mandarinism: "To insist narrow-mindedly on the ideals of liberty and equality, or to express the sentiment of universal brotherhood at such a time is like Lu Xiufu's insistence on teaching the classics as the Mongol armies attacked, isn't it?"[6]

Specific undercurrents of hostility toward China seethe beneath Chômin's text; in the end, Mr. Champion is headed in no uncertain terms for Shanghai. Champion's arguments cleverly employ rhetoric aimed at the emotions of honor and shame, in order to glorify the emperor above all else[7] and even to make light of the pains that soldiers experience in combat, since it is a soldier's highest honor to die nobly and beautifully.[8] A nation must at all costs avoid becoming what Champion calls "a big, fat sacrificial cow," waiting for other nations to lead it to slaughter.[9]

There is a semi-psychotic male vanity at work here—we have seen it lampooned in Suzuki's *Fighting Elegy*, for example—by which the imperative to kill or be killed turns the nation into a more or less literal body (kokutai). This body must be hard, impenetrable, self-sustaining; it must not show its flanks, as the naked Terumichi does in suicide at the end of Oshima's *The Ceremony*—the definitive abdication. It must also not fall for the distracting seductions of too much thought; Champion has a word for this particular weakness: nostalgia. The nostalgic body, which he associates with liberalism, is marked by everything that a warrior would wish to avoid: complacency, laziness, helplessness, passing the buck, wide open to the creeping predations of metaphorical cancers. Above all, nostalgia cannot seem to see the forest for the trees: it is so enamored with the ideal of goodness that it forgets how to achieve it, and in its unpreparedness it is doomed to end up massacred on some foreign battlefield.[10]

As their names suggest, "the Champion" is given greater weight than "the Gentleman"—he presents his argument second, thus being able to attack the Gentleman point by point—and in the end Nankai seems to side with him,[11] dismissing democracy as essentially too idealistic, radical and futuristic to apply to Japan.[12] At first unwilling to commit his views to the discourse, Master Nankai, when pressed, espouses a constitutional monarchy placing emphasis on "the dignity and glory of the emperor above," and with dynastic parliamentary leadership, the Upper House consisting only of aristocrats born to govern for life.[13]

Here is where we might imagine Oshima, for example, rolling his eyes at this text, even throwing the book across the room. Chômin's unsatisfactory, folksy recommendations were to have disastrous impact on Japanese history, beating the drums of war and imperialism from a lofty, blinkered, eternal comfort zone. In his wealth, Nankai has the luxury of staying drunk and playing at deciding the fate of the world with his friends. It is not he who will have to pay for these fanatical dreams, it is ordinary Japanese, and ordinary Asians across the mainland, Chinese, Koreans, Vietnamese, and others. This is something that Oshima was acutely sensitive to: he journeyed to Korea and Vietnam to witness first hand the human misery that Japanese adventurism in those nations had led to; he believed in pan–Asian unity and generally is aligned with Mr. Gentleman's belief that civilizations should rule with their best qualities, seeking the best in others (a kind of otherness-in-one on a global scale). When Oshima resurrects Chômin's "three drunkards" in his experimental satire *Three Resurrected Drunkards* (*Kaette kita yopparai*, 1968), he sets the debate in modern Japan, and makes all three of the protagonists poor young students, stuck on the business end of history rather than its masters. He also has them mistaken for Koreans and summarily executed.

Unlike Champion's rant in Chômin's treatise, war is very much a visceral, immediate problem in Oshima's film. The drunkards have a bitter, absurdist running joke about photojournalist Eddie Adams' then-sensation-causing, still landmark photograph of the execution of a Viet Cong prisoner by a South Vietnamese general; from a standing position with his hands tied, the young Viet Cong is shot point blank in the temple and falls over dead. The famous image captures the exact second when the gun is fired, the bullet blasts into the prisoner's head, and the pained consciousness of "dying" blooms fully in his twitching face. The South Vietnamese general said afterwards: "These guys kill a lot of our people, and I think Buddha will forgive me." But in 1968 public opinion turned against South Vietnam largely because of this single image.[14]

The executed prisoner's expression is one of flinching torment, and the drunkards seize on this. "This is how an Asian looks when he's dying," one of them says, pulling a contorted, undignified, crooked face. What is significant about this is not that they are making "fun" of a humanitarian crisis (they are the drunkards, after all, and anyway they hearken back to the insensitivities of Chômin's text); what is significant is that these Japanese are not saying, "This is how a Vietnamese looks." Quite the opposite; they are expressing solidarity with other, more oppressed Asian nations and ethnicities, seemingly unhappy that Asians are being killed anywhere, and that these Asians' deaths have also been exploited by the media, which codes them as cowardly, undignified, etc. This pan-Asian solidarity is in direct contradiction to what Champion had put forth as the duty of each nation to invade and conquer other nations, a policy which imperial Japan put into effect not long after the Meiji Restoration. 1968 was the year to revisit the Meiji Restoration, since modern unrest called for a time of new constitutions and social contracts.

In general, Oshima took a distinct interest in the idea of resurrection, seemingly intending it almost in its Christian meaning of a Christ-like rising from the dead. As soon as one begins to look, one notices references to Christ and Christianity nearly abounding in Oshima's cinema. In *Cruel Story of Youth*, a key scene is played out in a chapel with Oshima inserting a close-up of the chapel's stained glass window depicting the crucifixion. Christmas features in *Boy* as a moment of relative tranquility for the dysfunctional, abusive family; and it is "the Christmas spirit" which the formerly sadistic Lieutenant Hara comes to internalize in *Merry Christmas Mr. Lawrence*. In *Death by Hanging*, a Korean convict is literally resurrected after being executed by the state; this is no salvation, however, since he is only resurrected to endure more punishments, inequalities, and humiliations. Oshima also has some of the most corporeal ghosts in Japanese cinema (*Violence at Noon*; *Empire of Passion*): they are frequently male, in contradistinction to the trend of Japanese ghosts to be gendered as female, and could be seen as substitutes for Christ. *The Man Who Left His Will on Film* concerns an unending cycle of suicide and regeneration for a martyr-like young Japanese male. Finally, the continuous immersions into strangulation and yankings-back into breath and consciousness of the man in *In the Realm of the Senses* marks it as a ritual of fetishized resurrection, infused with Bataillean jouissance; much like the penis itself, flaccid then engorged, can be considered a "resurrection" in its miracle of erection—that shy, elusive phenomenon that seemed to obsess Japanese New Wave filmmakers and drive them to almost valorize the act of violent rape.

This is certainly a mixed gamut of signifiers, and hardly orthodox, but all the more intriguing for this reason. We might ask, was Oshima a kind of closet Christian, perhaps in solidarity with the Koreans whom he so defended? Christianity was the majority belief system in Korea, and the Japanese occupation persecuted and all but outlawed it. Colonized Korean Christians were forced by law to bow to Shinto shrines: "One Christian seminary told its people not to bow to the shrines and consequently they suffered continual persecution. Many [Koreans] did as they were told in order to survive."[15] Did Oshima's hatred of Japanese religions and the blood on their hands cause him to view his own rough and even semi-profane version of Christian resurrection as a superior goal to strive for? There is something incipiently revolutionary in Oshima's adoption, as a Japanese, of Christian imagery. In this sense, it is no different from Baudelaire's lovely, anguished benefit of the doubt toward the false gods of other nationalities, because he understood that "his own" god was no less false, no less blood-stained, and no less stridently proclaiming of its dubious and insufferable power: "I never pass by a wooden fetish, a gilded Buddha, a Mexican idol without reflecting: perhaps it is the true God."[16] This would also be an example of otherness-in-one, seeing the cultural other from inside, inside oneself as it were. Resurrections occur in Oshima's cinema almost as dress rehearsals for a revolution that would cause Japan itself to die and be reborn, a site of somewhat cynical magic where poverty and superstition devolve into a need for living matter to be redeemed somehow from nameless, faceless obliteration and void.

As I write this, there is an intriguing story from Honduras that is almost like the plot of an Oshima film. Neysi Perez collapsed at home and began to foam at the mouth; she was sixteen, a newlywed, and pregnant. Believing her to be possessed by demons, her mother took her to an exorcist; the exorcism killed her, or at any rate failed to save her, and Ms. Perez was buried in her wedding dress after being officially declared dead by doctors. The following day, members of her family, still keeping vigil at her grave, heard muffled screams from inside her tomb, pounding, and cries for help. Frantic, they broke open the sealed tomb with sledgehammers. Inside she was "motionless and cold to touch," yet the family carried her back to the doctor, who pronounced her dead a second time.

To Ms. Perez's mother, however, the doctors killed her daughter by wrongly declaring her dead the first time, leading to a live burial that she could not be rescued from in time. Either way, the hope held out by the family is that they did everything they could, and even, for a moment, resurrected young Neysi. "We were all so happy. I thought I was going to get my daughter back."[17] It would be easy to treat this story sardonically, yet I find it unbearably moving. Its demonstration of strong emotions derailing staid ceremonies recalls Oshima's films.

As for the Japanese, it is perhaps the Buddhist doctrine of regeneration itself that leads in some measure to what has been considered their streak of nihilism. If everything will die and come back, then nothing will die—hence, one is assured of living again, unlike in Christianity, here in the earthly realm. Even dead a spirit is considered as a physical thing, a possession that can either protect or burden, always with the living survivor. There is essentially little distinction between life and death. Nihilism may be little more than a confusion of tenses, past, present and future jumbled together into indistinguishability. But the human agent is hard to place in this; fate itself can hardly be described as possessing a capacity for evil. Under this logic a human can only view his or her own destructiveness impartially, from outside, as if this destructiveness were finally overcome by something beyond its own ability to endure; yet he or she is also aware that something does endure just as something else perishes. It is this that Kurosawa rebelled against, insisting on Western concepts of agency and the importance of living a higher quality life in the present tense; we recall a key line from *Rashomon*, "The demon here fled in fear of the ferocity of man." But in Zen, there would be no thought of flight, no need for it—nothing can flee nothing, just as nothing can harm nothing. It is almost like an early embodiment of Freud's insight into the connection between sensitivity and aggression: what is already "small" in its own eyes is apt to lash out to augment itself. In Zen, nothingness and reflexive violence are two sides of the same "enlightenment": to be nothing is to be able to kill at will; it is also to be able to be killed, since being killed cannot reduce one's nothingness any further. Needless to say, to kill a human is to kill nothing.

Yet we know that Zen never overruled Japanese humanity entirely; again, the films prove that the Japanese were and are ineluctably human. Ontology is a strange state of refuge, as Catherine Malabou might say. One begins to believe in one's own existence, conceive one's own consciousness, only in defiance of the fact that one is nothing, or reducible to nothing. All ontology stares across this onyx pool of damage and is nourished by it. Otherwise consciousness would go out, snuffed like a candle.

Cinema reiterates these movements of consciousness into being, into awareness; it is always a story, or it becomes one. Even non-narrative films enact the process of being coming into consciousness, and consciousness coming into being. Cinema, history, fiction, are different names we give to this ontological process, which is fluid and endless, only arbitrarily bordered by beginnings and endings. Gordon states that "individuals construct and reconstruct their memories in much the same way as nations do their histories, creating what Borges called a 'fictitious past' that they can live with.... But they were the same people, inhabiting the same self, status, and daily life, except that the frame of social meaning had been suddenly changed around them."[18] The Japanese have sometimes demonstrated an unusual need to reconstruct the content held within that frame of social meaning, to creatively remake it as something comfortably of their own image and understanding.

Indeed, in Japanese cinema, to rely too much on a past that cannot be changed, to remain too connected to it, is to become highly vulnerable. Chômin's detested "nostalgia" plays out in Japanese cinema as a literal killer. Trying to leave behind his criminal life in the slum, Ibuki in *Gate of Flesh* stops by a friend's place to pick up something he had left in safe keeping, the personal effects of a buddy of his who died in combat. He does not want them but cannot bring himself to burn them. Soon after, the police close in on Ibuki and kill him; when they search his body for the black-market penicillin that they were told he had, they find only this package of mementos from the dead friend. Suzuki does not blame his antihero for this, but it is as if Ibuki has died precisely for clinging to an untenable past, his "crime" the refusal to let go of the past, to let the dead remain buried.

At the same time, to be denied one's past can be horrible, too, in a different way. Sas explains, "The longing for tradition ... is a paradoxical but passionate desire for an active, living past, one to be discovered and grasped only from within 'the vital passion of our own lives,' in the physical and present moment."[19] In *Women of the Night*, Fusako

Nagisa Oshima, on set in the 1970s.

goes to collect her dead husband's belongings from the military. The official tells her, "His uniform was in tatters so I left it behind." In Mizoguchi's vision, the remnants of imperialism are not to be coveted and mourned; Fusako does not care that she cannot have the uniform, weeping over some small notebooks that her husband left, a sign of potential individualism (writing, drawing) rather than conformity. Buddhism describes a "world of continual rebirth,"[20] but the rebirth-from is all we can know to help us anticipate (or need, for that matter) the rebirth-into. It is not enough to go on, of course, but in the end, what could be? Simple problems are best, because they leave us enough energy to go on living an ordinary life after solving them. In the solving of complex problems, we may forget how to live, become unable to.

At the end of *Women of the Night*, Fusako is reunited with young Kumiko, and the two of them go off to begin again in a surrogate mother-daughter relation; they pass behind a stained-glass panel of Mary and the baby Jesus, the only erect thing (miraculously) in an urban field of rubble. The stained-glass, for Mizoguchi, is a simple but eloquent visual metaphor for a kind of door that will only admit the pure of heart or those willing to seek salvation. As with Oshima, Christianity is refreshing and new in Mizoguchi's work, seen (one wants to say) through eyes that are not jaded and even primitive. In *Sans Soleil*, Chris Marker visits a temple of cats in suburban Tokyo that is both kitschy (in the sense of some primitive art) and profound. People go there to pray for their own cats, whether living or deceased. The arrays of plump ceramic felines are cartoonish rather than realistic, and all give a one-paw salute that looks unmistakably quasi-fascist. One prominent cat has a broken-off paw; this cat (a kind of animal Christ) comes to denote how all the cats, though intact, are essentially emblems of woundedness in their blank sameness. Like the heaven suggested at the end of *Women in the Night*, the temple of cats is not a shrine to perfection but to woundedness, what the individual can do to teach herself to overcome trauma and nihilism.

Resurrections are finally not about the future, but an enshrinement of the past, Chômin's nostalgic body refusing to give up the ghost. In this, they can also be read as cycles of protest and entrenchment which mark the citizens of democracies. Without constantly changing and expanding, democracy withers and dies. It is one of the few political systems that we speak of either "taking root" or "not taking root" (like a living thing) in nations who try it, depending on the disposition of the people. In fact, we are not certain where it has ever taken root in a true movement of otherness-in-one. To state that democracy "did not take" in Japan is also, probably, to be forced to admit that it never quite took in the U.S. either, the proof being that our cycles rarely signal drastic change much less improvement to the status quo, but instead a condition of stillbirth indefinitely perpetuated and denied. This is what Oshima meant when he said that the question, "How can one die?" can only be answered by the more difficult question, "How can one live?"[21] Just as the question, "What does *death* matter?" can only be answered by a question whose stakes are much higher, "What does *life* matter?"—the two things, our most precious possessions, being inextricable. And in the end, for this reason if no other, we must love the Japanese, and also feel in some measure sorry for them; because, although their excellence has led them into historical delusions of specialness and honor, and chronic disappointment, still, excellence being excellence, they have come closer than many national cultures to laying bare the stark, profound, tragic and comedic essence of those two most important, bewildering, and only intermittently comprehensible things.

Chapter Notes

Preface

1. Roland Barthes, *Empire of Signs* (Trans. Richard Howard; New York: Hill and Wang, 1982), 95.
2. Nagisa Oshima, "Interview," *Cahiers du Cinéma* No. 218 (March 1970), 34.
3. For this reason, I am bucking the academic trend of reproducing Japanese names in the old-fashioned way, with the patronymic surname first and the given name second, because I see this as reflective of patriarchal culture.
4. Guided by the noble and groundbreaking work of Edward W. Said in *Orientalism* (New York: Vintage, 1979), Western scholars have been erring on the side of being distinctly noncritical of Eastern cultures, so as not to participate in that arrogant know-nothingism by which Asia was reduced, for centuries, to a system of Western-controlled representations, a wholly Western imaginary. But what this new piety tends to overlook is the same thing that the practice of "Orientalism" itself ignored and obscured: the fact that Asia is hardly a united entity. Even after we rescue it from all fictive claims by non–Asians, we must note the vast differences and even historical hostilities which exist among various ethnicities and races within the general "Asian" category.
5. "Through the bomb, the United States, gendered as male, rescued and converted Japan, figured as a desperate woman." (Yoshikuni Igarashi, *Bodies of Memory: Narratives of War in Postwar Japanese Culture, 1945–1970*; Princeton: Princeton University Press, 2000, 20).
6. J. Hoberman, *Vulgar Modernism: Writing on Movies and Other Media* (Philadelphia: Temple University Press, 1991), 310–311.
7. *Ibid.*, 314.
8. *Ibid.*, 315.
9. Marilyn Ivy, *Discourses of the Vanishing: Modernity, Phantasm, Japan* (Chicago: University of Chicago Press, 1995), 2.
10. *Ibid.*
11. Igarashi, *Bodies of Memory*, 73.
12. David Desser, *Eros Plus Massacre: An Introduction to the Japanese New Wave Cinema* (Bloomington: Indiana University Press, 1988), 14.
13. Miryam Sas, *Fault Lines: Cultural Memory and Japanese Surrealism* (Stanford: Stanford University Press, 1999), 7.
14. *Ibid.*, 8.
15. Hoberman, *Vulgar Modernism*, 313.
16. Chris D., *Outlaw Masters of the Japanese Cinema* (London: I. B. Tauris, 2005), 45.
17. Alain Badiou, *Cinema* (Trans. Susan Spitzer; Cambridge, UK: Polity Press, 2013), 91.
18. Barthes, *Empire of Signs*, 68.

Introduction

1. Alain Badiou, *Briefings on Existence: A Short Treatise on Transitory Ontology* (Translated by Norman Madarasz; Albany: State University of New York Press, 2006), 24.
2. *Ibid.*
3. *Ibid.*, 25.
4. *Ibid.*
5. *Ibid.*, 26–27.
6. The Japanese title of *The Man Who Left His Will on Film* translates as "Secret History of the Post Tokyo-War Period," a reference to the then-current cause célèbre in which Japanese police confiscated a film that a private citizen had taken of a leftwing demonstration.
7. I should say that the interpretation I am pursuing of *The Man Who Left His Will on Film* overlooks something that Oshima has built into the storyline: Motoki was, perhaps, the one who committed suicide, and will do so again, in an endless repetition. This aspect of Motoki as a character, while interesting, is not necessary to understanding Oshima's film the way I wish to, here, as an extended study of subjective consciousness coming into contact with filmed images, and undergoing a subject-object inversion. From what I have investigated, only Maureen Turim and John Mowitt, in an article from *Wide Angle* in 1977, have touched on such a meta-reading of this film, as an encounter "between a subject and a representational system ... whose 'signification' is generated emphatically through that subject's fragmentation and displacement" (cited in Desser, *Eros Plus Massacre*, 200). This suggests, however, that film is the enemy, the opposite of subjectivity in a dialectical struggle, whereas I see the film as being an interrupted, repeated cycle of expansions and contractions of subjectivity as it pursues and internalizes objectified otherness.
8. Maureen Turim, *The Films of Oshima Nagisa: Images of a Japanese Iconoclast* (Berkeley: University of California Press, 1998), 102.
9. Come to think of it, Hideo Nagata's *Ring (Ringu,* 1998)—about a haunted videotape that will kill whoever watches it in seven days, unless the watcher passes on the curse by showing the tape to someone else—plays like an extreme dumbing-down of the cinematic-ontological questions raised by Oshima's *The Man Who*

Left His Will on Film. In both, consciousness takes objective form in a recorded series of images that seem both random and at the same time charged with significance; at the same time, the images literally begin to change whoever watches them—in *Ringu* the watchers' faces grow progressively distorted in photographs of *them*. The living subjectivities trapped in the testament footage and in *Ring*'s haunted tape call out for the viewers to become part of the films, and finally to step into the role of one who presents images to others; but with both, the chain is never complete. One only spawns new seekers who must find their own place in, and thereby extend, the chain of cinematic-ontologies.
10. J. Victor Koschmann, *Revolution and Subjectivity in Postwar Japan* (Chicago: University of Chicago Press, 1996), 41.
11. *Ibid.*, 208.
12. *Ibid.*, 48.
13. Turim, *The Films of Oshima Nagisa*, 108.
14. Andy Warhol, *THE Philosophy of Andy Warhol (From A to B and Back Again)* (San Diego: Harcourt Brace & Company, 1977), 100–101.
15. Badiou, *Briefings on Existence*, 38.
16. Kelsey Wood, *Troubling Play: Meaning and Entity in Plato's* Parmenides (Albany: State University of New York Press, 2005), 47–48.
17. Badiou, *Briefings on Existence*, 29.
18. Wood, *Troubling Play*, 22.
19. *Ibid.*, 48.
20. Badiou, *Briefings on Existence*, 30.
21. *Ibid.*, 38.
22. Emiko Ohnuki-Tierney, *The Monkey as Mirror: Symbolic Transformations in Japanese History and Ritual* (Princeton: Prince University Press, 1987), 23.
23. Claude Lévi-Strauss, *The Raw and the Cooked: Mythologiques, Volume 1* (Translated by John and Doreen Weightman; Chicago: University of Chicago Press, 1983), 160.
24. *Ibid.*
25. Badiou, *Briefings on Existence*, 36.
26. *Ibid.*
27. Ohnuki-Tierney, *The Monkey as Mirror*, 151.
28. Norma Field, *In the Realm of a Dying Emperor: Japan at Century's End* (New York: Vintage, 1993), 186.
29. Nagisa Oshima, *Cinema, Censorship, and the State: The Writings of Nagisa Oshima, 1956–1978* (Translated by Dawn Lawson; Edited by Annette Michelson; Cambridge, MA: MIT Press, 1992), 66.
30. Wood, *Troubling Play*, 31.
31. *Ibid.*, 30.
32. *Ibid.*, 24.

Part One

1. Edward W. Said, *Orientalism* (New York: Vintage, 1979), 54.
2. Siegfried Kracauer, *Theory of Film* (London: Oxford University Press, 1960), 558.
3. Nicholas Ray, *I Was Interrupted: Nicholas Ray On Making Movies* (Edited and Introduced by Susan Ray; Berkeley: University of California Press, 1995), 54.

Chapter 1

1. Daisetz T. Suzuki, *Zen and Japanese Culture* (Princeton: Princeton University Press, 1993), 127.
2. *Ibid.*, 127.
3. *Ibid.*, 116.
4. *Ibid.*, 124.
5. Oshima, *Cinema, Censorship, and the State*, 30.
6. Ivy, *Discourses of the Vanishing*, 2.
7. *Ibid.*, 3n.
8. *Ibid.*, 2–3n.
9. *Ibid.*, 3n.
10. Badiou, *Briefings on Existence*, 39.
11. Catherine Malabou, *Ontology of the Accident: An Essay on Destructive Plasticity* (Translated by Carolyn Shread; Cambridge, UK: Polity, 2013), 11.
12. *Ibid.*, 29.
13. *Ibid.*, 4.
14. *Ibid.*, 14.
15. *Ibid.*, 14–15.
16. *Ibid.*, 85.
17. *Ibid.*, 87.
18. Freda Freiberg, DVD Special Features, *When a Woman Ascends the Stairs* (BFI, 2007).
19. Terayama's real-life father did fight in the Pacific Asian War as an imperial officer, but died unglamorously of dysentery.
20. Desser, *Eros Plus Massacre*, 24.
21. Koschmann, *Revolution and Subjectivity in Postwar Japan*, 63.
22. Malabou, *Ontology of the Accident*, 18.
23. Kôjin Karatani, *Architecture as Metaphor: Language, Number, Money* (Translated by Sabu Kohso; Cambridge, Massachusetts, and London: The MIT Press, 1995), 43.

Chapter 2

1. Badiou, *Briefings on Existence*, 47.
2. Wood, *Troubling Play*, 61.
3. Emmanuel Levinas, *Is It Righteous to Be?* (Edited by Jill Robbins; Stanford: Stanford University Press, 2001), 106.
4. *Ibid.*, 105.
5. *Ibid.*, 110.
6. At one point in *Suicide Club*, the leader of the girl group tells a TV interviewer, "Everybody's acting funny these days. We hope that this song cheers people up." This is the phenomenon of the young conservative pop star playing the double role of naïve concerned citizen and police-enforcer of cheery normalization.
7. Joseph L. Anderson and Donald Richie, *The Japanese Film: Art and Industry* (New York: Grove Press, 1960), 363–364.
8. Roger J. Davies and Osamu Ikeno (Eds.), *The Japanese Mind: Understanding Contemporary Japanese Culture* (Tokyo: Tuttle, 2002), 110.
9. Anderson and Richie, *The Japanese Film*, 364.
10. Kenneth Scott Latourette, *The History of Japan* (New York: Macmillan, 1951), 18.
11. Hugo Munsterberg, *The Arts of Japan: An Illustrated History* (Rutland, VT: Charles E. Tuttle Company, 1962), 29.
12. Joan Mellen, *The Waves at the Genji's Door: Japan Through Its Cinema* (New York: Pantheon Books, 1976), 59.
13. *Ibid.*, 28.
14. Anderson and Richie, *The Japanese Film*, 319.
15. Kaneto Shindô, *Kenji Mizoguchi: The Life of a Film Director [Aru eiga-kantoku no shogai]*, Kindai Eiga Kyokai, 1975.

16. Igarashi has compared postwar Japan to the figure of a languishing woman from melodrama, in need of rescue (see *Bodies of Memory*, 20; also 30–34). The concept of the women's picture as political allegory is also familiar to us in the West mainly through the Douglas-Sirk-influenced 1970s films of Rainer Werner Fassbinder, including most famously *The Marriage of Maria Braun* (*Die Ehe der Maria Braun*, 1978), in which West Germany is figured as a materially successful businesswoman driven insane by her own and others' deliberate suppression of an atrocious past.
17. Kenneth B. Pyle, *Japan Rising: The Resurgence of Japanese Power and Purpose* (New York: Public Affairs, 2007), 127.
18. Munsterberg, *The Arts of Japan*, 3.
19. Pyle, *Japan Rising*, 125.
20. *Ibid.*, 59.
21. Frederick Buell, *National Culture and the New Global System* (Baltimore: Johns Hopkins University Press, 1994), 67.
22. *Ibid.*, 47.
23. Ivy, *Discourses of the Vanishing*, 24.
24. Davies and Ikeno, *The Japanese Mind*, 38.
25. Buell, *National Culture and the New Global System*, 48.
26. Latourette, *The History of Japan*, 27.
27. Hoberman, *Vulgar Modernism*, 312.
28. Desser, *Eros Plus Massacre*, 21.
29. *Ibid.*
30. *Ibid.*
31. *Ibid.*
32. *Ibid.*, 109.
33. Sas, *Fault Lines*, 4.
34. In his exquisite memoir, *Fun in a Chinese Laundry* (San Francisco: Mercury House, 1988), Sternberg teases out a mordant précis of his experience making *Anatahan* (1953) in Japan; it is a tale that goes from serene triumph to the depths of misunderstanding and acrimony. Arriving in Japan he says he "was greeted like an old friend." He enjoyed the hospitality of a young film fan who lived on a mountaintop with a view "of grandeur and solemnity." This youth "had timidly arranged to provide food for me ... and when I thanked my host for bringing me to such a beautiful spot, he said, 'It is as beautiful as if you had directed it.'" (273). Sternberg relates that he "planned to picture the Japanese exactly as they were, not as they imagined themselves to be, and [...] to show that they were no different from any other race of people, much as they would like to be considered apart from the rest of mankind." (285) The language barrier was an obstacle from the start (286–287), but that does not seem to account for all the on-set frictions, as when Sternberg had to "inadvertently" stomp on a box of chocolates which his leading lady, rapidly putting on weight, had tried to hide from him. (115) "Half of my crew," Sternberg writes," had been trained as kamikazes, and the other half had been guerilla fighters in the Philippines, though this had not prepared them for the ordeal of working with me." (289) *Anatahan* portrayed Japanese soldiers as grubby, power-mad rapists, stabbing each other in the back over petty things and burying their heads in the sand when it came to Japan's wartime defeat; the film did miserably in Japan, but Sternberg got the last laugh, sort of, when a kind of anti-fan-club-cum-recovery-group was spawned in his wake: "a small group even went so far as to form a club in my name in order to immortalize my work with them, but [...]

failed to survive two or three meetings, and soon disintegrated into units that could only recall their bitterest moments." (115)
35. Anderson and Richie, *The Japanese Film*, 246.
36. Desser, *Eros Plus Massacre*, 254.
37. *Ibid.*, 179.
38. John W. Dower, *Embracing Defeat: Japan in the Wake of World War II* (New York: W. W. Norton & Company, Inc., 2000), 149.
39. Igarashi, *Bodies of Memory*, 78.
40. *Ibid.*, 41.
41. *Ibid.*, 40.

Chapter 3

1. Koschmann, *Revolution and Subjectivity in Postwar Japan*, 194.
2. Pyle, *Japan Rising*, 46.
3. Anesaki Masaharu, *History of Japanese Religion* (Rutland, VT, and Tokyo: Charles E. Tuttle Company, 1966), 4.
4. Tadao Sato, *Currents in Japanese Cinema* (Trans. Gregory Barrett; New York: Harper & Row, 1987), 74.
5. Koschmann, *Revolution and Subjectivity in Postwar Japan*, 13.
6. Buell, *National Culture and the New Global System*, 65.
7. Mellen, *The Waves at Genji's Door*, 75.
8. Sato, *Currents in Japanese Cinema*, 95–96.
9. Chris D., *Outlaw Masters of the Japanese Cinema*, 153.
10. https://en.wikipedia.org/wiki/Aum_Shinrikyo (accessed 7/31/15).
11. Pyle, *Japan Rising*, 121–122.
12. Mellen, *The Waves at Genji's Door*, 68.
13. Koschmann, *Revolution and Subjectivity in Postwar Japan*, 57.
14. *Ibid.*, 53.
15. Sato, *Currents in Japanese Cinema*, 173.
16. Even the wonderfully quixotic character of Toyo Odagiri (Miki Odagiri), the bored young madcap civil servant in Kurosawa's *Ikiru*, is essentially Hollywood-derived, a "Jean Arthur type."
17. Quoted in Koschmann, *Revolution and Subjectivity in Postwar Japan*, 66.
18. *Ibid.*, 97.
19. Pyle, *Japan Rising*, 52.
20. Mellen, *The Waves at Genji's Door*, 6.
21. Pyle, *Japan Rising*, 47.
22. Jacob M. Schlesinger, *Shadow Shoguns: The Rise and Fall of Japan's Postwar Political Machine* (New York: Simon & Schuster, 1997), 12.
23. *Ibid.*
24. *Ibid.*, 231.
25. *Ibid.*, 259.
26. *Ibid.*, 233.
27. *Ibid.*, 231.
28. *Ibid.*, 196.
29. *Ibid.*, 172.
30. *Ibid.*, 159–160.
31. The enterprising "snow-country village that arranged a special tour that would 'allow city people to experience clearing snow from roofs.'" (*Ibid.*, 200).
32. *Ibid.*, 12.
33. *Ibid.*, 235.
34. *Ibid.*, 12.
35. *Ibid.*, 231.

36. *Ibid.*, 245.
37. *Ibid.*
38. *Ibid.*, 12.
39. *Ibid.*, 13.
40. *Ibid.*, 15.
41. Jeff Kingston, *Contemporary Japan: History, Politics, and Social Change Since the 1980s* (Malden, MA: Wiley-Blackwell, 2011), 255.
42. Chris D., *Outlaw Masters of the Japanese Cinema*, 28.
43. A strikingly handsome, engaging actor, Kawaguchi modeled himself on James Dean and Montgomery Clift. He does something physical and strange in nearly every scene of *Kisses*, particularly when his character is brooding or uncomfortable: throwing himself against random cars in a parking lot as he delivers bitter lines about his rich parents' separation (cars were the premiere symbol of postwar economic wealth in Japan); bouncing wearily on a bed when speaking with his mother; finally, proudly taking a thrashing from the movie's villain in order to wrest the heroine from his clutches.
44. Sato, *Currents in Japanese Cinema*, 120.
45. Kingston, *Contemporary Japan*, 187.
46. *Ibid.*, 186.
47. Field, *In the Realm of a Dying Emperor*, 183.
48. Iris Chang, *The Rape of Nanking: The Forgotten Holocaust of World War II* (New York: Basic Books, 1997), 12.
49. Field, *In the Realm of a Dying Emperor*, 183.
50. This was the germ warfare division of the Japanese military, which, from 1936 to 1945, murdered over three thousand people, mainly Chinese, by experimenting on how best to infect large quantities of persons with deadly diseases (Igarashi, *Bodies of Memory*, 199).
51. Kingston, *Contemporary Japan*, 188.
52. *Ibid.*, 202–203.
53. *Ibid.*, 158.
54. Hoberman, *Vulgar Modernism*, 310.
55. Kingston, *Contemporary Japan*, 158.
56. *Ibid.*, 186.
57. Matthew Pennington, "Japan's 'whitewashing' of WWII history rankles some U.S. veterans," www.japantimes.com.jp, posted April 26, 2015.
58. Ohnuki-Tierney, *The Monkey as Mirror*, 16.
59. Kingston, *Contemporary Japan*, 20.
60. *Ibid.*
61. *Ibid.*, 153–154.
62. *Ibid.*, 21.
63. *Ibid.*, 23.
64. *Ibid.*
65. *Ibid.*, 115.
66. Badiou, *Briefings on Existence*, 45.
67. Mellen, *The Waves at Genji's Door*, 20.
68. Munsterberg, *The Arts of Japan*, 23.
69. *Ibid.*, 29.
70. Mellen, *The Waves at Genji's Door*, 21.
71. *Ibid.*, 105.
72. Sato, *Currents in Japanese Cinema*, 47.
73. Mellen, *The Waves at Genji's Door*, 21.

Chapter 4

1. Anderson and Richie, *The Japanese Film*, 318.
2. Igarashi, *Bodies of Memory*, 56.
3. Helen Hardacre, *Marketing the Menacing Fetus in Japan* (Berkeley: University of California Press, 1999), 148.
4. Mellen, *The Waves at Genji's Door*, 92.
5. *Ibid.*, 66–67.
6. Dower, *Embracing Defeat*, 105.
7. Marius B. Jansen, *The Making of Modern Japan* (Cambridge, MA: The Belknap Press of the University of Harvard Press, 2002), 681.
8. Davies and Ikeno, *The Japanese Mind*, 38.
9. Igarashi, *Bodies of Memory*, 79.
10. Mellen, *The Waves at Genji's Door*, 62.
11. Malabou, *Ontology of the Accident*, 6.
12. Donald Richie (with additional material by Joan Mellen), *The Films of Akira Kurosawa* (Berkeley: University of California Press, 1984), 75–76.
13. *Ibid.*, 76.
14. Lesley Downer, *Women of the Pleasure Quarters: The Secret History of the Geisha* (New York: Broadway Books, 2001), 1.
15. Erich Fromm, *To Have or to Be?* (London: Continuum, 2010), 98.
16. Dower, *Embracing Defeat*, 91.
17. *Ibid.*, 90.
18. *Ibid.*, 108.
19. *Ibid.*, 105.
20. Mellen, *The Waves at Genji's Door*, 47.
21. Malabou, *Ontology of the Accident*, 88.
22. Peter Tasker, *The Japanese* (New York: E. P. Dutton, 1987), 133.
23. What is fascinating, and trenchantly comedic, about Ozu's film is that the adults speak in the abstract about caring for children and pitying the plight of starving children in the postwar, and also about children's "pure-mindedness," but when confronted by an actual homeless child they become irritated and abusive toward him. Once they do soften, they must confront the magnitude of the problem, as Ozu implies by concluding his film with images of dozens of homeless boys, sprawled around a public monument, smoking cigarettes or scratching their flea-ridden clothes; Ozu's psychology anticipates, but is much, much subtler than, Hitchcock's *The Birds* (1963), in which the characters' fear of the birds seems to make them appear out of nowhere.
24. Mellen, *The Waves at Genji's Door*, 53.
25. Barthes, *Empire of Signs*, 102.
26. *Ibid.*, 65.
27. *Ibid.*, 67.
28. *Ibid.*, 80.
29. Kôjin Karatani reminds us that *Empire of Signs* is "nothing but a representation of the Western mind" (*Architecture as Metaphor*, 44). At the same time, we have already noted numerous instances of how Japan has been influenced by the ways in which Westerners view it.
30. Karatani, *Architecture as Metaphor*, 76.
31. *Ibid.*, 78.
32. Mellen, *The Waves at Genji's Door*, 54.
33. For a thorough treatment of the way normalizing, authoritative voiceovers are commonly gendered as male, see Kaja Silverman, *The Acoustic Mirror: The Female Voice in Psychoanalysis and Cinema* (Bloomington: University of Indiana Press, 1988).
34. It has always been my interpretation of *Taboo* that Soji is the attacker. Both Kano and Tashiro are convinced that the other has committed these crimes; Tashiro speaks of his dagger having been stolen and planted at the scene of the second attack to implicate him. Soji's violent hatred of gays and his surreptitious nature emerge fully by the end of the film.

35. Tom Mes, *Agitator—The Cinema of Takashi Miike* (Godalming, UK: FAB Press, 2004), 25–26.
36. Koschmann, *Revolution and Subjectivity in Postwar Japan*, 103.
37. Oshima, *Cinema, Censorship, and the State*, 215.
38. Koschmann, *Revolution and Subjectivity in Postwar Japan*, 65.
39. Dower, *Embracing Defeat*, 138.
40. Chang, *The Rape of Nanking*, 49.
41. Igarashi, *Bodies of Memory*, 32–33.
42. *Ibid.*, 35.
43. Desser, *Eros Plus Massacre*, 121.
44. Sato, *Currents in Japanese Cinema*, 81.
45. Igarashi, *Bodies of Memory*, 60.
46. Sato, *Currents in Japanese Cinema*, 81.
47. In nearly all aspects and details, however, Wakamatsu allows himself to depart liberally from the actual Speck murders.
48. Anderson and Richie, *The Japanese Film*, 264.
49. *Ibid.*, 265.
50. Turim, *The Films of Oshima Nagisa*, 36–37.
51. Desser, *Eros Plus Massacre*, 101.
52. Ohnuki-Tierney, *The Monkey as Mirror*, 13.
53. "Interview with Kaneto Shindô," *Onibaba* DVD Bonus Features (The Criterion Collection, 2004).
54. *Ibid.*
55. Igarashi, *Bodies of Memory*, 54.
56. Dower, *Embracing Defeat*, 107–108.
57. Richie, *The Films of Akira Kurosawa*, 59.
58. Mellen, *The Waves at Genji's Door*, 360–361.
59. The best description of the grandfather is unintentionally provided by Quentin Tarantino, in a line from *Kill Bill: Volume 1* (2003): "dressed like a villain on *Star Trek*."
60. Mellen, *The Waves at Genji's Door*, 361.
61. *Ibid.*, 360.
62. For Oshima's radical purposes, baseball must be an emblem of deracination, associated with Japan's surrender to the U.S. However, it should be said that baseball had been hugely popular in Japan almost as long as it had been in the U.S., as we see from Yasujirô Shimazu's 1934 film, *Our Neighbor, Miss Yae*. Baseball is also treated with affection in Kurosawa's *Stray Dog*.
63. It is similar to Sartre's insights into the meaning of incest in Nazi Germany, in his play *The Condemned of Altona*, in which incest becomes an objective-correlative for nationalist pride and racial purity, the interrelated clan being the ultimate closed, exclusivist society.
64. Mellen, *The Waves at Genji's Door*, 364.
65. *Ibid.*, 366.
66. *Ibid.*, 363.
67. *Ibid.*, 353.

Chapter 5

1. Badiou, *Briefings on Existence*, 57.
2. Suzuki, *Zen and Japanese Culture*, 112.
3. Keiji Nishitani, *Religion and Nothingness* (Trans. Jan Van Bragt; Berkeley: University of California Press, 1982), 6–7.
4. *Ibid.*, 7.
5. Malabou, *Ontology of the Accident*, 7.
6. Nishitani, *Religion and Nothingness*, 11.
7. *Ibid.*, 11.
8. *Ibid.*, 13–14.
9. Badiou, *Briefings on Existence*, 45.
10. Nishitani, *Religion and Nothingness*, 14.
11. Yukio Mishima, *Confessions of a Mask* (Trans. Meredith Weatherby; New York: New Directions, 1958), 34–35.
12. Nishitani, *Religion and Nothingness*, 11.
13. Mishima, *Confessions of a Mask*, 65.
14. Karatani, *Architecture as Metaphor*, 18–19.
15. *Ibid.*, 20.
16. Nishitani, *Religion and Nothingness*, 11.
17. *Ibid.*, 9.
18. *Ibid.*, 10.
19. *Ibid.*, 14.
20. *Ibid.*, 19.
21. Ohnuki-Tierney, *The Monkey as Mirror*, 57.
22. Suzuki, *Zen and Japanese Culture*, 5.
23. Suzuki, *Zen and Japanese Culture*, 61. For Suzuki, Zen is in fact the militarist's religion par excellence, a religion of swift violent actions that resolve problems of incommensurable thought. The violence of Zen is axiomatic, and borne out in numerous anecdotes, such as this: "A [Zen] monk, coming out of the monastery that was under the leadership of Rinzai (Lin-chi, d. 867), met a party of three traveling monks belonging to another Buddhist [non–Zen] school, and one of the three ventured to question the Zen monk: 'How deep is the river of Zen?' [...] The Zen monk, [...] who was noted for his direct actions, lost no time in replying. 'Find out for yourself,' he said, and offered to throw the questioner from the bridge. But fortunately his two friends interceded and pleaded for mercy, which saved the situation." (*Ibid.*, 5) Also: "When Rinzai was asked what the essence of Buddhist teaching was, he came right down from his seat and, taking hold of the questioner by the front of his robe, slapped his face, and let him go." (*Ibid.*, 8) We would view this as the "action" of a bully—at any rate, someone for whom physical assaults and even threats of death are *instructive* in and of themselves, as a way of asserting the ego-limits of what can and cannot be expressed or questioned.
24. Of course, we already have this, in artificial intelligence, cybernetics, the internet. Our sentimental tendency to want to anthropomorphize these entities into self-conscious or ontologic "beings" only shows how unsettled the question of ontology remains, in spite of post–Heideggerian claims that philosophy has passed from a state of content into an ungrounded state of form or formalism, something which Karatani discusses (in slightly different terms) in *Architecture as Metaphor: Language, Number, Money*. What is usually missing from current philosophy is cinema, which contains both romanticized and formalist versions of human ontology within it. When current philosophers contemplate cinema, they do it separately from philosophy as a whole; the opportunity is missed to connect the two, and in fact cinema itself often goes misunderstood. In my opinion, Badiou's and Deleuze's writings on *everything but film* are useful to the study of film; their actual writings on film, nearly useless. Film is both object and subject, but in reducing it only to object philosophy curtails the ontological possibilities of film, as well as its own sophistication (shown everywhere but in its film criticism) about how the distinction between object and subject has become meaningless and moot.

Part Two

1. Quoted in Downer, *Women of the Pleasure Quarters*, 25.

2. Takashi Fujitani, *Splendid Monarchy: Power and Pageantry in Modern Japan* (Berkeley: University of California Press, 1998), 21.

Chapter 6

1. Malabou, *Ontology of the Accident*, 41.
2. Anderson and Richie, *The Japanese Film*, 363.
3. Sato, *Currents in Japanese Cinema*, 52.
4. Jun'ichirô Tanizaki, *In Praise of Shadows* (Trans. Thomas J. Harper and Edward G. Seidensticker; Stoney Creek, CT: Leete's Island Books, 1977), 18.
5. Roland Barthes, *The Pleasure of the Text* (Trans. Richard Miller; New York: Hill and Wang, 1975), 44.
6. Malabou, *Ontology of the Accident*, 7.
7. *Ibid.*, 9.
8. Keiko I. McDonald, *Reading a Japanese Film: Cinema in Context* (Honolulu: University of Hawaii Press, 2006), 96.
9. Davies and Ikeno, *The Japanese Mind*, 47–48.
10. *Ibid.*, 42–43.
11. *Ibid.*, 43.
12. Suzuki, *Zen and Japanese Culture*, 111.
13. *Ibid.*
14. *Ibid.*
15. Catherine Russell, *Classical Japanese Cinema Revisited* (New York: Continuum, 2011), 45.
16. Davies and Ikeno, *The Japanese Mind*, 42.
17. Oshima, *Cinema, Censorship, and the State*, 49–50.
18. Davies and Ikeno, *The Japanese Mind*, 42.
19. Barthes, *Empire of Signs*, 7.
20. Davies and Ikeno, *The Japanese Mind*, 37.
21. *Ibid.*, 5.
22. Fromm, *To Have or to Be?*, 22.
23. Davies and Ikeno, *The Japanese Mind*, 37.
24. *Ibid.*
25. More than any other culture of which I am aware, the Japanese have many fascinating words to describe specific aspects of social relations. *Amae* is "depending on the benevolence of others." Every action between adults is modeled on the indulgence and fondness of parents for their child. "With people who are part of the inner circle ... the Japanese do not usually have as much of a sense of guilt, because they are so close that amae gives them confidence in any sin being forgiven...." There are inner circle relations marked by lack of *enryo* (restraint), and then relations of *giri* (social obligation) marked by differing degrees of *enryo*, and finally "outer circle" relations which are strictly marked by codes of politeness compelling *enryo* in all situations (Davies and Ikeno, *The Japanese Mind*, 17–19). For example, in Yasujirô Shimazu's *Our Neighbor, Miss Yae*, the sons of one family often break the next-door family's windows when they play catch in the yard; the mother next door says that she cannot draw the shutters of her windows because that would make the entire neighborhood resentful toward her; yet, someone else counters, if she were to get hit by a wild pitch, it would cause even worse "embarrassment" to both families.
26. Davies and Ikeno, *The Japanese Mind*, 9.
27. *Ibid.*, 37.
28. *Ibid.*, 12.
29. Andrew Gamble, "The Drifter's Escape," from *The Political Art of Bob Dylan* (Eds. David Boucher and Gary Browning; Charlottesville, VA: Imprint Academic, 2009), 45.
30. Malabou, *Ontology of the Accident*, 9.
31. Gamble, *The Political Art of Bob Dylan*, 45.
32. Mes, *Agitator*, 341.
33. *Ibid.*, 337–338.
34. Barthes, *Empire of Signs*, 14.
35. *Ibid.*, 15.
36. *Ibid.*
37. *Ibid.*, 16.
38. *Ibid.*, 18.
39. *Ibid.*, 24.
40. *Ibid.*, 25.
41. Davies and Ikeno, *The Japanese Mind*, 75–77.
42. Malabou, *Ontology of the Accident*, 5.
43. Anderson and Richie, *The Japanese Film*, 361 (my italics).
44. In an interview, director Teruo Ishii inadvertently confirms this, speaking about Mikio Naruse, whom he assisted in the late 1950s, and Hiroshi Shimizu, another director of the same period, stating that the difference between them as visual stylists is that Naruse positioned his camera at a slight "diagonal" angle to the action, while Shimizu filmed the action head-on. The effect for both was simply to achieve something "natural," without cluttered or freighted compositions ("Interview with Bernard Eisenschitz" [2004], *Late Chrysanthemums* DVD Bonus Features, BFI, 2007).
45. Chris D., *Outlaw Masters of the Japanese Cinema*, 147.
46. Takashi Miike suggests something like this when he says: "Normally, a director creates a character from his own point of view, his own frame of reference. But in my case, I think that human beings are strange. I don't believe you can understand them entirely, so I don't create the characters from my own point of view. There is the screenplay and there are the actors who play the characters, so I leave space for them to put their own vision into the character." (Mes, *Agitator*, 341).
47. This is why the samurai has been an escapist figure for the Japanese, because "all samurai had to live admirably and honorably in order not to have regrets when they died, since facing death was a daily occurrence." (Davies and Ikeno, *The Japanese Mind*, 45).
48. Barthes, *Empire of Signs*, 24.
49. *Ibid.*, 103.
50. Mellen, *The Waves at Genji's Door*, 102.
51. Anesaki Masaharu, *History of Japanese Religion* (Rutland, VT: Charles E. Tuttle Company, 1966), 67.
52. It is very Western to view Japanese cinema of the 1960s only or primarily as the time of the Japanese New Wave. For the most part, mainstream Japanese cinema (the kind of movies that actual Japanese people liked to go and see) consisted of light office comedies such as *The Travels of Scouting Workers* (1962), or period pieces such as *Young Boss Takeshi* (1965), the latter in fact being a celebration of feudal and patriarchal values. Art films come to international prominence, but they hardly reflect the total intentions of any national cinema. Japanese art films in particular are already more Westernized, meaning specifically more humanist and leftwing in attitude, than the bulk of mainstream Japanese culture. For the most part, the theories in this book are based on readings of Japanese art films.
53. McDonald, *Reading a Japanese Film*, 96.
54. Dower, *Embracing Defeat*, 22.
55. *Ibid.*
56. Anderson and Richie, *The Japanese Film*, 262.
57. Daikichi Irokawa, *The Age of Hirohito: In Search of Modern Japan* (Trans. Mikiso Hane and John K. Urda; New York: The Free Press, 1995), 64.

58. Mellen, *The Waves at Genji's Door*, 103–104.
59. Suzuki, *Zen and Japanese Culture*, 42.
60. *Ibid.*, 16.
61. *Ibid.*, 7.
62. *Ibid.*, 8.
63. *Ibid.*, 9.
64. Ivy, *Discourses of the Vanishing*, 165n22.
65. Tanizaki, *In Praise of Shadows*, 30.
66. The ghost of Gisaburo, the cuckolded and murdered husband in Nagisa Oshima's *Empire of Passion*, is a notable exception; he even drinks sake and eats. Also, the male ghost Genji who counsels Matsuko in Oshima's *Violence at Noon* is filmed without special effects or make-up, exactly as he is in the scenes where he is still a living man. In *Taboo*, a story is told about a samurai ghost who returns to console his male lover. But in this motif (as in other things) Oshima was an original who went against the grain.
67. Anderson and Richie, *The Japanese Film*, 262.
68. And it is not only that Japanese ghosts are usually female; it is that Japanese females themselves became associated with the ghostlike: uncanny, ethereal, haunted, demonic. Women were seen to move in an interior space of darkness, "the darkness in which ghosts and monsters were active, and indeed was not the woman who lived in it, behind thick curtains, behind layer after layer of screens and doors—was she not of a kind with them? The darkness wrapped her round tenfold, twenty fold, it filled the collar, the sleeves of her kimono, the folds of her skirt, wherever a hollow invited. Further yet: might it not have been the reverse, might not the darkness have emerged from her mouth and those black teeth, from the black of her hair, like the thread from the great earth spider?" (Davies and Ikeno, *The Japanese Mind*, 35).
69. Tanizaki, *In Praise of Shadows*, 3.
70. *Ibid.*, 4.
71. *Ibid.*, 5.
72. *Ibid.*
73. *Ibid.*, 4.

Chapter 7

1. Tanizaki, *In Praise of Shadows*, 8.
2. Mes, *Agitator*, 341.
3. Malabou, *Ontology of the Accident*, 18.
4. Richard B. Frank, *Downfall: The End of the Imperial Japanese Empire* (New York: Random House, 1999), 189.
5. Baudelaire, *Les Fleurs du Mal*, 120 (my translation): although this aspect of Matsumoto's study could be said to be dated, it is mainly Leda, the older and more old-fashioned of the film's two main queens, who displays this sort of self-defeatist wallowing in bad decision-making, more than the younger and more self-preserving Eddie.
6. Turim, *The Films of Oshima Nagisa*, 116.
7. Davies and Ikeno, *The Japanese Mind*, 46.
8. *Ibid.*
9. Mellen, *The Waves at Genji's Door*, 140.
10. *Ibid.*, 112.
11. Malabou, *Ontology of the Accident*, 19.
12. *Ibid.*, 18.
13. *Ibid.*, 22.
14. *Ibid.*, 24.
15. *Ibid.*, 18.
16. *Ibid.*, 4–5.
17. *Ibid.*, 19–20.
18. *Ibid.*, 20.
19. William J. Schull, *Effects of Atomic Radiation: A Half-Century of Studies from Hiroshima and Nagasaki* (New York: Wiley-Liss, 1995), 130.
20. Irokawa, *The Age of Hirohito*, 37.
21. Dower, *Embracing Defeat*, 47.
22. Schull, *Effects of Atomic Radiation*, 111–112.
23. *Ibid.*, 112.
24. *Ibid.*, 112.
25. *Ibid.*, 13.
26. *Ibid.*
27. *Ibid.*, 15.
28. *Ibid.*, 14.
29. *Ibid.*, 55.
30. *Ibid.*, 266.
31. *Ibid.*, 160.
32. *Ibid.*, 55.
33. *Ibid.*, 50.
34. *Ibid.*, 46–47.
35. *Ibid.*, 48.
36. *Ibid.*, 191–193.
37. Desser, *Eros Plus Massacre*, 149.
38. Schull, *Effects of Atomic Radiation*, 169–170.
39. Igarashi, *Bodies of Memory*, 49–50.
40. *Ibid.*, 50.
41. *Ibid.*
42. Schull, *Effects of Atomic Radiation*, 5.
43. *Ibid.*, 169.
44. *Ibid.*, 48.
45. *Ibid.*, 44.
46. *Ibid.*, 50.
47. Mellen, *The Waves at Genji's Door*, 203.
48. Richie, *The Films of Akira Kurosawa*, 109.
49. Davies and Ikeno, *The Japanese Mind*, 95.

Part Three

1. Emiko Ohnuki-Tierney, *Kamikaze, Cherry Blossoms, and Nationalisms: The Militarization of Aesthetics in Japanese History* (Chicago: University of Chicago Press, 2002), 3.
2. Field, *In the Realm of a Dying Emperor*, 58.
3. Chris Marker, *Sans Soleil* (Argos Films, 1983).

Chapter 8

1. Hoberman, *Vulgar Modernism*, 309.
2. Chang, *The Rape of Nanking*, 58.
3. Robert B. Edgerton, *Warriors of the Rising Sun: A History of the Japanese Military* (New York: W. W. Norton & Company, 1997), 239.
4. Buell, *National Culture and the New Global System*, 46–47.
5. Kenneth Scott Latourette, *The History of Japan* (New York: Macmillan, 1951), 10.
6. Fujitani, *Splendid Monarchy*, 6–9.
7. Latourette, *The History of Japan*, 10.
8. Mellen, *The Waves at Genji's Door*, 297.
9. *Ibid.*, 299.
10. *Ibid.*, 297–298.
11. Field, *In the Realm of a Dying Emperor*, 69.
12. Edgerton, *Warriors of the Rising Sun*, 323–324.
13. Field, *In the Realm of a Dying Emperor*, 179.
14. Fujitani, *Splendid Monarchy*, 15.
15. *Ibid.*, 26–27.

16. Ohnuki-Tierney, *Kamikaze, Cherry Blossoms, and Nationalisms*, 4.
17. Desser, *Eros Plus Massacre*, 84.
18. Sato, *Currents in Japanese Cinema*, 126.
19. Latourette, *The History of Japan*, 18.
20. *Ibid.*, 21.
21. *Ibid.*, 23.
22. *Ibid.*, 24.
23. *Ibid.*, 27–28.
24. Igarashi, *Bodies of Memory*, 51.
25. *Ibid.*, 52.
26. Chang, *The Rape of Nanking*, 32.
27. *Ibid.*, 31.
28. Sato, *Currents in Japanese Cinema*, 111.
29. Chang, *The Rape of Nanking*, 31.
30. *Ibid.*, 30.
31. *Ibid.*, 216.
32. Edgerton, *Warriors of the Rising Sun*, 244.
33. *Ibid.*, 250.
34. *Ibid.*, 250.
35. Chang, *The Rape of Nanking*, 35.
36. Edgerton, *Warriors of the Rising Sun*, 245.
37. Chang, *The Rape of Nanking*, 56.
38. *Ibid.*, 6.
39. Edgerton, *Warriors of the Rising Sun*, 246.
40. Chang, *The Rape of Nanking*, 4–5.
41. *Ibid.*, 6.
42. *Ibid.*, 56.
43. Edgerton, *Warriors of the Rising Sun*, 15.
44. Chang, *The Rape of Nanking*, 59.
45. *Ibid.*, 50.
46. Edgerton, *Warriors of the Rising Sun*, 247.
47. Chang, *The Rape of Nanking*, 90–91.
48. *Ibid.*, 6.
49. Edgerton, *Warriors of the Rising Sun*, 249.
50. *Ibid.*, 17.
51. Sato, *Currents in Japanese Cinema*, 35.
52. It is worth noting that Japan's militarism has not been historically monolithic. Kôjin Karatani writes about the attempt to impose a draft during the 19th century Meiji restoration: "There was, in fact, at least one example of a riot against mandatory military service, which arose from misunderstanding of it as a 'blood tax' (as some called it)." (*Origins of Modern Japanese Literature*, 130–131) Furthermore, Karatani argues that the military as an historical institution in Japan served a positive function of consolidating Japanese from different class strata, backgrounds and locales into a single category of "human beings." (*Ibid.*, 131) Whether this is true only as the function of a certain sophistry (whereby "the military" creates its own inevitable category by definition, without actually promoting meaningful changes either within itself or within the larger social order) is difficult to say with certainty. For our purposes, 20th century emperor worship drew upon traditional attitudes going back at least to samurai culture while at the same time presenting itself as sui generis and unprecedented, since modern technology (of airplanes, in the case of kamikaze pilots) gave rise to new conditions under which to exercise extreme forms of emperor worship as well as new ambivalences, in the sense that the warrior's "soul" was now interlinked with mechanistic technology. The will may have remained human, but the destructive force was now partly beyond the human—which is why the Japanese recognized in the atomic bomb a final or "perfected" countering of their own extremist military intentions. As Terumichi tells the hothead Tadashi in Oshima's *The Ceremony*, taking a samurai sword out of his hands: "With this old thing you will only kill one or two people.... Without the will to exterminate, it is useless to take up a weapon."
53. Ohnuki-Tierney, *Kamikaze, Cherry Blossoms, and Nationalisms*, 111.
54. *Ibid.*, 10.
55. Jeff Kingston, *Contemporary Japan: History, Politics, and Social Change Since the 1980s* (Malden, MA: Wiley-Blackwell, 2011), 188.
56. Irokawa, *The Age of Hirohito*, 122.
57. *Ibid.*

Chapter 9

1. Another example of a male character who grows emotionally is the junior executive Asahina (Jirô Tamiya) in Masumura's *Black Test Car* when he expresses real remorse in having become so deeply embroiled in business corruption, specifically forcing his fiancée Masako (Junko Kanô) to sleep with a competitor in order to steal his trade secrets. "I want to live like a decent human being," Asahina says as he resigns from the company.
2. Irokawa, *The Age of Hirohito*, 42.
3. Chang, *The Rape of Nanking*, 29.
4. Davies and Ikeno, *The Japanese Mind*, 263.
5. Irokawa, *The Age of Hirohito*, ix.
6. *Ibid.*, 121.
7. Dower, *Embracing Defeat*, 427.
8. *Ibid.*, 427–428.
9. *Ibid.*, 428.
10. *Ibid.*
11. Igarashi, *Bodies of Memory*, 36.
12. *Ibid.*
13. *Ibid.*
14. *Ibid.*, 37.

Chapter 10

1. Dower, *Embracing Defeat*, 34.
2. *Ibid.*, 36.
3. Jansen, *The Making of Modern Japan*, 660.
4. Ronald H. Spector, *In the Ruins of Empire: The Japanese Surrender and the Battle for Postwar Asia* (New York: Random House, 2007), 23.
5. Dower, *Embracing Defeat*, 38.
6. Spector, *In the Ruins of Empire*, 23.
7. Dower, *Embracing Defeat*, 37.
8. *Ibid.*, 36–37.
9. *Ibid.*, 38.
10. Fujitani, *Splendid Monarchy*, 241–242.
11. Dower, *Embracing Defeat*, 38.
12. Spector, *In the Ruins of Empire*, 23–24.
13. Igarashi, *Bodies of Memory*, 27–28.
14. Irokawa, *The Age of Hirohito*, 116.
15. Dower, *Embracing Defeat*, 23.
16. *Ibid.*, 22–23.
17. Igarashi, *Bodies of Memory*, 33.
18. Dower, *Embracing Defeat*, 25.
19. *Ibid.*, 24.
20. Andrew Gordon, Ed., *Postwar Japan as History* (Berkeley: University of California Press, 1993), 67.
21. Mellen, *The Waves at Genji's Door*, 316.
22. By contrast, Oshima avoids floor-level. In his films, whenever his characters do kneel or lie on the

floor, Oshima almost always raises the camera slightly above them and also places it at enough of a distance that we see the activity in wide angle, as if taking place on a stage-set. It is almost never a private or an intimate act. Noel Burch has noted this theatricality in relation to *The Ceremony* (Desser, *Eros Plus Massacre*, 188), though not specifically in relation to the camera's distance from the floor.

23. Maureen Turim calls these interludes in Ozu's films "pillow shots." (*The Films of Oshima Nagisa*, 93) Tadao Sato calls them "curtain shots," and says, "When Ozu's films are shown on Japanese television, these curtain shots are usually cut, a pity since they are indispensable for regulating the overall tone of an Ozu film." (*Currents in Japanese Cinema*, 190).

24. Anderson and Richie, *The Japanese Film*, 361.

25. Kuriyashi Kurosawa's acclaimed *Tokyo Sonata* is like an Ozu family drama where someone has spiked the sake with acid; like Ozu by way of Todd Solondz. The father Sasaki has been downsized at work and is too ashamed to tell his family; leaving the house every day in his suit, he changes into a jumper inside the mall where he now endures the humiliation of being a janitor. But his fate is shared by dozens of other displaced male workers, all changing clothes en masse at the start of the shift. Indeed, Sasaki discovers that there is an entire subculture of fake businessmen like himself: men who walk around all day in suits like uniforms, pretending to take urgent calls from companies that have forgotten them. Nonetheless, shame clings to his loss of status. Only children see through Sasaki's deception, as when a little girl asks him out of the blue: "You have it rough, don't you?" No longer patriarchs, older males are superfluous in current Tokyo, their charades of competence and authority easy to unravel. The young are nobler because they force no one to be dependent on them: no one is shamed, intentionally or not, for the sake of their egos. Ironically, at home, Sasaki cannot communicate with his sons, teenage Takashi who wants to join the U.S. army and young Kenji, a piano prodigy hiding his artistic talent from his parents. The wife, too, is beset by secret longings; she befriends an antisocial criminal and ends up running away with him. "Do you think I can start over?" she asks. Meanwhile her husband expresses the same desire to start anew, rolling in garbage on the street in his soiled janitor's uniform.

26. Dower, *Embracing Defeat*, 162–163.

27. Mellen, *The Waves at Genji's Door*, 321.

28. Sato, *Currents in Japanese Cinema*, 87.

29. This is similar to the initial displeasure which Setsuko (Ineko Arima) shows at the fact that her boyfriend Masahiko (Keiji Sada) has approached her father to ask for her hand in marriage without her knowledge, in Ozu's *Equinox Flower*: "Why did you see father without telling me?" she asks, clearly vexed at having been left out of the decision. In some ways, what is represented in Ozu is "family knowledge" rather than specifically male or patriarchal knowledge.

30. Sada played a similar "barefoot ingenu" in Ozu's *Equinox Flower*, so perhaps this was a case of the director permitting a favorite actor to express some of his own personality within his roles.

31. The food and drink left in offering to the dead have an oblivious and perverse quality, like the nonoperational display phones in the Ginza where Marker imagines picking up a receiver at random and hearing a dream voice of history. The voice that can only respond to and be summoned by technology that does not work, by inefficiency and uselessness, by surplus and luxury, suggests oppression; but what we in the West would be inclined to see as an issue of class war is, in Japan, more like a living paradox not meant to be rectified by social justice.

32. Even so, Ozu's sense of realism had been censored during the war: "They objected to the fact that the soldier eats ... everyday food instead of red rice to celebrate the special occasion of his departure. I wish I could have changed it, but it was ridiculous to write it that way, so I forgot it." (Mellen, *The Waves at Genji's Door*, 151).

33. Gordon, *Postwar Japan as History*, 69.
34. Dower, *Embracing Defeat*, 183.
35. Latourette, *The History of Japan*, 47.
36. Davies and Ikeno, *The Japanese Mind*, 37.
37. Latourette, *The History of Japan*, 47.
38. *Ibid.*, 47–48.
39. Dower, *Embracing Defeat*, 125–126.
40. *Ibid.*, 147.
41. *Ibid.*, 26.
42. Anderson and Richie, *The Japanese Film*, 267.
43. *Ibid.*, 251.
44. *Ibid.*, 268.

Chapter 11

1. Field, *In the Realm of a Dying Emperor*, 69.

2. Marker shows how the Japanese themselves have commodified and marketed their own traumatic history, as when he films "at the edge of the ditch where two hundred girls used grenades in 1945 to commit suicide rather than fall into American hands. People have their pictures taken here. Grenade-shaped cigarette lighters are sold nearby as souvenirs." These are what Marker calls "small fragments of war enshrined in everyday life." The little pacification, the tranquilizer, of a cigarette is placed incommensurably against an atrocity that is nonetheless strangely resolved within this very incommensurability; what for us in the West would probably be an insulting trivialization is actually a way of seeking closure, precisely in acknowledging that nothing can be done to help it, nothing can ever measure up. This also reassures the spirits of the dead, by allowing them to feel that they do not wound our thoughts and make us sad. Instead we have a little smoke in their honor. Our Western jadedness cannot account for ways in which the commodity-form culture has been a semi-organic offshoot of spiritualism in other cultures. This is not unlike Karatani's "inversion of semiotic constellation," in which, in order to see a thing true, we must first suppress the sign which has come to substitute for it, i.e., the social meaning.

3. Anderson and Richie, *The Japanese Film*, 360. In this complete lack of interest in romantic love, Ozu was very much of his time and society. We read, in a 1904 marriage manual written by Naomi Tamura, these rather extreme declarations: "It is very clear that we do not marry for love. If a man is known to have broken this rule, we look upon him as a mean fellow, and sadly lacking in morality. His own mother and father would be ashamed of him. Public sentiment places love for a woman very low on the scale of morals.... We place love and brutal attachment on the same plane." (Downer, *Women of the Pleasure Quarters*, 69).

4. Paul Willemen, DVD Special Features, *Floating Clouds* (BFI, 2007).

5. Freiberg, DVD Special Features, *Floating Clouds* (BFI, 2007).
6. Desser, *Eros Plus Massacre*, 23.
7. Field, *In the Realm of a Dying Emperor*, 186.
8. Freiberg, DVD Special Features, *Ibid.*
9. Levinas, *Is It Righteous to Be?*, 129.
10. Mellen, *The Waves at Genji's Door*, 225–226.
11. *Ibid.*, 225.
12. Freiberg, DVD Special Features, *Floating Clouds* (BFI, 2007).
13. Freiberg notes that *Floating Clouds* is "atypical" for Naruse in that the heroine "wallows in masochism" and is therefore "irritating." (DVD Special Features, *Floating Clouds*, BFI, 2007) She views this as partly deriving from Kabuki theater, in which women showed strength by enduring emotional pain. Tadao Sato takes a different view, maintaining that for Naruse the male-female relation is really "a kind of persistence, too tough for such a pretty label as love and much more precious than progress or intelligence. Thus, the apparently foolish woman in *Floating Clouds* is respected precisely because of her blind persistence. Japanese women are admired for this unglamorous emotion, and within it, unexpectedly, spiritual security can be achieved." (Sato, *Currents in Japanese Cinema*, 93).
14. Sato, *Currents in Japanese Cinema*, 47.
15. Alain Badiou, *Cinema* (Trans. Susan Spitzer; Cambridge, UK: Polity Press, 2013), 204.
16. See Jennifer Robertson, "The Politics of Androgyny in Japan: Sexuality and Subversion in the Theater and Beyond," *American Ethnologist*, Vol. 19, No. 3 (August 1992), 419–442.
17. Sato, *Currents in Japanese Cinema*, 17.
18. *Ibid.*, 19.
19. *Ibid.*, 22–23.

Chapter 12

1. Field, *In the Realm of a Dying Emperor*, 201–202.
2. Koschmann, *Revolution and Subjectivity in Postwar Japan*, 196.
3. *Ibid.*, 194.
4. *Ibid.*, 191.
5. In the early 1970s Imamura directed a series of documentaries for Tokyo TV with the theme of trying to locate (and interview if possible) Japanese soldiers who had never returned from former colonies after the war. *Outlaw Matsuo Comes Home* is the longest of these, the most developed, and the only one to feature a veteran repatriated to Japan.
6. The wealthy are not pleasant or nice in Imamura's film; in fact, they are ruthless and also miserable. About Fujio, Imamura comments, "His anger often seemed the reverse expression of his loneliness." This was the nouveau riche of the rebuilt Japan, scarred, isolated, haunted, and bordering on passive-aggressive psychosis in the way it sometimes pulled expensive strings. In the late 1980s, "Ryoei Saito, a paper mill magnate, stunned the art world by dropping $160 million in three days to buy *Au Moulin de La Galette* by Renoir and *Portrait of Dr. Gachet* by van Gogh; he caused another stir by declaring he wanted them cremated with him when he died." (Schlesinger, *Shadow Shoguns*, 195) Military means were not the only kind by which a certain war (for claims on history itself) could be waged against the West.
7. Irokawa, *The Age of Hirohito*, 120.
8. *Ibid.*, 118.
9. This motif was not unique to Oshima's film. The popular 1948 story on which Seijun Suzuki based *Gate of Flesh* has a scene of violent sexual coupling between a Japanese prostitute and a Japanese veteran-thief, in which she chokes him. "'I'm gonna kill you and I'll die too.' Ibuki saw two drab pupils that burn like phosphorus in the dark. 'Shin-chan, please die, die with me.'" One of the ways that such former illusions as emperor worship were finally stripped away was through a heterosexual liberation in which women became carnal aggressors, agents of sexual trauma and death. (Irokawa, *The Age of Hirohito*, 120) However, where the potboiler story resolved the tension in favor of the male regaining his potency and dominating the woman (*Ibid.*, 118), Oshima carries out the reversal of male power to its ultimate conclusion.

Conclusion

1. Quoted in Koschmann, *Revolution and Subjectivity in Postwar Japan*, 165.
2. *Absolutely Fabulous: Absolutely Everything* (BBC Video, 2008).
3. Nakae Chômin, *A Discourse by Three Drunkards on Government* (Trans. Nobuko Tsukui; Boston: Weatherhill, 2010), 96.
4. *Ibid.*, 95.
5. *Ibid.*, 94.
6. *Ibid.*, 95.
7. *Ibid.*, 100–101.
8. *Ibid.*, 96.
9. *Ibid.*, 100.
10. *Ibid.*, 114.
11. *Ibid.*, 98.
12. *Ibid.*, 129.
13. *Ibid.*, 136.
14. "Saigon Execution: Murder of a Viet Cong by Saigon Police Chief, 1968." http://rarehistoricalphotos.com/saigon-execution-murder-vietcong-saigon-1968/ (accessed 9/17/2015).
15. Hildi Kang, *Under the Black Umbrella: Voices from Colonial Korea, 1910–1945* (Ithaca, NY: Cornell University Press, 2001), 112.
16. Quoted in Walter Benjamin, *Reflections: Essays, Aphorisms, Autobiographical Writings* (Trans. Edmund Jephcott; Ed. Peter Demetz; New York: Harcourt Brace Jovanovich, 1979), 67.
17. Andy Campbell, "Family Breaks Open Teenager's Tomb, Saying They Heard Her 'Screaming,'" *The Huffington Post*, http://www.huffingtonpost.com/entry/dead-teen-screaming-in-tomb_55dcc238e4b04ae49704c32b (accessed 8/26/2015).
18. Gordon, *Postwar Japan as History*, 76.
19. Sas, *Fault Lines*, 167.
20. *Ibid.*, 129.
21. Oshima, *Cinema, Censorship, and the State*, 189.

Works Cited

Absolutely Fabulous: Absolutely Everything. BBC Video, 2008.
Adachi, Masao. *A.K.A. Serial Killer [Ryakushô renzoku shasatsuma].* 1969.
Anderson, Joseph L., and Donald Richie. *The Japanese Film: Art and Industry.* New York: Grove Press, 1960.
Aoyama, Shinji. *Eureka [Yurika].* DENTSU Music and Entertainment, 2000.
Badiou, Alain. *Briefings on Existence: A Short Treatise on Transitory Ontology.* Trans. Norman Madarasz. Albany: State University of New York Press, 2006.
_____. *Cinema.* Trans. Susan Spitzer. Cambridge, UK: Polity Press, 2013.
Barker, Clive. *Hellraiser.* Cinemarque Entertainment BV, 1987.
Barthes, Roland. *Empire of Signs.* Trans. Richard Howard. New York: Hill and Wang, 1982.
_____. *The Pleasure of the Text.* Trans. Richard Miller. New York: Hill and Wang, 1975.
Baudelaire, Charles. *Les Fleurs du Mal.* Paris: GF-Flammarion, 1991.
Benjamin, Walter. *Reflections: Essays, Aphorisms, Autobiographical Writings.* Trans. Edmund Jephcott; Ed. Peter Demetz. New York: Harcourt Brace Jovanovich, 1979.
Buell, Frederick. *National Culture and the New Global System.* Baltimore: Johns Hopkins University Press, 1994.
Campbell, Andy. "Family Breaks Open Teenager's Tomb, Saying They Heard Her 'Screaming,'" The Huffington Post. http://www.huffingtonpost.com/entry/dead-teen-screaming-in-tomb_55dcc238e4b04ae49704c32b (accessed 8/26/2015).
Chang, Iris. *The Rape of Nanking: The Forgotten Holocaust of World War II.* New York: Basic Books, 1997.
Chômin, Nakae. *A Discourse by Three Drunkards on Government.* Trans. Nobuko Tsukui. Boston: Weatherhill, 2010.
D., Chris. *Outlaw Masters of the Japanese Cinema.* London: I. B. Tauris, 2005.
Davies, Roger J., and Osamu Ikeno (Eds.). *The Japanese Mind: Understanding Contemporary Japanese Culture.* Tokyo: Tuttle, 2002.
Desser, David. *Eros Plus Massacre: An Introduction to the Japanese New Wave Cinema.* Bloomington: Indiana University Press, 1988.
Dower, John W. *Embracing Defeat: Japan in the Wake of World War II.* New York: W. W. Norton & Company, Inc., 2000.
Downer, Lesley. *Women of the Pleasure Quarters: The Secret History of the Geisha.* New York: Broadway Books, 2001.
Edgerton, Robert B. *Warriors of the Rising Sun: A History of the Japanese Military.* New York: W. W. Norton & Company, 1997.
Field, Norma. *In the Realm of a Dying Emperor: Japan at Century's End.* New York: Vintage, 1993.
Frank, Richard B. *Downfall: The End of the Imperial Japanese Empire.* New York: Random House, 1999.
Freiberg, Freda. DVD Special Features, *Floating Clouds.* BFI, 2007.
Fromm, Erich. *To Have or to Be?* New York: Continuum, 2010.
Fujitani, Takashi. *Splendid Monarchy: Power and Pageantry in Modern Japan.* Berkeley: University of California Press, 1998.
Fukasaku, Kinji. *Battle Royale [Batoru rowaiaru].* AM Associates, 2000.
Futagawa, Buntarô. *Serpent [Orochi].* Bando Tsumasaburo Production, 1925.
Gamble, Andrew. "The Drifter's Escape," in *The Political Art of Bob Dylan.* Edited by David Boucher and Gary Browning; Charlottesville, VA: Imprint Academic, 2009.
Godard, Jean-Luc. *My Life to Live [Vivre sa vie].* Les Films de la Pléiade, 1962.
Gordon, Andrew (Ed.). *Postwar Japan as History.* Berkeley: University of California Press, 1993.
Hani, Susumu. *Bad Boys [Furyo shônen].* Iwanami Productions, 1961.

Hara, Kazuo. *The Emperor's Naked Army Marches On [Yuki Yukite shingun]*. Imamura Productions, 1987.
———. *Goodbye CP [Sayonara CP]*. Shisso Production, 1972.
Hardacre, Helen. *Marketing the Menacing Fetus in Japan*. Berkeley: University of California Press, 1999.
Hoberman, J. *Vulgar Modernism: Writing on Movies and Other Media*. Philadelphia: Temple University Press, 1991.
Igarashi, Yoshikuni. *Bodies of Memory: Narratives of War in Postwar Japanese Culture, 1945–1970*. Princeton: Princeton University Press, 2000.
Imamura, Shôhei. *The Eel [Unagi]*. Eisei Gekijo, 1997.
———. *In Search of Unreturned Soldiers in Malaysia [Mikikan-hei o otte: Marei-hen]*. Imamura Productions, 1970.
———. *In Search of Unreturned Soldiers in Thailand [Mikikan-hei o otte: Tai-hen]*. Imamura Productions, 1971.
———. "Japan," segment of *September 11*. CIH Shorts, 2002.
———. *Outlaw Matsuo Comes Home [Muhomatsu kokyo e kaeru]*. Imamura Productions, 1973.
Irokawa, Daikichi. *The Age of Hirohito: In Search of Modern Japan*. Trans. Mikiso Hane and John K. Urda. New York: The Free Press, 1995.
Ishii, Gakuryû. *Isn't Anyone Alive? [Ikiterumono wa inainoka]*. Dragon Mountain, 2012.
Ishii, Teruo. "Interview with Bernard Eisenschitz (2004)." *Late Chrysanthemums* DVD Bonus Features (BFI, 2007).
———. *Japanese Hell [Jigoku]*. Teruo Ishii Production, 1999.
Ivy, Marilyn. *Discourses of the Vanishing: Modernity, Phantasm, Japan*. Chicago: University of Chicago Press, 1995.
Jansen, Marius B. *The Making of Modern Japan*. Cambridge, MA: The Belknap Press of the University of Harvard Press, 2002.
Kang, Hildi. *Under the Black Umbrella: Voices from Colonial Korea, 1910–1945*. Ithaca, NY: Cornell University Press, 2001.
Karatani, Kôjin. *Architecture as Metaphor: Language, Number, Money*. Trans. Sabu Kohso. Cambridge, MA: MIT Press, 1995.
———. *Origins of Modern Japanese Literature*. Translation edited by Brett de Barry. Durham: Duke University Press, 1993.
Kauffman, Linda S. *Bad Girls and Sick Boys: Fantasies in Contemporary Art and Culture*. Berkeley: University of California Press, 1998.
Kazuaki, Kiriya. *Casshern*. Tatsunoko Production, 2004.
Kingston, Jeff. *Contemporary Japan: History, Politics, and Social Change Since the 1980s*. Malden, MA: Wiley-Blackwell, 2011.
Kinugasa, Teinosuke. *A Page of Madness [Kurutta ippêji]*. Kinugasa Productions, 1926.
Kitano, Takeshi. *Brother*. RPC, 2000.
———. *Dolls*. Bandai Visual Company, 2002.
———. *Kids Return [Kizzu ritân]*. Bandai Visual Company, 1996.
———. *A Scene at the Sea [Ano natsu, ichiban shizukana umi]*. Office Kitano, 1991.
Kobayashi, Masaki. *Kwaidan [Kaidan]*. Bungei, 1964.
Koschmann, J. Victor. *Revolution and Subjectivity in Postwar Japan*. Chicago: University of Chicago Press, 1996.
Kracauer, Siegfried. *Theory of Film*. London: Oxford University Press, 1960.
Kurosawa, Akira. *Drunken Angel [Yoidore tenshi]*. Toho Company, 1948.
———. *High and Low [Tengoku to jigoku]*. Kurosawa Production Company, 1963.
———. *Ikiru*. Toho Company, 1952.
———. *The Quiet Duel [Shizukanaru kettô]*. Daiei Motion Picture Company, 1949.
———. *Ran*. Greenwich Film Productions, 1985.
———. *Rashomon [Rashômon]*. Daiei Motion Picture Company, 1950.
———. *Stray Dog [Noru inu]*. Film Art Association, 1949.
———. *Throne of Blood [Kumonosu-jô]*. Toho, 1957.
Kurosawa, Kiyoshi. *Bright Future [Akarui mirai]*. Uplink, 2003.
———. *Tokyo Sonata [Tôkyô sonata]*. Django Films, 2008.
Kwak, Jae-young. *Cyborg Girl [Boku no kanojo wa saibôgu]*. Amuse Soft Entertainment, 2008.
Latourette, Kenneth Scott. *The History of Japan*. New York: Macmillan, 1951.
Levinas, Emmanuel. *Is It Righteous to Be?* Ed. Jill Robbins. Stanford: Stanford University Press, 2001.
Lévi-Strauss, Claude. *The Raw and the Cooked: Mythologiques, Volume 1*. Trans. John and Doreen Weightman. Chicago: University of Chicago Press, 1983.
Malabou, Catherine. *Ontology of the Accident: An Essay on Destructive Plasticity*. Trans. Carolyn Shread. Cambridge, UK: Polity, 2013.
Marker, Chris. *Sans Soleil [Sans soleil]*. Argos Films, 1983.

Masaharu, Anesaki. *History of Japanese Religion*. Rutland, VT: Charles E. Tuttle Company, 1966.
Masumura, Yasuzô. *Black Test Car [Kuro no tesuto kaa]*. Daiei Studios, 1962.
_____. *Blind Beast [Môjû]*. Daiei Motion Picture Company, 1969.
_____. *Kisses [Kuchizuke]*. Daiei Studios, 1957.
_____. *Red Angel [Akai tenshi]*. Daiei Studios, 1966.
Matsumoto, Toshio. *Funeral Parade of Roses [Bara no sôretsu]*. Art Theatre Guild, 1969.
McDonald, Keiko I. *Reading a Japanese Film: Cinema in Context*. Honolulu: University of Hawaii Press, 2006.
Mellen, Joan. *The Waves at Genji's Door: Japan Through Its Cinema*. New York: Pantheon Books, 1976.
Mes, Tom. *Agitator—The Cinema of Takashi Miike*. Godalming, UK: FAB Press, 2004.
Miike, Takashi. *Andromedia [Andoromedia]*. Avex Inc., 1998.
_____. *Dead or Alive [Dead or Alive: Hanzaisha]*. Daiei Motion Picture Company, 1999.
Mishima, Yukio. *Confessions of a Mask*. Trans. Meredith Weatherby. New York: New Directions, 1958.
_____. *Patriotism [Yûkoku]*. Toho Company, 1966.
_____. *The Sailor Who Fell from Grace with the Sea*. Trans. John Nathan. New York: Vintage, 1994.
Mizoguchi, Kenji. *A Geisha [Gion bayashi]*. Daiei Studios, 1953.
_____. *The Love of Sumako the Actress [Joyû Sumako no koi]*. Shôchiku Eiga, 1947.
_____. *Osaka Elegy [Naniwa ereji]*. Daiichi Eiga, 1936.
_____. *Sansho the Bailiff [Sanshô Dayû]*. Daiei Studios, 1954.
_____. *Sisters of the Gion [Gion no shimai]*. Daiichi Eiga, 1936.
_____. *A Tale from Chikamatsu [Chikamatsu Monogatari]*. Daiei Studios, 1954.
_____. *Ugetsu [Ugetsu monogatari]*. Daiei Studios, 1953.
_____. *Women of the Night [Yoru no onnatachi]*. Shochiku, 1948.
Munsterberg, Hugo. *The Arts of Japan: An Illustrated History*. Rutland, VT: Charles E. Tuttle Company, 1962.
Nagata, Hideo. *Ring [Ringu]*. Omega Project, 1998.
Nakahira, Kô. *Crazed Fruit [Kurutta kajitsu]*. Nikkatsu, 1956.
Napier, Susan J. *From Impressionism to Anime: Japan as Fantasy and Fan Cult in the Mind of the West*. New York: Palgrave Macmillan, 2007.
Naruse, Mikio. *Apart from You [Kimi to wakarete]*. Shochiku, 1933.
_____. *Floating Clouds [Ukigumo]*. Toho, 1955.
_____. *Flunky, Work Hard! [Koshiben ganbare]*. Shochiku, 1931.
_____. *Late Chrysanthemums [Bangiku]*. Toho, 1954.
_____. *No Blood Relation [Nasanunaka]*. Shochiku, 1932.
_____. *Sincerity [Magokoro]*. Toho Eiga Gaisha, 1939.
_____. *When a Woman Ascends the Stairs [Onna ga kaidan wo agaru toki]*. Toho, 1960.
_____. *The Whole Family Works [Hataraku ikka]*. Toho Eiga, 1939.
Nishitani, Keiji. *Religion and Nothingness*. Trans. Jan Van Bragt. Berkeley: University of California Press, 1982.
Ohnuki-Tierney, Emiko. *Kamikaze, Cherry Blossoms, and Nationalisms: The Militarization of Aesthetics in Japanese History*. Chicago: University of Chicago Press, 2002.
_____. *The Monkey as Mirror: Symbolic Transformations in Japanese History and Ritual*. Princeton: Princeton University Press, 1987.
Okamoto, Kihachi. *The Sword of Doom [Dai-bosatsu tôge]*. Takarazuka Eiga Company, 1966.
Oshima, Nagisa. *Boy [Shônen]*. Art Theatre Guild, 1969.
_____. *The Ceremony [Gishiki]*. Art Theatre Guild, 1971.
_____. *Cinema, Censorship, and the State: The Writings of Nagisa Oshima, 1956–1978*. Trans. Dawn Lawson; Ed. Annette Michelson. Cambridge, MA: MIT Press, 1992.
_____. *Cruel Story of Youth [Seishun zankoku monogatari]*. Shochiku Ofuna, 1960.
_____. *Death by Hanging [Kôshikei]*. Art Theatre Guild, 1968.
_____. *Diary of a Shinjuku Thief [Shinjuku dorobô nikki]*. Sozosha, 1969.
_____. *Empire of Passion [Ai no bôrei]*. Argos Films, 1978.
_____. *In the Realm of the Senses [Ai no korîda]*. Argos Films, 1976.
_____. "Interview," *Cahiers du Cinéma* No. 218. March 1970.
_____. *Japanese Summer: Double Suicide [Muri shinjû: Nihon no natsu]*. Sozosha, 1967.
_____. *The Man Who Left His Will on Film [Tôkyô sensô sengo hiwa]*. Art Theatre Guild, 1970.
_____. *Merry Christmas Mr. Lawrence*. RPC, 1983.
_____. *Pleasures of the Flesh [Etsuraku]*. Sozosha, 1965.
_____. *Taboo [Gohatto]*. Oshima Productions, 1999.
_____. *Three Resurrected Drunkards [Kaette kita yopparai]*. Sozosha, 1968.
_____. *Violence at Noon [Hakuchû no tôrima]*. Sozosha, 1966.
Ozu, Yasujirô. *An Autumn Afternoon [Samma no aji]*. Shochiku, 1962.
_____. *Dragnet Girl [Hijôsen no onna]*. Shochiku Company, 1933.

_____. *Early Spring [Shôshun]*. Shôchiku Eiga, 1956.
_____. *Equinox Flower [Higanbana]*. Shôchiku Eiga, 1958.
_____. *Good Morning [Ohayô]*. Shochiku, 1959.
_____. *A Hen in the Wind [Kaze no naka no mendon]*. Shôchiku Eiga, 1948.
_____. *An Inn in Tokyo [Tôkyô no yado]*. Shôchiku Eiga, 1935.
_____. *Late Spring [Banshun]*. Shôchiku Eiga, 1949.
_____. *The Only Son [Hitori musuko]*. Shôchiku Eiga, 1936.
_____. *Record of a Tenement Gentleman [Nagaya shinshiroku]*. Shôchiku Eiga, 1947.
_____. *Woman of Tokyo [Tôkyô no onna]*. Shôchiku Eiga, 1933.
Pennington, Matthew. "Japan's 'whitewashing' of WWII history rankles some U.S. veterans." www.japantimes.com.jp, posted April 26, 2015.
Pyle, Kenneth B. *Japan Rising: The Resurgence of Japanese Power and Purpose*. New York: Public Affairs, 2007.
Ray, Nicholas. *I Was Interrupted: Nicholas Ray On Making Movies*. Edited and Introduced by Susan Ray. Berkeley: University of California Press, 1995.
Richie, Donald (with additional material by Joan Mellen). *The Films of Akira Kurosawa*. Berkeley: The University of California Press, 1984.
Robertson, Jennifer. "The Politics of Androgyny in Japan: Sexuality and Subversion in the Theater and Beyond." *American Ethnologist*, Vol. 19, No. 3 (August 1992).
Russell, Catherine. *Classical Japanese Cinema Revisited*. New York: Continuum, 2011.
Said, Edward W. *Orientalism*. New York: Vintage, 1979.
"Saigon Execution: Murder of a Viet Cong by Saigon Police Chief, 1968." http://rarehistoricalphotos.com/saigon-execution-murder-vietcong-saigon-1968/ (accessed 9/17/2015).
Sas, Miryam. *Fault Lines: Cultural Memory and Japanese Surrealism*. Stanford: Stanford University Press, 1999.
Sato, Tadao. *Currents in Japanese Cinema*. Trans. Gregory Barrett. New York: Harper & Row, 1987.
Schlesinger, Jacob M. *Shadow Shoguns: The Rise and Fall of Japan's Postwar Political Machine*. New York: Simon & Schuster, 1997.
Schroeter, Werner. *Eika Katappa*. Werner Schroeter Filmproduktion, 1969.
Schull, William J. *Effects of Atomic Radiation: A Half-Century of Studies from Hiroshima and Nagasaki*. New York: Wiley-Liss, 1995.
Shimazu, Yasujirô. *A Brother and His Younger Sister [Ani to sono moto]*. Shôchiku Eiga, 1939.
_____. *Our Neighbor, Miss Yae [Tonari no Yae-chan]*. Shôchiku Eiga, 1934.
Shindô, Kaneto. "Interview with Kaneto Shindô." *Onibaba* DVD Bonus Features (The Criterion Collection, 2004).
_____. *Kenji Mizoguchi: The Life of a Film Director [Aru eiga-kantoku no shogai]*. Kindai Eiga Kyokai, 1975.
_____. *Onibaba*. Kindai Eiga Kyokai, 1964.
Silverman, Kaja. *The Acoustic Mirror: The Female Voice in Psychoanalysis and Cinema*. Bloomington: University of Indiana Press, 1988.
Sono, Shion. *Suicide Club [Jisatsu sâkuru]*. Omega Project, 2001.
Spector, Ronald H. *In the Ruins of Empire: The Japanese Surrender and the Battle for Postwar Asia*. New York: Random House, 2007.
Sternberg, Josef von. *Anatahan*. Daiwa, 1953.
_____. *Fun in a Chinese Laundry*. San Francisco: Mercury House, 1988.
Suzuki, Daisetz T. *Zen and Japanese Culture*. Princeton: Princeton University Press, 1993.
Suzuki, Seijun. *Fighting Delinquents [Kutabare gurentai]*. Nikkatsu, 1963.
_____. *Fighting Elegy [Kenka ereji]*. Nikkatsu, 1966.
_____. *Gate of Flesh [Nikutai no mon]*. Nikkatsu, 1964.
_____. *Youth of the Beast [Yajù no seishun]*. Nikkatsu, 1963.
Syberberg, Hans-Jürgen. *Parsifal*. Gaumont, 1982.
Tanizaki, Jun'ichirô. *In Praise of Shadows*. Trans. Thomas J. Harper and Edward G. Seidensticker. Stoney Creek, CT: Leete's Island Books, 1977.
Tarantino, Quentin. *Kill Bill: Volume 1*. Miramax, 2003.
Tasker, Peter. *The Japanese*. New York: E. P. Dutton, 1987.
Terayama, Shûji. *Pastoral Hide and Seek [Den-en ni shisu]*. Art Theatre Guild, 1974.
Toyoda, Toshiaki. *9 Souls [Nain souruzu]*. Eisei Gekijo, 2003.
Tsukamoto, Shin'ya. *Vital*. Kaijyu Theater, 2004.
Turim, Maureen. *The Films of Oshima Nagisa: Images of a Japanese Iconoclast*. Berkeley: University of California Press, 1998.
Uegaki, Yasuaki. *Female Teacher: In Front of the Students [Onna kyôshi: Seito no me no maede]*. Nikkatsu, 1982.
Wakamatsu, Kôji. *Caterpillar [Kyatapirâ]*. Skhole Co., 2010.
_____. *Running in Madness, Dying in Love [Kyôsô jôshi-kô]*. Wakamatsu Production, 1969.
_____. *Violated Angels [Okasareta hakui]*. Wakamatsu Production, 1967.

Warhol, Andy. *THE Philosophy of Andy Warhol (From A to B and Back Again)*. San Diego: Harcourt Brace & Company, 1977.
Willemen, Paul. DVD Special Features, *Floating Clouds*. BFI, 2007.
Wood, Kelsey. *Troubling Play: Meaning and Entity in Plato's* Parmenides. Albany: State University of New York Press, 2005.

Index

Numbers in *bold italics* refer to pages with photographs.

Abe, Tetsuo 11
Absolutely Fabulous 197
Adachi, Masao 9
Adams, Eddie 199
A.K.A. Serial Killer (Adachi) 9
Akada, Mariko 171
Akagi, Ranko 86
Altman, Robert 16
Ameisen, Jean-Claude 135
Anatahan (Sternberg) 207*n*34
Anderson, Joseph L. 41, 44, 64, 109, 124, 169
Anderson, Lindsay 12
Andromedia (Miike) 38, 62, 102, 133–134, 177
Anger, Kenneth 89
Aoki, Hohi 168
Aoki, Tomio 71
Aoyama, Shinji 115, 132
Apart from You (Naruse) 160–162, 181
Ara, Masato 14, 55, 84
Arashi, Kanjûrô 175
Aratama, Michiyo 120
Araya, Hosui 94
Arima, Ineko 213*n*29
Aristotle 7
Artaud, Antonin 93
Arthur, Jean 207*n*16
Asano, Tadanobu 20, *79*, 79, 122, 173
Ashida, Shinsuke 87, *88*
Asô, Kumiko 192
Astaire-Rogers 50
An Autumn Afternoon (Ozu) 26, 149, *150*, 171–172, 188
Awaji, Keiko 40, *152*

Bad Boys (Hani) 42, 48, 84, 91
The Bad Sleep Well (A. Kurosawa) 59
Badiou, Alain 5, 6–7, 16, 18, 26–27, 62, 101, 102, 182, 209*n*24
Baishô, Mitsuko 192
Bandô, Tsurasaburô 181
Barker, Clive 194

Barthes, Roland 1, 62, 76–77, 109, 112, 116, 117, 125, 135
Bataille, Georges 199
Battle Royale (Fukasaku) 37, 38, *39*, 59, 66, 72–74, *73*, 114–115, 127, 131
Baudelaire, Charles 74, 130, 200
The Birds (Hitchcock) 208*n*23
Black Test Car (Masumura) 59, 78, 96, 189, 212*n*1
Blackmail Is My Life (Fukasaku) 59
Blanchot, Maurice 27
Blind Beast (Masumura) 130, 133
Blitzkrieg Operation Number Eleven 174
Blues Harp (Miike) 81
Borges, Jorge Luis 201
Bowie, David 128
Boy (Oshima) 11, 39–40, 56, 129, 153, 158–159, 173–174, 199
Brecht, Bertolt 129, 131
Briefings on Existence (Badiou) 6
Bright Future (K. Kurosawa) 72, 122, *123*, 131
Brother (Kitano) 128
A Brother and His Younger Sister (Shimazu) 47, 71, 149
Buell, Frederick 49, 54, 176
Burch, Noel 212*n*22

Cassavetes, John 91
Casshern (Kazuaki) 158
Caterpillar (Wakamatsu) 23, 192–195
The Ceremony (Oshima) 79, 96–100, *99*, 131, 155, 180, 198, 212*n*22, 212*n*52
Chang, Iris 147, 153, 154, 155, 163
China Night 165, 166
Chômin, Nakae 197–199, 201, 203
Citizen Kane (Welles) 39
Clift, Montgomery 208*n*43
The Condemned of Altona (Sartre) 209*n*63
Conti, Tom 112

Conversation Piece (Visconti) 12
Crazed Fruit (Nakahira) 51
Cruel Story of Youth (Oshima) 90–93, *91*, 199
Cukor, George 17
Cyborg Girl (Kwak) 177

Damasio 133
Dead or Alive (Miike) 36, 112
Dean, James 208*n*43
Death by Hanging (Oshima) 19, 199
Deleuze, Gilles 209*n*24
Descartes, René 102
Desser, David 4, 30, 93
Diary of a Shinjuku Thief (Oshima) *9*, 39, 85, 111, 128, 173
A Discourse by Three Drunkards on Government (Chômin) 197–199
Dolls (Kitano) 119, 122, 133
Dower, John W. 51, 165, 167, 170
Dragnet Girl (Ozu) 53, 80
Drunken Angel (A. Kurosawa) 53, 56, 70
Durbin, Deanna 51
Dziga-Vertov Group (Godard-Gorin) 7

Edgerton, Robert B. 147, 155
The Eel (Imamura) 60–62
Eika Katappa (Schroeter) 29
Eita 57
The Embryo Hunts in Secret (Wakamatsu) 93, 193
Emoto, Akira 192
The Emperor Meiji and the Great Russo-Japanese War 174, 175
The Emperor's Naked Army Marches On (Hara) 42, 171, 173, 184
Empire of Passion (Oshima) 28, 42, 45, *130*, *134*, 164, 199, 211*n*66
Equinox Flower (Ozu) 136, 213*n*29, 213*n*30
Etchan 163

221

Index

Eureka (Aoyama) 115, 132
Every-Night Dreams (Naruse) 50
Executive Koala (Kawasaki) 62

Fassbinder, Rainer Werner 12, 180, 207n16
Female Teacher: In Front of the Students (Uegaki) 37, 51
Field, Norma 60, 145, 151, 187
Fighting Delinquents (Suzuki) 69–70, 80
Fighting Elegy (Suzuki) 118, 153, 156–157, 198
Floating Clouds (Naruse) 28–29, 135, 141–142, 177, 178–181, 187, 191, 214n13
Floating Weeds (Ozu) 34, 41–42, *41*, 44
Flunky, Work Hard! (Naruse) 162–163
Frank, Richard B. 127, 147
Freiberg, Freda 29, 178, 214n13
Fromm, Erich 69
Fuji, Tatsuya 28, *134*
Fujitani, Takeshi 107, 148, 151
Fukasaku, Kinji 37, 38, *39*, 59, 66, 72–73, *73*, 114
Fukuoka, Sukio 10
Fuller, Samuel 165
Funakoshi, Eiiji 130
Funeral Parade of Roses (Matsumoto) 74–76, 130
Futagara, Buntarô 69

Gamble, Andrew 115
Gate of Flesh (Suzuki) 51, 96, 119, 124, 136, 137, 138, 181–182, 186, 201, 214n9
A Geisha (Mizoguchi) 40, 42, 45, 47, 79, 171
Genet, Jean 74
Gibson, William 62
God of War Admiral Yamamoto and the Combined Fleet 174
Godard, Jean-Luc 34
Good Morning (Ozu) 72
Goodbye CP (Hara) 46, 110–111, 132–133, 135, 138–139, 197
Gordon, Andrew 168, 201
Goto, Kazuo 10
Greenaway, Peter 194

Hair Extensions (Sono) 63
Hamlet (Shakespeare) 6
Hani, Susumu 42, 48, 84, 91
Hara, Kazuo 42, 46, 110, 111, 132, 135, 138, 171, 173, *184*, 184, 197
Hara, Setsuko 47
Hardacre, Helen 64
Harvey, Lillian 50, 51
Hasegawa, Masami 164
Hayama, Masao 170
Heidegger, Martin 103, 209n24
Hellraiser (Barker) 194
A Hen in the Wind (Ozu) 24–25, 26, 168–169, 176–177
High and Low (A. Kurosawa) 76
Hirayama, Hisyoshi 115

Hirohito 49, 58, 60, 94, 97, 139, 149, 154, 157, 158, 163, 165, 166–168, 174, 177, 183, 184, 187, 188, 192, 194
Hitchcock, Sir Alfred 208n23
Hoberman, J. 4, 49
Honda, Shûga 13
Honma, Noriko 78
House of Bamboo (Fuller) 165
The Human Condition (Kobayashi) 156

I Live in Fear: Record of a Living Being (A. Kurosawa) 141
Ichihara, Etsuko 61
Ichikawa, Kon 90
If... (Anderson) 12
Igarashi, Yoshikuni 4, 165
Igawa, Ureo 150
Iida, Chôko 55, 170
Ikiru (A. Kurosawa) 24, 27, 35–36, 38, 39, 42, 55, 72, 136, 170, 207n16
Imamura, Shôhei 33, 60, 62, 118, 138, 175, 187, 188–192, *189*, 192–193, 214n5, 214n6
In Search of Unreturned Soldiers in Malaysia (Imamura) 188, 189
In Search of Unreturned Soldiers in Thailand (Imamura) 190, 191
In the Realm of the Senses (Oshima) 68, 195, 199
An Inn in Tokyo (Ozu) 45, 55–56, 66, 71, 72, 163
Inoue, Masuo 32
Irie, Takako 164
Irokawa, Daikichi 119, 159, 162, 167
Iseya, Yûsuke 158
Ishihara, Shintaro 90
Ishii, Gakuryû 129
Ishii, Teruo 54–55, 112, 115, 210n44
Isn't Anyone Alive? (G. Ishii) 129
Isono, Âkio 160
Ivy, Marilyn 4, 25, 49
Iwashita, Shima *26*, 172

"Japan" (Imamura) 192–193
Japanese Hell (T. Ishii) 55, 112, 115
Japanese Summer: Double Suicide (Oshima) 56, 81–82

Kagawa, Kyôko 182
Kaku, Atsuko 98, *99*
Kamei, Fumio 164–165, 177
Kaneko, Nobuo 72
Kanô, Junko 212n1
Kanze, Hideo 85
Kaoru, Osanai 50
Kara, Juro 87
Karatani, Kôjin 25, 34, 77, 103, 208n29, 209n24, 212n52, 213n2
Karayuki-san (Imamura) 138
Kasai, Yukiko 127
Kasuya, Keigo 23
Kato, Seiichi 162
Kato, Teruko 164
Kawachi, Tamio 81

Kawaguchi, Hiroshi *41*, 59, 90, 208n43
Kawaguchi, Saeda 83
Kawahara, Sabu 193
Kawamura, Reikichi 149, 161
Kawarasaki, Kenzô 98, *99*
Kawasaki, Minoru 62
Kawazu, Yûsuke 85, 90, *91*
Kazuaki, Kiriya 158
Kids Return (Kitano) 71
King Lear (Shakespeare) 24, 66
Kingston, Jeff 59, 60, 62
Kinugasa, Teinosuke 31, 34, 36, 54, 75
Kisses (Masumura) 48, 59, 71–72, 98, 208n43
Kitano, Takeshi 60, 71, 73, *73*, 80, 113, *113*, 119, 122, 128, 133, 177, *178*
Kiwokata, Sôji 172
Kobayashi, Masaki 120, 156
Kogure, Michiyo 42
Kokushô, Sayuri 115
Kondô, Hiroshi 69
Koschmann, J. Victor 52
Kowano, Miyuki 90, *91*
Koyama, Akiko 82, 97, *99*, 158
Koyanagi, Keiko 89
Kracauer, Siegfried 3, 21
Kudo, Eiichi 4
Kuga, Yoshiko 93
Kurosawa, Akira 3, *3*, 4, 24, 27, 35, 39, 42, 53, 55, 56, 59, 62, 64, *65*, 66, 68, 69, 70, 72, 76, 78, 96, 114, 116, 135, 136, 141, 143, *152*, 170, 201, 207n16, 209n63
Kurosawa, Kiyoshi 65, 72, 122, *123*, 131, 213n25
Kuwano, Michiyo 149
Kwaidan (Kobayashi) 120, 180
Kwak, Jae-young 177
Kyô, Machiko 13, 65, *65*, *121*

Late Chrysanthemums (Naruse) 176–177, 181
Late Spring (Ozu) 47, 171, 172
Latourette, Kenneth Scott 174
Lévi-Strauss, Claude 17, 18
Levinas, Emmanuel 37, 180
Lily 173
Lost Sex (Shindô) 85, *86*
The Love of Sumako the Actress (Mizoguchi) 41, 63, 67–68, *67*, 117

Maki, Claude 177, *178*
Malabou, Catherine 27, 28, 30, 37, 63, 68, 70, 96, 102, 109, 110, 115, 116, 127, 132, 134, 135, 136, 201
The Man Who Left His Will on Film (Oshima) 7–13, 14–16, 27, 29, 32, 68, 129, 170, 199, 205n6, 205n7, 205n9
Marker, Chris 47, 62, 132, 147, 173, 177, 202, 213n31, 213n2
The Marriage of Maria Braun (Fassbinder) 207n16

Index

Maruyama, Masao 187
Masumura, Yasuzô 25, 27, 30, *33*, 48, 59, 71, 78, 85, *88*, 96, 98, 130, 155, 189, 212*n*1
Matsubara, Chieko 122
Matsuda, Ryûhei 19, *20*, *81*
Matsumoto, Toshio 74, 130
McDowell, Malcolm 12
Mellen, Joan 44, 54, 55, 57, 63, 65, 78, 97, 98, 100, 117, 120, 132, 141, 170, 180
Merry Christmas Mr. Lawrence (Oshima) 112–113, *113*, 127, 128, 199
Midori, Mako 130
Mifune, Toshirô *3*, 53, 64, *65*, 66, 96, 124, *152*
Mihashi, Tatsuyo 122
Miike, Takashi 34, 36, 38, 62, 81, 102, 112, 116, 127, 133, 177, 210*n*46
Minakami, Reiko 168
Minami, Eiko 31
Minamida, Yôko 182
Minnelli, Vincente 180
Mishima, Yukio 51, 89, 102–103, 130
Mito, Mitsuko 42, *43*
Mitsui, Kôji 53
Mitzukobo, Sumiko 161
Miyoshi, Eiko *152*
Mizoguchi, Kenji 13, *14*, 33, 40–41, 42, *43*, 44–45, 47–48, 50, 56, 62, 63, 67, *67*, 68, 78, 90, 177, *118*, 120, *121*, 121, 136, *140*, 140, 142, 147–148, 164, 171, 181, 182, 186–188, 202
Mori, Masayuki 13, *14*, 28, 65, *121*
Mowitt, John 205*n*7
Murase, Sachiko 163
Murata, Chieko 168
Muto, Yoko 54
My Life to Live (Godard) 34

Nagata, Hideo 119, 142, 205*n*9
Nakadai, Tatsuya 24, 40
Nakagawa, Yoshie 32
Nakahira, Kô 51
Nakamura, Atsuo 100
Nakamura, Katsuo 81
Nakamura, Nobuo 39
Nakane, Tôru 51
Naniwa, Tomoko 162
Narihira, Ariwara no 107
Naruse, Mikio 28, 33, 38, 40, 41, 44, 48, 50, 51, 77, 115, 135, 141, 142, 149, 160–165, 171, 172, 173, 176, 177, 178–180, 187, 191, 210*n*44, 214*n*13
Narushima, Yuri 97
Nashville (Altman) 17
Nezu, Jinpachi 24
Nezu, Yoshiko 69
Nihon'yanagi, Hiroshi 93
9 Souls (Toyoda) 56–57, 63, 115, 119, 135
Nishitani, Keiji 101, 102, 104

No Blood Relation (Naruse) 141, 163
Nogawa, Yumiko 124
Nozoe, Hitomi 59

Obinata, Den 173
Odagiri, Jô 122, *123*
Odagiri, Miki 170, 207*n*16
Ogasawara, Osamu 74
Ohnuki-Tierney, Emiko 17, 18, 61, 145, 151, 158
Oka, Joji 53
Okada, Yoshiko 150
Okamoto, Kihachi 78
Oko, Rina 51
Okura, Fumio 45
Okuzaki, Kenzo 42, 171, 184
O'Neill, Eugene 100
Onibaba (Shindô) 93–96, *95*, 132, 183–185
The Only Son (Ozu) 50, 170
Ono, Komachi 118
The Origin of Sex (Shindô) 85
Osaka Elegy (Mizoguchi) 44, 45, 47, 50, 147–148, 164
Oshima, Hiroko 177, *178*
Oshima, Nagisa 1, 7, 8–9, *9*, 11, 13, 15, *20*, 27, *28*, 29, 32, 33, 39–40, 42, 45, 56, 62, 68, *79*, 79, 81, 82, *83*, 83–85, 90–92, *91*, 93, 96–100, *99*, 111, 112–113, *113*, 118, 127, 128, 129, *130*, 131, *134*, *152*, 153, 155, 158, 164, 170, 171, 173, 180, 181, 184, 195, 198–200, *202*, 203, 205*n*7, 205*n*9, 209*n*63, 211*n*66, 212*n*52, 212*n*22, 214*n*9
Ota, Yoshikaki 100
Otowa, Nabuko 85, 94
Otskuka, Hisao 197
Our Neighbor, Miss Yae (Shimazu) 173, 209*n*63, 210*n*25
Outlaw Matsuo Comes Home (Imamura) 175, 188–192, 214*n*5
Ozu, Yasujirô 24–25, *26*, *26*, 33, 34, 41–42, *41*, 44, 45, 47, 48, 50, 51, 52–53, *53*, 55, 62, 66, 70, 71, 72, 80, 111, 116, 135, 149, *150*, 150–151, 160, 163, 164, 166–172, 176, 177, 188, 208*n*23, 213*n*23, 213*n*25, 213*n*29, 213*n*30, 213*n*32

A Page of Madness (Kinugasa) 31–33, 35, 36, 54, 75
Parsifal (Syberberg) 193
Pasolini, Pier Paolo 74
Pastoral Hide and Seek (Terayama) 29–30, 31, 89, 170
Patriotism (Mishima) 89, 130
Pitâ 74
Plato 5, 34
Pleasures of the Flesh (Oshima) 81
Polan, Dana 179
Punishment Room (Ichikawa) 90
Pyle, Kenneth B. 49, 52, 55, 56, 58

The Quiet Duel (A. Kurosawa) 66, 143

Rampo, Edogawa 130
Ran (A. Kurosawa) 4, 24, 40, 66, 72, 116
Rashomon (A. Kurosawa) 64–65, *65*, 66–67, 69, 70, 76, 77, 78, 81, 96, 114, 201
The Raw and the Cooked (Lévi-Strauss) 17
Ray, Nicholas 21
Record of a Tenement Gentleman (Ozu) 70
Red Angel (Masumura) *33*, 85–87, *88*, 155
Reich, Wilhelm 82
Renoir, Jean 66
Ringu (Nagata) 119, 142, 205*n*9
Ritchie, Donald 41, 44, 64, 68, 109, 124, 169
Rossellini, Roberto 180
Running in Madness, Dying in Love (Wakamatsu) 54
Ryan, Robert 165
Ryû, Chishû 170, 171
Ryû, Daisuke 66

Sada, Keiji 171, 213*n*29, 213*n*30
Said, Edward W. 21, 205*n*4
The Sailor Who Fell from Grace with the Sea (Mishima) 51
Sakamoto, Ryuichi 112
Sakamoto, Takeshi 55
Sakurai, Keiko 81, 82
Sanjô, Miki 66
Sano, Sûji 168
Sans Soleil (Marker) 47, 132, 147, 173, 177, 202
Sansho the Bailiff (Mizoguchi) 40–41, 63, 121
Santô, Rushia 37
Sartre, Jean-Paul 209*n*63
Sas, Miryam 4, 201
Satô, Kei 81, 94, *95*, 95, 97
Sato, Tadao 53, 56, 63, 86, 109, 151, 153, 171, 182, 213*n*23, 214*n*13
Saunders, Jennifer 197
Sawamura, Ichisaburo *14*, 120
A Scene at the Sea (Kitano) 177–178, *178*
Schlesinger, Jacob M. 58, 59
Schroeter, Werner 29
Schull, William J. 137, 138, 140
Scorpio Rising (Anger) 89
Senba, Jôtarô 86
Serpent (Futagara) 66, 181
Shibuya, Minoru 56
Shiganoya, Benkei 44, 45
Shimabukuro, Hiroko 102
Shimazu, Masahiko 72
Shimazu, Yasujirô 47, 48, 71, 149, 150, 173, 209*n*63, 210*n*25
Shimizu, Hiroshi 210*n*44
Shimizu, Mayumi 80
Shimizu, Miso 61
Shimura, Takashi *3*, 24, 56, 65, 66
Shindô, Eitarô 182
Shindô, Kaneto 85, *86*, 93, 94, *95*, 132
Shishido, Jô 81

Index

Shitara, Kôji 72
Sincerity (Naruse) 163–164, 171, 172
Sirk, Douglas 180, 207n16
Sisters of the Gion (Mizoguchi) 40, 44–45, 47, 50
Solondz, Todd 213n25
Sono, Shion 30, 37, 40, 63, 112, 122, 129, 131
Speck, Richard 87
Spinoza, Baruch 135
Springfield, Dusty 74
Sternberg, Josef von 50, 207n34
Story of the Last Chrysanthemums (Mizoguchi) 50
Stray Dog (A. Kurosawa) *3*, 96, *152*
Suematsu, Takayuki 71
Sugai, Ichirô 96
Sugimura, Haruko 72, 171, 176
Suicide Club (Sono) 30, 37, 38, 40, 74, 112, 122, 129, 131, 134, 206n19
The Sutra of 42 Sections 166
Suzuki, Daisetz T. 23, 101, 123
Suzuki, Seijun 34, 51, 69, 76, 80, 96, 116, 118, 119, 124, 136, 138, 153, 156, 173, 181, 186, 198, 201, 214n9
The Sword of Doom (Okamoto) 78, 124
Syberberg, Hans-Jûrgen 193

Taboo (Oshima) 19, *20*, *79*, 79–80, *81*, 153, 171, 208n34, 211n66
Taguchi, Tomorowo 171, 192
Takada, Minoru 163
Takahiro, Tamaru 164
Takamine, Hideko 28, 40, 141
Takano, Hiroyuki 29
Takasugi, Sanae 187
Takeda, Shinji *79*, 80, *81*
A Tale from Chikamatsu (Mizoguchi) 63, 182–183
Tamiya, Jirô 212n1
Tamura, Naomi 213n3
Tamura, Taijirô 64
Tanabe, Seichi 81
Tanaka, Kinuyo 13, *14*, 24, 47, 53, *67*, *67*, *140*

Tanizaki, Jun'ichirô 109, 110, 114, 124, 125–126, 127, 187
Terada, Chiho 61
Terajima, Shinobu 23
Terao, Akira 24, 158
Terayama, Shûji 29, 31, 89, 170, 206n19
The Third Generation (Fassbinder) 12
Thompson, Jim 81
Three Resurrected Drunkards (Oshima) 198
Throne of Blood (A. Kurosawa) 124
Tokugawa, Musei 149
Tokyo Sonata (K. Kurosawa) 65, 213n25
Tokyo Story (Ozu) 1, 135
Tominaga, Misako 181
Tonoyama, Taiji 94, *95*
Toura, Rokkô 54, 83
Toyoda, Toshiaki 56–57, 63, 115, 119, 135
The Tragedy of Japan (Kamei) 165
The Travels of Scouting Workers 210n52
Tsubaki, Ryuichi 97
Tsubaki, Yukihuro 100
Tsuchiya, Yoshio 74
Tsukioka, Yumeji 172
Tsukomoto, Shin'ya 132, 166
Tsunoda, Tomie *140*
Turim, Maureen 11, 90, 131, 205n7, 213n23

Uemura, Kenjiro 142
Ugetsu (Mizoguchi) 13, *14*, 42–44, *43*, 56, 90, 120–122, *121*, 125, 136
Umemoto, Katsui 56
Umemura, Yôko 44
Usami, Jun 171
Utamaro and His Five Women (Mizoguchi) 117, *118*

Violated Angels (Wakamatsu) 87–89, 93, 193
Violence at Noon (Oshima) 82–85, *152*, 153, 181, 199, 211n66
Visconti, Luchino 12

Vital (Tsukomoto) 132, 133, 166, 173

Wada, Kôji 69
Wakamatsu, Kôji 23, 24, 34, 54, 87–89, 93, 118, 192–195
Wakao, Ayako *33*, *41*, 47, 85, *88*, 90
Warhol, Andy 15
Watanabe, Fumio 153
Watanabe, Misako 120
The Waves at Genji's Door (Mellen) 44
West, Mae 50
When a Woman Ascends the Stairs (Naruse) 40, 48, 77, 115, 142
The Whole Family Works (Naruse) 149, 163, 172, 173
Willeman, Paul 178, 180
Woman of Tokyo (Ozu) 150, 160
The Women (Cukor) 17
Women of the Night (Mizoguchi) 47, 90, 136, *140*, 140, 142, 181, 186–188, 201–202, 203
Wood, Kelsey 16, 20
The Writing of the Disaster (Blanchot) 27

Yakusho, Kôji 61, 115
Yamada, Isuzu 40, 44, 124
Yamada, Yukio 84
Yamaguchi, Isamu 162
Yamaguchi, Shirley 165
Yamamura, Sô 41, *67*
Yokoo, Tadanori 39
Yokoyama, Rie 39
Yoshikawa, Mitsuko 160
Yoshimuro, Yitsuko 94
Yoshiyuki, Kazuko *28*, *130*, *134*
Yoshizawa, Ken 54
Young Boss Takeshi 210n52
Youth of the Beast (Suzuki) 53, 76, 80–81, 173
Yu, Do-yun 19
Yui, Masayuki 40

Zeami 116

www.ingramcontent.com/pod-product-compliance
Lightning Source LLC
Chambersburg PA
CBHW081553300426
44116CB00015B/2870